COLOSSIANS & PHILEMON

FOR PASTORS

JOHN A. KITCHEN

KRESS
BIBLICAL
RESOURCES

Colossians and Philemon for Pastors
© 2012 by John A. Kitchen

ISBN 978-1-934952-18-4

Published by Kress Biblical Resources
P.O. Box 132228
The Woodlands, TX 77393
www.kressbiblical.com

Cover photo: St. Paul the Apostle (oil on canvas), Vignon, Claude (1593-1670)
Copyright Galleria Sabauda, Turin, Italy / Alinari / The Bridgeman Art Library

Typesetting and cover design by Greg Wright (diamondpointmedia.com)

Printed in the United States of America

10 9 8 7 6 5 4 3 2 1

Dedicated to the little church in Gilbert, Iowa
whose influence upon the world is disproportionate to its numbers

Thank you for patiently enduring my first, fumbling attempts
to expound the epistle to the Colossians thirty years ago

Χριστὸς ἐν ὑμῖν, ἡ ἐλπὶς τῆς δόξης

—Colossians 1:27b

CONTENTS

CONTENTS

PREFACE

The first sermon I ever preached was from Colossians 2:6-10. The first expository series I ever attempted was from Colossians. One of the first series of messages I preached in the first church I served as a full-time pastor was from the letter to the Colossians. Colossians was the text for perhaps my favorite series of messages at the church I currently serve.

There is something about Colossians that keeps drawing me back, again and again. The journey of my Christian discipleship has never ventured very far from this letter. I find myself circling back here over and over for the good of my own soul. That which keeps drawing me back to this letter is its portrayal of Jesus in His glory and grace. Seeing as I have no hope but Jesus (and in Jesus, every hope!), inevitably I find myself back in Colossians time and time again. I pray you will as well.

I want to express my gratitude to my dear wife, Julie, and to our children, Melody, Joe, and Clint. Thank you for your patience with me and for your patience with seeing this project through to completion. Thank you to Dan Phillips for a critical reading of a good portion of the text of this commentary. Dan, your insights have been a great help. Thanks also goes to Charlotte Gunther and Stephanie Kern for their careful proofreading of the text. Thanks goes out to Rick Kress for the opportunity to share these gleanings in Colossians and Philemon with many others.

Most of all, thank You, Lord Jesus! You are the center, circumference, and substance of this letter and of all life. You are my life (Col. 3:4), my hope (1:27), my goal (1:28). To be found in You and to realize You in me is a gift of unspeakable grace and wonder!

Abbreviations

Old Testament

Gen.	Genesis	Eccl.	Ecclesiastes
Exod.	Exodus	Song of Sol.	Song of Solomon
Lev.	Leviticus	Isa.	Isaiah
Num.	Numbers	Jer.	Jeremiah
Deut.	Deuteronomy	Lam.	Lamentations
Josh.	Joshua	Ezek.	Ezekiel
Judg.	Judges	Dan.	Daniel
Ruth	Ruth	Hos.	Hosea
1 Sam.	1 Samuel	Joel	Joel
2 Sam.	2 Samuel	Amos	Amos
1 Kings	1 Kings	Obad.	Obadiah
2 Kings	2 Kings	Jonah	Jonah
1 Chron.	1 Chronicles	Mic.	Micah
2 Chron.	2 Chronicles	Nah.	Nahum
Ezra	Ezra	Hab.	Habakkuk
Neh.	Nehemiah	Zeph.	Zephaniah
Esth.	Esther	Hag.	Haggai
Job	Job	Zech.	Zechariah
Psa.	Psalm	Mal.	Malachi
Prov.	Proverbs		

New Testament

Matt.	Matthew	1 Tim.	1 Timothy
Mark	Mark	2 Tim.	2 Timothy
Luke	Luke	Titus	Titus
John	John	Philem.	Philemon
Acts	Acts	Heb.	Hebrews
Rom.	Romans	James	James
1 Cor.	1 Corinthians	1 Peter	1 Peter
2 Cor.	2 Corinthians	2 Peter	2 Peter
Gal.	Galatians	1 John	1 John
Eph.	Ephesians	2 John	2 John
Phil.	Philippians	3 John	3 John
Col.	Colossians	Jude	Jude
1 Thess.	1 Thessalonians	Rev.	Revelation
2 Thess.	2 Thessalonians		

Bible Translations

ESV	English Standard Version
GNB	Good News Bible
JB	Jerusalem Bible
KJV	King James Version
NAB	New American Bible
NASB	New American Standard Bible (1977)
NASU	New American Standard Bible: Updated Edition (1995)
NEB	New English Bible
NET	The NET Bible
NIV	New International Version
NJB	New Jerusalem Bible
NKJV	New King James Version
NLT	New Living Translation
NRSV	New Revised Standard Version
RSV	Revised Standard Version
TNIV	Today's New International Version

Miscellaneous

c.	*circa*, about
cf.	*confer*, compare
contra	contrary to
e.g.	*exempli gratia*, for example
etc.	*et cetera*, and the like
ff.	following (verses, pages, etc.)
ibid.	*ibidem*, in the same place
i.e.	*id est*, that is
LXX	Septuagint
n.d.	no date
NT	New Testament
OT	Old Testament
PE	Pastoral Epistles
rpt.	reprint

Footnotes

BAGD   *A Greek-English Lexicon of the New Testament and
                            Other Early Christian Literature*

NIDNTT   *The New International Dictionary of New Testament
                            Theology*

NIDNTT: Abridged *The New International Dictionary of New Testament
                            Theology: Abridged Edition*

Little Kittel   *Theological Dictionary of the New Testament* (abridged
                            in one volume)

HOW TO USE THIS BOOK

Allow me to share a word about how you may use this volume for your personal growth and for that of your congregation. Like my earlier commentary, *The Pastoral Epistles for Pastors*, this volume weaves three distinct features into the fabric of one volume. It will serve your needs in any number of different ways. Three of the most obvious ways it will serve you are as a commentary, a counselor, and a coach.

Commentary: you will find that *Colossians and Philemon for Pastors* provides a wealth of exegetical information regarding the text of these two NT epistles. This will aid you in personally understanding God's Word, in preaching and teaching these texts, and in explaining the meaning of these Scriptures to the people whom you shepherd.

Counselor: you will find dispersed throughout the text what I call Ministry Maxims. These are pithy, pointedly stated principles of ministry which arise from or are suggested by the verse where they are found. Each is stated in such a way as to distill the wisdom of the given Scripture into a pointed—and sometimes provocative—statement of principle which applies in ministry contexts of all cultures and at all times. Do you wonder if that is possible? Have a debate with one of the Ministry Maxims? Then they have served their purpose! They are stated in thought-provoking ways in order to stimulate thought and rouse you to interaction with the truth. While the commentary speaks facts into your mind, the Ministry Maxims are designed to speak truth into your heart.

Coach: this companion never allows you to leave a section of Scripture without stopping to ponder how its truth applies to your life and ministry. It provides bridges of application from the truths found in the text of Scripture to the work of ministry in your local church. You will find Digging Deeper questions dispersed throughout the text. My hope is that these will stimulate reflection on how the truths of Colossians and Philemon apply to life and local church ministry. If the commentary is designed to speak facts into your mind and the Ministry Maxims are designed to speak truth into your heart, then these Digging Deeper questions are intended to put skill into your hands as you serve the Lord by serving His people. Additionally, the appendices provide practical ideas on how you can use Colossians and Philemon in personal ministry growth, counseling, and preaching/teaching.

Finally, may I suggest that *Colossians and Philemon for Pastors*, just as with my earlier commentary, is suitable for diving, wading, and dipping. That is to say, you may want to dive in and immerse yourself in the fullness of its content. Or you may want to wade into a particular section of one of these two NT epistles by studying the commentary at that point in the text. Or you may simply want to dip into its contents by perusing the Ministry Maxim call-out boxes, and only then stopping to examine the exegetical work behind those statements which pique your interest. In my mind, the deeper you dive the better, but there is benefit in all these approaches.

COLOSSIANS

INTRODUCTION TO COLOSSIANS

The little letter of Colossians should be required reading for anyone seeking to live for Christ in these early years of the third millennium. Few portions of Scripture more powerfully and pointedly address many of the key issues confronting us in the current cultural climate in which we find ourselves. The faithful shepherd seeking to guide and guard the flock of God under his care will not want to miss the opportunity to carefully expound the truths of this epistle.

This diminutive epistle confronts ever-enduring but always-morphing expressions of heterodoxy. Old lies always find new lines of expression, but they remain fundamentally unchanged. God's people need to see these lies exposed again to the light of truth.

But the beauty and power of Colossians is not found merely in the negative (confrontation and denunciation of error), but even more wonderfully in the positive (affirmation of the truth). Held before us here are life-changing, soul-liberating truths about the possibilities and power of living out our union with Christ. Freedom from what binds and liberty for long-encumbered relationships is set before us.

Above all, Colossians provides us an unparalleled portrait of our Lord and Savior, Jesus Christ. In Colossians we are brought to fresh and breathtaking vistas of Him "who is our life" (Col. 3:4a). Such a look promises to bring new life to tired saints.

Before we dive into the text itself, it behooves us to survey the land we'll be traversing. That is the purpose of this introduction.

I have prepared the introduction with the pastor in mind. I am not primarily crafting this introduction for the academic community. Though the academic and the pastoral cannot and should not be separated entirely, my aim is that we might be well informed regarding the scholarly discussions without getting lost in technical debate. This introduction seeks to provide the pastor with what he needs in order rightly to approach the text of Colossians so as to engage that text robustly, gleaning from it what God has for him and for His flock. I will, therefore, from time to time direct the reader to other sources which will expand upon the issues at hand.[1]

This introduction will pursue answers to five questions:

1. Who wrote this epistle?
2. To whom was this epistle written?
3. What circumstances gave rise to the writing of this epistle?
4. Why did Paul write Colossians?
5. What does Colossians teach us?

Authorship: Who Wrote This Epistle?

At one level the answer to this question appears obvious. The text of the letter, in so many words, claims Paul as its author (Col. 1:1, 23; 4:18). That the Apostle may have employed an amanuensis to aid him in writing some of his letters is not largely in doubt (e.g., Rom. 16:22). At such times Paul would often affix his signature to the letter to assure that the scribe had faithfully conveyed his words (e.g., 1 Cor. 16:21; 2 Thess. 3:17). This may have been the case with the present letter (Col. 4:18).

That Paul was responsible for the writing of the letter to the Colossians stood as the largely unquestioned view until scholars in the nineteenth century presented alternative theories. Let us examine the points that have been raised in questioning Pauline authorship and then do the same with the view that the Apostle Paul is responsible for the composition of the letter.

Objections to Pauline Authorship

In more recent centuries some have hypothesized that someone other than the Apostle Paul is responsible for writing the letter to the Colossians. Other letters which claim to be written by Paul have similarly been questioned as to

---

[1] For those seeking a more detailed introduction I recommend Moo (25-71) and O'Brien (xxv-liv).

their authenticity. These include especially Ephesians, 2 Thessalonians and the Pastoral Epistles.[2] What is the evidence set forth in support of such a claim with regard to Colossians? Generally the claim centers around four basic lines of thought.

1. It is claimed that the vocabulary of Colossians is too markedly different from that of other letters which we know came from Paul's hand.

> O'Brien nicely surveys the differences, saying there are "thirty-four words appearing in Colossians but nowhere else in the NT, twenty-eight words which reappear in the NT but not in the other Pauline letters (not taking into account 2 Thess and the Pastorals), ten words which Colossians has in common only with Ephesians and a further fifteen appearing in Colossians and Ephesians as well as the rest of the NT, but not in the other Pauline letters."[3] Furthermore, certain words which have been deemed stock Pauline expressions are not found in Colossians. These include words such as *justify, believe,* and *salvation.*

2. It is claimed that the style of Colossians is significantly different from letters about which there is no doubt of Pauline authorship.

> Some call the style of Colossians "cumbersome, wordy, and marked by a multiplicity of genitival constructions, participles, and prepositional phrases."[4]

3. It is claimed that the error confronted in Colossians is full-blown Gnosticism and that scholarship has confirmed that Gnosticism was not fully developed until the second century AD.

> This would, of course, put the date of composition far beyond the lifetime of the Apostle Paul.

4. Furthermore, it is claimed that the theology of Colossians is different than what we find in the undisputed letters of Paul.

> Specifically the highly developed Christology of the letter is cited as evidence of a late date of composition. Opponents of Pauline authorship

---

[2] With regard to the authorship of the Pastoral Epistles see the author's *The Pastoral Epistles for Pastors,* 14-26.

[3] O'Brien, xlii.

[4] Vaughan, 11:164.

claim the theology of Colossians is more akin to that of the Apostle John (cf. John 1:1-18) and this, they insist, would require a post-Pauline date.

Evidence for Pauline Authorship

Not all scholars are convinced by the line of evidence set forth by those who oppose Pauline authorship. They cite several important lines of evidence that support the view that the Apostle Paul is responsible for the letter.

1. The letter claims to have been written by Paul (Col. 1:1, 23; 4:18).

Either the letter was or it was not penned by the Apostle. If the book was indeed written by someone other than Paul, then it is not what it claims to be and its veracity, legitimacy, and usefulness is called into question. If Colossians is in error on the matter of authorship, can we legitimately consider it without error in the other matters to which it speaks?

2. The earliest Christian writers believed the letter to have been penned by Paul, and his authorship has remained virtually unchallenged until relatively recent times.

Those church fathers who speak to the matter all attribute Colossians to the Apostle Paul. Justin (c.100-c.165) appears to have used Colossians. Irenaeus (c.125-c.202), Clement of Alexandria (d. c.215), and Origin (c.184-c.254) clearly assign it to Paul. It is cited in Marcion's list (c.146) and in the Muratorian Canon (c.170). The second-century Old Latin versions and the Chester Beatty codes of the Pauline Epistles (P[46]) in Egypt ascribe the book to Paul. In view of these facts, Vaughan testifies that "So far as we can determine from extant writings, Colossians was never suspect in ancient times."[5]

3. The close connection of Colossians to and similarities with the letter to Philemon (which is rarely ever considered non-Pauline) support Paul's authorship.

In both letters the author is in prison (Col. 4:3, 10, 18; Philemon 9-10, 13). Many of the same people are mentioned in both letters (Aristarchus, Mark, Epaphras, Luke, and Demas; cf. Col. 4:10-14; Philem. 23-24). Timothy is associated with Paul in the openings of

---

[5] Vaughan, 11:164.

both letters (Col. 1:1; Philem. 1). Archippus also is singled out in each (Col. 4:17; Philem. 2). Onesimus figures prominently in both letters (Col. 4:9; Philem. 10).[6] Harris says, "If Paul authored Philemon, it seems *a priori* likely that he also wrote Colossians, given these remarkable similarities of circumstance."[7]

4. The vocabulary and style of Colossians is typical of Paul's letters, especially those written to address real-time issues of importance in a particular location.

As noted above, some cite as evidence for non-Pauline authorship the fact that the vocabulary of Colossians shows some differences from what we find in his undisputed NT letters. Yet it seems that the variances in the vocabulary are easily attributable to the uniqueness of the issues being dealt with in Colossians. The parts of the letter in which both the vocabulary and syntax appears most un-Pauline are the very places where the Apostle deals most directly with the error that is being touted in Colossae.[8] The absence of key Pauline words (such as *justify, believe, salvation,* etc.) is not unlike some undisputedly Pauline letters.

5. The theology of Colossians appears consistent with Paul's thought as expressed in others of his letters.

Several areas of the theology in Colossians are said to be too highly developed for Paul's mind at this point. These include the letter's teaching on Christology, the church, and eschatology.[9] Opponents of Pauline authorship claim that the letter's exalted view of Christ (e.g., 1:15-20; 2:9-10, 15) betrays a Christology too well developed for Paul's mind at this time. They believe it is more akin to John's view of Christ (cf. John 1:1ff.).

Paul's Christology in Colossians does appear to be more fully developed than in his other letters. Yet Paul elsewhere shows signs of such an understanding of Christ (e.g., 1 Cor. 8:6; Phil. 2:5-11). And is it not possible that the fuller development in Colossians is due directly to the falsehood being countered? Certainly Paul and John can share

---

[6] Harris, 3.
[7] Ibid., 4.
[8] Vaughan, 11:164.
[9] Moo, 32.

the same view of Christ, can they not? The same Spirit inspired them both to write the Scriptures (2 Tim. 3:16)! Cannot He, whose calling it is to glorify Christ (John 16:14), equally inspire both Apostles to speak similarly of their Lord?

6. The profile we are able to reconstruct concerning the error being confronted in Colossae does not lead us to conclude that it is a full-blown Gnosticism requiring a time of composition in the second century.

For some time, many believed that the falsehood confronted in Colossians was a fully developed Gnosticism. The best evidence, however, seems to indicate that such Gnosticism did not exist prior to the second century. Such a late date for the composition for Colossians would, of course, prohibit Pauline authorship. These assumptions arose in part because of Colossian's use of words such as "fullness" (e.g., Col. 1:19; 2:9), words which would later play an important part in Gnostic thought. Though there may have been strains of thought that later developed into Gnostic ideology, scholarship has since largely dropped the case regarding identifying the falsehood in Colossae as this kind of pure, full-blown Gnosticism. A careful study of the nature of the heresy which was afoot in Colossae (see below) reveals that, while the seeds of what would later become Gnosticism may have been present at the time of the letter's composition, it was not the fully drawn heresy known more widely in the second century.

From where was Colossians written?

If, then, Paul did indeed pen the letter, where was he when he did so? Clearly the letter was penned from an imprisonment (4:3, 10, 18), but which one of Paul's imprisonments and from what location? Students of the Bible have championed three basic answers to this question.

1. Ephesus.

Some locate the letter's origin to what they believed was an imprisonment in Ephesus some time during his three to three-and-a-half years in Ephesus (Acts 19:10, 22; 20:31). This view may more easily explain the interchange and travel of Paul's associates such as Epaphras (Col. 1:7; 4:12; Philem. 23) and Onesimus (Col. 4:9; Philem. 10, 12) and even of Paul himself (Philem. 22). But there are concerns with this view. One might ask for the evidence that Paul was ever imprisoned in Ephesus. It is also of note that while Luke was present with Paul when he wrote Colossians (4:14), there is no evidence he was ever with Paul during his Ephesian ministry.[10]

2. Caesarea.

Others believe the letter came from the Apostle while he was incarcerated in Caesarea. Paul did spend two years under arrest in Caesarea prior to his appeal to Rome (Acts 23:31-24:27). But there is no evidence that during this time Paul organized any such dynamic missionary activity as that mentioned in Colossians 4:3-4, and 10-14.[11]

3. Rome.

After his two years of imprisonment in Caesarea and seeing that his case might proceed poorly, Paul appealed to Rome (Acts 25:11; 26:32; 28:19). Thus constrained, Festus sent Paul on to Rome (25:12). After a frightful voyage at sea in which God miraculously preserved the life not only of Paul, but the lives of all who journeyed with him, Paul and his captors arrived in Rome (Acts 27:1-28:14). "And he stayed two full years in his own rented quarters and was welcoming all who came to him, preaching the kingdom of God and teaching concerning the Lord Jesus Christ with all openness, unhindered" (Acts 28:30-31). The traditional and most widely held view is that Paul wrote the letter of Colossians (along with Philippians, Ephesians, and Philemon) from this first Roman imprisonment. Philippians may have been written during a different portion of this imprisonment, with Colossians, Ephesians, and Philemon—because of their similarities—probably being written at generally the same time. All three of the latter letters (along with a letter to the Laodiceans, Col. 4:16) were probably sent about the same time and carried by Tychicus (Eph. 6:21; Col. 4:7).

It is the view of this commentary that the most likely place of origin was Rome, during Paul's first imprisonment there. This means that Colossians and the other so-called Prison Epistles were probably written sometime between AD 60 and 62.

---

[10] Vaughan, 11:166.
[11] Ibid., 11:165.

Recipients: To Whom Was This Epistle Written?

Colossae was located in the interior of the Roman province of Asia Minor (modern-day western Turkey). In the first century, Colossae was, in regards to the larger world, a smallish, fairly insignificant community somewhat off the beaten path. Four or five centuries earlier, during the Persian and Greek periods, Colossae had been a thriving city—the most significant in the region. It had possessed a thriving economy which found at least part of its strength from the significant role it played in the textile industry of the day, particularly with regard to its woolen products. At the time it was in a position of strategic importance, at the crossroads of two major highways of the ancient world. One ran north and south. The other ran east to west, an artery for the larger cities of the East like the capital of Ephesus, which was approximately one hundred miles to the west.[12]

The fortunes of Colossae began to change when the north-south artery was repositioned to run through the neighboring community of Laodicea. Somewhere in the general time frame of Paul's letter to the Colossians, the region of the Lycus valley was ravaged by an earthquake, probably further debilitating the city. In Paul's day the cities of Laodicea (ten miles to the west; cf. Col. 2:1; 4:13, 15, 16; Rev. 3:14-22) and Hierapolis (thirteen miles to the northwest; cf. Col. 4:13) seem to have been more prominent.

It is unlikely that Paul had ever visited Colossae, though some hold out for the possibility that he in fact had journeyed through the city on his third missionary journey (Acts 18:23; 19:1).[13] Yet Paul seems to say clearly that he had never been to Colossae personally (Col. 1:4, 8; 2:1). However, he makes clear that he does intend to visit the city in the future (Philem. 22).

The area was likely evangelized and the church established during Paul's extended ministry in Ephesus, the capital city of Asia Minor (Acts 19). "This took place for two years, so that *all who lived in Asia heard the word of the Lord*, both Jews and Greeks" (v. 10, emphasis added). One of Paul's opponents in Ephesus told the citizens, "You see and hear that not only in Ephesus, but *in almost all of Asia*, this Paul has persuaded and turned away a considerable number of people, saying that gods made with hands are no

---

[12] Moo, 26.
[13] Harris, 3.

gods at all" (v. 26, emphasis added). This was accomplished as Paul trained and sent out into the surrounding regions gospel workers who bore the message of Jesus. It was probably Epaphras who filled this role for the cities of the Lycus valley, establishing churches in at least Colossae and Laodicea (Col. 1:7; 4:12; Philem. 23).

The population was largely Gentile, but included a significant and perhaps influential minority of Jews as well. In keeping with this general demographic the church appears to have been primarily Gentile in makeup (Col. 1:27; 2:13), though perhaps with a significant Jewish element as well (cf. 2:11; 3:11; 4:11). It appears that the church members had given ear to some ideas that threatened their stability in Christ (1:23; 2:1-23). Epaphras seems to have come to Paul in the Apostle's imprisonment to report on the church, to express his concerns, and to seek answers for how to address the problems (1:7; 4:12). Paul, in response, penned this letter and sent it to the church in Colossae, carried by the hands of Tychicus who brought along Onesimus (4:7-9). Epaphras remained with Paul (4:12-13; Philem. 23) for reasons which are not explained.

Occasion: What Circumstances Gave Rise to the Writing of This Epistle?

Concerning the circumstances that gave rise to the writing of Colossians, we need to address the question both from the angle of the recipients and from that of the author of the letter.

The Circumstances of the Recipients

The church in the city of Colossae, at the time of Paul's writing, had probably been in existence for at least five years, having likely been founded by Epaphras (Col. 1:7) during the time of the Apostle's extended ministry in Ephesus (Acts 19), the capital of Asia Minor.[14] Since that time Epaphras likely had been nurturing their faith, teaching them the truth as it is in Jesus (Col. 2:7).

But in more recent days an aberrant form of spiritual teaching had come in among them. Epaphras, perhaps feeling inadequate to handle the threat himself, set out to visit the Apostle Paul, reporting not only the progress of

---

[14] Hiebert, 224.

the Colossian believers' faith (1:3-8), but also the new threat that had come upon them (see especially 2:8, 16-23). The letter to the Colossians forms the Apostle's Spirit-inspired response to their needs.

It is common to speak of false teachers (plural) influencing the believers in Colossae. Yet, we must ask, is this based on assumption or upon the text of Colossians? Dan Phillips has pointed out that every verse of Colossians that makes explicit mention of the opposition speaks of them in the singular form(s).

- "I say this so that *no one* [μηδείς] will delude you with persuasive argument." (2:4)
- "See to it that *no one* [μή τις] takes you captive through philosophy and empty deception" (2:8a)
- "Therefore let *no one* [Μὴ οὖν τις] act as your judge in regard to food or drink or in respect to a festival or a new moon or a Sabbath day—" (2:16)
- "Let *no one* [μηδείς] keep defrauding you of your prize by delighting in self-abasement and the worship of the angels, taking his stand on visions *he has seen* [ἑόρακεν], inflated without cause by *his* [αὐτοῦ] fleshly mind, and not holding fast to the head ..." (2:18-19a)[15]

He presents a nonexhaustive, though arresting, listing of references which Paul makes to false teachers in his other letters—all of them in the plural forms. He says, "So I conclude that there was one charismatic and potentially influential false teacher in Colosse, who was threatening to exert a dangerous influence among believers. I don't think we should speak of the false teachers in Colosse, but the false teacher. At any rate, that's all we have direct authority to identify."[16]

Other voices chime in to affirm this notion of a singular false teacher who has caught the attention of at least some of the church members in Colossae. Hiebert says, "Since the denunciations throughout this epistle are in the singular number, rather than in the plural as in Galatians, it seems

---

[15] Daniel J. Phillips, "Colossians studies 3: the false teachers (?)" *Pyro Maniacs* (blog), February 25, 2010, http://teampyro.blogspot.com/2010/02/colossians-studies-3-false-teachers.html.

[16] Ibid.

that this Colossian heresy rested on the authority of some single teacher rather than on an appeal to Scripture or tradition."[17] Clinton E. Arnold says, "An influential leader—perhaps a shaman-like figure—is attracting a following among the believers. This spiritual guide claims superior insight into the spirit realm and is insisting on certain rites, taboos, and practices as a means of protection from evil spirits and for deliverance from afflictions and calamities."[18] Commenting on Paul's choice of words in chapter two, Arnold says, "The language of this passage (esp. the Gk. Pronoun *tis*, 'a certain person'), may point to an influential teacher ... who is ringleader of this emerging faction."[19]

Similarly Robert W. Wall says, "The second section of Paul's theological polemic envisions a particular person who apparently is acting as a spiritual umpire, watching to see whether the community observes certain holy days and complies with certain dietary regulations and using these to determine the quality of their devotion to God."[20] Callow, throughout his analysis of chapter 2, always refers to the subject in the singular, and he specifically says that the subject of 2:18 is "a false teacher."[21] Abbott, commenting on the indefinite singular pronoun in 2:8, says "it appears to point to some particular person whom the apostle has in view but does not wish to name."[22]

The text of the letter points us toward envisioning one singular, prominent leader possessing the personal charisma to capture popular attention and to sway personal opinions among the believers in Colossae. Whether by one teacher or by a group of teachers, the believers in Colossae were faced with new ideas that challenged the apostolic gospel they had received. The threat was severe enough for their shepherd to leave them and travel to the Apostle Paul for counsel. What the Apostle learned was serious enough for him to pen a personal letter to counteract the falsehood.

Just what was the nature of the false teaching? This has been the subject of much debate. Nowhere in the letter does Paul formally outline the tenets of the falsehood. We are left to sketch its shape from his comments in this

---

[17] Hiebert, 226.
[18] Arnold, *Bible Backgrounds Commentary*, 3:375.
[19] Ibid., 3:388.
[20] Wall, 121.
[21] Callow, 104.
[22] Abbott, 246.

letter. Here is what we are able to infer from Paul's words about the shape and substance of the falsehood:[23]

- It may have sold itself as something mysterious (1:27; 2:2).
- It may have claimed to have exclusive or special insight/ wisdom/ knowledge.
  - ° "knowledge" (1:9, 10; 2:3); "true knowledge" (2:2; 3:10)
  - ° "wisdom" (2:3, 23)
- It is called "philosophy" (2:8).
- It seems to have been enamored with angels, giving them an exalted status ("the elementary principles of the world, 2:8, 20; "disarmed the rulers and authorities," 2:15; "the worship of angels," 2:18).
- It appears to have been highly persuasive ("delude you with persuasive argument," 2:4).
- It appears to have assigned Jesus a diminished role, though perhaps not openly so.
  - ° Paul emphasizes Jesus as Lord (e.g., 2:6).
  - ° It held an exalted view of angels ("rather than according to Christ," 2:8b).
  - ° Paul emphasizes "in Him all the fullness of Deity dwells in bodily form" (2:9) and the full-sufficiency of Jesus (2:10) and that Christ is "Head" (2:19).
- Their teaching was "empty deception" (2:8).
- Rather than representing higher insight and heavenly treasures, their teaching simply amounted to "the tradition of men" (2:8).
- The rite of circumcision appears to have played a key role in their system (2:11) and may hint at an admixture of Jewish and pagan thought.
- Strands of Jewish thought may also be hinted at in Paul's reference to "the certificate of debt consisting of decrees against us and which was hostile to us" (2:14a).

---

[23] I will leave it to the text of the commentary to expand upon each of these as they are encountered in the flow of the letter.

- The exclusivity of the false teaching resulted in a legalistic tendency which may be pointed to in statements such as "let no one act as your judge" (2:16) and "why ... do you submit to decrees, such as ..." (2:20b).
- The false teacher(s) forced dietary restrictions upon adherents (2:16a).
- Sabbath and Jewish calendar observance was apparently mandatory (2:16b).
- It seems to have possessed esoteric strands of thoughts in which the spiritual was exalted over and above the physical ("the substance belongs to Christ," 2:17b).
- There were also ascetic elements to their thought.
  - "Self-abasement" (2:18, 23)
  - "Do not handle, do not taste, do not touch" (2:21)
  - "severe treatment of the body" (2:23)
- The false teacher appears to have come off as hyperspiritual, with an emphasis upon his visions ("taking his stand on visions he has seen," 2:18).
- Yet at the core all this was driven by "his fleshly mind" (2:18b).
- The resulting line of thought was nothing more than "the commandments and teaching of men" (2:22b).
- For all the "appearance of wisdom" (2:23), it was at root a "self-made religion" (2:23).
- And it was, as such, powerless against "fleshly indulgence" (2:23).

From this we might conclude that the false teaching was most likely some combination of Jewish and pagan ideas. It is not easy to distinguish and definitively assign each strand of thought to one or the other camp. But it seems likely that these statements point to a Jewish element:

- "circumcision" (2:11)
- "the certificate of debt consisting of decrees against us, which was hostile to us" (2:14a)
- "let no one act as your judge" (2:16) and "why ... do you submit to decrees, such as" (2:20b, pointing to legalism)

- "food or drink" (2:16a, Jewish dietary restrictions)
- "a festival or a new moon or a Sabbath day" (2:16b, Jewish Sabbath and calendar observance)

Similarly these elements may point to a pagan (perhaps pre-Gnostic) line of thought:

- "knowledge" (1:9, 10; 2:3); "true knowledge" (2:2; 3:10); and "wisdom" (2:3, 23a)
- "philosophy" (2:8)
- "the substance belongs to Christ" (2:17b, esoteric thought; the spiritual over and above the physical)
- "self-abasement" (2:18, 23); "Do not handle, do not taste, do not touch" (2:21); and "severe treatment of the body" (2:23)
- "taking his stand on visions he has seen" (2:18)
- "fleshly mind" (2:18b)
- "self-made religion" (2:23)

Most scholars seem to acknowledge some mixture of Jewish and pagan (pre-Gnostic) elements present in the falsehood in Colossae, though they may differ over which element is the more dominant and in some cases they may differ over whether a particular statement by the Apostle points to a Jewish or a pagan background. It is safe, however, to conclude that what the believers in Colossae faced was a syncretistic blend of falsehoods melded together uniquely into a spiritually toxic brew.

In all of this, the false teacher(s) nevertheless seems to have claimed he was teaching the way of Christ (2:3-10), or perhaps a higher, greater fulfillment of the way of Christ. He may have held that his line of teaching was where the trajectory of Christ and His gospel should logically and naturally lead. This very emphasis is part of what makes Colossians so vital for the church in our day. Warren Wiersbe nicely states the matter:

> This is an age of "syncretism." People are trying to harmonize and unite many different schools of thought and come up with a superior religion. Our evangelical churches are in danger of diluting the faith in their loving attempt to understand the beliefs of others. Mysticism, legalism, Eastern religions, asceticism, and man-made

philosophies are secretly creeping into churches. They are not denying Christ, but they are dethroning Him and robbing Him of His rightful place of preeminence.[24]

And of course doctrine is never divorced from daily life. True doctrine has authoritative implications for life and godliness which rest with divine authority upon God's people (Titus 2:1ff.). Similarly, false doctrine has an ethical trajectory and finds expression in the lives of its adherents. The two greatest failures of the teaching in Colossae were that it disparaged Christ and therefore distorted Christian living. Paul most directly addressed their diminishing of Christ in 1:15-20 (and see 2:9-10). He seems to address their resulting failures in conceptualizing Christian living in 2:16-23. In these verses Paul crystallizes the falsehood as embracing:

- a false legalism (2:16-17);
- a false spirituality (2:18-19); and
- a false asceticism (2:20-23).

While the false teaching had found some traction (or there would have been no call for the level of concern in Epaphras and Paul), thankfully the false teacher(s) had not been entirely successful among the Colossians (2:4, 8, 20).

It is important to do our best at reconstructing the tenets of the falsehood in Colossae. But it is equally important to note just *how* the Apostle went about combating this falsehood. Paul did not primarily confront the falsehood or its teacher(s) head-on, both barrels blazing with Scriptural and logical argumentation—which would have had the ancillary and lamentable consequence of giving it greater visibility.

Rather, Paul, for the most part, chose to combat the falsehood and its proponent(s) by positively setting forth the truth. There are times when false teachers (e.g., 2 Tim. 2:17) and their false teachings (e.g., Jude and 2 Peter 2) must be directly denounced and debunked. But the more regular practice, without naively ignoring either the false teachers or their falsehoods, is simply to consistently and thoroughly set forth the truth of Christ from the Scriptures in the power of the Holy Spirit. This allows

---

[24] Wiersbe, 2:105.

the truth itself to destroy falsehood (Col. 1:5-6; 2:8), the light to drive out the darkness (1:12-13), and Jesus to triumph over the devil and his minions (1:13; 2:15).[25]

The Circumstances of the Author

Consider also the circumstances of the Apostle Paul himself as he wrote this letter. As we have noted, he was in prison (Col. 4:3, 10, 18). We understand this to be his house arrest in Rome (see above) as he awaited trial before the emperor (Acts 28:30-31). During this time he received a visit from Epaphras (Col. 1:7; Philem. 23), who probably founded the church in Colossae and perhaps the other churches of the Lycus valley. Epaphras informed him of conditions in the church in Colossae generally (Col. 1:3-8; 2:5) and of the threats that confronted the believers. Paul, then, wrote in response to word about their growing faith and the challenges they faced as they sought to continue faithfully in the way of Christ.

Lightfoot has famously said: "Without doubt Colossae was the least important church to which any epistle of Paul is addressed."[26] What are we to make of such a statement? Is there not encouragement for us here? Some readers of this commentary may pastor large, significant churches in strategic locations which afford them tactical influence for the Kingdom. Yet most of us, this author included, probably labor in places and among people who seem at times distantly removed from the power centers of influence and change. We are reminded that virtually every problem faced in a large, influential church is met also in the smaller church—only oftentimes with fewer earthly resources to address those challenges. Colossians reminds us that the fullness of the glorious Christ is ours, regardless of our local circumstances!

The Relationship of Colossians and Ephesians

Even the casual reader of the NT will quickly note the marked similarities of Ephesians and Colossians. Both letters were written from imprisonment (Eph. 3:1; 4:1; 6:20; Col. 4:10, 18). Both appear to be carried to their destination by a common courier (Eph. 6:21; Col. 4:7). The general shape

---

[25] See below for more on the positive development of truth in Colossians (see Theology: What Does Colossians Teach Us?).

[26] Lightfoot, 16.

of the letters is much the same. Many of the themes are strikingly similar: the church as the body of Christ, Christ as the head of the church, ethical demands being made, relationships stressed, instructions concerning prayer.[27] And much of the vocabulary in the two letters is the same. Harris says that some thirty-two words in the Greek text are identical in the two letters.[28] Themes such as wisdom, knowledge, fullness, mystery, principalities and powers are shared by the two letters.[29]

All this leads one to wonder over the relationship between these two epistles. Is one dependent upon the other? Is one an extrapolation of the other? Which, if either, is to be considered dependent upon the other?

Not surprisingly, scholars differ in their answers to these questions. Some believe Ephesians was written first and that Colossians followed, calling upon some of the same ideas developed in the first letter.[30] Others give chronological priority to Colossians, believing that Ephesians then refined and further developed and polished those ideas.[31]

Ultimately, we do not know the answer in any sense which warrants dogmatism. And we don't need to know. We do know that the Holy Spirit inspired the Apostle Paul to pen both and because He did we are all the richer.

While there are profound similarities between the two letters, we should also note their distinctive styles and approaches. In this regard Vaughan wisely says, "Colossians is terse and abrupt; Ephesians is diffuse and flowing. Colossians is specific, concrete, and elliptical; Ephesians is abstract, didactic, and general. Finally, there is a difference in mood. Colossians, argumentative and polemical, is a letter of discussion; Ephesians, calm and ironical, is a letter of reflection.[32]

Purpose: Why Did Paul Write Colossians?

It would appear that Paul penned this letter in response to a report from Epaphras, who had arrived with word about some troubling conditions at

---

[27] Vaughan, 11:169; cf. Kent, 12.
[28] Harris, 4.
[29] Vaughan, 11:169.
[30] E.g., Wright, 37-39.
[31] E.g., Vaughan, 11:169.
[32] Ibid.

the church in Colossae (Col. 1:7; 4:12; Philem. 23). A thorough view of the motives behind the Apostle's letter would include at least these:

1. Paul wished to establish a personal connection with the believers in Colossae and to express his pastoral concern for their spiritual health and well-being.

> Paul apparently had never been to the city (Col. 1:4, 8; 2:1), had not founded the church (1:7), and did not personally know many of its people. Yet because the church was apparently founded during his extended ministry centered in Ephesus and by one whom he had probably personally trained (Epaphras), he clearly felt an affinity to and a responsibility and concern for the well-being of its believers.

2. Paul purposed to counteract false teaching that had arisen in the church in Colossae.

> The Apostle heard from Epaphras of ideas and teachings that were being circulated among the believers in Colossae (see above). Epaphras likely did not feel prepared to confront these teachings and sought the counsel of his mentor. Paul spends the first chapter and a half of the letter presenting the positive doctrinal foundation from which these falsehoods were to be understood, confronted, and overcome (1:1-2:7).

3. Paul wanted to warn the believers in Colossae about several wrong-headed approaches to the Christian life and ministry that were the result of the false teaching.

> It is not until 2:8 that Paul addresses these problems directly, but he spends the rest of the second chapter confronting several of its tenets head-on (2:8-23). What is more, he then outlines (Col. 3-4) divinely authoritative ethical implications of these truths as applied to daily life and relationships.

Theology: What Does Colossians Teach Us?

Though in writing the letter to the Colossians Paul touches upon many aspects of truth and in doing so brings in the wide-ranging concerns of his broader theology, he nevertheless does so with a distinctive emphasis. The two greatest failures of the false teacher(s) in Colossae were his diminished view of Jesus and, as a result of this, his distorted view of the Christian life. Not surprisingly then, perhaps the two great contributions Colossians makes to us are along the same two lines, only from a positive standpoint.

Christology

The portrait of Christ in Colossians is unparalleled in all of Paul's writings. This is a remarkable statement in its own right, for Paul throughout all his letters consistently holds Christ up to the highest place. Yet here, in Colossians, he soars to heights of truth and expressions of fact that are beyond compare.

Christ is everywhere in Colossians; Christ is everything in Colossians. Certainly the letter is Trinitarian. The Father (1:2, 3, 12, 19; 3:17) and the Spirit (1:8) are vital and present. But Christ shines most brilliantly. He is designated as "Christ" (eighteen times; e.g., 1:2; 2:2; 3:11; 4:4:3), "Jesus Christ" (1:1; 4:12), "Christ Jesus" (1:4), "Christ Jesus the Lord" (2:6), "the Lord Jesus" (3:17), and "the Lord Jesus Christ" (1:3). He is God's "beloved Son" (1:13). He is God's "mystery" (1:27). He is the sphere in which our maturity will be realized (1:28). In Him "are hidden all the treasures of wisdom and knowledge" (2:3). He is the sphere in which the believer lives his life (2:6). He is the soil in which we thrive and the arena in which we are built up to become what we were designed to be (2:7).

Christ has died (2:20), been buried (2:11-12), is risen (3:1), and is now exalted to the place of supreme authority in the entire universe (3:1). Thus Christ has utterly defeated Satan and all demonic powers (2:10, 15). Remarkably, Paul tells us that with Christ *we* have died (2:20), been buried (2:12), and been raised (3:1). Thus we share in His victory and authority. Indeed, "you have died and your life is hidden with Christ in God" (3:3).

Christ is the substance and reality of all God's purposes and grace (2:17). He is "the head" of the body, the church (2:19), and as such is both the supply line of all we need and the binding support which holds us together as His people. At His return we will "be revealed with Him in glory" (3:4). Christ is the goal and pattern after which God is remaking us and to which He is conforming us (3:10). Christ overcomes all human, earth-bound distinctions that separate people (3:11). He has forgiven us all our sins (2:13; 3:13). His word is to become the substance of our thoughts, the meditation of our hearts, the song on our lips, the theme of our conversations, and the substance of our worship (3:16). His name is to be stamped over everything we say or do (3:17a). He is the channel of our ever-flowing stream of thanksgiving to the Father (3:17b). He governs and defines marriage (3:18-19), parenting (20-21), and our employer/employee relationships (3:22-4:1).

Christ is worth being imprisoned for (4:3). To Him we bend the direction of our lives, rendering our service (4:7, 12), and from Him we receive our ministries (4:17).

While He reigns supreme through the whole of the letter, the highest heights are reached in the first and second chapter, where Paul lays the doctrinal foundation from which he will launch his vigorous polemic against the false teacher and his false gospel (2:8, 16-23).

As to His relationship to God, *Jesus is the invisible God made visible.* That is to say He is "the image of the invisible God" (1:15a). He is no mere resemblance or reproduction of God, but shares the very essence of the one true Deity. Jesus manifests to us the otherwise invisible God. The Father delights for "all the fullness to dwell in Him" (1:19). In case there is any question as to what he means, the Apostle clarifies: "in Him all the fullness of Deity dwells in bodily form" (2:9). Nothing missing. No mere emanation of God. Not a mere reflection. Not merely a portrait of God. Jesus Christ is God and shares completely in the fullness of the divine essence.

As to Christ's relationship to all created reality, He is the *origin* of all creation ("He is before [πρὸ] all things," v. 17a); the *sphere* of all creation ("by [ἐν] Him all things were created, both in the heavens and on earth, visible and invisible, whether thrones or dominions or rulers or authorities," v.16a); the *agent* of all creation ("all things have been created by [δι'] Him," v. 16b); the *goal* of all creation ("all things have been created ... for [εἰς] Him," v. 16c); and the *sustainer* of all creation ("in [ἐν] Him all things hold together," v. 17b). Indeed, He is the *King* of all creation ("the firstborn of all creation," 1:15b)!

STOP! Reread that last paragraph. This time substitute the word "reality" for the word "creation." Now pause. Consider and be amazed! Ponder and fall down in worship and rise in service! What folly to attempt to live independent of Christ!

As to Christ's relationship to God's new creation, the church, He holds first place over *new life* ("the beginning, the firstborn from the dead," v. 18b); over *a new people* ("the head of the body, the church," v. 18a); and over *a new creation* ("He Himself will come to have first place in everything," v. 18c).

STOP! Consider this: Before it is all over, Jesus "will come to have first place in everything"! If this defines our destination (and that of all created reality), ought it not also describe our current journey? This very Jesus is first in the Father's heart ("good pleasure," v. 19a). Ought He not hold the same position in ours?

It is hard to imagine how the primacy and preeminence of Christ could be more fully or beautifully set forth. The Apostle, caught up in the wonder, finally flings human language to its farthest horizon and concludes: "Christ is all, and in all" (3:11b)!

Sanctification

For Paul orthodoxy always leads to orthopraxy. That is to say, right doctrine is not an end in itself. Truth transforms. Everything changes when one embraces the truth of who Jesus Christ is. Just as with the heresy, the truth of who Christ is and what He has done works itself out along an ethical and moral trajectory.

Progressing through the text of Colossians, we do not meet an imperative until 2:6. We are, then, to understand 1:1-2:5 as providing the theological/ doctrinal/ instructional foundation for the moral imperatives that are laid upon us from 2:6 onward. Those imperatives are only understandable and reasonable in light of the truths set forth in 1:1-2:5. They are only achievable by the resources and relationship set before us in 1:1-2:5. The imperatives of 2:6ff. would be a means of despair apart from the provisions set forth in 1:1-2:5. But with those foundational provisions in place, the imperatives become a pathway to life and liberty. Gospel imperatives always rest on gospel grace.

So what are those provisions which the Apostle sets forth, provisions which make moral and ethical effort both possible and pleasing? The reality that makes life-change possible, that which makes moral imperatives into pathways of hope is set before us along two lines of one great truth. That truth is the believer's union with Christ.

This is a real union, though it is something of a mystery and is ultimately unexplainable in the fullest sense. This union with Christ is not something that exists merely in a line of mental cognition, doctrinal syllogisms, or logical rationale. It is a *real* union. That living, actual union with Jesus Christ is life altering. This is a game changer. This single great truth is set before us, then, along two lines. They are drawn out most simply in this way:

- You "in Christ" (1:28)
- "Christ in you" (1:27)

Paul's emphasis of the believer being "in Christ" has been identified as the single and most simple way of summing up all of Paul's theology. John Murray has said, "Union with Christ is really the central truth of the whole doctrine of salvation."[33] James S. Stewart has written, "Union with Christ, rather than justification or election or eschatology, or indeed any of the other great apostolic themes, is the real clue to an understanding of Paul's thought and experience."[34]

Union with Christ is pervasive throughout all Paul's letters. It is no less an essential theme of his communication with the believers in Colossae. He opens the letter by identifying its recipients as "the saints and faithful brethren *in Christ*" (1:2, emphasis added). This is no mere convention. It is at the heart of Paul's understanding of what salvation achieves and what this salvation produces in believers.

Indeed, Paul can say that the fullest view of reality includes both our physical address and the circumstances that come with it at any given time (ἐν Κολοσσαῖς, "at Colossae," lit., "in Colossae") as well as the realities of our spiritual union as those "in Christ" (ἐν Χριστῷ,, v. 2). We are simply not in touch with a full view of reality until we understand both, and the latter informs and holds sway over the former. It is in union with Christ (ἐν ᾧ, "in whom") we come to enjoy and possess "redemption, the forgiveness of sins" (v. 14).

The great goal of Paul's ministry (and all gospel ministry) is to "present every man complete *in Christ*" (ἐν Χριστῷ, 1:28, emphasis added). The whole of our Christian life, from regeneration to resurrection and

---

[33] Murray, 161.
[34] Stewart, vii.

glorification is "in Him" (ἐν αὐτῷ, 2:6b). Indeed, it is "in Him" that we are called to "walk"—the moment-by-moment, step-by-step unfolding of our Christian experience and life is conducted and experienced in this real union with Christ.

To be thus in union with Christ is to be also, then, "in the Spirit" (ἐν πνεύματι, 1:8). The Holy Spirit is "the Spirit of Jesus" (Acts 16:7; Rom. 8:9; Gal. 4:6; Phil. 1:19; 1 Peter 1:11). Being indwelt by "the Spirit of Christ" (Rom. 8:9) is an essential defining element of truly being a participant in God's salvation. The Spirit actualizes, applies, and makes real the living union with Christ into which God has brought us.

To thus be "in Christ" means we have been given an entirely ***new identity***. We are not who we once were. We have been made new (Col. 3:10), born again (John 3:3, 7), regenerated to a new life (Titus 3:5) with a new heart (Ezek. 36:26; Col. 3:12) and a new mind (Col. 3:2). The Christian life (2:6ff.) demands a new identity, for "the old self" (Rom. 6:6) cannot perform that which characterizes the new life which God works in us. The "mind set on the flesh is death" (Rom. 8:6a). Indeed, "the mind set on the flesh is hostile toward God; for it does not subject itself to the law of God, for it is not even able to do so" (v. 7). We must change our minds about who we are for "the mind set on the Spirit is life and peace" (v. 6b).

The foundation for sanctification is, then, first of all a new identity. The old "me" is not being asked to perform the commands laid upon us in 2:6ff. (or any of the rest of the Scriptures). It is to the new "me" that exists by God's grace in union with Christ that these imperatives are given. In such a context they become a path of life, liberty and hope.

To the foundation of a new identity, we might add the second line of truth which Paul presents to us regarding our union with Christ. This is not only that you are "in Christ," but that "Christ [is] in you" (1:27). If the first holds before us the fact of our new identity, this second line of truth holds before us the reality of a ***new presence*** in our lives. Not only am I "in Christ," but Christ is in me. The first changes my identity, the second changes my possibilities. The first changes who I am, the second changes what is possible, for I am not left to my own devices, but am the residence of a new presence and thus a new power and thus a new potential and thus a whole new life of possibilities. Christ Himself, by His indwelling

Spirit (1:8; cf. Rom. 8:1-11; Gal. 5:16-26; Eph. 5:18), actualizes His presence and power in our lives. This requires recalibrating what I understand as possible. This requires that I reevaluate all potentialities by the standard of a new identity and possibility that is mine by virtue of being brought into union with Christ Himself.

Review again what Paul, in this letter to the Colossians, has claimed for Christ. Contemplate what it means then to be in union with Christ! It is impossible to take in all the implications!

How then are we to understand these two truths so that our hearts and minds embrace them in a life-changing way? How can we be "in Christ" and at the same time have Christ in us? When we hear the word *"in"* we think spatially, and being *in* something and that something being *in* you do not seem to be possible at the same time in the same way. But our union with Christ is not a spatial reality, but a relational and spiritual reality. This, however, does not make it any less *real*.

Realizing that no illustration is perfect (including this one), allow me to paint a picture which might crack the door of our understanding. Christ is infinite (1:15ff.). The Pacific Ocean *seems* infinite to us. The Pacific Ocean is not infinite, but it *seems* to be from our perspective. The Mariana Trench reaches depths of over six and a half miles. Whether you are four foot eleven or seven foot six, the water definitely would be over your head. Thus for the sake of illustration the waters of the Pacific might help us.

Picture a helicopter flying you into the middle of the Pacific Ocean. You ask the pilot to bring the helicopter to a standstill, hovering just above the surface of the water. Then you leap from the helicopter. You are now *"in* the Pacific." You signal the pilot, and he turns the craft and speeds away. Your entire identity is now wrapped up in the fact that you are "in the Pacific." You are surrounded by seemingly endless miles of open water. There are an estimated 622 million cubic kilometers of water in the Pacific. You are now *in* those waters. This now defines your existence. This answers the question of your identity.

But this only helps us with one line of this foundational truth of our union with Christ. It aids us in seeing ourselves "in Christ." But what of the other essential strand of truth—"Christ in you"?

Picture yourself now taking an action that will be completely counter-intuitive. It will go against everything that you've come to deem rational and logical. It will cut cross-grain against everything you've ever known as sanity and in accord with reality. It will defy what seems to be "life." Yet now, by an act of your will, you draw in a deep breath, turn yourself downward and swim with all your might. You kick and use your arms—going as deep as you are able with one breath. There you are, twenty or thirty feet below the surface of the Pacific. You are "*in* the Pacific." Now you open your mouth and … draw in a huge breath!

To this point you have been "in the Pacific." But now "the Pacific is in you"!

"Ah," you say, "but now I am also dead!"

Precisely. You have died with Christ (Col. 2:20; 3:3). In fact you were buried with Him (2:12a). But you have also been made alive with Him (2:12b; 3:1). In fact it is "Christ who is your life" (3:4a, ESV)! This has been and continues to be actualized by His indwelling Spirit (1:8). "Therefore if you have been raised up with Christ, keep seeking the things above, where Christ is, seated at the right hand of God. Set your mind on the things above, not on the things that are on earth" (3:1-2). In other words, think in accordance with reality—the new reality established for you by God in bringing you into union with Christ! A reality that provides you …

- **A New Identity**: *You "in Christ"*
- **A New Presence**, and thus a new **power**, and thus an entirely new **potential**, and thus a life defined by completely new **possibilities**: *"Christ in you"*

Now, in conscious awareness of your new identity as one "in Christ" and in faith-filled dependence upon the Christ who indwells you by His Spirit, turn to the text of Colossians, asking God to press the truth upon you until you have been conformed to His image (3:10), walking with Him until everything and everyone proclaims that "Christ is all, and is in all" (3:11b)!

Bibliography[35]

Abbott, T. K. *The Epistles to the Ephesians and to the Colossians*. The International Critical Commentary on the Holy Scriptures of the Old and New Testaments. Edited by Samuel Rolles, Alfred Plummer, and Charles Augustus Briggs. Edinburgh: T. & T. Clark, n.d., last impression 1991.

Alford, Henry. *Alford's Greek Testament: An Exegetical and Critical Commentary*. 5 vols. Grand Rapids, MI: Baker Book House, reprint 1980 from the 1871 version.

Arnold, Clinton E. "Colossae." In *The Anchor Bible Dictionary: Volume 1*. New York: Doubleday, 1992.

Arnold, Clinton E. "Colossians." In *Zondervan Illustrated Bible Backgrounds Commentary: Volume 3, Romans to Philemon*. Grand Rapids, MI: Zondervan, 2002.

Arnold, Clinton E. *The Colossian Syncretism*. Grand Rapids, MI: Baker Books, 1996.

Barclay, William. *The Letters to the Philippians, Colossians, and Thessalonians*. The Daily Study Bible. Philadelphia: The Westminster Press, 1959.

Bauer, Walter, *A Greek-English Lexicon of the New Testament and Other Early Christian Literature*, 2nd ed. Translated by William F. Arndt and F. Wilbur Gingrich. Chicago: The University of Chicago Press, 1979.

Brown, Colin, ed. *The New International Dictionary of New Testament Theology*. 3 vols. Grand Rapids, MI: Zondervan, 1975.

Bruce, F. F. *Paul, Apostle of the Heart Set Free*. Grand Rapids, MI: William B. Eerdmans, 1977.

---

[35] See Appendix E for an annotated bibliography of commentaries.

Bruce, F. F. *The Epistles to the Colossians, to Philemon, and to the Ephesians.* The New International Commentary on the New Testament, F. F. Bruce, general editor. Grand Rapids, MI: William B. Eerdmans, 1984.

Bullinger, E. W. *Figures of Speech Used in the Bible: Explained and Illustrated.* GrandRapids, MI: Baker Book House, 1898, reprinted in 1988.

Callow, John. *A Semantic Structure Analysis of Colossians,* 2nd ed. Dallas: SIL International, 2002.

Carson, Herbert M. *The Epistles of Paul to the Colossians and Philemon: An Introduction and Commentary.* Tyndale New Testament Commentaries, R. V. G. Tasker, general editor. Grand Rapids, MI: William B. Eerdmans, 1960, reprint 1981.

Dana, H. E. and Julius R. Mantey. *A Manual Grammar of the Greek New Testament.* Toronto: Macmillan, 1927, 1955.

Davids, Peter H. "Colossians." In *Cornerstone Biblical Commentary – Volume 16: Ephesians-2 Thessalonians, Philemon.* Carol Stream, IL: Tyndale House, 2008. WORDsearch CROSS e-book.

Demarest, Gary. *Colossians: The Mystery of Christ in Us.* Waco, TX: Word Books, 1979.

Dunn, James D. G. *The Epistles to the Colossians and to Philemon: A Commentary on the Greek Text.* Grand Rapids, MI: William B. Eerdmans, 1996.

Eadie, John. *A Commentary on the Greek Text of the Epistle of Paul to the Colossians.* Birmingham, AL: Solid Ground Christian Books, first published in 1885, new edition July 2005.

Fee, Gordon. *God's Empowering Presence: The Holy Spirit in the Letters of Paul.* Peabody, MA: Hendrickson Publishers, 1994.

Friberg, Timothy, Barbara Friberg, and Neva F. Miller. *Analytical Lexicon of the Greek New Testament*. Victoria, British Columbia: Trafford Publishing, 2005.

Garland, David E. *The NIV Application Commentary: Colossians and Philemon*. Grand Rapids, MI: Zondervan, 1998.

Geisler, Norman L. "Colossians." In *The Bible Knowledge Commentary: New Testament*. Edited by John F. Walvoord and Roy B. Zuck. Victor Books, 1983.

Guthrie, Donald. "Colossians." In *The New Bible Commentary: Revised*. Edited by Donald Guthrie and J. A. Motyer. Grand Rapids, MI: William B. Eerdmans, 1970.

Harris, Murray J. *Colossians and Philemon*. Exegetical Guide to the Greek New Testament. Edited by Murray J. Harris. Grand Rapids, MI: William B. Eerdmans, 1991.

Hendriksen, William. *Philippians, Colossians and Philemon*. New Testament Commentary. Grand Rapids, MI: Baker Book House, 1962.

Henry, Matthew. *Matthew Henry's Commentary on the Whole Bible: Complete and Unabridged in One Volume*. Peabody, MA: Hendrickson Publishers, 1991.

Hiebert, D. Edmond. *An Introduction to the Pauline Epistles*. Chicago: Moody Press, 1954.

House, H. Wayne. "The Christian Life According to Colossians." *Bibliotheca Sacra* 151, no. 604 (October 1994): 440-454.

_____. "The Doctrine of Christ in Colossians." *Bibliotheca Sacra* 149, no. 594 (April 1992): 180-192.

_____. "The Doctrine of Salvation in Colossians." *Bibliotheca Sacra* 151. no. 603 (July1994) 325-238.

_____. "Heresies in the Colossian Church." *Bibliotheca Sacra* 149, no. 593 (January 1992): 45-59.

Ironside, H. A. *Lectures on the Epistles to the Colossians*. Neptune, NJ: Loizeaux Brothers, 1981.

Johnson, S. Lewis. "Beware of Philosophy." *Bibliotheca Sacra* 119, no. 476 (October, 1962): 302-311.

_____. "Christian Apparel." *Bibliotheca Sacra* 121, no. 481 (January, 1964): 22-33.

_____. "Christ Pre-eminent." *Bibliotheca Sacra* 119, no. 473 (January, 1962): 12-19.

_____. "The Complete Sufficiency of Union with Christ." *Bibliotheca Sacra* 120, no. 477 (January, 1963): 13-23.

_____. "From Enmity to Amity." *Bibliotheca Sacra* 119, no. 474 (April, 1962): 139-149.

_____. "Human Taboos and Divine Redemption." *Bibliotheca Sacra* 120, no. 479 (July, 1963): 205-213.

_____. "The Minister of Mercy." *Bibliotheca Sacra* 119, no. 475 (July, 1962): 227-237.

_____. "The New Man in the Old Relationships." *Bibliotheca Sacra* 121, no. 482 (April, 1964): 107-116.

_____. "The Paralysis of Legalism." *Bibliotheca Sacra* 120, no. 478 (April, 1963): 109-116.

_____. "Paul's Final Words to the Colossians." *Bibliotheca Sacra* 121, no. 484 (October, 1964): 311-220.

_____. "Spiritual Knowledge and Walking Worthily of the Lord." *Bibliotheca Sacra* 118, no. 472 (October, 1961): 334-346.

_____. "Studies in the Epistle to the Colossians," *Bibliotheca Sacra* 118, no. 471 (July, 1961): 239-250.

Kent, Homer A., Jr. *Treasures of Wisdom: Studies in Colossians and Philemon,* rev. ed.: Grand Rapids, MI: Baker Book House, 2006. First published 1978 by BMH Books, Winona Lake, IN.

King, Martha. *An Exegetical Summary of Colossians.* Dallas: Summer Institute of Linguistics, 1998.

Kitchen, John. *Revival in the Rubble.* Fort Washington, PA: CLC Publications, 2006.

Kitchen, John A. *The Pastoral Epistles for Pastors.* The Woodlands, TX: Kress Biblical Resources, 2009.

Kittel, Gerhard and Gerhard Friedrich. *Theological Dictionary of the New Testament.* Translated and abridged in one volume by Geoffrey W. Bromiley. Grand Rapids, MI: William B. Eerdmans, 1985.

Knox, John. *Philemon among the Letters of Paul.* London: Collins, 1960.

Lenski, R. C. H. *The Interpretation of St. Paul's Epistles to the Colossians, to the Thessalonians, to Timothy, to Titus and to Philemon.* Minneapolis: Augsburg. Copyright 1937, Lutheran Book Concern; 1946, The Wartburg Press. Copyright assigned to Augsburg, 1961.

Liddell, Henry George, Robert Scott, Henry Stuart Jones, and Robert McKenzie. *A Greek-English Lexicon,* 9th rev. ed. Copyright © Oxford University Press, 1996. Bibleworks 7.

Liefeld, W. L., "Mystery." In *The Zondervan Pictorial Encyclopedia of the Bible,* vol. 4. Merrill C. Tenney, general editor. Grand Rapids, MI: Zondervan, 1975, 1976.

Lightfoot, John B. *Saint Paul's Epistle to the Colossians and to Philemon.* London: MacMillian, 1892.

Lohse, Eduard. *Colossians and Philemon*. Hermeneia. Philadelphia: Fortress Press, 1971.

Louw, J. P. and E. A. Nida, eds., *Louw-Nida Greek-English Lexicon of the New Testament Based on Semantic Domains*, 2nd ed. New York: United Bible Societies, 1988. Electronic version.

MacArthur, John. *MacArthur New Testament Commentary: Colossians and Philemon*. Chicago: Moody Press, 1992. WORDsearch CROSS e-book.

Martin, Ralph P. *Colossians and Philemon*. New Century Bible Commentary. Grand Rapids, MI: William B. Eerdmans, 1973.

Melick, Richard R. *New American Commentary – Volume 32: Philippians, Colossians, Philemon*. Nashville, TN: Broadman Press, 1991. WORD*search* CROSS e-book.

Moo, Douglas J. *The Letters to the Colossians and to Philemon*. The Pillar New Testament Commentary. Grand Rapids, MI: William B. Eerdmans, 2008.

Moule, C. F. D. *The Epistles to the Colossians and Philemon*. The Cambridge Greek Testament Commentary. Cambridge: Cambridge University Press, 1957.

Moule, H. C. G. *Studies in II Timothy*. Grand Rapids, MI: Kregel, 1977.

Mounce, William D., general editor. *Mounce's Complete Expository Dictionary of Old and New Testament Words*. Grand Rapids, MI: Zondervan, 2006.

Muller, Jac. J. *The Epistles of Paul to the Philippians and to Philemon*. New International Commentary. Grand Rapids, MI: Zondervan, 1955.

Murray, John. *Redemption—Accomplished and Applied*. Grand Rapids, MI: William B. Eerdmans, 1955.

Newman, Barclay M., Jr., *A Concise Greek-English Dictionary of the New Testament,* Copyright © 1971 by the United Bible Societies (UBS) and 1993 by Deutsche Bibelgesellschaft (German Bible Society), Stuttgart. Used by permission. MRT ASCII version reformatted, corrected, and updated in 1987 by CCAT, University of Pennsylvania. Barclay, Newman, electronic edition.

O'Brien, Peter T. *Colossians and Philemon.* Word Biblical Commentary, vol. 44. Nashville, TN: Nelson Reference & Electronic, 1982.

Phillips, Daniel J. "Colossians studies 3: the false teachers (?)" *Pyro Maniacs* (blog), February 25, 2010 , http://teampyro.blogspot.com/2010/02/colossians-studies-3-false-teachers.html.

Piper, John. *This Momentary Marriage.* Wheaton, IL: Crossway Books, 2009.

Rienecker, Fritz. *A Linguistic Key to the Greek New Testament.* Translated by Cleon L. Rogers, Jr. Grand Rapids, MI: Zondervan, 1976, 1980.

Robertson, Archibald Thomas. *Grammar of the Greek New Testament in the Light of Historical Research,* 3rd ed. London: Hodder & Stoughton, 1919.

Robertson, Archibald Thomas. *Word Pictures in the New Testament.* 6 vols. Grand Rapids, MI: Baker Book House, reprint n.d. from 1930 Sunday School Board of the Southern Baptist Convention.

Rupprecht, Arthur A. "Philemon." In *The Expositor's Bible Commentary,* vol. 11. Grand Rapids, MI: Zondervan, 1978.

Salter, Martin. "Does Baptism Replace Circumcision? An Examination of the Relationship between Circumcision and Baptism in Colossians 2:11-12." *Themelois* 35, no. 1 (2010): 15-29.

Stewart, James S. *A Man in Christ.* New York: Harper and Row, 1955.

Stott, John R. W. *Men Made New.* Grand Rapids, MI: Baker Book House, 1966.

Thayer, Joseph H. *Thayer's Greek-English Lexicon of the New Testament.* Peabody, MA: Hendriksen Publishers, reprinted 2003 from the 4th ed. Originally published by T&T Clark, Edinburgh, 1896.

Thomas, Major W. Ian. *The Saving Life of Christ.* Grand Rapids, MI: Zondervan, 1989.

Vaughan, Curtis. "Colossians." In *The Expositor's Bible Commentary,* vol. 11. Grand Rapids, MI: Zondervan, 1978.

Verbrugge, Verlyn D., ed. *New International Dictionary of New Testament Theology: Abridged Edition.* Grand Rapids, MI: Zondervan, 2000.

Vincent, Marvin R. *A Critical and Exegetical Commentary on the Epistles to the Philippians and to Philemon.* The International Critical Commentary. Edinburgh: T. & T. Clark, 1897.

Vincent, Marvin R. *Vincent's Word Studies in the New Testament.* McLean, VA: MacDonald Publishing Company, n.d.

Vine, W. E. *Vine's Expository Dictionary of New Testament Words.* McLean, VA: MacDonald Publishing Company, n.d.

Wallace, Daniel B. *Greek Grammar: Beyond the Basics.* Grand Rapids, MI: Zondervan, 1996.

Wiersbe, Warren W. *The Bible Exposition Commentary: New Testament,* vol. 2. Colorado Springs: Victor Books, 2001.

Wright, N. T. *The Epistles of Paul to the Colossians and Philemon: An Introduction and Commentary.* Tyndale New Testament Commentaries, Leon Morris, general editor. Downers Grove, IL: IVP Academic, 1986.

Zacharias, Ravi, "Pleasure at a Price," *A Slice of Infinity,* March 30, 2000. http://www.rzim.org/slice/slicearticleprint.aspx?aid=9044

COLOSSIANS 1

1:1 Paul, an apostle of Jesus Christ by the will of God, and Timothy our brother,

The wording of this verse is matched precisely in 2 Corinthians 1:1. The opening clause (Παῦλος ἀπόστολος Χριστοῦ Ἰησοῦ διὰ θελήματος θεοῦ, "Paul, an apostle of Jesus Christ by the will of God") is identical to Ephesians 1:1 and 2 Timothy 1:1.

The author's name (Παῦλος, "Paul") is the first word encountered, as is the case in all thirteen of Paul's NT epistles. "Paul" was born as the son of a Roman citizen (Acts 22:28) and was given both a Roman name (Παῦλος, "Paul") and a Hebrew name (Σαῦλος, "Saul"). Early in the biblical record he is referred to by his Hebrew name (e.g., Acts 7:58; 8:1, 3; 13:1, 2, 7, 9), for he was still primarily associated with the Jewish people. When he was called and sent as a missionary to the Gentiles, his Roman name became the normal way reference was made to him.

He is "an apostle of Christ Jesus" (ἀπόστολος Χριστοῦ Ἰησοῦ). The word "apostle" (ἀπόστολος) refers to one sent with a message and endowed with the full authority of the sender in delivering it. The outworking of this commission has landed Paul now in prison (4:3, 10, 18). In his letters Paul often referred to his apostleship in order to establish his authority in the face of opposition or internal division. This is likely part of his purpose here as he will confront false teaching (2:4, 8, 16-23) and lay down authoritative instruction for the church. And this to a congregation he has never met personally (2:1) and in whose founding he played no direct role (1:4, 7-9). He may also, however, want the readers to know that his imprisonment is a part of his ambassadorship for "Christ Jesus" (Χριστοῦ Ἰησοῦ). Paul uses this order three times in the letter (1:1; 2:6; 4:12) as compared to one time for the reverse order ("Jesus Christ"; 1:3). Among the writers of Scripture, only Paul uses this order (though see the slightly different form in Acts 24:24). He employs it eighty-nine times, in every letter he penned except 2 Thessalonians. The special import of this order is not easily discernable. Moule comments regarding its use in 2 Timothy, "this Pauline order breathes a certain feeling of worshipping while intimate *affection* towards the blessed Lord."[36]

This divine commissioning was "by the will of God" (διὰ θελήματος θεοῦ). This same expression is used often in the salutations of Paul's letters (1 Cor. 1:1; 2 Cor. 1:1; Eph. 1:1; 2 Tim. 1:1; cf. also Rom. 15:32; 2 Cor. 8:5). Romans has Paul "called as an apostle" (1:1) and 1 Timothy has Paul an apostle "according to the command of God our Savior" (1:1). Here the preposition διὰ ("by") signals the "efficient cause"[37] of Paul's apostleship and, by extension, all that comes from it. The point here is that his apostleship is direct from the hand of God, and that all the events that have flowed from fulfilling that role are also from the hand of God. This would include his current imprisonment and this present letter of instruction to the Colossian church.

Paul is not alone in writing and thus adds "and Timothy" (καὶ Τιμόθεος). Timothy is similarly designated in the salutations of 2 Corinthians, Philippians, 1 and 2 Thessalonians, and Philemon. Paul met Timothy and discovered him to be a disciple when he made his return to Lystra (Acts 16:1-2). On his first visit to the city, the Apostle had been taken initially for a god, after healing a lame man. But soon the populace turned on him, stoning him nearly to death at the provocation of the local Jewish citizenry (Acts 14:8-20). The Apostle spent only a short time there before moving on. There is no word of Timothy's conversion at that time. Had he been one listening at the fringes of the crowd as Paul preached? It is possible his heart

---

[36] H. C. G. Moule, 30 (emphasis original).
[37] BAGD, 180.

had been moved and, when he witnessed the Apostle's resolute faith in the face of death (2 Tim. 3:11), he put his faith in Christ.

Whenever the genesis of his faith might be placed and whatever the final impetus to trust in Christ, Timothy was a well-known disciple of Christ at the time of Paul's return to Lystra. He was known in his hometown (the same locale in which the Apostle had been stoned to the point of death!) and throughout the region as an effective disciple of Christ (Acts 16:2). Paul desired that Timothy travel at his side in the cause of the gospel, so that he might further nurture his faith and equip him for ministry (Acts 16:3).

Perhaps a decade had transpired between that time and this. Paul and Timothy had logged many miles together and had experienced much of life and ministry side by side. With Paul in a Roman prison, Timothy is found faithfully at his side. It is not expressly clear whether Timothy was likewise imprisoned or simply available as his servant and associate. It seems likely it was the latter. In any case Timothy was present to care for the Apostle's needs and to carry out his instruction, facilitating ministry under his direction.

Certainly Timothy was present with Paul at the time of writing, but does the expression (καὶ Τιμόθεος, "and Timothy") indicate that he played a role in the composition or recording of this letter to the Colossians? The expression may point to his service as an amanuensis, penning down the words as Paul dictated them. It is also possible that Paul may have provided the gist of his thoughts, leaving to Timothy the task of fleshing out a draft of the letter which the Apostle would later review and revise. However, passages such as 1:23-25, 29; 4:18 point to Paul's personal ownership of the letter. Certainly in the end the letter belonged to Paul, and he took responsibility for its contents.

In 2 Corinthians and Philemon, as here, Timothy is also designated "our brother" (ὁ ἀδελφὸς; more lit., "the brother"). This is the position Timothy holds toward Paul and the Colossians as they stand together in Christ. Paul, speaking of Timothy in relationship to himself personally, calls him "my true child in the faith" (1 Tim. 1:2), "my beloved son" (2 Tim. 1:2), and

Ministry Maxim

We all live vertically under divine authority and providence and horizontally in spiritual fellowship.

simply "my son" (2 Tim. 2:1). Such an esteemed brother alongside Paul would provide the clear indication that Paul was not simply representing his own ideas in this letter. Apparently Timothy was personally unknown to the Colossian church, as was Paul (though surely they knew of him and his faithful ministry). In view of the fact that Paul will call the Colossian believers "faithful brethren" (v. 2), he may designate Timothy "our brother" to bring a warm, familial atmosphere to the letter. Though there is no denying Paul is "an apostle of Jesus Christ by the will of God" and though he clearly writes out of that authoritative commission, he wishes to approach these fellow believers on the ground of shared faith in Christ.

Paul presents himself as a man under divine authority ("an apostle"), under divine providence ("by the will of God"), and in spiritual fellowship ("and Timothy our brother").

1:2 To the saints and faithful brethren in Christ who are at Colossae: Grace to you and peace from God our Father.

As Paul identifies the recipients of the letter, his first word is the definite article (τοῖς, "the"). This one definite article governs an adjective used as a substantive (ἁγίοις, "saints"; contra NIV) and a noun and its accompanying adjective (πιστοῖς ἀδελφοῖς, "faithful brethren").[38] That all three words are dative masculine plurals in form signals that Paul intends by these designations not two distinct groups, but one group described by the double descriptive terms.

By πιστοῖς Paul means "faithful" (as in the NASU), not "believing," for

> **Ministry Maxim**
>
> Though at present we live in two spheres, the spiritual must always rule the earthly.

that would be a needless redundancy alongside both "saints" (ἁγίοις) and "brethren" (ἀδελφοῖς). Paul intends that we understand "the saints" and "faithful brethren" as identical with one another.[39] The former describes the recipients in regard to their standing before God. The latter describes them in regard to their standing with Paul and other believers (note the proximity of the statement "Timothy, our brother" in v. 1). God has

---

[38] Harris, 9.

[39] This understands the καί ("and") as epexegetical. The intent then is to say "the saints at Colossae, namely, the faithful brothers."

made them holy in His sight by His justifying work in Christ (Rom. 3:21-28). All those who are thus justified, God has made one new family of believers "in Christ" (ἐν Χριστῷ). As in so many of Paul's letters, so here too the phrase (ἐν Χριστω, "in Christ") is loaded with theological intensity. The precise form is found seventy-three times in Paul's letters; the concept is found many more times from his pen.

Tucked in the attributive position are "at [lit., "in"] Colossae" (ἐν Κολοσσαῖς). It should not pass without notice that the recipients are at one and the same time "in Christ" and "in Colossae." This is not to say that ἐν ("in") is used in precisely the same way in both expressions, but to indicate that both relations are true at precisely the same time. Is this not true of us as well? We are truly—not simply theologically or spiritually, but truly—"in Christ." Yet we are in fact "in" some physical, geographical, political, and social place as well. The latter is not surer than the former. We are dual residents of two realms, of two kingdoms. The recipients had long been residents of Colossae. By virtue of being placed "in Christ" by God's grace received through faith, they had only more recently become citizens of the kingdom of God. Yet their position "in Christ" must in fact have the dominant influence over their residence in any geographical place they might find themselves. This may have been the subtle hint intended by the Apostle when choosing his wording. The good news is it is possible to live fully "in Colossae" (or whatever other physical location you may find yourself in, with all its attendant challenges and temptations) and at the same time remain and abound as "saints and faithful brethren in Christ Jesus"! As Johnson so articulately points out: "Utter secularism (in Colosse only) or complete monasticism (in Christ) are not the only alternatives."[40]

Paul adds his customary blessing: "Grace to you and peace from God our Father" (χάρις ὑμῖν καὶ εἰρήνη ἀπὸ θεοῦ πατρὸς ἡμῶν). These words are repeated precisely at the head of Romans (1:7), 1 Corinthians (1:3), 2 Corinthians (1:2), Galatians (1:3), Ephesians (1:2), Philippians (1:2), 2 Thessalonians (1:2), and Philemon (3). Yet in every one of those cases Paul included "and the Lord Jesus Christ" (καὶ κυρίου Ἰησοῦ Χριστοῦ). Why did he make Colossians 1:2 the exception? In this letter in which he so delights to exalt Christ (e.g., 1:15-20; 2:2-3, 9-10), why not set His full

---

[40] Johnson, "Spiritual Knowledge and Walking Worthily," 337.

designation ("our Lord Jesus Christ") next to that of "God our Father" as he so often did elsewhere? The definitive answer to this is not available to us. Dunn suggests that "it may be deliberate that before embarking on the exposition of Christ's full significance, the ultimate supremacy of the one God and Father is thus given prominence. The likelihood is strengthened by the formulation used in the thanksgiving in 1:3."[41]

Note that the designation of God as "Father" is now the third time familial language is used in the first two verses ("our brother," v. 1; "faithful brethren," v. 2) and with the next stroke of his pen, Paul will designate God as "the Father of our Lord Jesus Christ" (v. 3). Grace" (χάρις) gathers up in one word the germ of all Paul's theology. It signals that all which comes to us from God in salvation is a free, unmerited gift. The word "peace" (εἰρήνη) echoes the Hebrew *shalom* with its emphasis not so much on tranquility of heart, but on the full-orbed wholeness of a life at rest with God. Wright well says, "The scene is set for a letter through which Paul intends, by his writing, to be a means of that grace, and so to bring about that rich and mature peace (see, e.g., 3:15)."[42]

Digging Deeper:

1. Though we are not called as apostles as Paul was, in what sense are we under authority as God's "sent ones"?
2. What implications does this have for your ministry right now?
3. What has the will of God brought upon you now which you could wish different? How does Paul's example in the midst of imprisonment challenge you in your present circumstances?
4. How does the earthly sphere of your existence challenge your enjoyment of the spiritual sphere of your existence?
5. What demands does the spiritual sphere of your existence make right now upon the physical sphere of your existence?

---

[41] Dunn, 52.
[42] Wright, 48.

1:3 We give thanks to God, the Father of our Lord Jesus Christ, praying always for you,

The Apostle now begins a complex sentence that will not come to a conclusion until the end of verse 8. The main verb is "We give thanks" (Εὐχαριστοῦμεν). The present tense points to the ongoing nature of the gratitude. The plural form indicates that this is thankfulness shared in jointly by both Paul and Timothy,[43] though it is possible that this serves as an example of the so-called epistolary plural.[44]

Gratitude forms a rich theme throughout Colossians (1:3, 12; 2:7; 3:15–17; 4:2).[45] Here the gratitude is directed "to God" (τῷ θεῷ) as the source and origin of that which brings delight to their hearts. Indeed, God is the Giver of all good gifts (John 1:16; 1 Tim. 4:4; James 1:17). All things are "from Him and through Him and to Him" (Rom. 11:36).

This gracious, giving, good God is "the Father of our Lord Jesus Christ" (πατρὶ τοῦ κυρίου ἡμῶν Ἰησοῦ Χριστοῦ). As a Father He delights to give to His children (Matt. 7:11; Luke 11:13). Some manuscripts contain textual variants surrounding πατρὶ ("Father"), with some adding τῷ and others adding καὶ in what appears to be an attempt to clarify the shorter and likely original reading (τῷ θεῷ πατρὶ). The absence of the article with πατρὶ ("Father") points to "God, in the character of the Father of Christ, that we thank, for He is in this relation our Father-God."[46] The gift of His Son is the ultimate expression of His goodness (John 3:16; Rom. 8:32; 2 Cor. 9:15; 1 John 4:10) and, as such, the ultimate provocation to gratitude for us, the beneficiaries of His gift.

The precise and full title "our Lord Jesus Christ" (τοῦ κυρίου ἡμῶν Ἰησοῦ Χριστου) is found twenty-seven times in Paul's letters. The full title is probably used here as a precursor of the great extent to which the Apostle will go throughout this epistle to elevate Jesus Christ to the highest possible place in the face of the false teacher(s) who seeks to make Him just one more (even if the highest) emanation of God.

---

[43] Bruce, NIC, 40-41; Eadie, 5; O'Brien, 9.
[44] Harris, 15.
[45] O'Brien, 108.
[46] Eadie, 5.

This gratitude naturally found its expression in the "praying" (προσευχόμενοι) of both Paul and Timothy (the participle is plural in form). A grateful heart is a praying heart. Gratitude cannot be long contained or constrained. Thankfulness moves us God-ward as the realization of the origin of the satisfying blessing breaks upon us. The present tense points to the ongoing nature of the praying. This is a deponent verb so the middle voice is active in meaning. The participial form may be used with regard to time, denoting activity concurrent with that of the main verb—every time Paul prayed, he gave thanks for the Colossian believers.[47]

This gratitude is "for you" (περὶ ὑμῶν; the pronoun is plural in form; i.e., the Colossian believers). The preposition περὶ, when used with words for prayer, takes the place of ὑπὲρ and means "on behalf of."[48] Paul characteristically began his letters to churches with expressions of gratitude.[49] The exceptions are 2 Corinthians and Galatians, and the omission signals the grave concern to be expressed in those letters.[50] In verse 4 the Apostle will explain the reason for his thankfulness over the Colossian believers.

> **Ministry Maxim**
>
> True gratitude won't rest easy until it finds a way to make itself known.

The adverb "always" (πάντοτε) may modify either "We give thanks" (Εὐχαριστοῦμεν) or "praying" (προσευχόμενοι). The fact that it comes before "for you" (περὶ ὑμῶν) may indicate that it should be understood to modify the former (cf. ESV, NIV, NRSV). Elsewhere Paul speaks both of praying always (Eph. 6:18; Col. 1:9; 1 Thess. 5:17; 2 Thess. 1:11) and of giving thanks always (Eph. 5:20; 1 Cor. 1:4; Eph. 5:20; 1 Thess. 1:2; Philem. 4). Since he speaks here of gratitude finding expression in prayer, it ultimately and practically matters little which one we determine it is meant to modify.

1:4 since we heard of your faith in Christ Jesus and the love which you have for all the saints;

This thanksgiving, says the Apostle, had risen to God "since we heard" (ἀκούσαντες). The aorist tense looks back to the moment of hearing. The

---

[47] Ibid.
[48] BAGD, 644.
[49] Abbott, 194.
[50] Kent, 22.

plural form again encompasses both Paul and Timothy. The participial form is likely used in a temporal way, thus the rendering "*since* we heard" (emphasis mine; cf. ESV, NET, NKJV, KJV), though it could possibly be used in a causal sense ("because," NIV; "for," NLT, NRSV). The context's emphasis on time elements seems to point to the former (cf. "since the day," v. 6).[51]

Paul had never personally met or visited the Colossian believers (Col. 2:1). Thus the verb looks back to the report(s) the Apostle had received—either verbal or written, or both—regarding the work of God among those residing in Colossae. At least the initial report probably came to the Apostle through Epaphras (Col. 1:7-8), who likely founded the church in Colossae as a part of the Apostle's strategy of sending church planting evangelists throughout Asia Minor during his extended ministry in the capital city of Ephesus (Acts 19:10, 26).

Paul heard a twofold report concerning the Colossians. The news, firstly, was "of your faith" (τὴν πίστιν ὑμῶν). By using the definite article the Apostle does not make this a reference to the body of truth sometimes referred to as "the faith" (cf. Col. 1:23). Rather it distinguishes the particular faith (not "faithfulness") which belongs to the Colossian believers (ὑμῶν, "of your"). Their trusting confidence was "in Christ Jesus" (ἐν Χριστῷ Ἰησοῦ). The preposition ἐν ("in") with the dative probably points to "the sphere or realm in which their faith operated or was evident."[52]

Coupled with (καὶ, "and") this faith was "the love" (τὴν ἀγάπην) of the Colossian believers. That these two virtues are held in parallel is evident by their both being accusative in form. The report of the Colossians' love came to Paul through Epaphras (v. 8). There this love is said to be "in the Spirit" (ἐν πνεύματι). The Spirit-produced love, says the Apostle, is that "which you have for all the saints" (ἣν ἔχετε εἰς πάντας τοὺς ἁγίους). The relative pronoun (ἣν, "which") clearly finds its antecedent in "the love" (τὴν ἀγάπην) as both are in the accusative case. The verb "have" (ἔχετε) is in the present tense, pointing to the ongoing nature of the love which they possess. The plural form points to all those who make up the

> **Ministry Maxim**
>
> Vertical faith unfailingly produces horizontal love.

---

[51] NET Bible.

[52] Harris, 16.

church in Colossae. Paul speaks of love "for all the saints" (εἰς πάντας τοὺς ἁγίους) when writing to the Ephesians (Eph. 1:15) and to Philemon (Philem. 5). Clearly the Apostle put great value upon mutual love among believers as a sign of the reality of their new life in Christ (cf. John 13:35).

Sometimes Paul speaks of a triad of virtues: faith, hope, and love (e.g., 1 Cor. 13:13; Gal. 5:5-6; 1 Thess. 1:3; 5:8). Here, the third virtue ("hope") will come with the Apostle's next pen stroke (v. 5).

1:5 because of the hope laid up for you in heaven, of which you previously heard in the word of truth, the gospel

The Apostle continues by giving the cause (διὰ, "because") of something. But to what does this prepositional phrase connect? It is possible that it links backward to the main verb (Εὐχαριστοῦμεν, "give thanks," v. 3). In this case Paul would provide here the ground for which his thanksgiving takes place—the hope that awaits the Colossian believers in heaven. But the prepositional phrase may alternatively link with the Colossian believers' "faith" (τὴν πίστιν), or with both their "faith" and "love" (τὴν ἀγάπην, v. 4), given that they are all accusative, singular, feminine nouns. Given the frequency with which these three virtues are linked throughout the NT (see above under v. 4), it seems more likely that the latter option was in the Apostle's mind (cf. the NIV's interpretational rendering, "the faith and love that spring from the hope").[53]

If this be the case, then Paul sees and draws out a unique interconnectedness among these virtues: love grows out of faith (v. 4) which in turn arises out of hope (v. 5). The everlasting, objective hope of eternal life in God's presence in heaven is the fertile soil in which faith grows. Such sure and certain faith is free then from striving, self-protection, and worry. Such faith can look outward from that place of rest and peace of heart and can take up the cares and concerns of others around about, loving them selflessly, just as Christ has loved us. If we lose our assurance of eternal life, if our confidence of being welcomed into God's heavenly presence wanes, then our fruitfulness in God's purposes here in this world suffers. The claim that some are too heavenly minded to be of any earthly good misses

---

[53] Ibid., 17; Moo, 85.

the point entirely. Quite the opposite, it is only those who are heavenly minded (cf. Col. 3:1ff.) that are of any earthly good!

While this is true, we must also stop here and recognize the dynamic interplay among the three virtues in the context of all Paul's writings. Would hope ever exist without faith? Can faith survive without hope? Will there be true, active love without either faith or hope? Did Paul not say, "But now faith, hope, love, abide these three; but the greatest of these is love" (1 Cor. 13:13)? Indeed, Moo says, "only here does he make hope the basis for love and faith."[54] Paul's emphasis here is true, yet we must read this passage in light of all Paul's other usages of this triad of virtues and draw our conclusions regarding their interrelationships from the larger context of his writings.

It is specifically "the hope laid up for you in heaven" (τὴν ἐλπίδα τὴν ἀποκειμένην ὑμῖν ἐν τοῖς οὐρανοῖς) that the Apostle has in mind. It is not just any hope which is in the Apostle's mind, but "*the* hope" (emphasis added); note the intentional use of the definite article (τὴν ἐλπίδα) here, just as it was used with "faith" and "love" in verse 4. This hope is intimately twined with and arises from the gospel itself (1:23). It is, ultimately, "the hope of glory" (1:27).

> **Ministry Maxim**
>
> When we speak the gospel we set reality before our hearers and steer them away from a delusion.

Here this hope is said to be "laid up" (τὴν ἀποκειμένην). The verb is used by Paul only here and in 2 Timothy 4:8 where he says "in the future there is laid up for me the crown of righteousness." The verb means to be laid away or reserved. With the dative of person, as it is here, it has the sense of "reserved for one" or "awaiting him."[55] It was used with reference to the rewards bestowed upon the champions of the Greek athletic games as well as metaphorically with reference to rewards for civic service.

Clearly, then, the hope which Paul intends here is not merely a state of mind, an inward disposition, a kind of hopefulness. No, he is looking to something objective—an inheritance to be gained. This objective "hope" is the firm ground, then, upon which the inward, subjective virtues of "faith"

---

[54] Moo, 85.
[55] Thayer, 63.

and "love" find a solid base from which to launch themselves. The present tense points to the abiding nature of this hope—it is ever there before us, awaiting us. The passive voice indicates that it was another—our God—who "laid up" this sure future for us. This "hope" is not merely a personal antici-pation, but one that is true of all believers (ὑμῖν, "you," plural) and enjoyed, strengthened, and grown in community with other believers.

The precise phrase (ἐν τοῖς οὐρανοῖς, "in heaven") is used only four times by Paul, three of those in this letter, and all of those in this chapter (2 Cor. 5:1; Col. 1:5, 15, 20). The noun is in the plural form (as in vv. 16, 20; reflecting the Hebrew practice of using a plural form) and is thus more liter-ally "in the heavens," but note his use of the singular form in Colossians 1:23 and 4:1. In total Paul uses the plural form ten times and the singular eleven without any difference in meaning between the two.[56]

Paul speaks of heaven more in Colossians than in any other of his letters. Why? Perhaps it has to do with his awareness of the pre-Gnostic heresy that threatens the Colossian church. The false teacher(s) seemed to indicate that Christ could only provide so much and that the heresy would bring to completion what Christ only began in the Colossian believers. The Apostle stands utterly opposed to this notion, insisting that their full hope is already on reserve for them, being kept in heaven for a later unveiling and enjoyment. Peter and Paul echo one another on this point, for Peter speaks of "an inheritance which is ... reserved in heaven for you ... for a salvation ready to be revealed in the last time" (1 Peter 1:4-5).

Paul then asserts to the Colossians that this hope is one "of which you previously heard" (ἣν προηκούσατε). The relative pronoun (ἣν, "of which") is in the accusative form, confirming that it is "the hope" to which it refers. The verb is used only here in the NT. It is a compound word comprised of πρό (before) and ἀκούω (to hear). The aorist tense points to that moment in the past when they heard the gospel announced to them by Epaphras (vv. 7, 23). They heard the truth, not just before this letter was written, but also before the false gospel now afflicting them came to their ears. The Colossian believ-ers must beware in the present of abandoning something they have heard, embraced, and been transformed by in the past.

---

[56] Moo, 85-86.

This hope is heard, asserts the Apostle, "in the word of truth, the gospel" (ἐν τῷ λόγῳ τῆς ἀληθείας τοῦ εὐαγγελίου). Paul speaks of "the word of truth" also in 2 Corinthians 6:7, Ephesians 1:13, and 2 Timothy 2:15 (cf. also James 1:18). That this word is "truth" stands in direct opposition to the words of the false teacher(s) in Colossae which are no more than "empty deception" (2:8) and "idle notions" (2:18, NIV), which amount to nothing more than the "commandments and teachings of men" (2:22). The expression "the gospel" (τοῦ εὐαγγελίου) is placed in apposition to "the word of truth" (τῷ λόγῳ τῆς ἀληθείας), indicating that the two expressions refer to the same reality. The gospel is truth; the truth is good news. When we speak the gospel we set reality before our hearers and steer them away from a delusion.

1:6 which has come to you, just as in all the world also
it is constantly bearing fruit and increasing, even as
it has been doing in you also since the day you heard
of it and understood the grace of God in truth;

The gospel which Paul has in mind (v. 5) is the one, he says, "which has come to you" (τοῦ παρόντος εἰς ὑμᾶς). The participle "has come" (τοῦ παρόντος) is from a compound verb comprised of παρά ("beside") and εἰμί ("I am").[57] The verb has the basic sense of *"to be by, be at hand, to have arrived, to be present."*[58] Debate regarding its precise nuance here ranges from "has come to you" (most English translations) to "is present among you" (Lohse).[59] Rienecker strikes a balance, saying that the preposition in compound "combines the idea of the gospel being present w[ith] the idea of the gospel coming to them."[60] As the Colossians are confronted by a heretical, false gospel, the Apostle reminds them that they have already welcomed the truth into their midst and that it remains among them even as he writes.

The gospel arrived in Colossae "just as in all the world also it is constantly bearing fruit and increasing" (καθὼς καὶ ἐν παντὶ τῷ κόσμῳ ἐστὶν καρποφορούμενον καὶ αὐξανόμενον). The fruitful coming of the gospel of Christ to the citizens of Colossae was "just as" (καθὼς) others

---

[57] Mounce, 536.
[58] Thayer, 487.
[59] Harris, 19.
[60] Rienecker, 564.

across the world are receiving the truth. This conjunction serves as a comparative which expresses the manner in which something happens.[61] In this case the coming of the gospel to Colossae was in the same manner as it was currently coming "also in all the world" (καὶ ἐν παντὶ τῷ κόσμῳ). This descriptive phrase did not intend to designate every square inch of the terrestrial globe. It may describe the broader world as the citizens of Colossae would have understood it in their day (intending something like "the entire Roman world" or "the entire known world") or it may be merely a "rhetorical exaggeration."[62]

Paul spoke similarly to the believers in Rome—though employing a different word—saying that their faith was being proclaimed "throughout the whole world" (ἐν ὅλῳ τῷ κόσμῳ, Rom. 1:8). He spoke to the Roman believers with other expressions in broad, almost universal terms of the spread of the gospel or the reach of his ministry (Rom. 10:18; 15:19; 16:26), but in the same letter could also describe his longing to go on to another as yet unreached region (15:28). Thus Paul's intent may not be to reference each and every place or person upon the earth, but to describe the universal effect of the gospel wherever in the world it is proclaimed. Yet Paul could also say the gospel "was proclaimed in all creation under heaven" (Col. 1:23). These expressions may have been intended to contrast the universal applicability and spread of the gospel with the more local and regional appeal of the heresies being peddled in Colossae at that time.[63]

Indeed, "it is constantly bearing fruit and increasing" (ἐστὶν καρποφορούμενον καὶ αὐξανόμενον). The verb finds its subject in "the gospel" (τοῦ εὐαγγελίου) of verse 5. The present indicative form of the verb ("is," ἐστὶν) points to the present and continuous reality of this effect wherever in the world the gospel is being made known. The verb is followed now by two present-tense participles. Again the present tenses point to the regular, continuous effect of the gospel upon its hearers ("constantly"). Both participles appear again in combination in verse 10. Here they describe the growth of the gospel itself; there they describe the prayer of the Apostle for the progress of the Colossian believers. Here they are used in thanksgiving;

---

[61] Friberg, 211.
[62] BAGD, 446; cf. Moo, 89.
[63] Abbott, 197.

in verse 10 they are used in petition. O'Brien says this double use of the words expresses Paul's desire "that the dynamic of the gospel may characterize the lives of the Colossian believers themselves."[64]

The first such effect is "bearing fruit" (καρποφορούμενον). The word is a compound comprised of "fruit" (καρπός) and "to wear/bear" (φορέω). Paul is responsible for four of its eight NT usages (Rom. 7:4, 5; Col. 1:6, 10). In verse 10 it describes the ideal lives the Colossian believers are to lead. Here it describes "practical conduct as the fruit of the inner life."[65] The middle voice is used here (cf. the active voice employed in v. 10) and "may imply the intrinsic potency of the gospel in producing its own fruit."[66] Indeed, "*All by itself* the soil produces grain" (Mark 4:28, NIV, emphasis added). Paul elsewhere states that "the gospel ... is the power of God for salvation to everyone who believes" (Rom. 1:16).

To this Paul joins (καὶ, "and") a second participle: "increasing" (αὐξανόμενον). The word means simply "to grow," here figuratively in a spiritual sense. The passive voice points to the work of God in bringing this effect through the preaching of the gospel. The present tense once again indicates the perpetual effect of the gospel among those to whom God sends it with His blessing.

This combination of verbs sounds an echo of OT language, particularly from the creation account (Gen. 1:28), the mandate following the flood (Gen. 8:17; 9:1, 7), and God's communication with Abraham and the patriarchs (Gen. 17:20; 28:3; 35:11).[67] In Jesus' parable of the sower (Mark 4), He spoke of the seed (the word, v. 14) which "grew up and increased [αὐξανόμενα]" (v. 8), and then in His explanation of the parable He spoke of those who hear the word and "bear fruit [καρποφοροῦσιν]" (v. 20).[68] Some commentators assert that "bearing fruit" (καρποφορούμενον) points to the work of the gospel within the believers and "increasing" (αὐξανόμενον) points to its outward growth in reaching more and more people.[69]

---

[64] O'Brien, 14.
[65] BAGD, 405.
[66] Harris, 19.
[67] Moo, 88.
[68] O'Brien, 13.
[69] E.g., Hendriksen, 50-52; Kent, 26; Vaughan, 11:175.

Paul now moves from the general (the world) to the particular (the believers in Colossae): "even as it has been doing in you also" (καθὼς καὶ ἐν ὑμῖν). The NASU translators have added the words "it has been doing" for smoother translation. A more wooden translation is simply "even as also in you." The combination καθὼς καὶ ("even as ... also") is employed again (see "just as ... also" earlier in the verse). The gospel's fruit bearing and increasing effect—they could testify themselves—has taken place "in you" (ἐν ὑμῖν). The personal pronoun (ὑμῖν, "you") is plural. The idea here is "among you" (ESV, NIV), not "in you" individually, though that is where the gospel makes its changes personally. The inward reality of the gospel's ongoing life and fruitfulness is something the Colossian believers cannot deny. Their shared experience is at one and the same time both intimately personal and wonderfully shared with each other and other believers they have never met from across the world. "What the gospel produced and achieved in the world, it produces and achieves among you."[70] This moves the Apostle to expressions of profound gratitude.

> **Ministry Maxim**
>
> Every person needs not only the God-ordained opportunity to *hear* the gospel, but also the Spirit-enabled ability to *listen* to it.

And this has been the case "since the day you heard of it and understood the grace of God in truth" (ἀφ' ἧς ἡμέρας ἠκούσατε καὶ ἐπέγνωτε τὴν χάριν τοῦ θεοῦ ἐν ἀληθείᾳ). Just what period of time had passed "since the day" (ἀφ' ἧς ἡμέρας) is hard to say with any precision. But from that first day (lit., "from which day") and throughout that span of time—however long or short it may have been—the gospel had been bearing fruit and increasing in their midst. That which set in motion this dynamic was that on that critical day they both "heard of" the gospel and "understood the grace of God in truth." Both verbs are aorist tense. They look back to the pivotal moment when the Spirit of God illumined their hearts to hear, see, and believe the truth of the gospel. By God's doing they "heard of it" (ἠκούσατε) through Epaphras (v. 7). One must clearly hear the gospel before one can embrace it in faith (Rom. 10:14; cf. Acts 19:2).

---

[70] Eadie, 14.

Belief is essential to salvation (Rom. 10:9; 1 Cor. 1:21; 15:2; 1 Tim. 4:10). But here the Apostle also (καὶ, "and") speaks of how they "understood" (ἐπέγνωτε). The aorist is likely ingressive. The compound word is comprised of ἐπί ("upon") and γινώσκω ("to know"). It points to a knowledge which is full, deep, and complete. Here it is used "especially in relation to higher and spiritual knowledge received through revelation *fully know, perfectly know*."[71]

Paul likely used this intensified form because of the false teaching which was rife in Colossae. The false teacher(s) claimed a corner on the truth (2:4, 8, 18). Thus by employing this verb Paul could underscore that the false teacher(s) had nothing to offer the believers. In Christ they already possessed fullness of knowledge and insight and did so, at least as a birthright, from the moment they put their faith in Him. Indeed, Paul could say that the Colossian believers possessed "the full assurance of understanding, resulting in a true knowledge of God's mystery, that is, Christ Himself, in whom are hidden all the treasures of wisdom and knowledge" (Col. 2:2b-3).

What should we make of Paul's use of both "heard" (ἠκούσατε) and "understood" (ἐπέγνωτε)? Clearly hearing the gospel is not sufficient in itself. We must hear with understanding; there must be both Spirit-ordained *hearing* of the gospel and Spirit-enabled *listening* to the gospel. The ministry of illumination is essential, for our darkened hearts and minds cannot hear with faith apart from the gracious ministry of the Holy Spirit (2 Cor. 4:3-6; Eph. 2:8). Jesus Himself said, "For many are called, but few are chosen" (Matt. 22:14).

That which was thus understood is "the grace of God" (τὴν χάριν τοῦ θεοῦ). This appears to be a shorthand designation for the gospel itself. And this they were enabled to grasp "in truth" (ἐν ἀληθείᾳ). The noun may mean something like "reality."[72] And as such it may stand in contrast to the fanciful assertions of the false teacher(s). Paul has just spoken of "the word of truth, the gospel" (v. 5). Opponents often chide believers as escapists, but it is only in the gospel that the light of God breaks through to reveal the reality of matters as they stand before Him.

---

[71] Friberg, 163; cf. BAGD, 291.
[72] BAGD, 36.

The Apostle takes a two-pronged approach to verifying the gospel itself
and the Colossian believers' experience of it. He appeals both to the inherent
truth of the gospel and the reality of their experience of that gospel. As Moo
states it, "The gospel is authenticated not by truth only nor by its power in
people's lives only but by both working in tandem."[73]

1:7 just as you learned it from Epaphras, our beloved fellow bond-servant, who is a faithful servant of Christ on our behalf,

For the third time in this extended sentence (twice in v. 6) Paul uses καθὼς
("just as"), another evidence of the complicated nature of this extended
sentence. The Apostle is now expanding upon their reception of the gospel
(described in v. 6) by centering on the one through whom it came. He tells
them "you learned" (ἐμάθετε) the gospel. This is a
somewhat unusual expression for Paul. The
customary way for him to describe the reception of
the gospel is as "believing," "hearing," or "obeying."[74]
The verb describes learning through the instruction
of another.[75] The aorist tense looks back to that time
when Epaphras instructed them in the gospel and
views it as a whole. The verb is cognate with the
noun μαθητής ("disciple"). Paul sent Epaphras in
Jesus' Name, and in His Name and by His grace
Epaphras made disciples of Christ from among the
citizens of Colossae. O'Brien asserts that the use of
this verb "probably indicates that Epaphras had
given them systematic instruction in the gospel rather than some flimsy
outline and that these Colossians had committed themselves as disciples to
that teaching (cf. 2:6, 7)."[76]

> **Ministry Maxim**
>
> The gospel is not simply something non-Christians must *hear* and new Christians have *believed*, but it is that which growing Christians continue to *learn*.

This knowledge came "from Epaphras" (ἀπὸ Ἐπαφρᾶ). The name
Epaphras is a shortened version of the longer name Epaphroditus
(Ἐπαφρόδιτος), though it had become a recognizable name in its own right.
This Epaphras is thus to be distinguished from the Epaphroditus mentioned

---

[73] Moo, 89.
[74] O'Brien, 15.
[75] BAGD, 490.
[76] O'Brien, 15.

by Paul in Philippians 2:25 and 4:18. The latter is always associated with the Philippian church, while Epaphras is always connected to the Colossian church. Indeed, the only references we have to Epaphras in the NT are in this letter (1:7; 4:12) and the letter to Philemon (Philem. 23). He appears to have been a citizen of Colossae for Paul designates him "one of your number" (Col. 4:12). Certainly his heart was bound up with those of the Colossian believers for Paul can tell them that Epaphras was "always laboring earnestly for you in his prayers, that you may stand perfect and fully assured in all the will of God" (Col. 4:12). It appears he had been imprisoned with the Apostle (Philem. 23). Whether that was a present imprisonment (in Rome) or perhaps in the past (perhaps in Ephesus) we cannot be certain, though the former seems more likely given that in the letter to Philemon he sends his greetings to Philemon via the Apostle Paul at this time (Philem. 23). (See the introduction for more on the connection of the two letters.) Clearly Epaphras had been separated from his beloved Colossian believers and longed for their welfare and growth in grace.

We can safely conjecture that Epaphras was a trustworthy fellow-servant along with Paul and had likely evangelized in and around Colossae during Paul's tenure of ministry in Ephesus. During that time we know that "all who lived in Asia heard the word of the Lord, both Jews and Greeks" (Acts 19:10). At that time Paul's opponent could testify, "not only in Ephesus, but in almost all of Asia, this Paul has persuaded and turned away a considerable number of people" (Acts 19:26). And in much of that territory the work was doubtless carried out by faithful colaborers like Epaphras who were trained and sent out by the Apostle. Epaphras may have been responsible for not only the founding of the Colossian church, but also for the churches in other cities of the Lycus valley, such as Laodicea and Hierapolis (Col. 4:13).

Paul designates Epaphras with significant labels, probably in an attempt to certify that through him the Colossians had heard the authentic apostolic gospel. The first is "our beloved fellow bond-servant" (τοῦ ἀγαπητοῦ συνδούλου ἡμῶν). The word behind "fellow bond-servant" (συνδούλου) is a compound, made up of σύν ("with") and δοῦλος ("bond-servant"). Though Paul is fond of designating coworkers with words compounded with σύν-, his only other use of this word is found in Colossians 4:7 where he similarly designates Tychicus. But notice here the use of the definite article, further setting Epaphras apart as "*the* fellow bond-servant," indeed "the fellow bond-servant" who is so "beloved"! Paul uses the root word (δοῦλος, "bond-servant") thirty-two times. This root word describes a slave (Col. 3:22; 4:1), not simply a servant. Such a one serves at and according to the will of another. Paul frequently chose this word as a self-designation (e.g., Rom. 1:1; Gal. 1:10; Phil. 1:1; Titus 1:1). The addition of the prefix (σύν) indicates that Epaphras had joined Paul in abandoning his will to the will of God and had taken up the Great Commission of Christ as his marching orders.

In the fellowship of this common service Epaphras had become "beloved" (ἀγαπητοῦ). This adjective is in the attributive position (slipped between the definite article and the noun), emphasizing the nature of Epaphras as a bond-servant. It emphasizes the intimate connection that had arisen between the two. Paul uses the adjective four times in this letter, not only designating Epaphras as their "beloved fellow bond-servant" (1:7), but also Tychicus (4:7) and Onesimus (4:9) each as a "beloved brother," and Luke as "the beloved physician" (4:14).

Paul further describes Epaphras by adding "who is a faithful servant of Christ on our behalf" (ὅς ἐστιν πιστὸς ὑπὲρ ὑμῶν διάκονος τοῦ Χριστοῦ). The present tense of the verb (ἐστιν, "is") points to the consistent and abiding character of Epaphras. In designating Epaphras as "faithful" (πιστὸς), Paul is indicating he both believes in Christ and allows that trust to control everything in his life. Specifically, at this juncture, he points to how Epaphras's faith is seen as a "servant of Christ" (διάκονος τοῦ Χριστου). The previous word (συνδούλου, "fellow bond-servant") pointed to what we would designate a slave. Now the word "servant" (διάκονος) points simply to one who voluntarily serves or ministers to or for another. The service of Epaphras was not grudging, but glad and willing. The word can refer to the office of deacon (1 Tim. 3:8), but here no such narrowing of the meaning is in view. Epaphras simply and consistently humbles himself to address the needs of others.

This service, says the Apostle, is for Christ but is displayed "on our behalf" (ὑπὲρ ὑμῶν). There is some debate as to whether the correct reading is the first-person plural (ἡμῶν, "us") or the second-person plural (ὑμῶν, "you"). Though the Nestle-Aland twenty-seventh edition employes the latter, the manuscript evidence seems to favor the former. The English translations are divided with some opting for the first-person plural (e.g., NASU, NIV, NLT) and others adopting the second-person plural (e.g., ESV, NRSV). It seems to me that the evidence favors the former. Thus the first-person plural pronoun indicates that Epaphras had well served the body of believers in Colossae on Paul's behalf. In obeying Paul's directives to evangelize the region, Epaphras had led a number of the Colossians to Christ and saw a church founded.

Paul closely aligns Epaphras with himself and Timothy by designating him both a "fellow bond-servant" and as "a faithful minister of Christ on our behalf." For the Colossians to now jettison the faith they had received through Epaphras in favor of the teaching of the heretical teacher(s) would be tantamount to rejecting the Apostle Paul himself, and indeed, the very Lord who commissioned Paul.

Interestingly, while here Epaphras is called a "beloved fellow bond-servant, who is a faithful servant of Christ," in Colossians 4:7 the terms are inverted and Tychicus is called "beloved brother and faithful servant and fellow bond-servant in the Lord" (4:7).

1:8 and he also informed us of your love in the Spirit.

The extended and complicated sentence begun in verse 3 now comes to an end. In verse 7 Paul describes Epaphras's ministry on Paul's behalf to the Colossians. Here in verse 8 he describes Epaphras's ministry in the reverse direction—communicating to the Apostle the reality of the Colossian's faith. Referring to Epaphras (v. 7), Paul says "he also informed us" (ὁ καὶ δηλώσας ἡμῖν). The articular participle probably functions as a relative clause.[77] The verb itself is fairly rare, occurring only three times in Paul's writings (1 Cor. 1:11; 3:13; Col. 1:8) for a total of seven times in the

> **Ministry Maxim**
>
> Nothing displays the power of the gospel or presence of the Spirit more than a life of love.

NT (Heb. 9:8; 12:27; 1 Peter 1:11; 2 Peter 1:14). It means to reveal, make clear, or show something.[78] Thayer says it means "to render evident to the

---

[77] Harris, 22-23.
[78] BAGD, 178.

mind, of such disclosures as exhibit character or suggest inferences; hence, especially of prophetic, typical, or other supernatural disclosures."[79] The Apostle is asserting that the reality of the Colossian believers' commitment to Christ was made manifestly clear. The plural "us" (ἡμῖν) probably refers to himself and Timothy (1:1) and perhaps others to whom this word arrived through Epaphras.

The report Epaphras communicated was "of your love" (τὴν ὑμῶν ἀγάπην). This kind of love (τὴν ... ἀγάπην) describes the very nature of God Himself ("God is love," John 4:8, 16). It is the word that describes God's stance toward the world of people He created, a love that moved Him to the greatest self-sacrifice (John 3:16). More specifically it is employed to describe the unconditional, covenant love of God for His people (Eph. 1:4-5). It, then, becomes the identifying mark of God's presence in those who have come to experience His salvation (1 John 4:7). In the truly redeemed, this love has gained the ascendancy in mind, emotions, and will, bringing them in glad submission to God and His service. In this letter Paul has already told the readers that he rejoices over "the love which you have for all the saints" (Col. 1:4). This kind of love is divine, describing the very love of the Father for His Son (v. 13). It is the binding cord which God uses to hold His people, the church, together (2:2; 3:14).

Such love operates "in the Spirit" (ἐν πνεύματι). The uppercase "Spirit," despite the absence of the definite article, is the correct translation of Paul's intent here.[80] The same expression is used often by Paul to refer to God the Spirit (e.g., Eph. 2:22; 3:5; 5:18; 6:18). The preposition (ἐν, "in") is probably instrumental in use.[81] Their love became a reality through the instrumentality of the Holy Spirit (cf. "called forth by the Spirit"[82]). The first fruit of the Spirit is this kind of love (Gal. 5:22), and "the love of God has been poured out within our hearts through the Holy Spirit" (Rom. 5:5).

This is the only direct reference to God the Spirit in this epistle (though cf. the adjective πνευματικός in v. 9). This is a matter of some interest, for compare Ephesians where the Holy Spirit is mentioned at least ten times. It is true that the ministry of the Holy Spirit is to bring glory to Jesus Christ

---

[79] Thayer, 131-132.
[80] BAGD, 677.
[81] Harris, 23; Moo, 92.
[82] BAGD, 677.

(John 16:13-14)[83], and He does so marvelously in this letter. Rather than signaling that the letter may not be genuinely Pauline this idiosyncrasy leaves us wondering if it reveals something about the nature of the falsehood being peddled in Colossae and therefore prompted the Apostle to this emphasis.

Digging Deeper:

1. From what you observe in your own life and in the lives of those you minister to, what is the interrelationship of faith, hope, and love? Which is primary? Which are derivatives?
2. In what way does the gospel bring people back to reality?
3. In what sense must the gospel be not only heard, but also understood and learned?
4. What implications does this have for how we evangelize?
5. What implications does it have for how we make disciples?

1:9 For this reason also, since the day we heard of it, we have not ceased to pray for you and to ask that you may be filled with the knowledge of His will in all spiritual wisdom and understanding,

Paul now begins a new sentence, running through verse 14. He turns from giving thanks (vv. 3-8) to the content of his petitions for the Colossian believers (vv. 9-14). The transition is made with the words "For this reason" (Διὰ τοῦτο). Just what is "this reason"? The Apostle seems to be looking back over the whole of vv. 4-8 where he describes the ground of his thanksgiving over the Colossians. The demonstrable reality of their faith in Christ moves him and Timothy (note the plural forms throughout, "we") now to not only give thanks for them, but to intercede on their behalf. The connective "also" (καὶ) belongs with the verb.[84] Not only do they give thanks for the Colossians and their faith in Christ (vv. 4-8), but they "also" intercede for them (vv. 9-12).

---

[83] Kent, 28.
[84] Rienecker, 565.

Douglas Moo outlines the numerous parallels between the thanksgivings of verses 3-8 and the petitions of verses 9-14:

- "since the day you heard" (v. 6) and
  "since the day we heard" (v. 9)
- "give thanks" (v. 3) and "giving thanks" (v. 12)
- "always" (v. 3) and "not ceased" (v. 9)
- "praying … for you" (v. 3) and "pray for you" (v. 9)
- "understood" (v. 6) and "knowledge" (vv. 9, 10)
- "bearing fruit and increasing" (v. 6) and "bearing fruit … and increasing" (v. 10).[85]

Not only does this reason undergird their praying, but it is "since the day we heard" (ἀφ' ἧς ἡμέρας ἠκούσαμεν). The words "of it" are added by the translators since the direct object is left off in the original text and is assumed by the context. But just what does the context suggest here? Is "it" the Colossian's "love in the Spirit" (v. 8)? Or could it be an echo of Paul's previous statement in verse 4: "since we heard of your faith in Christ Jesus and the love which you have for all the saints"?[86] This latter seems preferable as it is another signal that the Apostle is gathering up the whole of his previously expressed thoughts and transitioning from thanksgiving to intercession.

The main verb is "we have not ceased" (οὐ παυόμεθα). Paul uses the verb three times (1 Cor. 13:8; Eph. 1:16; Col. 1:9). It is a favorite of Luke, who uses it nine times in his Gospel and the book of Acts. It is in the middle voice (as it is in fourteen of its fifteen NT usages, except for 1 Peter 3:10) which can yield the meaning not just of ceasing, but of stopping oneself.[87] The plural no doubt includes both Paul and Timothy (1:1). The present tense points to continuous action. The negation (οὐ) denies a thing categorically or absolutely.[88] Paul and Timothy never stop themselves from praying on behalf of the Colossians. This, of course, does not mean that their expression of prayer is continuous, but that when they pray they regularly include the Colossian believers in those prayers.

---

[85] Moo, 92.
[86] NET Bible.
[87] BAGD, 638.
[88] Thayer, 408.

Two complementary participles modify this main verb: "to pray" (προσευχόμενοι) and (καὶ) "to ask" (αἰτούμενοι). That which they do not cease to do is, first of all, "to pray" (προσευχόμενοι). The word has already been used in verse 3, which you can see for further comments. It will be used again in 4:3 as the Apostle asks that the Colossian believers reciprocate and pray for him. It is the most general word for prayer in the NT. Here the middle voice has an active meaning. The present tense underscores the unceasing nature of the prayers of Paul and Timothy on behalf of the Colossian believers.

The second participle is "to ask" (αἰτούμενοι). Paul employs this word far less often, only four times (1 Cor. 1:22; Eph. 3:13, 20; Col. 1:9). It is used often in contexts of prayer, usually with the sense of a subordinate asking for something from a superior.[89] By this time the middle voice had come to differ little in meaning from the active voice.[90] The present tense again underscores the unceasing nature of the activity. The former word describes prayer more generally while this latter word describes the activity more specifically in terms of requesting something from God on behalf of the Colossians. Indeed, Paul makes plain that their prayers are "for you" (ὑπὲρ ὑμῶν). On behalf of the believers in Colossae, the Apostle and Timothy exerted conscious, consistent, continuous prayer. What an investment! Particularly when it is remembered that he had never met them face-to-face (2:1)!

What was at the heart of these petitions on their behalf? It was "that you may be filled" (ἵνα πληρωθῆτε). The conjunction (ἵνα) with the subjunctive mood of the verb is used to indicate the content of the prayers, rather than a purpose statement.[91] The verb is used eighty-six times in the NT and can be used both spatially and figuratively. It is in a figurative sense that he employs it here.[92] When used figuratively it can mean to fill persons with

> **Ministry Maxim**
>
> The insight essential to walking with God is alien to my soul—only His Spirit can give it to me.

---

[89] Mounce, 41-42.
[90] BAGD, 25.
[91] Harris, 30; Moo, 93.
[92] Mounce, 251.

some kind of powers or qualities.[93] Paul speaks of believers being filled with the Holy Spirit (Eph. 5:18), indeed, with God Himself (Eph. 1:23; 3:19)! The qualities with which Paul speaks of people being filled include joy and peace (Rom. 15:13), knowledge (Rom. 15:14), comfort (2 Cor. 7:4), and the fruit of righteousness (Phil. 1:11). This verb becomes a significant word in Paul's communication with the Colossians (1:9, 25; 2:10; 4:17). Here the aorist tense views the action as an event rather than a process. The passive voice signals that this filling is something God Himself works in us. O'Brien has traced out the emphasis Paul gives in this letter, through various terms, to the idea of fullness: "fullness" (1:19), "filling up" (1:24), "fully" (1:25), "full" (2:2), "fullness" (2:9), "made complete" (2:10; "given fullness," NIV), "fully" (4:12), "fulfill" (4:17).[94]

Specifically here, that with which they are to be filled is "the knowledge of His will" (τὴν ἐπίγνωσιν τοῦ θελήματος αὐτοῦ). The word for "knowledge" (ἐπίγνωσιν) is a compound word comprised of ἐπί ("upon") and γνῶσις ("knowledge"). The prefix intensifies the root word and points to fullness, depth, and completeness of knowledge. Paul has just used the cognate verb in verse 6. As there, Paul may use the noun here as a jab against the false teacher(s) who claimed a corner on the truth (2:4, 8, 18). As already noted, Paul will soon say that the Colossian believers possessed "the full assurance of understanding, resulting in a true knowledge of God's mystery, that is, Christ Himself, in whom are hidden all the treasures of wisdom and knowledge" (Col. 2:2b-3).

Here the presence of the definite article (τὴν, "the") signals that it is not any and all knowledge which the Apostle has in mind, but knowledge "of His will" (τοῦ θελήματος αὐτου). This precise phrase is also used in Ephesians 1:5, 9, and 11. Those usages signal that this will is what encompasses the predestination of our adoption as sons of God (Eph. 1:5), the kindness of God in setting His grace upon us (1:9), and guaranteeing us an inheritance in Christ (1:11).

Thus it seems that Paul's intent here is that the Colossians would be filled with a deep, full, rich understanding of the grace of God that is theirs in Christ, a grace that stretches from eternity past when God set His will and

---

[93] BAGD, 671.
[94] O'Brien, 20.

predestined them to adoption as sons all the way through the present and into the future where they will spend eternity discovering the wonders of their inheritance in Christ as sons of God. Later we will find that Epaphras also is "always laboring earnestly for you in his prayers, that you may stand perfect and fully assured in all the will of God" (Col. 4:12).

And this filling is to be "in all spiritual wisdom and understanding" (ἐν πάσῃ σοφίᾳ καὶ συνέσει πνευματικη). What will it take for this to become reality? Such a knowledge of God's will requires being "in" (ἐν) relationship to "all spiritual wisdom and understanding." But just how one should translate the preposition (ἐν) is a matter of some debate. Some believe it describes the manner[95] or mode[96] by which God fills the Colossians ("through," NIV). Others see it as instrumental[97] (describing the instrument of God's filling the Colossians) and still others as associative[98] (describing that which accompanies the knowledge already spoken of).

What is clearer is that which is described by the words "wisdom and understanding" (σοφίᾳ καὶ συνέσει). The former describes that wisdom which only God can impart and which comes only to those who live in close relationship with Him. It is the good judgment that enables a person to engage the demands of life on the physical, relational, and spiritual planes.[99] The background of the OT probably shines through and emphasizes wisdom as the practical application of the knowledge of God's will to the demands of earthly life.[100] It was in such wisdom that Paul taught all people (Col. 1:28) and with which all believers are to edify one another from the Word of God (Col. 3:16). This wisdom is to govern our every relationship and all our interactions (Col. 4:5). All such wisdom is found only in Christ (Col. 2:3).

Again the Apostle likely rescues this word from the abuse of the false teacher(s) who claimed special insight, deeper knowledge, and higher wisdom than the Colossians were getting through the simple gospel of Christ. Having described some of his basic tenets, Paul will concede that they may possess "the appearance of wisdom," but must conclude that they

---

[95] Abbott, 202.
[96] Eadie, 22.
[97] Bruce, NIC, 45; Harris, 30.
[98] Bruce, NIC, 45; Moo, 94.
[99] BAGD, 759.
[100] Rienecker, 565-566.

are "of no value" (Col. 2:23). What the false teacher(s) claimed to possess is in fact found only in Christ through the gospel which has already been preached to them by Epaphras. The latter word (συνέσει, "understanding") is a compound ("with," σύν; "bring," εἰμί) and is used to describe the coming or sending together of two things. It is used to describe the union of two rivers that flow together.[101] Thus it "refers to putting together the facts and information and drawing conclusions and seeing relationships."[102] Paul prays and labors in ministry because he knows that a believer's deep assurance comes through such understanding (Col. 2:2). These twins "wisdom and understanding" are often found together in the OT (e.g., Exod. 31:3; 35:31, 35; Deut. 4:6; 1 Chron. 22:12; Job 8:10; 12:13; Psa. 49:3; 111:10; Prov. 1:7; 2:2-3, 6; Isa. 10:13).[103]

These two treasures Paul prays will be the possession of the Colossian believers in fullest measure (πάση, "all"), or perhaps better, that they will experience wisdom and understanding "of every sort."[104] Both of these are "spiritual" (πνευματικη) in nature. This adjective is emphatic by its position in the sentence. The word is used in the NT with reference to that which is caused by, filled with, or pertaining or corresponding to the Holy Spirit.[105] This is thus not far from Paul's command that the Ephesian believers be "filled with the Spirit" (Eph. 5:18). Here he views the fruit of such a filling, there the root which produces this fruit of "spiritual wisdom and understanding." This "spiritual wisdom" stands in contrast to the "fleshly mind" (Col. 2:18) of the false teacher(s) which had only "the appearance of wisdom" (2:23).

1:10 so that you will walk in a manner worthy of the Lord, to please Him in all respects, bearing fruit in every good work and increasing in the knowledge of God;

The goal of the knowledge for which Paul and Timothy pray (v. 9) is "so that you will walk" (περιπατῆσαι) in a particular way. The infinitive is used to express either purpose[106] or result.[107] It expresses the outcome of the filling

---

[101] Friberg, 366.
[102] Rienecker, 566.
[103] Dunn, 70.
[104] O'Brien, 22.
[105] BAGD, 678-679.
[106] Moo, 95; O'Brien, 22.
[107] Dunn, 71; Harris, 31; Lenski, 35.

requested in verse 9. This word is used figuratively to describe one's conduct through daily life (Col. 2:6; 3:7; 4:5)[108] and is a reflection of Hebraic thought (e.g., Prov. 2:20; 4:12; 6:22). The aorist tense "views the Christian's whole life and conduct as a unit, without reference to individual or repeated acts."[109]

The desired way of living is "in a manner worthy of the Lord" (ἀξίως τοῦ κυρίου). The adverb means "worthily," "suitably," or, as it is rendered here, "in a manner worthy of."[110] It has the basic notion of "bringing into balance,"[111] and in classical Greek it was often used to describe the balancing of the two sides of a scales in which two entities are brought into equilibrium.[112] It is found six times in the NT, five of which are by Paul (Rom. 16:2; Eph. 4:1; Phil. 1:27; Col. 1:10; 1 Thess. 2:12; 3 John 6) and three of which are found in combination with περιπατέω (Eph. 4:1; Col. 1:10; 1 Thess. 2:12), as here.

The genitive of person, "the Lord" (τοῦ κυρίου), designates who sets the standard by which such conduct is measured. In this case, in view of the definite article's presence, the referent is probably the Lord Jesus Christ.[113]

This is further explained as "to please Him in all respects" (εἰς πᾶσαν ἀρεσκείαν). The noun (ἀρεσκείαν, "please") occurs only here in the NT, though the cognate verb is used fourteen times by Paul (e.g., 1 Thess. 2:4, 15; 4:1; 2 Tim. 2:4). In classical Greek the noun was often, though not exclusively, used in a negative sense. In that sense it could describe "trying to gain favor from someone and describes that cringing subservient attitude which one has who would do anything to please a benefactor."[114] Here, however, it is used in a positive sense. The indefinite adjective (πᾶσαν, "all") broadens the goal and means "every" or "every kind of."[115] The entire clause seems to parallel the previous one and here εἰς ("in") serves to introduce a second purpose statement.[116]

The precise details of what it means to walk worthy of the Lord is now explained in verses 10b-12a by the use of four participles describing what

---

[108] NIDNTT: Abridged, 453.
[109] Harris, 31.
[110] BAGD, 78.
[111] Little Kittel, 63.
[112] NIDNTT, 3:348.
[113] Harris, 31.
[114] Rienecker, 566.
[115] BAGD, 631.
[116] Harris, 31-32.

this lifestyle looks like.[117] The first is "bearing fruit" (καρποφοροῦντες). Paul uses the verb only four times, one being in verse 6 (Rom. 7:4, 5; Col. 1:6, 10). Though Paul gave thanks for the fruit the gospel had borne and is bearing in the Colossians and others around the world (v. 6), he continues to pray for further fruit to be produced through them (v. 10). Yesterday's grace must become today's fruit. Paul will echo something of this again when he commands them "as you have received Christ Jesus the Lord, so walk in Him" (Col. 2:6).

The present tense indicates that such growth is to be continuous and ongoing. True believers never rest in yesterday's harvest of righteousness, but ever press forward for continued growth in Christ. Far from creating a mind-set wherein there is never peace or attainment in the Christian life, this rather sets forth the Christian life as a joyful adventure of always having new horizons of grace to explore and new lands of fruitfulness to cultivate.

In verse 6 the verb is used in the middle voice, while here it is found in the active voice. Some think this indicates that the gospel bears fruit of itself (middle voice, v. 6), but that the believer does not bear fruit of himself, but only by reliance upon the Holy Spirit.[118] Other commentators, however, caution that Paul likely intended no such nuance of meaning between the middle and active voices in this context.[119]

This fruit is to be borne "in every good work" (ἐν παντὶ ἔργῳ ἀγαθῷ). Salvation is not gained by good works (Gal. 2:16; Eph. 2:8-9; 2 Tim. 1:9; Titus 3:5), but its reality is witnessed to by the presence of good works (Eph. 2:10; 1 Tim. 5:10; 6:18; 2 Tim. 2:21; 3:17). Thus such works will be the ongoing presentation of evidence that the gospel of Jesus Christ has taken possession of those who claim faith in Him. We each used to perform "evil deeds" (Col. 1:21), but now our standard is "Whatever you do in word or deed, do all in the name of the Lord Jesus,

> **Ministry Maxim**
>
> Yesterday's grace must become today's fruit.

giving thanks through Him to God the Father" (Col. 3:17). In this way the reality of one's salvation is attested.

---

[117] Moo, 92.

[118] Kent, 36.

[119] E.g., Moo, 96; O'Brien, 23.

The second (καὶ, "and") mark of the person living in a manner worthy of the Lord is that he or she is "increasing in the knowledge of God" (αὐξανόμενοι τῇ ἐπιγνώσει τοῦ θεοῦ). This verb (αὐξανόμενοι, "increasing") is a favorite of the Apostle. He most often employs it in an agricultural metaphor (1 Cor. 3:6, 7; 2 Cor. 9:10; 10:15) but can also use it of architectural (Eph. 2:21) and physiological (Eph. 4:15; Col. 2:19) growth. It signals the natural increase of that which is living. Such increase and growth is continuous, as the present tense indicates. Here again Paul is echoing in petition (v. 10) that which he has already thanked God for regarding the Colossian believers (v. 6). The passive voice also signals that such increase is worked by a person or force outside the individual himself. In this case it is God who gives the growth (1 Cor. 3:6).

The use of the passive is fitting, for the growth is "in the knowledge of God" (τῇ ἐπιγνώσει τοῦ θεοῦ). There is great debate over just how to interpret the meaning of the dative form. Some argue that it is a dative of means ("growing by means of the knowledge of God").[120] Some see it as instrumental in use ("by the knowledge of God").[121] Still others see the dative as indicating the sphere in which such growth takes place ("growing in the knowledge").[122] It seems to me that the latter is likely the best option, given the emphasis in this context on the importance of knowing God (vv. 6, 9).

So here again (see comments on v. 9) we meet the noun ἐπίγνωσις, which describes a deep, full knowledge (cf. Col. 2:2; 3:10). The heretical teacher(s) in Colossae was emphasizing his knowledge of things spiritual (2:4, 8, 18), but Paul makes clear that in Christ "are hidden all the treasures of wisdom and knowledge" (Col. 2:3). It is in this knowledge of Christ—who possesses all knowledge—that Paul prays the Colossian believers will increase and abound. Here the noun is accompanied by the definite article to make specific what knowledge is under consideration. The genitive (τοῦ θεου, "of God") should be understood as an objective genitive ("the knowledge of God Himself") rather than a subjective genitive ("the knowledge which God Himself possesses").[123] Indeed, it is, more literally, the

---

[120] Dunn, 72; Kent, 36; Lenski, 37.
[121] Abbott, 203.
[122] Harris, 32; Moo, 97.
[123] Moo, 97.

knowledge of "the God" (τοῦ θεοῦ)—the one and only God is known only by a faith relationship with Him through Jesus Christ.

Whatever the false teacher(s) is peddling will fail to deliver on the knowledge he promises. The Colossian believers already have possession of this knowledge potentially and are continuously on the path toward this knowledge in actuality through the Christ they encountered in the gospel.

1:11 strengthened with all power, according to His glorious might, for the attaining of all steadfastness and patience; joyously

The third mark of the person living in a manner worthy of the Lord is now set before us in this third of four participles: "strengthened" (δυναμούμενοι). Here again the present tense points to that which is continuously true. The passive voice indicates that the strength is not self-generated, arising from somewhere within the individual by force of will or determination. Rather the strengthening comes to the individual from outside himself—from God who imparts His Spirit to those who are His own. Such individuals move "from strength to strength" (Psa. 84:7). They move "from glory to glory, just as from the Lord, the Spirit" (2 Cor. 3:18). "Yet those who wait for the LORD Will gain new strength; / They will mount up with wings like eagles, / They will run and not get tired, / They will walk and not become weary" (Isa. 40:31).

This particular verb occurs only here and in Hebrews 11:34 in the NT. The word group, however, is used often in the NT—the noun δύναμις being used one hundred nineteen times and the verb δύναμαι being used over two hundred times—and is a favorite of the Apostle Paul.[124] The strengthening envisioned is "with all power" (ἐν πάσῃ δυνάμει). The preposition (ἐν, "with") with the dative indicates the instrument by which the strengthening becomes reality. The noun "power" (δυνάμει) is cognate to the previous verb and could yield a translation something like "strengthened with all strength" or "empowered with all power."[125] The adjective "all" (πάσῃ) designates the highest degree of something and thus points to power in its fullest or greatest expression.[126] As the believer

---

[124] NIDNTT: Abridged, 154.
[125] Robertson, *Word Pictures*, 4:476.
[126] BAGD, 631.

chooses to take a step forward in the will of God, he will never fail for lack of power to do so.

The measure of this strengthening is to be "according to His glorious might" (κατὰ τὸ κράτος τῆς δόξης αὐτοῦ). The noun "might" (τὸ κράτος) is used in the NT only of God's power, except in Hebrews 2:14. It points to "the possession of force or strength that affords supremacy or control"[127] or, as Robertson puts it, "perfect strength."[128] It is sometimes rendered "dominion" (1 Tim. 6:16; 1 Peter 4:11; 5:11; Jude 25; Rev. 1:6; 5:13). Such ruling power is the possession of Christ (αὐτοῦ, "His"). It is "the inherent strength which displays itself in the rule over others."[129] This ruling power of Christ is "glorious" (τῆς δόξης). This is power *expressed*, power *seen* in its radiance and outshining. These two nouns (κράτος, "might" and δόξα, "glory") occur together in five of the former noun's twelve usages in the NT (Col. 1:11; 1 Peter 4:11; Jude 25; Rev. 1:6; 5:13).

Should this phrase be translated as it is here ("His glorious might," qualitative genitive), or should it be rendered "the might of His glory" (possessive genitive, NASU margin)? Either is possible. Most English translations follow the former.[130] Most commentators follow the former as well.[131] Yet Moo makes a compelling case for the possessive genitive, noting that the genitive δόξης is used to qualify a noun or pronoun twenty other times in the NT and in virtually every case (except, perhaps, Eph. 1:17) "glory" is seen as a significant entity itself.[132] God's "glory" is the outshining of Himself as He shows His nature in action and deed. Thus "the might of His glory" is "the power which is declared to us when God reveals Himself"[133] to us in our need. The best parallel to Paul's prayer here is his prayer for the Ephesian believers (Eph. 1:17-21).

This divine empowerment is "for the attaining of all steadfastness and patience" (εἰς πᾶσαν ὑπομονὴν καὶ μακροθυμίαν). God's power is given "for" (εἰς) a certain end. Or we might say God's strength is provided to move the believer "into" a certain quality or kind of life.

---

[127] Friberg, 236.
[128] Robertson, *Word Pictures*, 4:476.
[129] Rienecker, 566.
[130] BAGD, 203.
[131] Bruce, NIC, 47; Dunn, 73.
[132] Moo, 98; cf. Eadie, 28; Kent, 37; Vaughan, 11:179.
[133] Carson, 37.

Two nouns are paired to describe the life for which believers are strengthened. First, there is "steadfastness" (ὑπομονὴν). This is a compound word comprised of ὑπο, ("under") and μονη, ("stay"). It means then to "remain under." It pointed to a patient endurance which held out long under difficulty with hope and courage. To this is added (καὶ, "and") "patience" (μακροθυμίαν). The word is used by Paul in ten of its fourteen NT appearances. It is often used of human patience (2 Cor. 6:6; Eph. 4:2; Col. 3:12; 2 Tim. 3:10; 4:2), but also of God's (Rom. 2:4; 9:22; 1 Tim. 1:16). Such patience is produced in us only by the indwelling Holy Spirit (Gal. 5:22). The word generally refers to a longsuffering endurance in the face of indignities and injuries by others. Wright puts it aptly, "The former

> **Ministry Maxim**
>
> God grants His power for His purposes, not ours.

["steadfastness"] is what faith, hope and love bring to an apparently impossible situation, the latter ["patience"] what they show to an apparently impossible person."[134] Both of these are possible without reserve (πᾶσαν, "all"). Here again the word points to something in its highest degree.[135] The power of God operating in a believer through the indwelling Holy Spirit will never come up against the far wall of patience and steadfastness and be forced to abandon them.

The phrase translated "joyously" (Μετὰ χαρᾶς) can be read with what precedes ("endurance and patience with joy," ESV; cf. KJV) or with what follows in verse 12 (NASB, NASU, NIV, NRSV). In the former it describes the attitude and demeanor in which hardship and wrong are suffered. In the latter it denotes the character of the gratitude which is fitting before God and which pleases Him. It seems most fitting to read it with the fourth participle, which is found in verse 12.[136] This maintains the symmetry of each of these four participles being joined by a modifying phrase.

---

[134] Wright, 60.
[135] BAGD, 631.
[136] Abbott, 205; O'Brien, 25.

1:12 giving thanks to the Father, who has qualified us to share in the inheritance of the saints in Light.

The fourth and final participle used to describe just what it means to "walk in a manner worthy of the Lord" (v. 10) now confronts us: "giving thanks" (εὐχαριστοῦντες). The present tense underscores that such active gratitude should be our abiding and ongoing attitude. This should take place "joyously" or "with joy" (Μετὰ χαρᾶς, v. 11b). No grudging expressions of gratitude will do. This must bubble up from the depths of one's heart.

Such thanksgiving is to be directed "to the Father" (τῷ πατρὶ). Paul has given thanks to the Father for the Colossian believers (v. 3) and now he calls them to a similar outlook in all things. That such gratitude should be broad in its embrace is underscored in the only other use of this verb in Colossians: "Whatever you do in word or deed, do all in the name of the Lord Jesus, giving thanks through Him to God the Father" (3:17). The scope of our thanks is all-encompassing. The object of our thanks is "the Father." Our thanks are expressed "through Him" (i.e., Jesus Christ). Gratitude becomes a rich vein running through Colossians (1:3, 12; 2:7; 3:17; 4:2).

The Father is the correct object of our gratitude (cf. 1:3; 3:17) for it is He "who has qualified us" (τῷ ἱκανώσαντι ὑμᾶς). The second-person personal pronoun (ὑμᾶς, "you") is likely the correct reading (ESV, NIV, NRSV, and most English versions) rather than the first-person plural (ἡμᾶς, "us"; KJV, NASB, NASU, RSV). This verb is found only two times in the NT (2 Cor. 3:6; Col. 1:12). It means "to make sufficient" or "to qualify." The latter idea may begin to blend into the notion of empowering or authorizing.[137] The cognate noun, however, is used thirty-nine times, six of those by Paul. The Apostle did not see himself as "fit to be called an apostle" (1 Cor. 15:9) nor adequate to fulfill the duties of such (2 Cor. 2:16). Rather, he knew well, "our adequacy is from God" (2 Cor. 3:5). Whether it is Paul as an apostle or any one of us as simple believers, all we are, have, and perform is by the grace of God.

The aorist tense marks this as a present, settled reality.[138] "The suggestion is that the qualifying is not a process but an instantaneous act."[139] The

---

137 BAGD, 374.
138 O'Brien, 26.
139 Vaughan, 11:179.

Colossian believers did not need to strive to be qualified or sufficient, for the Father had already determined them to be so qualified through the sacrifice of Jesus Christ. This truth calls for restful trust, not relentless effort on the part of the believer.

We are qualified "to share in the inheritance of the saints in Light" (εἰς τὴν μερίδα τοῦ κλήρου τῶν ἁγίων ἐν τῷ φωτί). The preposition (εἰς, "to") is used to denote reference to something and might be rendered "with respect to" or "with reference to."[140] That which we have been qualified with respect to is a "share in the inheritance" (τὴν μερίδα τοῦ κλήρου). The former word (τὴν μερίδα, "share") is used only five times in the NT, two by Paul (2 Cor. 6:16; Col. 1:12) and three by Luke (Luke 10:42; Acts 8:21; 16:12). It refers to "part of a whole that has been chosen or divided up" or "an assigned portion" (i.e., a share).[141] The article may be intended as possessive (i.e., "your share").[142] The latter word (τοῦ κλήρου, "the inheritance") is used only here by Paul. It is what is assigned by lot. Thus it refers to a portion or a share.[143] The genitive form is either epexegetical ("the portion which consists in the lot") or partitive ("to have a share in the lot").[144] These two words are found in combination elsewhere only in Acts 8:21. This entire expression is an overt allusion to the language of the OT where it is applied to Israel claiming her inheritance in the Promised Land. So too as NT believers we have an inheritance which we also must claim, enter into, and enjoy by faith.

Indeed, this inheritance is "of the saints" (τῶν ἁγίων). The genitive is possessive ("the saint's inheritance").[145] In the light of parallels in both the Scriptures (Deut. 33:3; Psa. 38:6) and the writings of Qumran, some view this as a reference to angels.[146] This may be an enticing option in light of the Apostle's opposition to the heretics who preach the worship of angels (Col. 2:18). Yet every other use of the expression in Colossians clearly makes reference to believers (1:2, 4, 22, 26; 3:12), and so it is best to read it in this

---

[140] BAGD, 230.
[141] Friberg, 258.
[142] Harris, 34.
[143] BAGD, 435.
[144] Rienecker, 566.
[145] NET Bible.
[146] Lohse, 35-36.

way here as well.[147] Note also the close parallels of the themes of this verse in Acts 26:18.[148] By the grace of God, Gentile believers like the Colossians have come to have a legitimate share in the inheritance which God had set on His chosen people, Israel (cf. Eph. 2:11-22). "And if you belong to Christ, then you are Abraham's offspring, heirs according to promise" (Gal. 3:29). We are "saints" (τῶν ἁγίων) by virtue of the cleansing work of Christ's blood applied to our lives. We are, however, not only cleansed of sin, but declared righteous on the ground of Christ's blood (Rom. 3:24-26). In this way God legitimately declares us "saints."

The sphere (ἐν, "in") in which this inheritance is found and enjoyed is "in Light" (ἐν τῷ φωτι). There is some debate about just what the Apostle intended by this expression. But we should note the presence of the definite article (lit, "in *the* light").[149] This signals that the answer is found in the contrast with "the domain of darkness" which Paul will mention in the next verse. God Himself "dwells in unapproachable light" (1 Tim. 6:16). Indeed, "He Himself is in the light" (1 John 1:7). The New Jerusalem will have no need for sun or moon, "for the glory of God has illumined it, and its lamp is the Lamb" (Rev. 21:23) and there "the nations shall walk by its light" (v. 24).

As we put our faith in Jesus Christ, His blood cleanses us from our sins and God the Father declares us righteous by imputing to us the righteousness of Christ. In this way we are transferred out of the kingdom of darkness (v. 13), where Satan rules and sin dominates, and we are ushered into the kingdom of God where the light of truth and righteousness is manifest. Thus we become "sons of light and sons of day" (1 Thess. 5:5; cf. Luke 16:8; John 12:36). As part of this new kingdom we enjoy the full blessings of God's children along with those who have been similarly ushered into this kingdom through like faith. This is a kingdom entered

> **Ministry Maxim**
>
> The inheritance becomes yours not by relentless effort, but by restful trust.

---

[147] O'Brien, 26.

[148] Bruce, NIC, 50n51.

[149] Could this be behind the NASU's decision to capitalize "Light"? In so doing it stands alone among English translations, including the original NASB. Compare NASU at John 1:4, 5, 7, 8, 9; 3:19, 20, 21; 8:12; 9:5; 12:35, 36, 46; 2 Cor. 4:6; Eph. 5:8, 9; 1 John 1:5, 7; 2:8, 9, 10.

and enjoyed here and now, but in fuller experience when Christ returns. In Colossians, only here does Paul speak of "light." But in Ephesians, where so many parallels with Colossians exist, he uses it more frequently (Eph. 5:8, 9, 13, 14).

Paul makes clear that a life lived "in a manner worthy of the Lord" (v. 10) includes the right use of our hands ("bearing fruit"), our minds ("increasing in the knowledge of God"), our wills ("strengthened"), and our hearts ("giving thanks").

Digging Deeper:

1. How can you use verse 9 to answer the next person who comes to you with questions about how to know the will of God?
2. How does one identify a life that is conducted "in a manner worthy of the Lord" (v. 10)? Who do you know who fits the bill?
3. If God's power is released to His people when they find themselves in difficult circumstances and difficult relationships (v. 11), what does that tell us about the effect of trying to live out our faith in a culture bent on affluence and comfort?
4. How are we, in daily, practical terms, to apply the truth of our inheritance in Christ (v. 12)?

1:13 For He rescued us from the domain of darkness, and transferred us to the kingdom of His beloved Son,

Though in Greek the sentence flows on directly from verse 12, the NASU breaks to begin a new English sentence. The pronoun ὅς is here represented with "He" for it finds its antecedent in "the Father" (τῷ πατρὶ) of verse 12. Paul is further expanding upon that which incites believers to a life of joyful gratitude. The Father "rescued us" (ἐρρύσατο ἡμᾶς). In the NT the verb is always used of God as the deliverer and a person as the object of that rescue.[150] At the close of his life, Paul used the verb to look back over a lifetime at God's perfect record of rescuing him from persecution and

---

[150] Friberg, 343.

hardship (2 Tim. 3:11; 4:17) and to look forward to God's faithfulness in the future, final deliverance (2 Tim. 4:18). Here the aorist tense views the rescue as an accomplished fact, achieved in the death and resurrection of Jesus Christ. Our salvation is God's work completely, from conception to consummation. Paul now moves from the second-person plural (ὑμᾶς, "you") in verse 12 to the first-person plural (ἡμᾶς, "us"). He has the same ground for gratitude as do the Colossians. He was saved in precisely the same manner as they were.

Our rescue was "from the domain of darkness" (ἐκ τῆς ἐξουσίας τοῦ σκότους). God has brought us "from" [ἐκ] this awful state. The preposition has the force of "out from,"[151] signaling complete and total deliverance. The expression "the domain of darkness" stands in contrast to "the inheritance of the saints in light" (v. 12). Generally speaking the noun "the domain" (τῆς ἐξουσίας) speaks of authority and power. Here it points to "ruling power" or "official power," and particularly the domain in which that power is exercised.[152] It is made specific by the presence of the definite article.

Paul told the Ephesians that in our natural state we "formerly walked (περιεπατήσατε) according to the course of this world, according to the prince of the power [τῆς ἐξουσίας] of the air" (Eph. 2:2). Indeed, Paul designates it the domain "of darkness" (τοῦ σκότους). The genitive is qualitative, describing the nature and quality of this dominion. It is spiritually dark for it is the kingdom of the prince of darkness, Satan. In our natural state we love the darkness and hate the light, because our deeds are evil (John 3:19). Indeed we used to reside under "the power of darkness" (Luke 22:53). Darkness can describe the unillumined state of the unsaved (Luke 1:79; John 1:5). They "walk in darkness" (John 8:12; 12:35), performing "deeds of darkness" (Rom. 13:12; cf. Eph. 5:11). Indeed, Paul can say, "you were formerly darkness" (Eph. 5:8).

This kingdom is ruled by the devil, but it is administered through other dark forces under his direction: our "struggle is not against flesh and blood, but against the rulers, against the powers, against the world forces of this darkness, against the spiritual forces of wickedness in the heavenly places" (Eph. 6:12). But "God is Light, and in Him there is no darkness at all"

---

[151] Robertson, *Word Pictures*, 4:477.
[152] BAGD, 278.

(1 John 1:5). Through Jesus Christ He delivers from this domain of dark-

<table>
<tr><td>

Ministry Maxim

We are saved not just *from*, but *to*.

</td><td>

ness. So thorough is our deliverance that Paul can tell the Thessalonian believers "But you, brethren, are not in darkness ... for you are all sons of light and sons of day. We are not of night nor of darkness" (1 Thess. 5:4-5). Peter can declare that God "has called [us] out of darkness into His marvelous light" (1 Peter 2:9). Those who do not take advantage of God's rescue will face ultimate punishment in "outer darkness" (Matt. 8:12; 22:13; 25:30), also called

</td></tr>
</table>

"the black darkness" (2 Peter 2:17; Jude 13).

The transfer from darkness to light comes through faith in Jesus Christ (John 12:46). God alone can give us "the Light of the knowledge of the glory of God in the face of Christ" (2 Cor. 4:6). Jesus told Paul that He was saving and sending Him to the Gentiles "to open their eyes so that they may turn from darkness to light and from the dominion of Satan to God" (Acts 26:18). Thus the Colossians, though Paul had not met them face-to-face (Col. 2:1) and had not been the one to directly evangelize them (Col. 1:5), were a very real proof of his apostleship.

We were not just saved *from*, but *into*. In addition (καὶ, "and") to deliverance from the domain of darkness, God "transferred us" (μετέστησεν) into a different kingdom. The verb means "literally *remove* from one place to another."[153] It was used frequently to speak of the deportation and removal of a group of people from one location to form a new community elsewhere.[154] The aorist tense sees this transfer as having already been accomplished.

That "into" (εἰς) which God transferred us is "the kingdom of His beloved Son" (τὴν βασιλείαν τοῦ υἱοῦ τῆς ἀγάπης αὐτοῦ). Paul probably makes no distinction between the kingdom of God (Rom. 14:17; 1 Cor. 4:20; 6:9, 10; 15:50; Gal. 5:21; Col. 4:11; 1 Thess. 2:12; 2 Thess. 1:5) and the kingdom of Christ ("the kingdom of Christ and God," Eph. 5:5; cf. 2 Tim. 4:1). As Paul describes it here, in this kingdom, Christ is above all. He is not simply one more intermediary between earth and heaven, as the false teacher(s) may have been suggesting. The Father "put all things in subjection under His feet, and gave Him as head over all things

---

[153] Friberg, 256.
[154] Eadie, 37.

to the church" (Eph. 1:22). Christ is to "have first place in everything" (Col. 1:18). Christ is Lord and King over all!

The genitive (αὐτοῦ, lit., "of him") is objective, meaning "the Son who is the object of His love."[155] The entire expression "His beloved Son" (τοῦ υἱοῦ τῆς ἀγάπης αὐτοῦ; note the piling up of the genitives, lit., "of the Son of the love of Him") echoes the Father's voice at the time of Jesus' baptism (Matt. 3:17) and Transfiguration (Matt. 17:5). As we bow under the rule of Jesus Christ, we, being in Christ, come under the infinite favor and love of God the Father. God saved us "to the praise of the glory of His grace, which He freely bestowed on us in the Beloved" (Eph. 1:6). The kingdom of God is thus a present reality in the lives of those who belong to Christ. Perhaps it is not yet in its final, most glorious form, but it is nonetheless real and present in the lives of those with faith in Jesus Christ.

This "rescue" and "transfer" could be understood sequentially—the one following upon the other. But it is probably better to understand the two actions as concurrent: "rescue by transference."[156]

1:14 in whom we have redemption, the forgiveness of sins.

The relative clause (ἐν ᾧ, "in whom") looks back to "His beloved Son" (v. 13) and thus is a reference to Christ. To be "in" (ἐν) Christ is stock Pauline thought. It is only in union with Christ[157] that we partake of the benefits of His saving work. It is there that "we have redemption" (ἔχομεν τὴν ἀπολύτρωσιν). The present tense of the verb (to which the best manuscript evidence points) views the present and continuous reality of the believer, yet it is also true that there is a coming "day of redemption" (Eph. 4:30) which will bring us more fully into all Christ died to make ours. This includes our bodies (Rom. 8:23). The precise expression used here is found also in Ephesians 1:7. Seven of the ten NT usages of the noun are by Paul (Rom 3:24; 8:23; 1 Cor. 1:30; Eph. 1:7, 14; 4:30;

> **Ministry Maxim**
>
> Redemption is a present possession that passage of time only enables us to enjoy more fully.

---

[155] Abbott, 208.
[156] Moo, 102-103.
[157] Harris, 37.

91

Col. 1:14). The word is a compound comprised of ἀπό ("from") and λυτρόω ("free by paying a ransom"). It was used to describe the action of freeing a slave or captive through payment of a ransom price. God did not wink at our sin. The price was real; that price was death (Rom. 6:23). Jesus Christ paid that price by dying that death for each one of us, thus paying our sin debt so that we might be set free.

The definite article makes specific the redemption that can only be had in relationship to Christ. This redemption took place "through His blood" (Eph. 1:7). A few manuscripts of Colossians 1:14 include this phrase, but copyists likely were attempting to bring the shorter (and surely original) text here into conformity with that of the longer expression in Ephesians (cf. Col. 1:20). The Holy Spirit seals the believer permanently in this redemption (Eph. 4:30).

This redemption is more fully explained by the clause placed in apposition: "the forgiveness of sins" (τὴν ἄφεσιν τῶν ἁμαρτιῶν). Under the Old Covenant God temporarily overlooked sins (Rom. 3:25; πάρεσις, meaning "passing over" or "overlooking").[158] But under the New Covenant He does infinitely more. When Paul speaks of "the forgiveness" (τὴν ἄφεσιν), he uses a word which can refer to either release from captivity or forgiveness. The former sense is found only two times in the NT (Luke 4:18), while the latter is found fifteen times.[159] Paul uses the word only here and in Ephesians 1:7. It describes our sin's *"removal* from the mind of God."[160] The word points to *"letting them go,* as if they had not been committed."[161] Note the presence of the definite article, pointing to the one and only such pardon for sin. Paul "sees the forgiveness of sins not only as the removal of past guilt but the total deliverance from the power of sin and restoration to fellowship with God."[162]

Of the seventeen times ἄφεσις ("forgiveness") is used in the NT, twelve of those times it is accompanied by the genitive "of sins" (τῶν ἁμαρτιῶν), though Ephesians 1:7 has "of our trespasses" (τῶν παραπτωμάτων). The connotation of our word here is the transgression of the Law (cf. 1 John 3:4).

---

[158] Friberg, 83.

[159] NIDNT: Abridged, 81.

[160] Friberg, 83.

[161] Thayer, 88.

[162] Mounce, 267.

It is the most frequently used word for "sin" in the NT. Paul uses it sixty-four times in his writings.[163] The definite article may indicate possession (i.e., "our sins").[164] Surprisingly, Paul speaks of the saving work of Christ in terms of forgiveness of sins only in Ephesians (1:7; 4:32) and Colossians (1:14; 2:13; 3:13), except for Rom. 4:7 (which is a quotation from the OT).[165] This does not, as some contend, point to non-Pauline authorship of these letters, but more likely is a sign that the Apostle was making specific the message of Christ to local conditions at the time (cf. Acts 13:38; 26:18).

Paul, then, enumerates three reasons for thanksgiving to God by the believer: qualification for an inheritance (v. 12b), deliverance from the domain of darkness (v. 13a), and transference into the kingdom of God's beloved Son (vv. 13b-14).[166] In celebrating what the Father has done in saving us (vv. 12-13), Paul has moved into a description of Christ's role in this salvation (v. 14) and will next launch into a majestic declaration about the Person and work of Christ (vv. 15-20).

Digging Deeper:

1. How does preaching salvation truth in the first-person plural ("us," cf. v. 13) rather than the second person ("you") change the preaching event?

2. How does a watering down of the dire nature of our preconversion state (v. 13a) diminish the joy of our present experience of salvation?

3. How does "redemption" (v. 14) as a possession as opposed to a pursuit change one's entire experience of salvation in this world?

4. Who do you know who, though professing faith in Christ, lives under an Old Covenant mind-set ("passed over," Rom. 3:25) rather than a New Covenant experience ("forgiveness," Col. 1:14b)? How can these verses help set them free?

---

[163] Ibid., 656-657.
[164] Harris, 37.
[165] Moo, 106.
[166] Harris, 36.

1:15 He is the image of the invisible God, the firstborn of all creation.

In the previous verses the Apostle began a transition which is now fully made in this present verse. The attention is now completely set upon God the Son, Jesus Christ. We enter now into an extended section (vv. 15-20) which guides us onto holy ground. Here Jesus Christ is extolled in the loftiest of terms.

Though scholars differ in their opinions, this section gives the impression of having hymnic or poetic qualities about it. Some opine that what we have here is a fragment of a Christian hymn of the most ancient kind and that Paul has borrowed from words familiar to the early Christians. Alternatively, it is possible that Paul used a piece composed with his own hand at an earlier time and then adapted it to the present need.[167] It is also possible that Paul composed this piece expressly for this letter.[168] Whatever we decide on these matters, we understand that the Holy Spirit was fully in charge of the Apostle's selection/writing process and breathed out the exact words as He saw fit (2 Tim. 3:16; 2 Peter 1:20-21). Indeed, it is the Spirit's great delight to exalt Christ (John 16:14) as He does here. Christ is here extolled as supreme over the present creation (15-17) and in the new creation (18-20). There are clear signs of an intentional literary design within the pericope:

- "who is" (ὅς ἐστιν, vv. 15, 18)
- "firstborn" (πρωτότοκος, vv. 15, 18)
- "all/everything" (πᾶς, vv. 15, 16 [2x], 17 [2x], 18, 19, 20)[169]
- "things ... in the heavens and on earth" (v. 16); "things on earth or things in heaven" (v. 20)
- the use of prepositions: ἐν (vv. 16a, 19), διά (vv. 16b, 20a)
- εἰς (vv. 16b, 20)
- statements and elaborations using ὅτι (vv. 16, 19).[170]

---

[167] See O'Brien (32-42) for an excellent discussion of these matters.
[168] Moo, 109.
[169] Moo calls this use of πᾶς "the thread that binds the verses together" (111).
[170] Ibid., 115.

There appear, then, to be two main stanzas (vv. 15-16; 18b-20) with an additional stanza of two parallels lines in the middle (vv. 17-18a).[171] The first and last stanzas are marked by their opening (ὅς ἐστιν; "He is," vv. 15a, 18b). The middle stanza has its two lines marked out by the repeated καὶ αὐτός ἐστιν ("And He is," v. 17a; "He is also," v. 18a). A rudimentary representation of this basic structure might look like this:

ὅς ἐστιν ... (vv. 15-16)

καὶ αὐτός ἐστιν ... (v. 17)
καὶ αὐτός ἐστιν ... (v. 18a)

ὅς ἐστιν ... (vv. 18b-20)

The opening and closing stanzas, then, both contain these key words: "firstborn" (πρωτότοκος, vv. 15b, 18b), "things ... in the heavens and on earth" (ἐν τοῖς οὐρανοῖς καὶ ἐπὶ τῆς γῆς, v. 16) and "things on earth or things in heaven" (εἴτε τὰ ἐπὶ τῆς γῆς εἴτε τὰ ἐν τοῖς οὐρανοῖς, v. 20), and "by [δι'] him and for [εἰς] him" (v. 16b) and "through [δι'] Him ... to [εἰς] Himself" (v. 20a).

The relative pronoun (ὅς) is rendered "He" and points back to "His Beloved Son" (τοῦ υἱοῦ τῆς ἀγάπης αὐτοῦ) in verse 13 as did ᾧ ("whom") in verse 14. Note the relative pronoun ὅς ("He") in verse 18 which also refers to Christ. In addition, from verses 14 to 20 there are eleven instances of the personal pronoun αὐτός, each referring to Christ.[172] Christ is the great obsession of this paragraph. Indeed, as Paul will declare, "Christ is all" (3:11)!

The Apostle goes on to speak of what Christ "is" (ἐστιν). The present tense points to what Christ is continuously, without end, eternally in both past and future. He is, first, "the image of the invisible God" (εἰκὼν τοῦ θεοῦ τοῦ ἀοράτου). The fact that the noun is anarthrous does not mean it is not definite, for a predicate noun following εἰμί often lacks the article, though it is definite in meaning.[173]

---

[171] cf. Moo, 116; Wright, 65f.

[172] Harris, 37.

[173] Ibid., 43.

The noun "image" (εἰκὼν) was used in various contexts outside of the NT to speak of an image such as that found in a painting, statue, idol, or upon a coin. In the Gospels we find it used in this way (Matt. 22:20; Mark 12:16; Luke 20:24).[174] But the use in the present context indicates more than that which simply bears a resemblance to something else. "In the NT the original is present in the image, which gives it visible manifestation."[175] Thus in Greek thought "an image shares in the reality of what it represents. The essence of the thing appears in the image; e.g., the god is himself present and operative in his image."[176] So it is accurate to say that (cf. 2 Cor. 4:4) "there is no difference here between the image and the essence of the invisible God, for in Christ we see God (cf. Jn. 14:9)."[177] As another scholar puts it, "the stress is on the equality of the eik□n with the original. Christ is the form of God and equal to God (cf. Phil. 2:6)."[178] O'Brien says, "The term points to his revealing of the Father on the one hand and his pre-existence on the other—it is both functional and ontological."[179] Jesus is viewed "as an embodiment or living manifestation of God."[180]

Paul will go on to say that "it was the Father's good pleasure for all the fullness to dwell in Him" (1:19) and "in Him all the fullness of Deity dwells in bodily form" (2:9). As the "image" of God, Jesus is both "an exact, as well as a visible, representation of God."[181] With different words, but with the same intent another writer says that "He is the radiance of His glory and the exact representation of His nature" (Heb. 1:3). It is little wonder, then, that Satan works to blind people to the light of the gospel of the glory of Christ, who is the image of God" (2 Cor. 4:4).

Jesus is this physical manifestation "of the invisible God" (τοῦ θεοῦ τοῦ ἀοράτου). God Himself is "invisible" (1 Tim. 1:17) and "no man has seen or can see" Him (1 Tim. 6:16). The word used here is a compound made up of ἀ (not) and ὁρατός (visible). For the only use of this root word

---

[174] NIDNTT: Abridged, 164.
[175] Little Kittel, 205.
[176] NIDNTT: Abridged, 164.
[177] Ibid.
[178] Little Kittel, 206.
[179] O'Brien, 44.
[180] Friberg, 131.
[181] Harris, 43.

see verse 16, where it stands as the opposite of our current word. The present word appears five times in the NT, four of those in Paul's writings. God's attributes are "invisible," yet they "have been clearly seen, being understood through what has been made" (Rom. 1:20). Jesus created all things "visible and invisible" (Col. 1:16). Moses found courage to leave Egypt and persevere on the road through the wilderness because he was "seeing Him who is unseen" (Heb. 11:27). Indeed, "No

Ministry Maxim
If you miss on your doctrine of Christ, you'll miss on everything else.

one has seen God at any time; the only begotten God who is in the bosom of the Father, He has explained Him" (John 1:18). Not only *is* God not seen, He *cannot* be seen. Yet Christ "has made Him known" (John 1:18b, ESV, NET, NIV, NRSV).

Academics have long and contentiously debated the connection between Paul's words here and the wisdom/logos connection made with OT texts like Proverbs 8:22-31 as well as both Jewish writers and Philo.[182] Clearly there is some reflection of Genesis 1:26-28 here: "Then God said, 'Let us make humankind in our image, after our likeness, so they may rule over the fish of the sea and the birds of the air, over the cattle, and over all the earth, and over all the creatures that move on the earth.' God created humankind in his own image, in the image of God he created them, male and female he created them. God blessed them and said to them, 'Be fruitful and multiply! Fill the earth and subdue it! Rule over the fish of the sea and the birds of the air and every creature that moves on the ground.'" Colossians 3:10 is also significant in this regard. There Paul speaks of the believer's new self "who is being renewed to a true knowledge according to the image of the One who created him." It is probably correct to make the distinction that Christ *is* (ἐστιν; not "became") the image of God and humans were *made* in that image. Even now believers are being renewed "according to" the image of God.[183]

Christ is also "the firstborn of all creation" (πρωτότοκος πάσης κτίσεως). Like the noun in the previous clause, "firstborn" (πρωτότοκος) is definite in meaning though it is anarthrous. The adjective "firstborn"

---

[182] See Moo (111-113) for a good synopsis of the debate.
[183] Ibid., 117-118.

(πρωτότοκος) is a compound from πρωτό- (first) and -τόκος (from τίκτω, give birth to).

The term is used both literally and metaphorically. Its literal sense is seen when it refers to a firstborn child, in terms of birth order and time (Heb. 11:28). Jesus is thus Mary's firstborn son (Luke 2:7). Some have wanted to see this literal meaning in the present passage. But the context must control whether the literal or metaphorical understanding of the word is intended. Here it cannot point to Christ as the first created being, since "by Him all things were created" (v. 16) and "He is before all things" (v. 17). Clearly the term is used metaphorically in our present passage. In this way it designates not temporal order, but honored status and suprema-cy.[184] In such cases the prefix πρωτο- carries, not a temporal meaning, but a superlative sense.[185]

This metaphorical meaning was already present in the LXX (e.g., Psa. 89:27)[186] and was perpetuated in the pseudepigrapha and in the rabbinic writings (where it is used of the favored position of Israel, the law, Adam, and the Messiah).[187] Of Isaac's son Jacob, though second born in time, the Lord could say, "Israel [i.e., Jacob] is My son, My firstborn" (Exod. 4:22). Furthermore, the title is used in the OT of the Messiah: "I also shall make him My firstborn, The highest of the kings of the earth" (Psa. 89:27). Thus Jesus is also the "firstborn from/of the dead" (Col. 1:18; Rev. 1:5). In saving, transforming, and glorifying the redeemed, Jesus is the "firstborn among many brethren" (Rom. 8:29). "The point, then, is not that Christ is the first creature. This would demand a stress on the *–tokos* and would also bring birth into conflict with creation. What is stated is Christ's supremacy over creation as its mediator. The term *prōtótokos* is used, then, because of its importance as a word for rank."[188]

> As a title of honor for Jesus [it] expresses more clearly than almost any other the unity of God's saving will and acts: 'the firstborn over all creation' (Col. 1:15), 'the firstborn from among the dead' (1:18), and 'the firstborn among many brothers' (Rom. 8:29; cf. Heb. 12:23).

---

[184] Mounce, 255.
[185] Robertson, *Word Pictures*, 4:468.
[186] NIDNTT: Abridged, 502.
[187] Little Kittel, 967.
[188] Ibid, 968.

Creator and Redeemer are one and the same, the all-powerful God in Jesus Christ, 'the First and the Last, the Beginning and the End' (Rev. 22:13), who binds his own to himself from all eternity and is their surety for salvation, if they remain in him. This goes beyond the limits of what can be logically asserted: The man Jesus of Nazareth is the mediator of creation; he who was executed on the cross as a criminal is the first to experience resurrection and the one who leads us to life. In the man Christ Jesus, the *prōtotokos*, God has brought his divine power and glory to its climax (Col. 1:19-20), and he has given a share in this to the church.[189]

The term also has created a great deal of scholarly discussion regarding its connection to the discussion of wisdom from both the OT (cf. especially Prov. 8:22-31) and Philo's writings. The personification of wisdom in Proverbs is not regarded by the NT writers as a prophecy whose details may be pressed to yield Christological conclusions, however much they may draw on its phraseology in depicting Christ as the "Wisdom of God."[190] Similarly, scholars have made much of the use of the term in connection with the use of the logos (λόγος) in other writings, both biblical (e.g., John 1:1, 14) and philosophic (particularly Philo).[191] As Moo points out, "there could also be allusion here to the wisdom/word tradition."[192] But he also quickly makes note of weak linguistic links to absolutely confirm such a connection, describing any such association as "a conceptual parallel" at best.[193]

Jesus is thus firstborn "of all creation" (πάσης κτίσεως). Some translators render the genitive as "of" all creation (ESV, KJV, NASB, NASU, NRSV) and others as "over" all creation (NET, NIV, NLT). The former are more wooden in their translation of the genitive while the latter correctly allow the meaning of the πρωτό- prefix of the accompanying adjective to flavor the understanding of the genitive. The latter ("over") gives the clearer intention of the passage as understood in its context.

---

[189] NIDNTT: Abridged, 502-503.
[190] Bruce, NIC, 60; cf. also the author's *Proverbs: A Mentor Commentary*, 189ff.
[191] For references to the latter see O'Brien, 44.
[192] Moo, 119-120.
[193] Ibid., 119.

The false teacher(s) who had infiltrated the church in Colossae was likely teaching that Jesus was just another emanation from God, one more (even if the highest) step on the ladder leading to God. In using this word Paul was likely refuting his diminished recognition of Christ's person and elevating Him to the highest place. Paul used both this word and εἰκών ("image") to "help express the deity of Jesus Christ in his relation to the Father as *eikōn* (Image) and to the universe as *prōtotokos* (First-born)."[194] Robertson can also say, "As *image* points to *revelation*, so *first-born* points to *eternal preexistence*."[195]

> **1:16 For by Him all things were created, both in the heavens and on earth, visible and invisible, whether thrones or dominions or rulers or authorities — all things have been created through Him and for Him.**

Paul moves now to explain (ὅτι, "For") or expand upon what he means that Christ is "the firstborn of all creation" (v. 15b). The cause for this title is that "by Him all things were created" (ἐν αὐτῷ ἐκτίσθη τὰ πάντα). The preposition "by" (ἐν) might more literally be rendered "in" (NRSV, RSV, TNIV). The preposition is used locally and points to the person of Christ as the sphere in which all things came into being.[196] Within the sphere of Christ's own person "all things were created."

The little phrase ἐν αὐτῷ ("in Him") becomes a repeated refrain throughout this letter and carries powerful theological implications regarding the supremacy of Christ over all things (Col. 1:16, 17, 19; 2:6, 7, 9, 10, 15). We might compare Paul's expression in Ephesians 1:4: "He chose us in Him [ἐν αὐτῷ] before the foundation of the world." Bruce says, "God's creation, like his election, takes place 'in Christ' and not apart from him."[197]

The "all things" (τὰ πάντα) is just as far-reaching and all-encompassing as it sounds. The presence of the article indicates that Paul is viewing all of creation as a whole, as one entity in its entirety.[198] Thus he speaks in the absolute sense of "the whole of creation."[199]

---

[194] Robertson, *Word Pictures*, 4:468.
[195] Ibid.
[196] BAGD, 259.
[197] Bruce, NIC, 62.
[198] Wright, 71,
[199] BAGD, 633.

The verb ("created," ἐκτίσθη) is used in the NT to point to God as the Creator (Rom. 1:25) and what He originally created (1 Cor. 11:9; Eph. 3:9; 1 Tim. 4:3). He also employs it to speak of the new creation which takes place through an individual's spiritual rebirth (Eph. 2:10; 4:24; Col. 3:10) as well as the formation of the church itself (Eph. 2:15). The aorist tense looks back either to creation as a single event or to a series of events as one whole.[200] The passive voice views the action as being taken by God through Christ. Nothing in all creation had existence prior to His work to bring it into being.

This is truly an overwhelming statement. Lightfoot comments, "All the laws and purposes which guide the creation and government of the universe reside in" Christ.[201] As Rienecker says, "He is not in all things but all things are in Him and this difference is not insignificant."[202] However far the most distant point of dark outer space may be from here, Christ resides beyond it. All the powers and laws of nature find their origin in, reside within, and are engulfed by the person of Jesus Christ.

This includes all that is "in the heavens and on the earth" (ἐν τοῖς οὐρανοῖς καὶ ἐπὶ τῆς γῆς). So all-encompassing is Paul's intent that he includes things "visible and invisible" (τὰ ὁρατὰ καὶ τὰ ἀόρατα). The exact relationship of these two clauses is not spelled out. There may be a chiastic arrangement which would yield "heavens" being paired with "invisible" and "earth" being paired with "visible." On the other hand, as Harris states it, we may "have here two different partially overlapping classifications of reality—one by locality (earth—heaven), the other by essence (visible—invisible ...)."[203]

> **Ministry Maxim**
>
> Christ is the sphere, agent, and goal of all creation—He must hold the same exalted relationship to all we create.

The word "invisible" (τὰ ἀόρατα) has just been met in v. 15. See our comments there. Now its opposite (simply subtracting the alpha privative) is introduced as well: "visible" (τὰ ὁρατα). Both words are accompanied by the definite article. Those unseen things are now

---

[200] Harris, 44.
[201] Lightfoot, 148.
[202] Rienecker, 567.
[203] Harris, 44.

enumerated through four plural nouns. The first is "thrones" (θρόνοι). The word can be used of literal thrones (Luke 1:32) and metaphorically of the heavens as God's throne (Matt. 5:34). It also can be used as a substitute for that which the throne symbolizes and thus be translated with words like dominion, rule, and sovereignty. But in the plural, as it is here, it points to "powerful spirit-beings who rule."[204] The second word is "dominions" (κυριότητες). The word points to dominion, power, and lordship.[205] It is used here and elsewhere in the NT of angelic powers (Eph. 1:21; 2 Peter 2:10; Jude 8).

The third term is "rulers" (ἀρχαὶ). The word carries the notion of primacy.[206] It points to that which is the beginning or one who comes to stand as first, and is thus a ruler. Here it is used "of angelic and demonic powers, since they were thought of as having a political organization."[207] And the fourth plural noun is "authorities" (ἐξουσίαι). Similarly this points to "rulers and functionaries of the spirit world" (cf. Eph. 3:10; 6:12; Col. 2:15).[208]

Elsewhere Paul similarly piles up nouns to speak of angelic beings (Col. 2:10; Eph. 1:21; 3:10; 6:12), even adding an additional word (δυνάμεως, Eph. 1:21). We should not make too fine a distinction between the meanings of the words nor use them to construct complex schemes of angelic hierarchy. Rather, Paul's point in using these four designations is to gather up the entire spirit world, comprised of both holy and malevolent angels, and declare Christ's supremacy over them. The broad and all-encompassing nature of the wording of this entire pericope (vv. 15-20) points to this being a reference to all angelic beings.

Paul will soon take on the false teacher(s) who delights in "the worship of angels" (Col. 2:18) by asserting that Christ "is the head over all rule and authority" (2:10) and that God through Christ has "disarmed the rulers and authorities" and "made a public display of them, having triumphed over them" (2:15). In a precursor to the direct battle the Apostle will wage in chapter two, he is here establishing Christ as not only supreme over all

---

[204] Friberg, 199.
[205] Thayer, 366.
[206] Friberg, 76.
[207] BAGD, 112.
[208] Ibid., 278.

such spirit beings, but as the agent of their creation, the sphere in which they have come into being and continue to exist, and the goal for which they were brought into being.

Once again Paul gathers up "all things" (τὰ πάντα) and makes a grand assertion as to their relation to Christ. They all "have been created" (ἔκτισται). This is the same verb found at the head of this verse. Here again we meet a chiastic structure in the Greek text: "ἐκτίσθη τὰ πάντα ... τὰ πάντα ... ἔκτισται."[209] In the first instance the verb has an aorist tense pointing to the event of creation. Here it is in the perfect looking back to that event, but also stressing the abiding nature of the work—all these things have been and still stand today as created "by Him" (δι' αὐτοῦ). This may suggest that the universe has an ongoing relationship to and dependence upon the person of Christ—an anticipation of "in Him all things hold together" (v. 17b).[210]

The preposition (διά) marks out Christ as the intermediate agent through which all of creation came into being (John 1:3; 1 Cor. 8:6; Heb. 1:2).[211] Certainly the Scriptures at times present wisdom personified as the agent of creation (e.g., Psalm 104:24; Prov. 3:19; 8:22-31; Jer. 10:12; 51:15). As has already been stated, wisdom in these contexts should not be understood as a reference to the preincarnate Christ per se. Rather, Christ is the One "in whom are hidden all the treasures of wisdom and knowledge" (Col. 2:3). The attribute of God's eternal wisdom is spoken of in personified terms at some points in the OT and is found incarnate and in its fullest manifestation in the person of Jesus Christ.

Additionally, all things are "for Him" (εἰς αὐτόν).[212] This preposition marks out Christ as the ultimate goal of all creation.[213] This is a notion which finds no parallel in any of the OT writings about wisdom personified nor in any other Jewish literature.[214] Clearly, to whatever extent Paul may have been drawing upon OT themes and ideas, he has come into a new, heaven-given understanding of the mystery which is Christ (Col. 1:27; 2:2; 4:3).

---

[209] Harris, 45.
[210] Ibid.
[211] Wallace, 433-434.
[212] Rienecker, 567.
[213] Lohse, 52.
[214] O'Brien, 47.

Note then the powerful message conveyed in the three prepositional phrases of this verse: Christ is the sphere in which all things came into being (ἐν), He is the agent through whom they came into being (διά), and He is the ultimate goal toward which the trajectory of their creation has launched them (εἰς)! Note also that these same three prepositions are found in this same order in the last stanza of this poetic portion, testifying again to the symmetry of this portion: "all the fullness to dwell in [ἐν] Him, and through [δι'] Him to reconcile all things to [εἰς] Himself" (vv. 19b-20a).[215]

1:17 He is before all things, and in Him all things hold together.

We come now to the middle stanza of this intricately arranged poem of praise to our Lord Jesus Christ (vv. 17-18a). These two lines are marked out by the repeated and parallel (καὶ αὐτός ἐστιν, "He is"). The NASB includes the "And" (καὶ) in verse 17, but translates it "also" in verse 18. The NASU fails to translate it in the first instance (v. 17), but retains the "also" in verse 18. The ESV translates it "And" in both cases.

The first of these middle stanzas asserts "He is before all things" (αὐτός ἐστιν πρὸ πάντων). The pronoun "He" (αὐτός) is emphatic, stressing "He and no other."[216] Christ is being set in a class of His own in relationship to all created things.

The preposition πρὸ is accurately rendered "before." It can mean "before" in terms of physical proximity and place (e.g., Acts 12:6), in terms of significance or rank (e.g., James 5:12), and in terms of time (Luke 11:38). But here it probably combines the latter two and means "before" both in terms of time and rank/preeminence.[217] Jesus predated "all things." God the Son, along with God the Father and God the Spirit, existed prior to the existence of every other thing. This "is" (ἐστιν) true of Jesus Christ. The present tense points to eternal, timeless existence. Paul did not say that Christ "was" (past tense) before all things, but that He "is" (present tense) before all things. What and who Jesus was in eternity past, He is now. Who and what Jesus is now, He always has been. "Jesus Christ is the same yesterday and today and forever" (Heb. 13:8).

---

[215] Moo, 120.
[216] Rienecker, 568.
[217] Harris, 46-47; BAGD, 701.

And He has been this in relationship to "all things" (πάντων). Here the adjective is found without a definite article, in contrast to its usage in verse 16 and the end of this present verse. Without the article it designates everyone without exception.[218] In a moment, as in verse 16, it will be used with the article and will designate the whole of creation in an absolute sense—the universe.[219] But presently Paul sets forth Christ as preexisting all individual people and parts of the created order.

The Apostle John emphatically sets Jesus apart from all others by means of His preexistence: "Jesus said to them, 'Truly, truly, I say to you, before Abraham was born, I am'" (John 8:58; cf. John 1:1-2; 17:5, 24). "I am the first and the last, and the living One" (Rev. 1:17b-18a; cf. 2:8). "'I am the Alpha and the Omega,' says the Lord God, 'who is and who was and who is to come, the Almighty'" (Rev. 1:8; cf. 21:6). "I am the Alpha and the Omega, the first and the last, the beginning and the end" (Rev. 22:13). Paul also affirms and adds his support to this exalted view of Christ (2 Cor. 8:9; Phil. 2:6-11).

In addition (καὶ, "and"), "in Him all things hold together" (τὰ πάντα ἐν αὐτῷ συνέστηκεν). By "all things" (τὰ πάντα) Paul includes everything absolutely. He speaks of the entire universe. The verb translated "hold together" (συνέστηκεν) is a compound made up of σύν (with) and ἵστημι (to put/place/stand). It has the basic sense of "putting together."[220] It is used transitively by Paul often in 2 Corinthians (3:1; 4:2; 5:12; 6:4; 7:11; 10:12, 18; 12:11) with the sense of commending someone (or one-self) to another person. But here he uses it intransitively with the meaning "continue, endure, exist, hold together"[221] or "to cohere, to hold together."[222] Mounce asserts that this means that were it not for Christ "this entire universe would fall apart."[223] Indeed, there is "creatorial coherence in the sustaining power of Christ."[224]

The perfect tense of the verb views this as an abiding state, the action initiated in the past, but with continuing results in the present—"the uni-

---

[218] BAGD, 632.
[219] Ibid., 633.
[220] Little Kittel, 1120.
[221] BAGD, 791.
[222] Thayer, 605.
[223] Mounce, 126.
[224] NIDNTT, 3:1186.

verse owes its continuing coherence to Christ."[225] The standing fact is that Jesus Christ "upholds all things by the word of His power" (Heb. 1:3). This entire universe finds its ongoing continuance "in Him" (ἐν αὐτῷ). The preposition is used in the local sense of "sphere." To the Athenians Paul could say, "in Him we live and move and exist" (Acts 17:28).

We owe both our existence and our continuance to Christ. Life as we know it, including all the so-called laws of nature, is dependent upon the ongoing, ever-present, continuous command of Christ which holds all the elements of the universe together in an ordered reality. On the macroscale this includes the orbits of planets around stars. On the microscale this includes the dynamic powers that hold atoms and their subatomic particles in whirling consistent wholeness. Christ is the "glue" that holds all things together. He is the tuning fork to which all created reality adjusts and conforms.

> **Ministry Maxim**
>
> Christ is the glue that holds all reality—around and in me—in constant, ordered existence.

"He is the principle of cohesion in the universe."[226]

Here too we find similarities to the writings of Platonic and Stoic philosophers, particularly the latter. Philo asserted that the divine logos "is the bond of all things, the one who holds them together indissolubly and binds them fast, when in themselves they are dissoluble."[227] There are also affinities with the writings of Hellenistic Judaism, particularly the LXX. The Book of Wisdom states, "The spirit of the Lord, indeed, fills the whole world, and *that which holds all things together* knows every word that is said" (1:7, JB, emphasis added). Similarly Ecclesiasticus tells us that "all things hold together by means of his word" (43:26, JB).[228] Scott also asserted a link here to the thought of Proverbs 8:30.[229] These similarities should not shake our confidence in the Apostle's assertions. The fact that "the Word became flesh and dwelt among us" (John 1:14), was crucified, buried, and raised again to life, and then ascended and was seated at the right hand of

---

[225] Moo, 125.

[226] Rienecker, 568.

[227] *Rer. Div. Her.* 23, quoted in Lohse, 52.

[228] O'Brien, 48.

[229] Scott, R. B. Y., "Wisdom in Creation: The *'Āmôn* Proverbs viii.30," *Vetus Testamentum* 10 [1960], 213-223, cited in Martin, 59.

God takes Paul's statements beyond anything asserted in other writings. The Christ described here and elsewhere by the Apostle (and the whole of the NT) soars infinitely beyond all others described with similar verbiage.

As already stated, verses 17 and 18a form a middle stanza of the poem/ hymn. Lines 17a and 18a both begin with καὶ αὐτός ἐστιν ("And He is" and "He is also" respectively, NASB). This leaves verse 17b as the high point of these middle lines, and indeed of the entire poem/hymn itself.[230] It functions, therefore, as something of a Janus—looking both backward to what has been asserted regarding Christ's place over this present creation (vv. 15-17a) and forward to His rightful place in the new creation (vv. 18a-20). Not only does Christ cause the created order to cohere, but spiritual life is held in order only as Christ is placed at the center of each life and of all things.[231]

Christ not only predates and has precedence over all things, but He is the arena in which all things exist and hold together in ordered reality.

Digging Deeper:

1. If Christ is preeminent over all creation (v. 15), what does that say about who and what I am and am not?

2. If Christ is the sphere in which all creation resides (v. 16a), what does that say about the context of all my thoughts, desires, and actions?

3. If Christ is the goal of all creation (v. 16c), what does that say about who and what I am and am not?

4. If Christ is the sustainer of all creation (v. 17b) what does that say about the possibility of living a successful life apart from Him?

---

[230] Moo, 125.
[231] Ibid., 126.

1:18 He is also head of the body, the church; and He is the beginning, the firstborn from the dead, so that He Himself will come to have first place in everything.

The second of the two lines which make up the middle stanza now opens precisely as did the first: καὶ αὐτός ἐστιν ("He is also," cf. v. 17a). This both maintains symmetry and moves the poem/hymn into its second half where Christ is seen as supreme over not only the first created order (vv. 15-17), but now also over the new creation (vv. 18-20). The first He demonstrated through creation and providential preservation. The latter He demonstrated through redemption and divine grace. He moves from cosmology (vv. 15-17) to soteriology (vv. 18-20). Once again (as in v. 17) the pronoun (αὐτός, "He") is emphatic and marks Christ as in a class all His own. No less than the one described in verses 15-17 is now held forth in His relationship to His redeemed people. This preeminent One holds this singular position and rank as "head of the body, the church" (ἡ κεφαλὴ τοῦ σώματος τῆς ἐκκλησίας). The present tense of the verb underscores the present, ongoing, abiding nature of Christ in this supreme relationship to His body the church.

Christ is designated the "head" (ἡ κεφαλὴ). Note the presence of the definite article marking Christ as *the* "head of the body." The word κεφαλή ("head") has been the center of intense debate in the past half century. Its meaning, however, was largely undisputed until Stephen Bedale introduced a novel assertion in his 1954 article in the *Journal of Theological Studies*.[232] His innovation was to suggest that the word carries no notion of authoritative leadership as traditionally understood. He suggested instead that it meant "source" or "origin." This had massive impact upon the understanding of Scripture's teaching with regard to gender roles.

In more recent years, however, a series of studies have convincingly set forth that the word does indeed carry a sense of authoritative leadership.[233]

---

[232] Bedale, Stephen, "The Meaning of *kephale* in the Pauline Epistles," *Journal of Theological Studies* 5 (1954), 215.

[233] See H. Wayne House, *The Role of Women in Ministry Today* (Grand Rapids, MI: Baker Book House, 1995), 25-33; and especially Wayne Grudem, "Does Kephale ('Head') Mean 'Source' or 'Authority Over' in Greek Literature? A Survey of 2,336 Examples," appendix I in George W. Knight III, *The Role Relationship of Men and Women* (Chicago: Moody Press, 1985), 49-80. Also Dr. Grudem's "The Meaning of 'Kephale ("Head"): A Response to Recent Studies'," Appendix I in John Piper and Wayne Grudem, *Recovering Biblical Manhood and Womanhood*

Wayne Grudem, for example, has profitably shown that there is not one example in all of extant ancient Greek literature in which the word is used to refer to a person and still carries the sense of "non-authoritative source."[234] Certainly here the word carries the notion of authoritative leadership as it pictures the relationship of Christ to His redeemed people. It is used figuratively "to mean a higher position of authority."[235]

The whole tenor of the poem/hymn (indeed, the entire letter!) is to place Christ in the most exalted place, supreme over all—first over all the created order (vv. 15-17) and now over all the redeemed new creation (vv. 18-20). Paul uses the word three times in this letter. He designates Christ not only head of His body (1:18), but "head over all rule and authority" (2:10). He also uses the word to speak of the false teacher(s) who is "not holding fast to the head" (2:19).

The organic imagery of the word is evident when the head is described as He "from whom the entire body, being supplied and held together by the joints and ligaments, grows with a growth which is from God" (2:19). He whose mind conceived of, whose voice spoke into being, and whose will presently governs and providentially sustains all of creation is most directly linked to those whom He has redeemed—as a head to a body. And indeed we are to Christ "the body" (τοῦ σώματος). What mystery! What grace! In earlier letters Paul had spoken of the church as Christ's body, but there dwelt more upon the interrelationship of the members (Rom. 12:4-5; 1 Cor. 12:12-31). Here in Colossians (1:24; 2:19; 3:15 and in Eph. 1:22-23; 4:4, 12, 16; 5:23, 30) Paul develops more of the relationship of the whole of the body to Christ Himself as head.

To further explain (by means of a genitive placed in apposition to the previous noun) what he means by "the body," Paul adds "the church" (τῆς ἐκκλησίας). The word can be used to designate a local fellowship of believers (Col. 4:15, 16). Here it seems that Paul refers to the church not in this limited, local sense, but in a more universal sense to the whole of those redeemed by Christ.[236] This seems also to be his intent later in this

---

(Wheaton, IL: Crossway Books, 1991), 425-468.

[234] Grudem, Wayne, "The meaning of 'head' in the Bible,' in *CBMW News*, Vol. 1 No. 3
(Libertyville, IL: Council on Biblical Manhood and Womanhood, December 1996), 1, 3-5.

[235] Mounce, 323.

[236] BAGD, 241.

chapter when again he speaks of "His body, which is the church" (1:24). A body cannot live without its head. The head rules and governs the body. The head directs and guides the body. The head coordinates the various functions of the body and enables them to work together toward meaningful and productive ends.

These notions only begin to touch on the meaning implicit in Paul's metaphor of Christ as the head of His people, His body. A good many commentators believe that they find here evidence that Paul (or another in his name) has adopted an earlier, non-Christian hymn and edited in the words "the church" (τῆς ἐκκλησίας). Because of similarity in language with certain ancient writings, many believe that what they call the original hymn spoke of the "body" (σῶμα) as referring to the cosmos.[237] All the ink spilt in an attempt to reconstruct the "original" hymn has yet to provide consensus regarding its earliest shape and structure. This should give us pause in too quickly assuming Paul, under the inspiration of the Holy Spirit, was incapable of original thought. As Moo states it, "We must deal with the text as it stands."[238]

The Apostle continues[239] by saying "He is the beginning, the firstborn from the dead" (ὅς ἐστιν ἀρχή, πρωτότοκος ἐκ τῶν νεκρῶν). We again meet the combination ὅς ἐστιν ("He is," cf. 1:7, 15, 18; 2:10; 4:9). The relative pronoun (ὅς, "He") is clearly a reference to Christ, harking back to αὐτός ("He"). It may have a causal sense to it, meaning "in that he is."[240] Note the parallel use of the same pronoun in verse 15.

The present tense of the verb (ἐστιν, "is") points to what Christ is continuously by virtue of His resurrection "from the dead" (ἐκ τῶν νεκρῶν). The preposition (ἐκ, "from") conveys the notion of "out from." Christ was, by virtue of His atoning death, once among the dead, but now He has finally and victoriously come "out from" the dead, never to die again.

By virtue of His resurrection Jesus is rightly designated "the beginning" (ἀρχή) and "the firstborn" (πρωτότοκος) from the dead. The former noun was just used in verse 16 to designate "rulers" (ἀρχαί), similar to how it will be used to designate all "rule" (ἀρχῆς) and authority in 2:10 and "the rulers" (τὰς ἀρχὰς) in 2:15. When the word appears as a predicate, as it does

---

[237] For good coverage of these ideas see Bruce, NIC, 66-67; Moo, 126; O'Brien, 48-49.
[238] Moo, 126.
[239] There is no corresponding conjunction for the NASU's "and."
[240] Robertson, *Word Pictures*, 4:480.

here, it is considered absolute within itself and does not require the definite article.[241] The word carries the basic idea of primacy. This can be understood in terms of physical place (Acts 10:110), time (John 2:11), or a position of power (as it is used elsewhere in Colossians).[242] Thayer asserts that here it designates "*the person or thing that commences, the first person or thing in a series, the leader*:"[243] Harris says that Christ's relationship to the church is that of the "originating cause and the source of its life."[244] Christ can justifiably say, "I am the Alpha and the Omega, the first and the last, the beginning [ἀρχὴ] and the end" (Rev. 22:3). Everything the church is and has and hopes for finds its origin and beginning in the Person of God the Son, Jesus Christ. Christ stands at the head, not only of the old created order (vv. 15-17), but also of the new humanity redeemed as a part of the new creation.[245]

The NIV inserts the word "and" here, seemingly pointing to two designations. There is no such corresponding word in the Greek text. Rather, the second word (πρωτότοκος, "the firstborn") seems to expand upon and explain the first (ἀρχή, "the beginning"). Indeed, others had been raised to life, only to face death again (e.g., the widow's son in Luke 7 and Lazarus in John 11). But Christ was the first to rise from the dead, never to die again. This latter word (πρωτότοκος, "the firstborn") was just used in verse 15 where Christ is said to be "the firstborn over all creation." As noted in our discussion there, the word is a compound and can designate either (or both) a temporal order or an honored status and supremacy. The latter was the primary sense in verse 15. Sound hermeneutics would counsel that the same word used twice in the same context would normally have the same meaning in both cases unless there is an additional signal from the context that another meaning is intended. Here the word ἀρχή

> **Ministry Maxim**
>
> The church's call is to make the *doctrinal fact* of Christ's supremacy an *experiential reality* in time and space.

("beginning") seems to have covered the temporal aspect. It would, therefore, appear redundant to read πρωτότοκος ("firstborn") in that sense. It

---

[241] O'Brien, 50.
[242] Friberg, 76.
[243] Thayer, 77.
[244] Harris, 48.
[245] O'Brien, 50.

appears that Paul's primary emphasis here is in declaring Christ as, not only the first one raised from the dead to never die again, but also (and thereby) the supreme Lord over all resurrection life. Is this not precisely what the next clause asserts?

Christ's resurrection took place for a specific purpose (ἵνα, "so that"). That purpose was that "He Himself will come to have first place in everything" (γένηται ἐν πᾶσιν αὐτὸς πρωτεύων). The verb (γένηται, "will come to have") is aorist subjunctive. The tense points to what was achieved at a point in time—through Christ's death, resurrection, and ascension. There is probably a contrast intended between "will come to have" (γένηται) here and "is" (ἐστιν) in verse 17a. In relationship to the universe, Christ is and always has been supreme (v. 17). In relationship to the church, however, Christ "became" preeminent by virtue of His resurrection from the dead (v. 18).[246]

What had always and forever been God the Son's by divine right, He secured in actual fact and experience by defeating sin, Satan, and death through His atoning death and resurrection from the dead. He "was declared the Son of God with power by the resurrection from the dead" (Rom. 1:4a). Christ is supreme over both the old creation and the new. Yet there is a sense in which we do not yet see Him as having finally subdued all of rebellious creation under His feet (1 Cor. 15:25-28; Heb. 2:8; cf. Phil. 2:11).[247] This victory is assured by Christ's resurrection, but is being worked out in time and space, looking to that day when He will have "put all His enemies under His feet" (1 Cor. 15:25).

Christ's resurrection achieved for Him "first place" (πρωτεύων). The word is used only here in the NT. It means to "be first, have first place, hold highest rank or *dignity*."[248] It picks up on the previously twice used πρωτότοκος ("firstborn," vv. 15, 18a), and together they stress Christ's place of primacy at the head of the new creation. The pronoun (αὐτὸς, "He Himself") is again emphatic—Christ and Christ alone, no other, is preeminent. His preeminence is found "in everything" (ἐν πᾶσιν). The preposition designates the sphere in which Christ's preeminence is exer-

---

[246] Harris, 49; Johnson, "Christ Pre-eminent," 18.
[247] Moo, 130.
[248] Friberg, 337.

cised. The bounds of this sphere are "everything." The anarthrous neuter adjective, as in verse 17a, designates everyone and everything without exception.[249] From all eternity and by divine nature, Christ is and always has been preeminent over the entire created order, and by virtue of His resurrection, He has become preeminent over the entire new creation.

1:19 For it was the Father's good pleasure for all the fullness to dwell in Him,

The conjunction (ὅτι, "For") is explanatory (note its parallel in v. 16). It signals that Paul is about to set forth more fully (in vv. 19-20) the basis for Christ rightly having "first place in everything" (v. 18b). Christ's supremacy in both creation and redemption rests upon His deity.

There is a debate over the subject of the sentence. The NASU adds "Father's" (as does the KJV); the NET, NIV, and NLT read "God." Clearly Paul intended God to be the subject, for throughout his writings the one who was working reconciliation through Christ (v. 20) was God the Father (Rom. 5:10-11; 2 Cor. 5:18-19; Eph. 2:16). This reading takes the subject as implied, rather than stated. An alternative is to read the clause "all the fullness" (πᾶν τὸ πλήρωμα) as the subject. This, of course, is understood to be a reference to God, thus ending with a translation of "all the fullness of God" (ESV; cf. NLT; RSV, NRSV).[250] This does create awkwardness when one arrives in verse 20 and discovers "the fullness" is said to be the reconciler. In either case the referent is clearly God the Father, either as the implied subject or by designation of "all the fullness [of God]."

> **Ministry Maxim**
>
> The Father took pleasure in incarnating the divine fullness in Jesus Christ, and we bring Him pleasure when we exalt Christ.

The verb translated "it was the ... good pleasure" (εὐδόκησεν) can be used of either human or divine good pleasure. When attributed to Deity, it always refers to God the Father (Matt. 3:17; 12:18; 17:5; Mark 1:11; Luke 3:22; 12:32; 1 Cor. 1:21; 10:5; Gal. 1:15; Heb. 10:6, 8, 38; 2 Peter 1:17).[251] It "designates the pleasure a person takes in another person

---

[249] BAGD, 632.
[250] Abbott, 218-219; Harris, 49; Lohse, 56-57; Moo, 131; O'Brien, 51.
[251] Vincent, *Word Studies*, 3:472.

or in doing something."[252] It is often found in close connection to the idea of choice or election (Luke 12:32; 1 Cor. 1:21; Gal. 1:15). So Moo can paraphrase, "God in all his fullness has chosen to dwell in Christ."[253] The aorist tense is constative.[254] The precise time when God made this decision and took this pleasure is not specified.

That which aroused such pleasure within God the Father was "for all the fullness to dwell" (πᾶν τὸ πλήρωμα κατοικῆσαι) in Christ. The articular noun τὸ πλήρωμα ("the fullness") describes the "sum total" or "fullness" of something.[255] What is that something? The definite article makes the reference specific—this is the fullness of God Himself. In 2:9 Paul will designate it "the fullness of Deity" (τὸ πλήρωμα τῆς θεότητος). God in all his glory, wisdom, character, and divine nature is resident in Christ. The word became a key word in the Gnosticism of the second century, but Paul is too early to link his usage directly to that later development. Yet it is possible that he is using the word to debunk a key component of the false teaching in Colossae.[256] The false teacher(s) apparently viewed the universe as filled with an ascending order of spiritual beings that marked levels approaching God. God's attributes and powers were thought to be shared with these aeons or emanations of the divine.

In direct opposition Paul, by his wording, demands that Christ is the fullness of all that God is. When one comes into relationship to Christ, He has come into relationship with God. Christ is the sole mediator between God and man (1 Tim. 2:5). He alone reconciles people to God (v. 20). The all-inclusive nature of the fullness is signaled by πᾶν ("all"). When found with a singular, articular noun it designates "the whole" or all of whatever the accompanying articular noun is.[257] Nothing of the divine fullness, nature, character, or attributes are left outside of Christ. All the "fullness" that the false teacher(s) may have been inciting the Colossian believers to find elsewhere is found in Christ.

---

[252] Mounce, 519.
[253] Moo, 132.
[254] Harris, 50.
[255] BAGD, 672.
[256] Moo, 132; O'Brien, 52.
[257] BAGD, 631.

All the fullness of Deity was made "to dwell" (κατοικῆσαι) in Christ. Abbott says this verb "implies permanent, or rather 'settled' residence."[258] And he adds, "It is probable ... that the false teachers maintained only a partial and transient connection of the πλήρωμα with the Lord."[259] The verb is used forty-four times in the NT, but only three of those are by Paul. He uses it both here and in 2:9 to describe the divine nature fully dwelling in Christ. He also uses it in Ephesians 3:17 when he prays that the Spirit will strengthen them in their inner man "so that Christ may dwell in your hearts through faith." The aorist tense is constative, simply signaling the fact that God's fullness dwells in Christ.[260] In Colossians 2:9 it will be used in the present tense to underscore the continuous, unceasing nature of deity dwelling in Christ.

Throughout this verse the language is reminiscent of the OT's description of God's good pleasure in dwelling in the temple in Zion (Psa. 67:17).[261] Now, the true Temple has come—Christ, the very Son of God—and the Father is pleased to dwell ultimately in His fullness in Him. The temple of old was only a pattern of Christ. Indeed, all this was and is true "in Him" (ἐν αὐτῷ). The phrase is positioned forward so as to make it emphatic. The referent, as throughout the hymn, is clearly Jesus Christ. The preposition designates the sphere in which the fullness of God dwells—the person of Jesus Christ. A stronger statement of Christ's deity is scarcely imaginable. This prepositional phrase begins a sequence which parallels that already encountered in verse 16 and which is repeated here in a statement running into verse 20: "in [ἐν] Him ... through [δι'] Him ... to [εἰς] Himself ..."

1:20 and through Him to reconcile all things to Himself, having made peace through the blood of His cross; through Him, I say, whether things on earth or things in heaven.

The parallel pattern of prepositions (compare v. 16) now continues (καὶ, "and") with the second in the series: "through Him" (δι' αὐτοῦ). Christ is again the great referent of the personal pronoun. The preposition denotes

---

[258] Abbott, 220.
[259] Ibid.
[260] Harris, 50; NET Bible.
[261] Lohse, 58; Moo, 132-133; Wright, 78.

agency. As Christ was the personal agent of creation (cf. same wording in v. 16), so He is God's personal agent in redemption.

Through Christ, God the Father was at work "to reconcile" (ἀποκαταλλάξαι). The word is a compound comprised of ἀπό (from) and καταλλάσσω (to reconcile). The root verb, minus the preposition, is used six times in the NT, all by Paul (Rom. 5:10 [twice]; 1 Cor. 7:11; 2 Cor. 5:18, 19, 20). The preposition in compound is intensive and thus has the emphasis of either "to reconcile completely" or "to reconcile *back again*, bring back to a former state of harmony."[262] The compound verb is used only three times in the NT (Eph. 2:16; Col. 1:20, 22). This reconciliation is effected by God the Father through Jesus Christ by virtue of His death on the cross. Through Christ this reconciliation is a reality on both the individual ("you," v. 22) and cosmic levels ("all things … whether things on earth or things in heaven"). The same Christ through the same sacrificial death also reconciles Jews and Gentiles to one another (Eph. 2:16).

The infinitive form shows us that it is coordinate with the previous infinitive (κατοικῆσαι, "to dwell," v. 19). Together both are dependent upon the verb εὐδόκησεν ("good pleasure"). God the Father was pleased, ontologically, to have His fullness dwell within Christ. He was equally pleased, soteriologically speaking, through Christ to reconcile to Himself all things. Here too, as in the previous aorist infinitive, the tense is constative. Harris rightly states, "The indwelling was a prerequisite for the reconciliation as well as continuing beyond it. Here … soteriology finds its basis in ontology."[263]

Presently Paul has reconciliation on a cosmic level in view, for it is "all things" (τὰ πάντα) that God through Christ is said to reconcile to Himself. As in verses 16 and 17 (where the expression is used three times) he speaks in the absolute sense of "the whole of creation."[264] The whole of created reality is in view.

Just how we are to understand εἰς αὐτόν ("to Himself") is a matter of some debate. Does this refer to Christ? Or, as the NASU translation seems to intimate, to God the Father? BAGD favors the former ("*reconcile*

---

262 Thayer, 63.
263 Harris, 50.
264 BAGD, 633.

everything in his own person, i.e., the universe is to form a unity, which has its goal in Christ"), but also notes that "many prefer to transl[ate] *reconcile everything to himself* (i.e., God)."[265] Since throughout the NT it is always God the Father who reconciles others to Himself through His Son Jesus Christ (Rom. 5:10; 2 Cor. 5:18-20), the NASU (and most other English versions) seems to capture the Apostle's idea.

To this Paul now adds a participial phrase (εἰρηνοποιήσας, "having made peace") describing the means by which the aforementioned reconciliation was accomplished.[266] The reconciliation and the peacemaking were not two distinct events, but one event. Peacemaking explains how the reconciliation was effected. Paul speaks of God the Father "having made peace." This is the only occurrence of the word in the NT. It is a compound made up of εἰρήνη (peace) and ποιέω (to do/make). These two root words are found in combination in Ephesians 2:15: "establishing peace" (ποιῶν εἰρήνην).[267] The aorist tense looks back to that moment when Christ was crucified. The participle describes the means of reconciliation.[268]

This peace was established "through the blood of His cross" (διὰ τοῦ αἵματος τοῦ σταυροῦ αὐτοῦ). Here the preposition διὰ ("through") indicates the means or instrument through which God the Father established peace with us sinners.[269] That means or instrument employed by the Father (at His good pleasure, v. 19) was "the blood of His cross" (διὰ τοῦ αἵματος τοῦ σταυροῦ αὐτοῦ). In Paul's writings the blood of Christ is seen to effect propitiation (Rom. 3:25), justification (Rom. 5:9), redemption, the forgiveness of our trespasses (Eph. 1:7), and, as here, reconciliation (Eph. 2:13). It is the ground of all the blessings of the new covenant (1 Cor. 11:25).

When Paul speaks of Christ's blood, he is using a figure of speech known as *metalepsis*. Thus, in the first place, "blood" stands for blood-shedding (i.e., the death of Christ). Then, secondly, Christ's death stands for the full and complete satisfaction which is made by it and for all the merits of the atonement which is brought about by it. Thus, says Bullinger, to speak of

---

[265] Ibid., 92.
[266] Harris, 51.
[267] Vincent, *Word Studies*, 3:474.
[268] Rienecker, 568.
[269] BAGD, 180.

the blood of Christ "means not merely the actual blood corpuscles, neither does it mean His death as an act, but the merits of the atonement effected by it and associated with it."[270] Here Christ's blood is called "of His cross" (τοῦ σταυροῦ αὐτοῦ) simply to indicate that it was, of course, upon the cross where Jesus gave up His life in death to effect these manifold blessings of the new covenant.

In many ancient manuscripts there is next a repeated occurrence of δι' αὐτοῦ ("through Him"). Yet the phrase is absent in many other ancient manuscripts. There is considerable debate as to its authenticity. The external evidence is fairly evenly divided, with significant and weighty support on both sides of the question. The word immediately preceding the phrase is αὐτοῦ, which would have made it easy for the eyes of copyists to have skipped over the second occurrence, having glanced away in their writing (a phenomenon known as *homoioteleuton*).[271] It seems more likely that the longer text is original, since the omission of the phrase makes for smoother reading. Another possible explanation is that a well-meaning but misguided scribe may have sought to "improve" the text by the omission of the seemingly awkward or redundant phrase.[272]

Thus, assuming the authenticity of the phrase, Paul is doubling back over his previous words for emphasis. The Apostle sets our eyes clearly and singularly upon Christ as the sole agent of reconciliation. This includes, as he has just said, "all things." Now Paul enlarges on and clarifies what he meant by asserting "whether things on earth or things in heaven" (εἴτε τὰ ἐπὶ τῆς γῆς εἴτε τὰ ἐν τοῖς οὐρανοῖς). The repeated εἴτε … εἴτε ("whether … or") is employed when "bringing together two objects in one's thoughts while keeping them distinct from each other."[273] Thus Paul spreads his arms and puts them around the farthest reaches of man's world: "things on earth" and "things in heaven." In verse 16 Christ was named as He in whom all things "in the heavens and on the earth" were created. Thus here a parallel is made (though the order is reversed) as His supremacy in the realm of redemption is set forth. All things within these bounds have been not only created by and in Christ, but have been reconciled by God through Christ on the ground of

---

[270] Bullinger, 610.
[271] NET Bible.
[272] Ibid.
[273] Friberg, 134.

His atoning blood shed on the cross. In the realm of creation this included both animate and inanimate things, including all spiritual beings (v. 16b).

Reconciliation is normally discussed within the realm of humanity. In what sense might it be said that God through Christ reconciled the entire cosmos to Himself? Similarly, in what sense can He be said to have reconciled all spiritual beings to Himself? The reconciliation has been secured and established by God through Christ's death. Yet it will involve and require the faith of the individual human being to enter those benefits (vv. 21-23). The Apostle can rightly say that "at the name of Jesus EVERY KNEE WILL BOW, of those who are in heaven and on earth and under the earth" (Phil. 2:10). Yet this does not mean each and every one will do so willingly, nor in a saving way.

> **Ministry Maxim**
>
> We order and submit ours lives under Christ now in anticipation of the day when this chaotic, rebellious universe will join us in this glad act of worship.

Scripture rightly asserts, "'YOU HAVE PUT ALL THINGS IN SUBJECTION UNDER HIS FEET.' For in subjecting all things to him, He left nothing that is not subject to him. But now we do not yet see all things subjected to him" (Heb. 2:8). Indeed, "He must reign until He has put all His enemies under His feet" (1 Cor. 15:25), and "When all things are subjected to Him, then the Son Himself also will be subjected to the One who subjected all things to Him, so that God may be all in all" (v. 28).

God's gracious, kind—though prior to Christ, mysterious—purpose has always been "the summing up of all things [τὰ πάντα, same expression as here] in Christ, things in the heavens and things on the earth" (Eph. 1:10). At present even the inanimate physical creation "groans and suffers the pains of childbirth," longing for this to be accomplished (Rom. 8:22). Paul speaks of "the anxious longing of the creation" as it "waits eagerly" for this final, sovereign triumph in Christ (v. 19). Somehow even this creation will enter "into the freedom of the glory of the children of God" (v. 21). God the Father, through the blood of Christ, has purchased back a perfectly ordered and submissive universe. The price has been paid; the transaction completed. Now we await only the final delivery of the guaranteed product.

Digging Deeper:

1. In what way is Christ's relationship to the cosmos shadowed in His relationship to His church?

2. If Christ by right of His divine nature was already "firstborn" (v. 15), why then did He come, live, suffer, die, and rise again to become "firstborn" (v. 18)?

3. If the Father's "good pleasure" was wrapped up in the incarnation of Christ (v. 19), how can we serve His "good pleasure" by our response to Christ?

4. How does our western bent on individualism hinder us in understanding what the Apostle says with regard to God's reconciling "all things to Himself … whether things on earth or things in heaven" (v. 20)?

1:21 And although you were formerly alienated and hostile in mind, engaged in evil deeds,

Paul now begins a new sentence, but he continues ("And," Καὶ) on the theme of reconciliation in this sentence which runs through verse 23. What has been said to be true of "all things" (v. 20) is now emphatically (Καὶ ὑμᾶς, "And you" thrust to the front of the sentence) made specific to the condition of the Colossian believers. (Note the transition from the third-person throughout vv. 15-20 to the second-person here in vv. 21-23.)[274] As Dunn and others have pointed out, the present sentence (vv. 21-23) may serve both to gather up what has been said and to anticipate the remainder of the letter. In terms of summarizing what has gone before, the following connections may be observed: verses 22a and 20, 22b and 12b, 21-22 and 13, 23 and 4-6. As far as outlining the remainder of the letter, verses 21-22 may relate to 1:24-2:5, verse 23a may correspond to 2:6-23, and verse 23b may connect with 3:1-4:1.[275]

The main verb of the present sentence is "He has … reconciled" (ἀποκατήλλαξεν) in verse 22. The present verse describes the conditions in which He found us prior to this act of grace. The personal

---

[274] Moo, 138.
[275] Dunn, 105.

pronoun (ὑμᾶς, "you") makes clear that Paul is transitioning from cosmic reconciliation (v. 20) to personal reconciliation to God (vv. 21-23). Together Καὶ ὑμᾶς ("And ... you") stand emphatically at the head of the sentence and thus "indicate that the central purpose in Christ's reconciling work has to do with the Christian readers at Colossae."[276] The goal of Christ's cosmic reconciliation of heaven and earth is the reconciliation of the congregation, and thus of all Christians.[277]

We were "formerly" (ποτε) in a state of alienation. This word points to some indefinite period of time in the past. It anticipates the νυνὶ δὲ ("yet ... now") of verse 22. The Apostle is describing the abiding condition each of us was in before God's grace through Christ broke into our lives. This condition related to what we "were" (ὄντας), not just what we had done. The present tense of the finite verb combines with the perfect participle (ἀπηλλοτριωμένους, "alienated") to intensify the idea of the abiding nature of the condition described.[278] The condition is viewed as an abiding, ongoing state. It is what we were without fail. The anarthrous adverbial participle is understood by the translators of the NASU as concessive ("although you were").[279] But most English versions do not render it this way (cf. ESV, NIV, RSV, NRSV). Translating the participle as a concessive may actually weaken the stark contrast that Paul intends between the condition of the Colossians before and after God's reconciling grace. Moo offers this rendering: "it is precisely you who were alienated whom God has reconciled."[280]

Our problem was twofold. First, we were "alienated" (ἀπηλλοτριωμένου). The word is a compound, being made up of ἀπό ("from") and a root related to the adjective ἀλλότριος ("belonging to another").[281] Abbott asserts that the prefix indicates that it was our movement away from God in rebellion which made us belong to another.[282] The verb

> **Ministry Maxim**
>
> In our natural state our problem is not just what we do, but who we are—so salvation changes the latter to deal with the former.

---

[276] O'Brien, 65.
[277] Lohse, 62.
[278] Dana and Mantey, 232.
[279] Harris, 57.
[280] Moo, 139.
[281] Kent, 51.
[282] Abbott, 225.

is used only three times in the NT, here and in Ephesians 2:12 and 4:18. In all three cases it is in the perfect passive form. It points, thus, to an abiding, unchanging state pictured as starting in the past and running right up until the time considered. The passive voice pictures this alienation having been set upon a person by another—to be separated from something or to be made a stranger to someone. It was our sin which estranged us from God.

Then, second (καὶ, "and"), we were "hostile in mind" (ἐχθροὺς τῇ διανοίᾳ). The definite article can be read with the sense of a possessive pronoun ("your minds," NIV). It may be better to understand it to be making definite the state of mind here described. The mind is to be devoted, with all the rest of a person's being, to loving God (Matt. 22:37; Mark 12:30; Luke 10:27). It is the place God longs to place His Law (Heb. 8:10; 10:16). Yet humanity has universally rebelled against God, becoming "darkened in their understanding [τῇ διανοίᾳ]" (Eph. 4:18) and "indulging the desires of the flesh and of the mind [τῶν διανοιῶν]" (Eph. 2:3). The word here describes a kind or way of thinking. It is descriptive of one's disposition,[283] mind-set,[284] or the way one thinks. In the LXX διάνοια most often is used where the Hebrew has לֵב (lēb, "heart").

Before God's grace in Christ came to us, our disposition was "hostile" (ἐχθροὺς) toward God. The NASU understands the word adjectivally ("hostile"), but it should probably be understood in the active sense as a substantive—enemies of God in our minds (cf. KJV, NET, NIV, NLT).[285] The word pictures one who is active in opposition to another.[286] It is the position the devil has taken toward God (Matt. 13:39; Luke 10:19). All who are not reconciled to the Father through His Son Jesus Christ stand as enemies of God, actively opposing God and His purposes (Rom. 5:10; Phil. 3:18).

This alienation and enmity soon enough shows up in our actions. Our problem was not just what we were, it also included what we did: "in evil deeds" (ἐν τοῖς ἔργοις τοῖς πονηροῖς). There seems to be little consensus regarding the intent of the preposition ἐν ("in"). Some contend that it is causal ("because of"), others locative ("in the midst of"), others

---

[283] BAGD, 187.
[284] Moo, 140.
[285] BAGD, 331.
[286] Mounce, 215.

circumstantial ("and engaged in"),[287] and still others see it as expressing the means by which our hostile minds find expression ("by means of").[288] It seems most likely to be used either in the locative sense, "the practical sphere in which the preceding characteristics exhibited themselves,"[289] or as describing the means by which the hostile mind is expressed.

Paul has already used the noun (τοῖς ἔργοις) to indicate that the goal of the gospel is that we might bring pleasure to God by bearing fruit "in every good work" (ἐν παντὶ ἔργῳ ἀγαθῷ, 1:10). Indeed, Abbott says it is "a striking contrast to the description of the Christian walk in ver. 10."[290] Every word and "deed" (ἔργῳ) is to be done in the name of Jesus (3:17).

Both the noun and adjective are articular. The adjective (τοῖς πονηροῖς) is in the attributive position, emphasizing the intrinsic nature and quality of the works. The adjective is used to describe the ethical nature of the actions—wicked, evil, bad, base, worthless, vicious, and degenerate.[291] Note then the clear path—what we think with our minds shows up in our actions. Our cognitions are the seedbed of our deeds. Not only what we think (our thoughts), but how we think (our minds) give rise to what we do. As has been suggested, perhaps the line of thought in Romans 1:21-32 is Paul's own best commentary on what he is describing more succinctly here.[292]

1:22 yet He has now reconciled you in His fleshly body through death, in order to present you before Him holy and blameless and beyond reproach —

Paul continues the sentence begun in verse 21 with a contrast in a form typical of his writings (νυνὶ δὲ, "yet ... now"; cf. Rom. 3:21; 6:22; 7:6, 17; 15:23, 25; 1 Cor. 12:18; 13:13; 15:20; 2 Cor. 8:11, 22; Eph. 2:13; Col. 3:8; Philem. 9, 11). The word νυνὶ is an intensified form of νῦν, though with the same meaning.[293] It means "in the present order of things, not 'at the present moment.'"[294] Having looked to their pre-Christian past (v. 21), Paul now speaks of their present spiritual reality in Christ.

---

[287] Harris, 57.
[288] Moo, 140; NET Bible.
[289] Abbott, 225.
[290] Ibid.
[291] BAGD, 691.
[292] Wright, 81.
[293] BAGD, 546.
[294] Abbott, 225.

He comes presently to the main verb of the sentence (ἀποκατήλλαξεν, "He has … reconciled). The subject of the verb, though not explicitly stated in the Greek text, is God the Father.[295] It is the same verb used in verse 20, so see our comments there. The difference is found in that in verse 20 Christ is said to have reconciled "all things" (τὰ πάντα). What is there spoken of in relation to the entire cosmos is now made personal and individual. The object of the verb is found all the way back in verse 21 (ὑμᾶς, "you").[296] The aorist tense is constative, setting forth the state of things as now established through Christ.

There is division among the manuscripts as to whether the correct verbal form is passive ("you were reconciled") or active ("He has … reconciled"). Though the passive is supported by some strong manuscript evidence, in total the external evidence more strongly supports the active form. The passive is the more difficult form, which would perhaps lend support for it as the original. Yet all the scenarios for the passive can also be supported when viewing the active as the original wording. The overall evidence seems to favor considering the active form the original text.

This reconciliation was effected "in His fleshly body" (ἐν τῷ σώματι τῆς σαρκὸς αὐτοῦ). A more literal translation would be "in the body of the flesh of Him." Note the double use of definite articles, making specific the body and flesh which are in view. The all-glorious One set forth in verses 15ff. took to Himself a body of flesh and became a human being. It was a very real body, made of "flesh" (τῆς σαρκὸς) and "blood" (v. 20). The combination here of τῷ σώματι and τῆς σαρκὸς underscore the actual nature of the incarnation of Christ. The genitive (τῆς σαρκὸς, lit., "of flesh") is qualitative.[297] His was no mere appearance, but true enfleshment. The personal pronoun (αὐτοῦ) clearly refers to Christ and governs the entire preceding expression.

Paul's use of the preposition ἐν ("in") is telling. It is "in [ἐν] Him" that "all things were created" (v. 16) and "in [ἐν] Him all things hold together" (v. 17). He who brought all things into being in Himself and in Himself holds together all reality—He who is the very sphere in which all things exist and continue—at a specific point in time and in a specific place limited Himself

---

[295] Harris, 57; Lohse, 64; Moo, 141.
[296] Lohse, 64.
[297] Harris, 58.

to a fleshly human body within that creation so that "in" (ἐν) that body He might reconcile us to the Father. It staggers the mind! Here the preposition is probably used instrumentally, meaning that Christ's physical body was the means by which the reconciliation was effected.[298]

But the Apostle is quick to say that the incarnation alone, as ultimately incomprehensible as it is, was not that which reconciled us to God the Father. It was by means of that body and "through death" (διὰ τοῦ θανάτου) that Jesus bore the penalty of our sins and made a perfect atonement for those sins. The wages of sin is death (Rom. 6:23), and so He poured out the life-blood that animated that very real human body, doing so in my place. This is what effected and realized our reconciliation to God the Father. In fact the only other place Paul uses the precise phrase διὰ τοῦ θανάτου ("through the death") is when he tells the Romans, "For if while we were enemies we were reconciled to God through the death [διὰ τοῦ θανάτου] of His Son, much more, having been reconciled, we shall be saved by His life" (Rom. 5:10; cf. also Heb. 2:14). Indeed, as Paul has already said in verse 20, it is "through the blood of His cross" that Jesus has made peace with God and brought about our reconciliation.

Here the preposition (διὰ) expresses the manner by which the reconciliation was achieved.[299] The definite article should be understood as possessive (τοῦ θανάτου, "his death," ESV). This entire clause seems to be "loaded" and may have been directed toward specific errors within the Colossian heresy (e.g., denial of Christ's true incarnation, depreciation of the necessity of Christ's death, etc.).

Paul now adds an infinitive clause which is translated as an expression of purpose by the NASU: "in order to present you" (παραστῆσαι ὑμᾶς). Other English translations also see it as a purpose statement (ESV, KJV, NET, NIV), but still others see it as expressing result (NLT, RSV). The word "to present" (παραστῆσαι) is a compound word with a basic meaning of "to place beside": παρὰ ("beside") and ἵστημι ("to place"). It can be used to describe the presentation of a sacrifice upon the altar (Rom. 12:1) or to picture a bride being presented to her husband (2 Cor. 11:2). The word, however, carries broad nuances of meaning and here becomes a near equivalent

---

[298] O'Brien, 67-68.
[299] Abbott, 226.

of "make" or "render."[300] Paul will use this verb again in verse 28 of this same chapter to explain the ultimate goal of his ministry: "We proclaim Him, admonishing every man and teaching every man with all wisdom, so that we may present [παραστήσωμεν] every man complete in Christ." The aorist tense used here is constative, but, given the condition set down in verse 23, should probably be understood as looking forward to what will take place at some point in the future, rather than as describing a present reality.[301] What is thus placed is "you" (ὑμᾶς).

The believing citizens of Colossae to whom Paul writes are viewed as being set "before Him" (κατενώπιον αὐτοῦ, i.e., God the Father). This phrase is actually found at the end of the clause in order to make it emphatic—

> **Ministry Maxim**
>
> In order to save us, He, *in* whom all things exist and are sustained, lived and died *in* a single human body.

it is before the very presence of God the Father Himself we are made to be the things he is about to state. The adverb used as a preposition (κατενώπιον, "before") is found only three times in the NT. The other two usages are as powerful as the present usage. "He chose us in Him before the foundation of the world, that we would be holy and blameless before [κατενώπιον] Him" (Eph. 1:4). "Now to Him who is able to keep you from stumbling, and to make you stand in the presence of [κατενώπιον] His glory blameless with great joy," (Jude 24). It means to be "*over against, opposite, before the face of, before the presence of, in the sight of, before.*"[302] The entire expression may be paraphrased as "in the sight of God on his heavenly throne."[303]

Our status, as we are set before God, is described in three adjectives. Some have viewed the latter two as descriptive of the first (e.g., "holy in his sight, without blemish and free from accusation," NIV). However, given the presence of καὶ ("and") between the adjectives, it is better to view them as parallel with one another. The first is "holy" (ἁγίους). The adjective has already been used three times in this chapter, each time to refer to the believers in Colossae as "saints" (vv. 2, 4, 12), and it will soon be used

---

[300] BAGD, 627-628.
[301] Harris, 59.
[302] Thayer, 339.
[303] BAGD, 421.

in that way again (v. 26). Its use here is similar to the only other use in this letter (3:12).

The second is "blameless" (ἀμώμους). The word was used literally to speak of the absence of defect in an animal bound for sacrifice. Christ was, as the Lamb of God, blameless (Heb. 9:14; 1 Peter 1:19). It came then to be used in a religious and moral sense to speak of that which is without fault or, as the NASU translators have rendered it here, "blameless."[304] Believers are chosen from eternity past for this purpose (Eph. 1:4). We are to prove ourselves blameless (Phil. 2:15), yet it is ultimately Christ who keeps us so that He may present us to Himself in this state (Jude 24), a glorious, beautiful bride (Eph. 5:27).

The third word is "beyond reproach" (ἀνεγκλήτους). The term is used to describe the requirement for both overseers (Titus 1:6, 7; cf. the synonym in 1 Tim. 3:2) and deacons (1 Tim. 3:10). In both cases it seems to summarize all the other qualifications required in these leaders. The word comes from the legal world and strictly it means not having been called up or arraigned before a judge.[305] It then has the sense of being without charge or accusation, and thus irreproachable.[306] In the only remaining NT appearance (1 Cor. 1:8), it describes the state in which all believers will stand before God at Christ's return.

The whole of this latter part of the sentence could be viewed under the imagery of religious sacrifice since the first two adjectives, and even the verb itself, were at times used in that context. However, this latter word does not come from the world of cultic ritual, but from the legal world. The verb likewise could be used to describe a case being set before the court. Thus it is preferable to view this as legal imagery and Paul as looking to present the Colossians before the bar of God in the condition described by these adjectives.

---

[304] Friberg, 47.
[305] Ibid., 54.
[306] Rienecker, 623.

1:23 if indeed you continue in the faith firmly established and steadfast, and not moved away from the hope of the gospel that you have heard, which was proclaimed in all creation under heaven, and of which I, Paul, was made a minister.

The reality of Christ's presentation of us to the Father (v. 22) is now qualified by a conditional statement. The first-class conditional statement (εἰ + present indicative) expresses the Apostle's confidence that the Colossian believers will "continue in the faith." Though the condition is real and must, by God's grace, be fulfilled, Paul is confident in the reality of the spiritual state of the Colossian believers and views their fulfillment of this condition as certain. The conditional conjunctive (εἰ) is joined by the particle γε, which is added for emphasis: "if indeed" (ESV, NASU, NET).[307] Robertson says it adds "a touch of eagerness" to the condition laid down.[308]

The condition Paul presents to the Colossian believers is whether "you continue" (ἐπιμένετε). The verb is a compound, composed of ἐπί ("upon") and μένω ("remain"). The preposition in compound "adds to the force of the linear action of the pres. tense 'to continue and then some.'"[309] The word conveys the active sense of persisting in something, rather than the passive notion of simply continuance.[310]

The direct object of this continuance is "in the faith" (τῇ πίστει). The locative demonstrates the sphere or realm in which the Colossians must continue. It could refer to "the faith" as a settled body of apostolic truth or to the Colossian believers' personal trust in Jesus Christ. In this case it seems to point to the former, without entirely losing any sense of the latter. The true gospel must truly be trusted.

This continuance in the faith is now qualified several times over. First, it is qualified by the perfect passive participle "firmly established" (τεθεμελιωμένοι). Paul uses the verb only twice, here and in Ephesians 3:17. In both cases the perfect tense looks at the action as having taken place in the past and its results as continuing in the present. This was not a work that needed yet to be inaugurated in the experience of the Colossian believers,

---

[307] BAGD, 152.
[308] Robertson, *Word Pictures*, 4:483.
[309] Rienecker, 569.
[310] Harris, 60.

but a state in which they needed to remain. The passive voice pictures God acting upon them in order to bring them to this state. Literally it meant to provide something with a foundation, to lay a foundation, or thus to found something (Matt. 7:25). Then figuratively it describes "providing a firm base for belief or practice" and can be translated with words such as "establish," "strengthen," "settle," "cause to be firm or unwavering."[311]

Continuing (καὶ, "and") the imagery Paul adds the adjective "steadfast" (ἑδραῖοι). The word comes from the noun ἕδρα ("a seat," "a chair"). In classical Greek the adjective has the notion of sitting or being sedentary. In the NT it speaks metaphorically of those who are fixed in purpose and are therefore firm, steadfast, or immovable.[312] It is used only here and in 1 Corinthians 7:37 and 15:58. The perfect participle establishes the abiding state into which believers have been brought; the adjective pictures the inward conviction of those believers.

Paul now adds (καὶ, "and") a balancing comment which views the matter from a negative perspective: "not moved away" (μὴ μετακινούμενοι). The word is found only here in the NT and is a compound made up of μετά ("in the midst of") and κινέω ("move"). The present tense pictures the ongoing nature of the action. The voice could be either middle (ESV, NET, NLT, NRSV) or passive (NASU, NIV). The former views the subject as taking action upon himself, while the latter pictures another person or force acting upon the subject. The negation (μὴ, "not") reverses all of this—indicating that believers do not allow this to happen. That from which believers refuse to be moved is "from the hope of the gospel" (ἀπὸ τῆς ἐλπίδος τοῦ εὐαγγελίου). The genitive "of the gospel" (τοῦ εὐαγγελίου) means *"the hope that is kindled by the gospel"*[313] or the *"hope that is based on the gospel."*[314]

The Apostle qualifies "the gospel" with four expressions. First, it is charged with hope. Paul appears to be echoing what he said in verse 5 when he referred to "the hope laid up for you in heaven, of which you previously heard in the word of truth, the gospel." Paul is clear—to abandon the gospel and to follow the false teacher(s) would be to throw all hope to the wind. The ground upon which the false teaching stood was fraught, not with hope,

---

[311] Friberg, 196.
[312] Thayer, 168.
[313] BAGD, 318.
[314] Ibid., 253.

but with judgment. Indeed, through the indwelling Christ, the gospel gives "the hope of glory" (v. 27).

<table>
<tr><td>

Ministry Maxim

The gospel is hopeful, personal, universal, and authoritative in its appeal— we must both embrace and communicate it as such.

</td><td>

Second, it is the gospel "that you have heard" (οὗ ἠκούσατε). The gospel was not a strange message to the Colossians. They had heard the words of life through Epaphras (v. 7). And, "the day you heard" that gospel, Paul can say, is the day you "understood the grace of God in truth" (v. 6).

Third, it is also the gospel "which was proclaimed in all creation under heaven" (τοῦ κηρυχθέντος ἐν πάσῃ κτίσει τῇ ὑπὸ τὸν οὐρανόν). This is generally understood in one of two ways: "in all creation" (NASU; cf. ESV, NET, NLT) or "to every creature" (NIV; cf. KJV, NRSV). The adjective πᾶς when found with a singular noun without the definite article usually emphasizes the individual members

</td></tr>
</table>

of the class ("every," "each," "any").[315] The latter translation facilitates this.

In what sense can Paul honestly assert this global, universal proclamation of the gospel? Paul personally ministered in Ephesus, the capital of Asia Minor, for over two years. Luke could write that during this time "all who lived in Asia heard the word of the Lord, both Jews and Greeks" (Acts 19:10). Colossae was located in Asia Minor, approximately one hundred miles east of Ephesus. One of Paul's greatest opponents in Ephesus could testify that "not only in Ephesus, but in almost all of Asia, this Paul has persuaded and turned away a considerable number of people" (Acts 19:26). Clearly the spread of the gospel throughout Asia was significant and thorough, not only in the eyes of the Apostle but also in those of his enemies. Concerning the statement here, Robertson says, "It is hyperbole, to be sure, but Paul does not say that all men are converted, but only that the message has been heralded abroad over the Roman Empire in a wider fashion than most people imagine."[316] Paul has already told the Colossians that the same gospel they embraced through faith "in all the world also … is constantly bearing fruit and increasing" (v. 6). The reconciliation which Christ effected

---

[315] Ibid., 631.
[316] Robertson, *Word Pictures*, 4:483.

has universal implications ("all things," v. 20), and thus the gospel of Christ must be proclaimed universally (v. 23).[317]

Fourth, and further still, the gospel is that "of which I, Paul, was made a minister" (οὗ ἐγενόμην ἐγὼ Παῦλος διάκονος). Paul speaks of himself emphatically: "I, Paul" (ἐγὼ Παῦλος). He is still amazed at God's grace in salvation and appointment as an apostle to proclaim this gospel. To name himself here singles Paul out from Timothy (v. 1) as taking responsibility for what now is being stated.[318]

The noun "a minister" (διάκονος) originally described a servant who waited at tables. The breadth of the word expanded over time. Paul delighted to use the word to describe his appointment in service by God. He variously viewed himself as having been appointed a servant of the new covenant (2 Cor. 3:6), of righteousness (11:15), of Christ (Col. 1:7), of God (2 Cor. 6:4), of the gospel (Eph. 3:7; Col. 1:23), and of the church (Col. 1:25).[319] It is interesting that Paul does not here designate himself an apostle, but "a minister." By designating himself in this way in the context of this letter, Paul is placing himself side by side with Epaphras (1:7) and Tychicus (4:7).

Yet it is more than this. By emphatically referring to himself, in distinction from Timothy whom he has listed as coauthor (v. 1), Paul is likely underscoring his authority as an apostle without dropping the title "apostle" in a heavy-handed manner. He had not met these Colossian believers (2:1) and wished to finesse the situation rather than demand compliance. He may be underscoring his authority even while framing the office and ministry of apostle as that of a servant. This gospel, says Paul, was attested hopefully, personally, universally, and authoritatively.

Then also Paul's use of "minister" (διάκονος) to refer to himself opens the way for the next section of the letter, where he describes his ministry first generally (1:24-29) and then specifically as it relates to the Colossians (2:1-5).[320]

---

[317] Moo, 147.
[318] Bruce, NIC, 80.
[319] Mounce, 632.
[320] Moo, 148.

Digging Deeper:

1. If my *doing* grows out of my *being* (v. 21), what does this change about my understanding of both salvation and sanctification?

2. How does God's commitment to change not only my status ("reconciled") but my nature ("holy and blameless and beyond reproach," v. 22) change the way I think about salvation? About sanctification?

3. How does Paul's "if" relate to "the hope of the gospel" (v. 23)? Does the condition ("if") change the nature of the hope? Or does the hope change the way we understand the condition?

4. If the gospel is hopeful, personal, universal, and authoritative (v. 23) how does this show up in my thinking about the gospel? In my sharing the gospel?

1:24 Now I rejoice in my sufferings for your sake, and in my flesh I do my share on behalf of His body, which is the church, in filling up what is lacking in Christ's afflictions.

Often Νῦν ("Now") is used in a temporal sense, referring to the present time or, in this case, the state of affairs at the moment of his writing. Paul was at that time imprisoned for His faith in and service to Christ (4:3, 10). Many commentators understand the word in this way.[321] He may also have been thinking not merely of that moment or his immediate circumstances, but of the general order of the present time in which he was living out his life for Christ. It seems more likely, however, that in this case the word is used in its more limited sense as a transitional conjunction. In this case it would simply move the conversation along to the next logical idea.[322] His last statement referred to the gospel "of which I, Paul, was made a minister" (οὗ ἐγενόμην ἐγὼ Παῦλος διάκονος). "Now" (Νῦν) Paul takes up just what this calling as a "minister" of the gospel requires of him.[323]

---

[321] Abbott, 228; Alford, 3:209; Eadie, 86; Harris, 65.
[322] Moo, 149; Wright, 89-90.
[323] Johnson, "The Minister of the Mystery," 228.

In verse 23 Paul, by use of the emphatic first-personal pronoun (ἐγὼ Παῦλος), set himself apart from Timothy and zeroed in on his relationship to the gospel. This served as another signal that he was closing out the previous section (vv. 15-23) and preparing for this new section (1:24-2:5) where Paul sets forth the nature and objective of his ministry, first generally (1:24-29) and then specifically to the Colossians (2:1-5). Paul is fond of the first-person singular throughout this section (1:24-25, 29; 2:1, 4-5; the first-person plural in 1:28 may be simply for variety's sake).[324]

There appears to be a well-built and clearly developed chiastic arrangement around which this section is built:

A	"rejoice," "flesh" (σάρξ)	1:24
B	"make known," "riches" (πλοῦτος) "mystery"	1:27
C	"struggling"	1:29
C	"struggling"	2:1
B	"knowledge," "wealth" (πλοῦτος), "mystery"	2:2
A	"rejoicing," "body" (σάρξ)	2:5[325]

The Apostle makes the remarkable assertion "I rejoice in my sufferings" (χαίρω ἐν τοῖς παθήμασιν). By the use of the first-person singular form, he again narrows the spotlight to himself alone (in contrast to the previous plurals "we give thanks," v. 3 and "we do not cease to pray for you," v. 9).[326] The preposition (ἐν, "in") points to the sphere in which Paul's joy was experienced. This is remarkable to us, but seems to have been his abiding attitude (Acts 16:25; Rom. 5:3; 2 Cor. 11:16-33; Phil. 2:18) and that of the other apostles (Acts 5:41). The plural form of the noun underscores the repeated nature of Paul's sufferings. The definite article (τοῖς) before the noun (παθήμασιν) is used in a possessive sense ("my").

And these sufferings, he says, are "for your sake" (ὑπὲρ ὑμῶν). Paul had never met the Colossian believers (2:1), and yet he could say that he had suffered multiple times on their behalf. Did this come as surprising news to them? In what sense had Paul suffered for the Colossian believers? No doubt he could count the many sufferings he encountered while in Ephesus

---

[324] Moo, 148.
[325] Dunn, 128; Moo, 148.
[326] O'Brien, 75.

(Acts 19:1-41; 20:13-38; 1 Cor. 15:32) as being on their behalf, since it was likely from the base of gospel operations in that capital city that the mission which brought the gospel to Colossae had been launched. Had Paul not endured those difficulties, it is possible the gospel would never have reached the citizens of Colossae (cf. Eph. 3:1, 13).

As remarkable as that statement may have been, Paul explains (καὶ, "and") that through this suffering, "I do my share … in filling up what is lacking in Christ's afflictions" (ἀνταναπληρῶ τὰ ὑστερήματα τῶν θλίψεων τοῦ Χριστοῦ). From any perspective, this is an extraordinary claim! In what sense can Paul make such an assertion?

The Apostle uses a rare double compound word found only here in the NT: ἀνά ("up"), ἀντί ("in turn"), and πληρόω ("to fill").[327] Thus it has the notion of to fill up in turn.[328] But because of its rarity, the word is somewhat difficult to define more precisely. It may mean to *fill up, complete* for someone else."[329] It may describe "mutually and representatively making up a lack within a community."[330]

The noun "what is lacking" (τὰ ὑστερήματα) describes a deficiency in something. Paul uses the word eight of the nine times it is found in the NT (Luke 21:4; 1 Cor. 16:17; 2 Cor. 8:14; 9:12; 11:9; Phil. 2:30; Col. 1:24; 1 Thess. 3:10). It refers to "a measurable deficiency, which implies a predetermined quota or fullness."[331]

That which is being measured is "Christ's afflictions" (τῶν θλίψεων τοῦ Χριστοῦ). Nowhere else in the NT is the expression "used of his redemptive act or general experience of suffering."[332] Paul's sufferings (πάθημα) were a smaller but real part of Christ's greater "afflictions" (θλῖψις). The former word describes suffering generally while the latter points to distress brought on by outward circumstances and pressure.[333] The "afflictions" (τῶν θλίψεων) is probably a genitive of reference ("what is still lacking

---

[327] Robertson, *Word Pictures*, 4:484.
[328] Thayer, 49.
[329] BAGD, 72, emphasis original.
[330] Friberg, 58.
[331] Harris, 65.
[332] O'Brien, 77.
[333] BAGD, 362.

in regard to Christ's afflictions") and "Christ's" (τοῦ Χριστοῦ) is probably possessive genitive ("the tribulations that relate to Christ").[334]

Certainly there was nothing deficient or left undone with regard to Christ's atoning work on the cross. There was no redemptive merit in the things which Paul suffered. Nor is there any such merit in anything endured or suffered by any person. Christ alone bore once for all the penalty of our sins, making perfect atonement which can never be supplemented, augmented, or improved upon (1:19-20 and 2:15).

But, having affirmed this, there was clearly something which Paul in his suffering achieved. Just what was that? Christ left nothing undone regarding the atonement for our sins, but in His earthly life and ministry He did not complete everything regarding the advancement of that message. He commissioned His disciples to complete the Great Commission (Matt. 28:19-20). This, as was made abundantly clear, would involve suffering (Acts 9:16; 14:22; Rom. 8:17; 1 Thess. 3:3; 2 Tim. 3:12; 1 Peter 5:10). There was no merit in such hardship, but it was nevertheless a part of the suffering necessary for the gospel to advance, the Kingdom to spread, and the church to grow (2 Cor. 1:5-8; 2 Tim. 2:9-10). In this, Paul was glad to "do [his] share." We must each be ready to carry our load in this regard. As the Apostle told others, "the sufferings of Christ are ours in abundance" (2 Cor. 1:5).

Paul longed to know Christ, including "the fellowship of His sufferings" (Phil. 3:10). Such "fellowship" was real, for, as he discovered even at his conversion, when His body suffered, Christ suffered (Acts 9:4). Paul's sufferings, he said, were accomplished "in my flesh" (ἐν τῇ σαρκί μου). His was not merely emotional or psychological suffering, but that which is physical, tangible, and corporeal. Paul told the Corinthian believers that he had endured

> **Ministry Maxim**
>
> We are called to suffer, not for atonement of sin, but for advancement of the gospel.

in far more labors, in far more imprisonments, beaten times without number, often in danger of death. Five times I received from the Jews thirty-nine lashes. Three times I was beaten with rods, once I was

---

[334] Moo, 151.

stoned, three times I was shipwrecked, a night and a day I have spent in the deep. I have been on frequent journeys, in dangers from rivers, dangers from robbers, dangers from my countrymen, dangers from the Gentiles, dangers in the city, dangers in the wilderness, dangers on the sea, dangers among false brethren; I have been in labor and hardship, through many sleepless nights, in hunger and thirst, often without food, in cold and exposure. (2 Cor. 11:23-27)

All this was done "on behalf of His body, which is the church" (ὑπὲρ τοῦ σώματος αὐτοῦ, ὅ ἐστιν ἡ ἐκκλησία). Paul has already used the imagery of "body" for the church (1:18). Here "His body" is equated with "the church." Both describe the same entity, simply under different imagery. When Paul here considered "the church" (ἡ ἐκκλησία), he has in mind the universal church, not merely the local congregation in Colossae.[335] All Paul's hardship and suffering was "on behalf of" (ὑπὲρ) this entity. Here the preposition has the sense of "for" or "in behalf of."[336]

Standing behind Paul's words is probably the concept of the "messianic woes" which had been developed in the intertestamental period and by rabbis from seed thoughts scattered throughout the OT. The notion understood all time divided into two great eras—the present evil age and the age to come. The transition from the one age to the next was understood to include great suffering by the people of God (Rom. 8:18-25). These sufferings were necessary if the age to come was to ever dawn in the fullness of its promise. Some conceived of a predetermined amount of suffering that was necessary, though apparently not all embraced this view.

This was the milieu into which Paul was born and in which he was raised. Upon his conversion to Christ, these views surely were matured and refined under the new revelation granted him, but it is unlikely that they were abandoned entirely. It was thus in this sense that Paul could rejoice in his sufferings (cf. Rom. 5:3), for suffering meant progress toward the return of Christ and the dawn of the new age. His sufferings were not atoning, for that work had been done in its entirety by Christ (cf. "It is finished," John 19:30). Nevertheless, by his sufferings he performed a definite service "on behalf of [Christ's] body" in that he played a vital part in moving events

---

[335] BAGD, 241.
[336] Ibid., 838.

along to the fulfillment of the Messiah's sufferings and the dawning of the age to come. Paul saw a sense in which all believers might think in these terms (Rom. 8:18-25), but here he likely views his role as unique because of his apostleship and his appointment as a minister of the gospel (v. 23) and of the church (v. 25).[337]

1:25 Of this church I was made a minister according to the stewardship from God bestowed on me for your benefit, so that I might fully carry out the preaching of the word of God,

The Apostle continues the sentence and the thought by use of the relative pronoun (ἧς). The antecedent is "the church" (ἡ ἐκκλησία) in verse 24 which is likewise a feminine singular. Thus the NASU translators are right in adding the words "this church" in making good English of the Greek text.

Paul speaks emphatically of himself (ἐγώ, "I") in relation to the church (as he did in verse 23 in his relation to the gospel). He "was made a minister" (ἐγενόμην … διάκονος). Paul has just used the noun to designate himself a servant of the gospel (v. 23, see our comments on the word there), and now he balances that thought by designating himself "a minister" of the church. He has used it to designate Epaphras "a faithful servant of Christ" (v. 7) and will use it again of Tychicus as a "faithful servant" (4:7). This, Paul "was made" (ἐγενόμην). The verb was also just used in verse 23, in the same form as well. As there, the aorist tense describes an event which took place at a point in time. As a deponent verb the middle form has an active meaning.

This was "according to the stewardship" (κατὰ τὴν οἰκονομίαν). The preposition (κατὰ) may be understood to indicate either the standard ("according to," ESV, NASU, NET, NRSV), the means ("by," NIV), or the cause ("as a result of," "by virtue of," NEB).[338] The noun "stewardship" (οἰκονομίαν) is a favorite Pauline word (1 Cor. 9:17; Eph. 1:10; 3:2, 9; 1 Tim. 1:4; elsewhere only in Luke 16:2-4). It refers to the administration of a household or the one charged with carrying out that management. Paul then used it by extension to speak of God's administration of salvation through Christ (Eph. 1:10; 3:9) or the stewardship of service placed upon

---

[337] For further development of the concept of the "messianic woes" see Bruce, NIC, 83-84; Harris, 66; Lohse, 69-72; Martin, 70; Moo, 149-153; O'Brien, 78-81; Wright, 87-90.

[338] Harris, 67.

an individual to further that plan (1 Cor. 9:17; Eph. 3:2; Col. 1:25). It is in the latter sense that Paul uses the word here.

For Paul "the stewardship" was his apostolic ministry.[339] The definite article makes specific the responsibility. Paul further clarifies by indicating that this stewardship was "from God" (τοῦ θεοῦ). This may be understood as a subjective genitive ("the commission God gave to me," NIV)[340] or an objective genitive ("the divine office," RSV).[341] It is probably the former rather than the latter that is in view. Thus divine authority and resources were granted to him for this service just as divine accountability would hold him responsible for his faithfulness.

Paul further explains that this stewardship was "bestowed on me for your benefit" (τὴν δοθεῖσάν μοι εἰς ὑμᾶς). The aorist passive participle (τὴν δοθεῖσάν, "bestowed") points to a time when this stewardship was passed to Paul. The passive voice underscores that Paul did not take this honor and responsibility upon himself, but that God conferred it upon him. This giving of the stewardship was "to me" (μοι), but "for your benefit" (εἰς ὑμᾶς). The responsibility and accountability were Paul's. They were the goal of this endowment of God upon him.[342] This latter phrase (εἰς ὑμᾶς) could be taken with what follows ("to present *to you*," NIV [emphasis added]; cf. NLT), but, as per the NASU, probably should be taken with what precedes.[343] The preposition (εἰς) should be understood as a dative of advantage.[344]

> **Ministry Maxim**
>
> Divine authority and accountability are mine as I fully exhaust the gospel in seeking your greatest benefit.

And all this was "so that I might fully carry out the preaching of the word of God" (πληρῶσαι τὸν λόγον τοῦ θεοῦ). Paul uses the exact phrase ("the word of God") only two other times (2 Cor. 2:17; 4:2), but it is a favorite of Luke (Luke 5:1; 8:21; 11:28; Acts 4:31; 6:2; 8:14; 11:1; 13:5, 7, 46; 18:11) and is found throughout the NT (Matt. 15:6; Mark 7:13; Heb. 13:7; Rev. 1:2, 9; 6:9; 20:4). By this

---

[339] Moo, 154.
[340] Harris, 67.
[341] BAGD, 559; Lohse, 72.
[342] BAGD, 229.
[343] Lohse, 73.
[344] BAGD, 229.

expression Paul means simply the Christian message, the gospel.[345] The exact nuance of the verb (πληρῶσαι, "so that I might fully carry out") is more difficult to discern as the variety of translations makes obvious: "fully carry out" (NASU), "in its fullness" (NIV), "to make ... fully known" (ESV, NRSV), "his entire message" (NLT), "to fulfill" (KJV). The infinitive may be used to express purpose ("so that")[346] or it may be epexegetical and thus define the content of Paul's stewardship ("the commission ..., namely, to declare fully ...").[347] The verb means simply to make full or to fill. Here it probably has the nuance of bringing something to completion or to finishing something that has already been started.[348]

Does Paul have in mind the notion of proclaiming the word of God in its entirety: "I did not shrink from declaring to you the whole counsel of God" (Acts 20:27, ESV)? Or does he refer to preaching the word of God in every place: "from Jerusalem and round about as far as Illyricum I have fully preached the gospel of Christ" (Rom. 15:19)?[349] Or does he mean that the word of God is only preached fully when it achieves its desired effect (Col. 1:5-6; cf. Isa. 55:11)?[350] In view of Paul's unique status as the apostle to the Gentiles (Rom. 11:13; 1 Tim. 2:7) and in view of the way he elsewhere uses οἰκονομία in such close connection to the expression of that unique stewardship (Eph. 3:2, 9), it seems likely that here he intends us to understand his unique role in making sure that the full gospel goes fully to the Gentiles to whom he has been sent. In this sense Paul can count himself so directly tied to and responsible for the church in Colossae which he has never even visited.

Note throughout this section (1:25-2:5) the all-encompassing scope of Paul's language: "*fully* carry out" (25), "*every* man" (28), "*all* wisdom" (28), "*every* man" (28), "*all* those who have not personally seen my face" (2:1), "*all* the wealth" (2:2), "*full* assurance of understanding" (2:2), "*all* the treasures of wisdom and knowledge" (2:3, all emphases added).[351]

---

[345] Ibid., 478.
[346] Robertson, *Word Pictures*, 4:484.
[347] Harris, 68; Moo, 154.
[348] BAGD, 671.
[349] Lohse, 73.
[350] Moo, 155; O'Brien, 83.
[351] Moo, 149.

1:26 that is, the mystery which has been hidden from the past ages and generations, but has now been manifested to His saints,

What Paul just referred to as "the word of God" (v. 25), he now calls "the mystery" (τὸ μυστήριον) by setting this word in epexegetical apposition to the previous expression. The word was used extensively in the pagan "mystery religions" of the era. Yet it also had a rich usage in Jewish writings, including the LXX of the Apocrypha, the Pseudepigrapha, and the writings of Qumran.[352]

This noun appears twenty-eight times in the NT, twenty-one of those occurring in Paul's letters. In the twin epistles of Ephesians and Colossians we find an especially heavy concentration. The use of the word in the NT is more reliant upon the Jewish background of the word than the pagan usages. Yet it is only in the context of each passage that the meaning may be truly deduced.[353]

This is the word's first occurrence in Colossians (1:26, 27; 2:2; 4:3). Generally, in the NT use of the term, a mystery does not designate that which is unknowable, but what previously has been left undisclosed by God. But it is something that via revelation (Eph. 1:9; 3:3-5) God has now made known and yet is perceived and experienced only through faith. This mystery is centered in the person of Christ (Col. 2:2; 4:3; Eph. 3:4) and relates to His dwelling in His people (Col. 1:27). This is now seen to include Gentiles who, along with Jews, have come to repentance and faith in Jesus Christ (Col. 1:27; Eph. 3:6). It is used in close proximity with οἰκονομία ("stewardship" or "administration") both in Ephesians (1:9-10; 3:2-3, 9) and Colossians (1:25-26).

The false teacher(s) present in Colossae at this time may have used the term to indicate what initiates to his brand of religion had to look forward to, but this is conjecture. If so, Paul may have been commandeering his word to indirectly undermine his efforts among the believers in Colossae. Yet Paul has used the word extensively in his other letters (e.g., Rom.11:25; 16:25; 1 Cor. 2:1; 4:1; Eph. 1:9; 2 Thess. 2:7; 1 Tim. 3:9, 16) which demonstrates he may already have developed his teaching along this line. The plural

---

[352] Liefeld, 4:327-228.
[353] Ibid., 4:328, 330.

form was employed in the pagan mystery religions of the day.[354] Here "the mystery" (τὸ μυστήριον; singular) is wrapped up in the person of Christ Himself (v. 27).[355]

Two great truths are set forth regarding this mystery. First, it is that "which has been hidden" (τὸ ἀποκεκρυμμένον). The word is used only four times in the NT. In three of those it is found in combination with μυστήριον ("mystery," 1 Cor. 2:7; Eph. 3:9; Col. 1:26). It is a compound word comprised of ἀπό ("from") and κρύπτω ("to hide"). The uncompounded form is used in Colossians 3:3 to assert that "your life is hidden with Christ in God." Here the perfect tense indicates that the action was taken in the past and has continued to the time when Christ appeared. The passive voice indicates that someone acted upon this "mystery" to conceal it, in this case God Himself.

This mystery was hidden "from the past ages and generations" (ἀπὸ τῶν αἰώνων καὶ ἀπὸ τῶν γενεῶν). The first use of the preposition (ἀπὸ, "from") is probably used in a temporal sense.[356] Perhaps "throughout" (NRSV) or "during" captures the sense (cf. "for ages and generations," ESV, NIV, RSV). The plural (τῶν αἰώνων, "the past ages") points to successively unfolding periods of time, one after another. The expression "generations" (τῶν γενεῶν) can refer to "the sum total of those born at the same time, expanded to include all those living at a given time."[357] In this case the fuller expression would mean "through all the ages of time and from all the generations of men."[358] Or perhaps this latter expression also points to a period of time generally.[359] Thus it would be basically synonymous with the first term. In this case the second occurrence of ἀπὸ, like the first, is probably also used in a temporal sense. A generation is the more basic unit, many generations making up each age.[360] Some have suggested that these two nouns are not used to designate temporal spans of time, but spiritual beings or powers

---

[354] Lohse, 74.

[355] O'Brien, 84.

[356] Rienecker, 570.

[357] BAGD, 154.

[358] Carson, 53.

[359] BAGD, 154.

[360] Abbott, 234; Rienecker, 570.

(cf. "from angels and men," RSV margin).[361] Yet Paul nowhere else uses the words in this sense, and it seems unlikely that he does so here.[362]

The second point Paul now makes regarding "the mystery" stands in contrast to the first: it "has ... been manifested" (ἐφανερώθη). Paul suddenly changes the construction, transitioning from the participle (τὸ ἀποκεκρυμμένον, "has been hidden") to the finite verb. The verb is used frequently throughout the NT and depicts the act of making visible that which has heretofore been unseen.[363] In this letter Paul uses it to describe both the second coming of Christ and the revelation of believers in their new bodies at that time (Col. 3:4). He uses it also to solicit prayer that he might make "the mystery" of the gospel plain in his preaching (Col. 4:4). Here the Apostle makes clear that it is in Jesus Christ that the fullness of God's saving plan is finally made open, plain and clear for all to see. This has not always been the case, "but now" (νῦν δὲ) the good news of God's salvation is made manifest in Christ. This dramatic expression is another reason to understand the previous occurrences of ἀπὸ as temporal in meaning.[364] The aorist tense of the verb is constative, viewing the disclosures as one whole. It is here translated with an English perfect to give the sense.[365] The passive form designates this as God's doing.[366]

> **Ministry Maxim**
>
> The ability to "see" is a gift from God and does not grow by a preacher's increase in volume.

This manifestation is not general and all-encompassing, but only "to His saints" (τοῖς ἁγίοις αὐτοῦ). Many remain in darkness. Indeed, we "were formerly darkness, but now [we] are Light in the Lord" and are called to "walk as children of Light" (Eph. 5:8). Paul was personally commissioned by Jesus and sent to the Gentiles "to open their eyes so that they may turn from darkness to light and from the dominion of Satan to God, that they may receive forgiveness of sins and an inheritance among those who have been sanctified [the Greek word is from the same root as "saints"] by faith in Me"

---

[361] BAGD, 28.
[362] Moo, 156.
[363] Mounce, 439.
[364] Lohse, 74.
[365] Harris, 69.
[366] O'Brien, 84.

(Acts 26:18). Paul, by referring to "His saints" refers to all believers in Christ (1:2, 4, 12; 3:12), "not some select group of initiates."[367]

1:27 to whom God willed to make known what is the riches of the glory of this mystery among the Gentiles, which is Christ in you, the hope of glory.

It is to these "saints" (v. 26) that Paul turns his attention now. It was them "to whom" (οἷς) the great decision was made to unveil God's mystery. The relative pronoun's masculine plural form and dative case agrees with the "saints" of verse 26. The revelation of God's mystery was made known not to a few obscure clerics, to a select group of charismatics, or to a sage teacher of wisdom. Rather "God willed" (ἠθέλησεν ὁ θεὸς) a broader revelation to all God's people. The aorist tense is probably constative, depicting God's decision prior to the disclosure.[368] Thus Paul can say that he is "an apostle of Jesus Christ by the will of God" (v. 1).[369]

God determined "to make known" (γνωρίσαι) what had previously been hidden from the view of mortals. The aorist tense agrees with the main verb and views the decisive event of God's revelation of the mystery. Paul uses the verb often in Ephesians in the context of making known the mystery (Eph. 1:9; 3:3, 5, 10; 6:19) as he also does in Romans 16:26. Here the infinitive (γνωρίσαι, "to make known") describes the same action as "has now been manifested" in verse 26.[370]

Paul begins now to speak much in terms related to knowledge, wisdom, and insight: "to make known" (27), "wisdom" (28), "full assurance of understanding" (2:2), "knowledge" (2:2), "wisdom" (2:3), "knowledge" (2:3), and "delude" (2:4).[371] Thus Paul intensifies his polemic against the false teacher(s), who, in what may have been a pre-Gnostic ideology, seems to have claimed a corner on the market of wisdom and knowledge (2:23).

Paul tells us that God has made known "the riches of the glory of this mystery" (τί τὸ πλοῦτος τῆς δόξης τοῦ μυστηρίου τούτου). The interrogative pronoun (τί) introduces an indirect question which is difficult to

---

[367] Ibid., 85.
[368] Harris, 70.
[369] Vincent, *Word Studies*, 3:479.
[370] Harris, 70.
[371] Moo, 148.

translate into clear English.[372] In this context it emphasizes the value of the riches: "how great ... are the riches" (ESV, NRSV, RSV).[373]

The noun "the riches" (τὸ πλοῦτος) is used here figuratively to speak of a wealth or abundance of something.[374] That something is designated by the genitive (τῆς δόξης, "of the glory") which in turn is qualified by a second genitive: "of this mystery" (τοῦ μυστηρίου τούτου). The former genitive is probably to be understood as attributive, in the sense of "the glorious riches of this mystery" (NIV, cf. NET).[375] Yet, as Moo asserts, "the theologically 'weighty' word 'glory' [should] not be weakened to a mere adjective ... If we take the word as a description of 'riches,' we should at the same time insist that it connotes the presence of God himself."[376] The latter genitive seems probably to be possessive (the glorious riches which this mystery contains/holds).[377]

The glorious richness of God's mystery was made known "among the Gentiles" (ἐν τοῖς ἔθνεσιν). One question is just how to understand the preposition (ἐν). Should it be taken as "among" or "in"? The precise phrase employed here is used a total of eight times in the NT (Acts 15:12; 21:19; Rom. 2:24; 1 Cor. 5:1; Gal. 1:16; 2:2; Col. 1:27; 1 Peter 2:12). Each of these usages seems to point to "among" as the correct understanding.[378]

Another question is to determine to which phrase this is to be connected. Should it be connected to the verb ("make known among the Gentiles") or to the mystery ("the mystery [displayed] among the Gentiles")? The former seems the more likely, given Paul's hesitancy in Colossians to explicitly make "the mystery" about the inclusion of the Gentiles, as he does more frequently in Ephesians.[379] In fact while he uses the word ἔθνος five times in Ephesians (2:11; 3:1, 6, 8; 4:17), he uses the word only here in Colossians.

The precise content of the mystery is "Christ in you" (Χριστὸς ἐν ὑμῖν). The relative pronoun (ὅ, "which") points back to "this mystery"

---

[372] Harris, 70.
[373] Abbott, 234.
[374] BAGD, 674.
[375] Harris, 70.
[376] Moo, 157; cf. O'Brien, 86.
[377] Harris, 70.
[378] BAGD, 258.
[379] Moo, 158.

(τοῦ μυστηρίου τούτου), agreeing with it in gender and number, though differing in case because it functions here as the subject of the relative clause.[380] A few manuscripts have the masculine pronoun (ὅς) instead of the neuter, but this appears to have been an attempt at "correction" to make it conform to the gender of Χριστὸς ("Christ").[381] The expression ὅ ἐστιν ("which is") can at times mean "which/that is," "which means," or "that is to say" (cf. v. 24).[382]

We discover here that the mystery is not an impersonal program, but is centered in the person of "Christ" (Χριστὸς) Himself (cf. 2:2). This "is" (ἐστιν) continuously the case, as the present tense indicates, and has been all along, though it has only been revealed in these last times (v. 26). But the mystery is not simply Christ Himself, but "Christ in you" (Χριστὸς ἐν ὑμῖν).

Again we need to decide the precise nuance intended by the preposition (ἐν, "in"). Did he mean "among" the Gentiles as a collective group? Or "in" each one personally (referring either to individual Gentile believers or to both Jewish and Gentile believers), thus pointing to the mystical union of the believer with Christ through His personal indwelling? In related fashion we also need to determine just what the Apostle intended by the plural personal pronoun (ὑμῖν, "you"). Did Paul mean "you" personally (as individuals)? Or did he mean more generally "you" who are Gentiles? Some believe that the previous use of ἐν must govern this usage, meaning the same in both cases ("among [ἐν] the Gentiles" and "among [ἐν] you").[383] Yet one of those commentators immediately goes on to insist that the two uses of δόξα ("glory") do not have to be understood in the same sense in this passage.[384] It would seem the same logic should be applied to our understanding of the preposition (ἐν). Paul elsewhere speaks freely of the personal indwelling of Christ in the believer

> **Ministry Maxim**
>
> The unbounded Christ "in" whom all creation dwells (v. 16) and is held together (v. 17) takes up His dwelling "in" you (v. 27)!

---

[380] Harris, 71.
[381] Moo, 157.
[382] BAGD, 584; Harris, 71.
[383] Abbott, 235; Lohse, 76.
[384] Abbott, 235.

(Rom. 8:10; 2 Cor. 13:5; Gal. 2:20), and he probably does so here as well.[385] Robertson says, "He is addressing Gentiles, but the idea of *en* here is *in*, not *among*. It is the personal experience and presence of Christ in the individual life of all believers that Paul has in mind, the indwelling Christ in the heart as in Eph. 3:17."[386]

But in our efforts to understand the precise intent of the preposition and pronoun, let us not miss the majesty of this vast, nearly incomprehensible statement of the Apostle: *"Christ* in you"! Who is this Christ? None other than the One just set before us in verses 15-20! Breathe again those exalted words of this Exalted One. This is the One said to now reside "in you." The thought is staggering. The reality is breathtaking. Pause in worship and submission.

This One who thus indwells believers (Gentile as well as Jew) is "the hope of glory" (ἡ ἐλπὶς τῆς δόξης). The definite article (ἡ) may signify possession (*"your* hope").[387] The genitive (τῆς δόξης, "of glory") is objective ("the hope which consists in glory") rather than qualitative ("glorious hope").[388] Harris says that the entire phrase is in epexegetical apposition to "Christ in you" and signifies that "the indwelling of the exalted Christ in individual believers is their assurance of coming glory" (cf. Eph. 1:13-14).[389] Elsewhere Paul speaks of the Spirit and the deposit of God guaranteeing our future inheritance (Rom. 8:15-17, 23; 2 Cor. 1:22; 5:5; Eph. 1:13-14), but, since Paul speaks elsewhere interchangeably of the Spirit and of Christ indwelling the believer (Rom. 8:10-11), he is able here to preserve the Christological focus of Colossians and freely center our assurance on Christ.[390]

In Colossians "hope" is always directly tied to the gospel (1:5, 23). The gospel promises that "When Christ, who is our life, is revealed, then you also will be revealed with Him in glory" (Col. 3:4). Indeed, our hope is centered in the Person of the Son of God, who is called "Christ Jesus our hope" (1 Tim. 1:1, ESV). Paul elsewhere combines the notions of "hope" and

---

[385] Dunn, 122-123.
[386] Robertson, *Word Pictures*, 4:485.
[387] Harris, 71.
[388] Ibid.
[389] Ibid.
[390] Bruce, NIC, 86.

"glory." God teaches us to "exult in the hope of the glory of God" (Rom. 5:2). Paul prayed that the Ephesians "will know what is the hope of His calling, what are the riches of the glory of His inheritance in the saints" (Eph. 1:17). And as believers we are "waiting for our blessed hope, the appearing of the glory of our great God and Savior Jesus Christ" (Titus 2:13, ESV).

Indeed, "our citizenship is in heaven, from which also we eagerly wait for a Savior, the Lord Jesus Christ; who will transform the body of our humble state into conformity with the body of His glory, by the exertion of the power that He has even to subject all things to Himself" (Phil. 3:20-21). We will discover in that day what we should count to be true today: "the sufferings of this present time are not worthy to be compared with the glory that is to be revealed to us" (Rom. 8:18). Indeed, Moo says that "the hope of glory" signifies simply "the certainty that we will experience final glory."[391]

Digging Deeper:

1. In what way has God called you to "fill up what is lacking in Christ's afflictions" (v. 24)? How does this perspective transform how you see those sufferings?
2. How can we know when we have "fully carr[ied] out the preaching of the word of God" (v. 25)?
3. Knowing that the ability to "see" and understand God's "mystery" is a gift given by Him (vv. 26-27), how should that change your understanding of your role and practice in preaching?
4. How can all reality be "in" Christ (v. 16) and held together "in" Him (v. 17) and yet Christ be said to be "in you" (v. 27)?

1:28 We proclaim Him, admonishing every man and teaching every man with all wisdom, so that we may present every man complete in Christ.

Paul's message—indeed our message—is not simply a philosophy, principle, or program, but a person! The Apostle declares, "We proclaim Him" (ὃν ἡμεῖς καταγγέλλομεν). The relative pronoun (ὃν, "Him") finds its

---

[391] Moo, 159.

referent in "Christ" (v. 27). The plural form of the personal pronoun (ἡμεῖς, "we") could refer to Paul and the other apostles, but it is probably to be understood more broadly to include Timothy (1:1), Epaphras (1:7; 4:12), and all who proclaim the true apostolic gospel.

The verb was reserved for "solemn religious messages"[392] and means "to announce, declare, promulgate, make known; to proclaim publicly, publish."[393] The present tense underscores the continual nature of this proclamation. This main verb is now qualified by two participial phrases, each describing something of the manner in which the proclamation is carried out or the results gained through the proclamation.[394]

The first participial phrase states that this proclamation includes "admonishing every man" (νουθετοῦντες πάντα ἄνθρωπον). The root word comes from νουθετης, which in turn comes from νοῦς ("mind") and τίθημι ("to place/put"). Thus the literal sense of the word is "to put in mind."[395] It means to admonish, to warn, or to instruct in the sense of "giving instructions in regard to belief or behavior."[396] It is used exclusively by Paul, except where Luke uses it to quote Paul (Acts 20:31).

The ministry of admonishment requires a knowledge base and purity of motive within the one undertaking the instruction (Rom. 15:14). That knowledge must come from the Word of God (Col. 3:16). This is what a father does with his children (1 Cor. 4:14). This is a ministry all the members of the body of Christ are to undertake (Rom. 15:14; Col. 3:16), but local spiritual leaders have a special responsibility in this regard (1 Thess. 5:12). It can be undertaken not only conversationally, but musically (Col. 3:16). The unruly (1 Thess. 5:14) and disobedient (2 Thess. 3:15) are special objects of this kind of warning. But this must be done with a broken heart (Acts 20:31) rather than a condescending attitude. Here the present tense underscores the ongoing need and practice of the ministry of "admonish-

> **Ministry Maxim**
>
> My message is not a philosophy, program, or principle, but a Person!

---

[392] Friberg, 217.
[393] Thayer, 330.
[394] Reinecker, 571.
[395] Thayer, 429.
[396] Friberg, 273.

ing." No one is beyond the need of this ministry, for it is directed at "every man" (πάντα ἄνθρωπον), which is understood as inclusive of females and children.

The second participial phrase reveals that this proclamation also (καὶ, "and") involves "teaching every man" (διδάσκοντες πάντα ἄνθρωπον). Again the participle is in the present tense, underscoring the abiding, continuous nature of the ministry. The word is used at times to speak of official teaching of doctrine within the church, and the scope of those who are to undertake this ministry is limited (1 Tim. 2:12). However, Colossians 3:16 makes clear that it is also—like admonishing—a function which in some sense all believers undertake with one another—again, even through song. Again the instruction must be from the Word of God (Col. 3:16), not simply our own inventions, good ideas, or philosophies. Paul will momentarily use the word in the aorist tense to say that these Colossians already "were instructed" (2:7). He was probably looking back upon the ministry of Epaphras among them (1:7; 4:12). Thus we must receive such teaching both early (2:7) and often (1:28) in our Christian experience. We never outgrow the need for admonishment and instruction alike. When we cannot receive both of these ministries from either spiritual leadership or from other members of the body of Christ, we are on dangerous ground. This is, again, a ministry for "every man" (πάντα ἄνθρωπον). The two participles may point to "admonishing" regarding behavior and "teaching" regarding doctrine.[397]

But this is also a ministry which can fall victim to various abuses. How, then, is it to be undertaken? Is there any regulation for the exercise of these ministries? The Apostle answers by demanding that all such admonishment and teaching must be done "with all wisdom" (ἐν πάσῃ σοφίᾳ). Wisdom has a significant place in this letter (1:9, 28; 2:3, 23; 3:16; 4:5), a more prominent place than in Ephesians (1:8, 17; 3:10). This may be due to a special emphasis by the false teacher(s) in Colossae (2:23). The word occurs in relationship to the previous two words not only here, but also in Colossians 3:16. This signals a significant interrelationship between the two passages. The words occur in the opposite order in the latter passage. In 3:16 it would appear that the Apostle makes the responsibility of all believers to one

---

[397] Robertson, *Word Pictures*, 4:485.

another what he claims for himself here. Here Paul has in view "all" (πάσῃ), or every form or expression of God's wisdom.

The Apostle now affixes a purpose clause to indicate the goal of such ministry. It is "so that we may present every man complete in Christ" (ἵνα παραστήσωμεν πάντα ἄνθρωπον τέλειον ἐν Χριστῷ). The verb "we may present" (παραστήσωμεν) is a compound word with a basic meaning of "to place beside" (παρὰ, "beside" and ἵστημι, "to place"). It was used in verse 22 (see comments there) to describe the Father reconciling us to Himself through Christ in order to present us before Him without fault. This repetition of the verb reminds us that the Father's purpose must become the purpose of His minister, if he is to be found faithful.

Paul labors with God to present us before Him "complete" (τέλειον). The word generally describes something which has attained its appointed purpose or end. It is thus complete or perfect.[398] It was also used in the first century as a technical term in the pagan mystery religions. There it described an individual who had passed into the mystic rites as an initiate.[399] In those settings the word distinguished the fully instructed from the novice.[400]

Paul may well be using the term here as an intentional polemic against the false teaching now infiltrating the church in Colossae. Paul labors to present them fully mature, complete, initiated into the depths of God through Christ. He uses the word again later in the letter to describe Epaphras's labors in prayer for them to the same end (4:12). The verb is in the subjunctive mood, being combined with the conjunction (ἵνα) to form the purpose clause. The arrival at such a state is dependent upon being and remaining "in Christ" (ἐν Χριστῷ). It is only in the sphere of relationship to Jesus Christ that we find and experience the purpose and ultimate end for which we were created. The aorist tense is used to indicate that there will come a day when such completeness may be achieved and experienced. Paul is looking to that eschatological last day when we shall each stand before God.

We should take note of the Apostle's threefold repetition in this verse of the expression "every man" (πάντα ἄνθρωπον). This precise phrase is found only four times in the NT, three of them in this verse (cf. John 1:9). In

---

[398] BAGD, 809.
[399] Ibid.
[400] Vincent, *Word Studies*, 3:480.

each case Paul uses the adjective "every" (πάντα) to point to each individual member of those he is pointing out.[401] Paul is speaking in universal terms to counteract the narrow exclusiveness of the false teacher(s).[402] In his emphasis on ministry to "every man," Paul is rebuking the false teacher's tendency to divide the people of God through legalism (2:16-17), arrogant spirituality (vv. 18-19), and asceticism (vv. 20-23). The noun "man" (ἄνθρωπον) is used not in a gender-specific way. Rather Paul points to men and women—"every human," we might say.

1:29 For this purpose also I labor, striving according to His power, which mightily works within me.

When Paul begins by saying "For this purpose also" (εἰς ὃ καὶ), he is looking back to his purpose statement in verse 28 ("so that we may present every man complete in Christ Jesus"). The phrase εἰς ὃ implies "movement toward a goal" and thus speaks of purpose.[403] The use of καὶ ("also") suggests that Paul is adding to the expressions of the last sentence (v. 28) and gives greater independence to the relative clause which follows.[404]

Toward this goal of full maturity in Christ for every individual (v. 28), Paul can assert "I labor" (κοπιῶ). This verb emphasizes the wearisome nature of the toil. Paul uses it in 2 Timothy 2:6 to describe "the hard-working farmer." It might apply to the ministry of local church leadership generally (1 Thess. 5:12), to preaching specifically (1 Tim. 5:17), or to striving after godliness in one's personal life (1 Tim. 4:10).

Paul knew from experience what it meant to work to the point of weariness (1 Cor. 4:12; 15:10; Gal. 4:11; Phil. 2:16; 1 Tim. 4:10). The present tense underscores the habitual, unending nature of the toil. The cognate noun is found in Paul's next line (ἀγών, "a struggle"; 2:1).

Ministry Maxim
I am to schedule and address my ministry assignments not by what I can do, but by what Christ can do in and through me.

Together they form the center or high point of the chiastic construction that frames 1:24-2:5 (see comments on 1:24). Paul here turns to the first-person

---

[401] BAGD, 631.
[402] Vincent, *Word Studies*, 3:480.
[403] NET Bible.
[404] BAGD, 393.

singular ("I"), whereas in verse 28 he used the first-person plural ("We"). He will continue this emphasis as chapter two opens.

This labor involves "striving" (ἀγωνιζόμενος). The participle we meet here, when used literally, can describe either competing for a prize in an athletic contest (1 Cor. 9:25) or engaging another in a battle with weapons (John 18:36). When it is used figuratively, it often has the sense of contending or struggling with great effort against difficulties or dangers generally (Col. 1:29; 1 Tim. 4:10) or of striving after something with strenuous zeal (Luke 13:24; Col. 4:12).[405] Paul uses it to summarize the entire nature of his battle in this life, "I have fought the good fight" (2 Tim. 4:7). It is related to our words *agony* and *agonize*.

Here, too, the present tense stresses the continual nature of the action. Both verbs can have athletic overtones (the former in Phil. 2:16 and the latter in 1 Cor. 9:25). Paul uses this latter verb in Colossians 4:12 to describe Epaphras "laboring earnestly" for the Colossian believers in prayer. In all this Paul is not working in his own strength, but "according to His power" (κατὰ τὴν ἐνέργειαν αὐτοῦ). The word "power" (τὴν ἐνέργειαν) is used in the NT of supernatural or spiritual energy, operation, or working.[406] The personal pronoun (αὐτοῦ, "his") makes clear that it is divine power which is spoken of here. It speaks of the working of God in raising Christ from the dead (Col. 2:12). Paul pursued his work and strove toward this divine goal not "according to" his own strength or what he could calculate to achieve, but "according to" (κατὰ) the measure of God's power. This power, says the Apostle, is one "which mightily works within me" (τὴν ἐνεργουμένην ἐν ἐμοὶ ἐν δυνάμει). Paul was consciously aware (present tense) of the presence of God at work within (middle voice) and through him. He consciously depended upon God's power in and through him to produce what only God can produce and to do what only God can do. Note the play on words: "power" (ἐνέργεια) which "mightily works" (ἐνεργέω). We get our word *energy* from this word group, though we dare not read our twenty-first century meaning back into the first century

---

[405] Thayer, 10.
[406] Friberg, 150.

word.[407] This divine "energy," says the Apostle more literally, is operating "in me in power" (ἐν ἐμοὶ ἐν δυνάμει).

Digging Deeper:

1. In practical terms, what does it look like for you to preach a Person (Jesus) rather than principles, philosophies, or programs (v. 28a)?

2. Which is harder in your ministry context, to admonish people with regard to their behavior or to teach them sound doctrine (v. 28b)?

3. How are we to balance accepting ministry assignments based on Christ's strength working through us with knowing when to say "no" to certain opportunities or when we are in over our heads (v. 29)?

---

[407] Robertson, *Word Pictures*, 4:486.

COLOSSIANS 2

2:1 For I want you to know how great a struggle I have on your behalf and for those who are at Laodicea, and for all those who have not personally seen my face,

T hough a new chapter begins, the line of thought has already been under development. As noted above in 1:24, Paul began to unfold the nature and objective of his ministry at that point. This, as also noted, is developed along a chiastic arrangement (see above under 1:24). The first half of that chiasm has been set forth in 1:24-29. Now Paul begins to work through the second part of the chiasm, this time developing his thoughts more specifically with reference to his relationship with the Colossian believers. What was true of his ministry generally (1:24-29) is seen also in his concern and ministry to the Colossians specifically (2:1-5).

In chiasm the line of thought set forth in the first half is then reversed in the second half. Thus the thought here is the center point and corresponds to that held out in 1:29. There Paul piled up words related to work and power ("labor," "striving," "power," "mightily," "works"). So here too we find what this exertion of power looks like through Paul toward the Colossians.

Paul's use of the coordinating conjunction "For" (γὰρ) is a clear signal that he is continuing a previous line of thought. It is used here to introduce Paul's development, in a more personal way, of the things set forth generally in the previous section. When Paul says "I want" (Θέλω), he uses a verb that can have the sense of either "I wish" or "I will." It is the former which is in view here. Paul is expressing a personal desire, not imposing his will upon the believers in Colossae. The present tense points to an ongoing and enduring desire within the Apostle. His desire relates to the Colossians coming into an awareness of (ὑμᾶς εἰδέναι, "you to know") something going on within or through him. The personal pronoun is in the plural, indicating that he is thinking not just of an individual believer within the Colossian church with whom he may be acquainted, but all of them.

For the perfect infinitive (εἰδέναι, "to know"), Paul chose a verb which points to a knowledge of information rather than experience. He wants them to be cognizant of the facts regarding his intentions and actions toward them. The perfect tense has the present-tense meaning.

What is to be known is "how great a struggle I have" (ἡλίκον ἀγῶνα ἔχω). The word "struggle" (ἀγῶνα) links this verse with 1:29 where its verbal cognate is found (ἀγωνιζόμενος, "striving"). What is true of Paul's ministry generally (1:29) is true regarding his ministry to the Colossians (2:1). But this was no ordinary "struggle." He wanted them to know "how great" (ἡλίκον) was that which worked within him. This adjective is used as an interrogative in indirect questions. It is found only here and in James 3:5 in the NT. It speaks there of size, here of intensity.[408] And this great internal wrestling is something Paul can say "I have" (ἔχω), the present tense pointing to the ongoing nature of the "struggle."

This struggle is "on your behalf" (ὑπὲρ ὑμῶν), the plural again pointing to all who make up the church in Colossae. However it was not only for the Colossians, but also (καὶ) "for those who are at Laodicea" (τῶν ἐν Λαοδικείᾳ). The two communities were only about ten to twelve miles distant from one another. As near neighbors there would have been a good deal of interaction between the communities in general and all the more so for churches struggling in the face of common issues.

In fact this letter, after its reading in Colossae, was to be read in the Laodicean church, and a letter the Apostle was sending to that church was to be read here in Colossae (Col. 4:16). Epaphras, similarly to Paul, shared a concern for the believers in both communities (4:12-13). Yet not even this exhausts Paul's concern; it is also (καὶ) "for all those who have not personally seen my face" (ὅσοι οὐχ ἑόρακαν τὸ πρόσωπόν μου ἐν σαρκί).

---

[408] Friberg, 190.

This no doubt indicates that the Apostle had not personally founded or even visited the region and its churches. Among the many elements that bound all these believers together was the fact that they had "not personally seen [Paul's] face." This phrase would surely have included those in Hieropolis (Col. 4:13), a city which along with Colossae and Laodicea comprised the three greatest communities in the Lycus Valley. Some manuscripts added "and Hieropolis" at this point, apparently a copyist's attempt to round out the idea.

There is a great lesson here. Paul was constrained by an intense inward drive and struggle for people he had never even met (cf. "the daily pressure upon me of concern for all the churches," 2 Cor. 11:28). He could have easily concluded, "I've got enough to worry about! They are someone else's affair." But he took not only personal interest in, but personal responsibility for, these followers of Christ. God gives ministry at a number of levels. Certainly there are those we are directly linked with through personal interaction— as were, for example, the Thessalonians to Paul (1 Thess. 1:5-6). But there are also those we are seemingly more indirectly linked to, such as the Colossian and Laodicean believers were to Paul. Epaphras (Col. 1:7; 4:12) was likely the one who had brought the good news of Christ to both communities and the entire Lycus Valley (Col. 4:12). These would have been his direct responsibility.

> **Ministry Maxim**
>
> My responsibility may extend further than my eyesight.

We do not know the precise connection and relationship between Paul and Epaphras. We do know that Epaphras was with Paul here in his first Roman imprisonment and joined in his greetings to Philemon (Philem. 23). Epaphras had come to Paul with word of their "faith in Christ Jesus and the love which [they had] for all the saints" (Col. 1:4). Paul called Epaphras both "a faithful servant of Christ on our behalf" (1:7) and "a bondslave of Jesus Christ" (4:12).

Though Paul apparently entrusted the ministry in the Lycus Valley to Epaphras, he felt a personal responsibility for these Christ followers. The same spiritual cords bound both Epaphras and Paul to these believers. Paul was an apostle in a unique sense and this likely played a significant role in his concern.

We are not as Paul was, yet we all do well to ask whether there are some who are beyond our immediate sphere of contact and influence for whom we are nevertheless responsible before the Lord. We do well to ask how this "struggle" manifested itself in or through Paul. Surely it included prayer (1:3; cf. 4:12), but part of his "struggle," finding its way from inward distress to outward action, also included the writing of this very letter. Writing—personal letter writing in this case—is a legitimate expression of inward spiritual concern, even when directed toward those we have never met.

2:2 that their hearts may be encouraged, having been knit together in love, and attaining to all the wealth that comes from the full assurance of understanding, resulting in a true knowledge of God's mystery, that is, Christ Himself,

Paul continues the sentence begun in verse 1 and running through verse 3. The subordinating conjunction (ἵνα, "that") reveals that the Apostle is about to disclose the purpose for his struggle (v. 1). The verb "may be encouraged" (παρακληθῶσιν) is a compound word, coming from the verb καλέω ("to call") and the prepositional prefix παρὰ ("beside"). The bare combination might mean "to call alongside." It appears in all of the Apostle's letters (except Galatians). It has a range of meaning that can swing from the softer sense of "comfort" to the sharper edge of "exhort." It is translated variously according to context by words such as "appeal" (Philem. 9, 10), "comfort" (2 Cor. 1:4, 6), "encourage" (1 Cor. 16:12), "exhort" (1 Cor. 1:10), "implore" (2 Cor. 12:8), and "urge" (Rom. 12:1). The cognate noun, in the masculine singular form, became a title for the Holy Spirit (John 14:16, 26; 15:26; 16:7) and the Lord Jesus Christ (1 John 2:1).

Here the aorist tense of the verb points to a definite time when this encouragement may come to those believers, including the Colossians, whom Paul has never met. The passive voice indicates that this will not arise naturally from within them, but must come from outside of them as acted upon by another. The subjunctive moves this one step away from present reality, but looks to what Paul wishes may be and which he intends to make reality by his labors on their behalf. Paul prays that "their hearts" (αἱ καρδίαι αὐτῶν) may be encouraged. In the NT "heart" (καρδία) describes the seat of the mind (2 Cor. 4:6), emotions (John 16:22), and will (2 Cor. 9:7). The "heart" is the core and center of the individual.

It should not escape us that the Apostle viewed himself as being able to come alongside believers he had never met face-to-face. This he did through his prayers and writing ministry. Who might we come alongside of in similar ways?

How will their hearts be thus encouraged? Through Paul's labors (v. 1), yes. But what goes into actually encouraging a heart? Encouragement requires their "having been knit together" (συμβιβασθέντες). This old verb is the causal form of συμβαίνω ("to bring together").[409] Here, in the passive voice, it means "to be united together."[410] The root verb (βιβάζω) was used, among other things, to describe the most intimate of human acts.[411] The word here is used seven times in the NT. It may describe the body held together by its various sinews (Eph. 4:16; Col. 2:19). It can also be used of logical conclusions based upon inferences (Acts 16:10; 19:33) or arguments (Acts 9:2). Additionally, it can refer to instruction (1 Cor. 2:16). But in Colossians 2:19 it clearly has the meaning "to bring together" and thus likely does here as well.[412] So then the verb points here in a figurative sense to being united or knit together.[413] The participle

> **Ministry Maxim**
>
> Division and discouragement are fertile ground for deception.

is used to indicate the manner in which the encouragement will take place.[414] The aorist tense points to being "knit together" as a definite event. The passive voice indicates that this action will be achieved by another— presumably by God Himself.

Paul has three specific things to say about this being "knit together," one concerning the sphere of its realization and two as to its goal. First, it is to take place "in love" (ἐν ἀγάπῃ). The preposition (ἐν, "in") points to the sphere in which believers are knit together with one another. That sphere is "love" (ἀγάπη). Paul has already praised the Colossian believers' love "for all

---

[409] Liddell, #40389.
[410] Friberg, 361.
[411] Thayer, 595.
[412] Lohse, 80-81.
[413] BAGD, 777.
[414] Rienecker, 571.

the saints" (1:4); a love empowered by the Holy Spirit (1:8). Little wonder since we are now citizens of a kingdom ruled by God's "beloved Son" (1:13)! See our comments on 1:8 for more on this rich word.

This being "knit together" is also (καί, "and") described in two other ways, both of which are introduced by the preposition εἰς. Whereas ἐν indicated the sphere in which believers are "knit together," εἰς points to the goal or purpose of their being "knit together."[415]

The first goal is "to all the wealth that comes from the full assurance of understanding" (εἰς πᾶν πλοῦτος τῆς πληροφορίας τῆς συνέσεως). The word "wealth" (πλοῦτος) corresponds to its usage in 1:27, revealing the second level of the chiastic arrangement of these verses. It is used here, as in 1:27, to speak figuratively of a wealth or abundance of something.[416] That "something" is designated by a genitive (τῆς πληροφορίας, "the full assurance") which in turn is qualified by a second genitive: "of understanding" (τῆς συνέσεως). The former is a descriptive genitive, i.e., "the wealth consists" of this "full assurance."[417] The word means either "full assurance," "complete certainty," "conviction," or "fullness," "abundance."[418] English versions that follow the former include ESV, NASU, NET, NKJV, while those that follow the latter include NIV ("complete understanding"), and NLT ("complete confidence").

The second genitive (τῆς συνέσεως, "of understanding") is probably a subjective genitive, meaning that the "full assurance" is a result of possessing the "understanding."[419] A possible translation is "a wealth of assurance, such as understanding brings."[420] This latter noun is a compound ("with", σύν and "bring," εἰμί) and is used to describe the coming or sending together of two things. It is used to describe the union of two rivers that flow together.[421] Thus it "refers to putting together the facts and information and drawing conclusions and seeing relationships."[422] Paul prays and labors in ministry because he knows that such understanding is the fount of a believer's deep assurance.

---

415 Robertson, *Word Pictures*, 4:487-488.
416 BAGD, 674.
417 Rienecker, 571.
418 BAGD, 670; Thayer, 517.
419 Harris, 81.
420 BAGD, 670.
421 Friberg, 366.
422 Rienecker, 566.

Paul has already indicated how he prays that this will become a reality for the Colossian believers (Col. 1:9-10). And this, he believes, can be possessed in "all" (πᾶν) its possible fullness. Note the alliteration which Paul uses in the Greek (πᾶν πλοῦτος τῆς πληροφορίας), which is another way the Apostle identifies his emphasis upon these points. "Paul is again piling up words in order to hammer home the truth that Christ, and Christ alone, is the source of every conceivable bit of spiritual knowledge worth having."[423]

The second goal (εἰς) of being "knit together" is to be "in a true knowledge of God's mystery" (εἰς ἐπίγνωσιν τοῦ μυστηρίου τοῦ θεοῦ). The noun "true knowledge" (ἐπίγνωσιν) is a compound word (ἐπὶ, "upon" and γνῶσις, "knowledge") which intensifies the root and points to fullness, depth, and completeness of knowledge. Paul used the cognate verb in 1:6 and this same noun in 1:9, 10 (where Paul also spoke of his prayers for the realization of this knowledge in the Colossian believers' lives). As there, Paul may be using the word intentionally set as a barb against the false teacher(s) who claimed a corner on the truth (2:4, 8, 18).

Whereas in 1:9 the knowledge was "of His will" and in 1:10 it was "of God," here it is knowledge "of God's mystery" (τοῦ μυστηρίου τοῦ θεοῦ) which the Apostle has in view. This is another clue into Paul's chiastic arrangement of these verses. The genitive (τοῦ θεοῦ, "of God") is possessive and indicates that this mystery belongs to God. Paul uses μυστήριον ("mystery") in 1:26 and 27 (see the chiastic depiction under 1:24). This "mystery" is "Christ Himself" (Χριστοῦ). The abrupt nature of the Greek syntax is awkward in English and has led to a number of similar, though distinct, renderings in our versions: "which is Christ" (ESV), "namely Christ" (NET), "namely, Christ" (NIV), "that is, Christ himself" (NRSV). There are at least fifteen variants in the Greek manuscripts, probably the result of copyists' attempts to "correct" a difficult text. This is behind the KJV's "and of the Father, and of Christ." "Even though the external support for the wording τοῦ θεοῦ Χριστοῦ is hardly overwhelming, it clearly best explains the rise of the other readings and should thus be regarded as authentic."[424]

---

[423] Moo, 167.
[424] NET Bible; cf. O'Brien, 94-95.

2:3 in whom are hidden all the treasures of wisdom and knowledge.

The sentence continues with Paul now describing further the singular person of Christ just set before us as God's mystery (v. 2). Paul says it is Christ "in

> **Ministry Maxim**
>
> God's wisdom is a treasure hidden in a mystery revealed in Scripture.

whom are hidden all the treasures of wisdom and knowledge" (ἐν ᾧ εἰσιν πάντες οἱ θησαυροὶ τῆς σοφίας καὶ γνώσεως ἀπόκρυφοι). The relative pronoun (ᾧ) connects back to "Christ," not to the "mystery" (v. 2). Thus "whom" is the correct translation rather than "which."[425] When Paul speaks of "the treasures" (οἱ θησαυροι), he employs a noun which can speak of a place or container in which valuables are held, a treasure box (Matt. 2:11). We derive our word *thesaurus* from this noun.[426] It can also, as here, speak of the treasure itself (cf. also 2 Cor. 4:7).

These "treasures" are identified as "wisdom and knowledge" (τῆς σοφίας καὶ γνώσεως). Note the definite article making specific and definite that wisdom and knowledge which are intended—that true wisdom and knowledge which is above all that claims to be wisdom and knowledge. The single definite article serves both nouns. For the former word see our comments on 1:9 (where it is paired with a word different than its mate here) and 28 (and later at 2:23; 3:16; 4:5). The latter noun is used only here in Colossians. The cognate verb is the root word of "true knowledge" (ἐπίγνωσιν) in verse 2 (also used in 1:9, 10; 2:2; 3:10) and is found in its uncompounded form in 1:27; 4:7, 8, and 9.

These two words lay bare Paul's dependence upon the rich wisdom teaching of Israel. Note especially the repetition of key words here from the LXX of Proverbs 2:1-8.[427] They were also likely key words used by the false teacher(s) to speak of what he believed he could offer above and beyond Christ. The Apostle employs the words here, turning them back upon the false teacher(s) and robbing him of the ground he hoped to claim for his cause. Indeed, those who are in Christ already have in Him these treasures

---

[425] Moo, 169.
[426] Robertson, *Word Pictures*, 4:488.
[427] Cf. Moo, 170.

personally (ἐν ᾧ, "in whom"), presently (εἰσιν, "are"), and thoroughly and comprehensively (πάντες, "all").

Yet these treasures are "hidden" (ἀπόκρυφοι) in Christ. The adjective is found only two other times in the NT (Mark 4:22; Luke 8:17). The word should not be linked directly to the verb "are" (εἰσιν), as is the case in the NASU ("are hidden"). Its placement at the end of the sentence suggests rather that it should be viewed as an emphatic secondary predicate ("in whom are all the treasures of wisdom and knowledge, hidden").[428]

Christ Himself was a mystery for long ages (v. 2) and now these treasures are hidden in Him. Thus it might be legitimate to say, by slightly amending Winston Churchill's famous quote regarding the Jewish race, that God's wisdom and knowledge are riches hidden in a mystery revealed in Scripture. But now the secret is out; the treasury doors have been thrown open! The wealth of wisdom and knowledge is available to all who will bow in humble repentance to the person of Jesus Christ. Yet they are hidden from those without the eyes of faith (2 Cor. 4:4). The false teacher(s) who was offering secret, hidden wisdom only to the initiated was in fact blinded himself to the true wisdom and knowledge of God because of his failure to rightly exalt Christ and submit to Him. What he failed to realize is that a full knowledge of Christ leads to the discovery of all knowledge and wisdom.

So in the face of the world's seducing lies which claim new and as yet undiscovered wisdom and knowledge, God says that the answer for the believer is not "new," but "old." Not wider, but deeper. The answer is not in discovering something novel, but in seeing more thoroughly and accurately the One already present. As believers we need not strive to obtain something we don't yet have, but to understand more deeply what we already possess in Christ.

Thus to summarize the Apostle's thoughts in verses 1-3, he labored that believers he had never met might be encouraged. The manner in which he saw them being encouraged is through being "knit together" in unity. This takes place in the sphere of love and with the goal of understanding and knowing Christ who is the repository of all God's wisdom and knowledge.

---

[428] Vincent, *Word Studies*, 3:483.

Digging Deeper:

1. For whom may you be responsible before the Lord, though you have never personally met them?

2. How might a ministry of writing from your own hand serve to build up others in Christ?

3. How do loving relationships factor into one's knowledge of Christ?

4. Practically speaking, how does knowing Christ unlock the treasures of wisdom and knowledge for people today?

2:4 I say this so that no one will delude you with persuasive argument.

The Apostle now adds a brief explanatory statement. "I say this" (Τοῦτο λέγω) probably refers to the previous sentence, which runs from verse 1 to verse 3.[429] Since this sentence is, however, a personalized development of the same line of thought set forth more generally in 1:24-29, it is likely that the whole line of thought from 1:24 onward forms the background. Paul has set forth the nature and objective of his ministry generally (1:24-29) and now is setting it forth specifically with regard to the Colossians (2:1-3) with a purpose (ἵνα, "so that") in mind. The heart of it, however, is the all-encompassing sufficiency of Jesus Christ as the mystery of God now revealed (1:27; 2:2-3).[430]

> **Ministry Maxim**
>
> The truth is self-attesting while deception requires pressure to be persuasive.

That purpose is that "no one will delude you" (μηδεὶς ὑμᾶς παραλογίζηται). Now for the first time in this letter there is a negative note sounded, and we become aware overtly that danger has crept up upon the Colossian believers. Note the singular form of the indefinite pronoun (μηδεὶς, "no *one*," emphasis added).[431] The verb (παραλογίζηται, "will

---

[429] Cf. O'Brien, 97.

[430] Harris, 86.

[431] Is there one singular false teacher at work in Colossae? Cf. our comments at verse 8 and our Introduction under "Occasion: What Circumstances Gave Rise to the Writing of this Epistle?"

delude") is a compound, made up of παρά ("beside") and λογίζομαι ("to think/reason"). The preposition in compound "has the idea of counting 'beside' or counting 'aside' w[ith] the idea of 'miscalculating.'"[432] It means then to "delude," "deceive," or "lead astray." It has the sense of "to cheat by false reckoning, to deceive by false reasoning."[433] The word is found elsewhere in the NT only in James 1:22. The present tense points to a present and ongoing possibility. The subjunctive mood is used in combination with ἵνα to make this a purpose clause.

This delusion is marketed "with persuasive argument" (ἐν πιθανολογίᾳ). The preposition (ἐν) points to the means by which the delusion takes place. The noun (πιθανολογίᾳ, "persuasive argument") is a compound made up of πιθανός ("persuasive") and λόγος ("word, argument, speech").[434] It refers to "persuasive speech" or "the art of persuasion."[435] It is used in a negative sense here, its only occurrence in the NT. It is thus "speech, adapted to persuade, then speciously leading astray."[436] "The terminology used here is practically equivalent to our English expression, 'to talk someone into something.'"[437] Indeed, Plato associates it with "popular oratory" as opposed to "cogent proof."[438] As Moo aptly puts it, it is easy for believers to "be led astray by high-flown rhetoric (or, in our day, by 'multimedia presentations')" rather than being grounded in the "cogent proof" of Christ's all-sufficiency and exclusivity.[439] Indeed, the power of the true gospel is "not in persuasive words of wisdom, but in demonstration of the Spirit and of power" (1 Cor. 2:4). By choosing this verb, Paul artfully pulls back the veil on Oz and allows the reader to peer in on the marketing technique the false teacher(s) was employing in Colossae.

---

[432] Rienecker, 572.
[433] Robertson, *Word Pictures*, 4:488.
[434] Harris, 86.
[435] BAGD, 657.
[436] Robertson, *Word Pictures*, 4:488.
[437] Rienecker, 572.
[438] BAGD, 657; Dunn, 133; Moo, 172.
[439] Moo, 172.

2:5 For even though I am absent in body, nevertheless I am with you in spirit, rejoicing to see your good discipline and the stability of your faith in Christ.

Paul designates the reason (γὰρ, "For") why he feels at liberty to issue the warning of verse 4.[440] In doing so the Apostle begins with a concession (εἰ ... καὶ, "even though"). The combination of the conditional particle εἰ and the conjunction καὶ, forms a first-class conditional statement with concessive force.

The concession the Apostle makes is that "I am absent in body" (τῇ σαρκὶ ἄπειμι). The verb is one used often by Paul in his correspondence with churches during one of his absences (1 Cor. 5:3; 2 Cor. 10:1, 11; 13:2, 10; Phil. 1:27). It is a compound word whose parts tell well its meaning: ἀπό ("away from") and εἰμι ("to be").[441] The present tense signals what was the case at the time of Paul's writing. It is worthy of note that Paul used the same word to describe his absence from churches which he had personally founded or visited and from this church which he had neither founded nor visited. His love and concern for them was the same.

The use of σάρξ ("body") harkens back to its use in 1:24 and signals the rounding out of the chiastic arrangement begun there (see comments there and on 2:1). In his "flesh" Paul did his part in completing the sufferings of Christ for His body the church (1:24), and, though absent in the flesh (2:5) from the Colossian believers, he continued striving for their firmness and maturity in the faith.

But in marked contrast (ἀλλὰ, "nevertheless") to his bodily absence, Paul could say "I am with you" (σὺν ὑμῖν εἰμι). His presence, however, was "in spirit" (τῷ πνεύματι). This exact phrase is used in various connections. Paul uses it to speak of the Holy Spirit (Rom. 8:16; Eph. 1:13), a person's personal spirit (Rom. 1:9; 1 Cor. 7:34), and the nature of a person's attitude or inward disposition (Rom. 12:11). The idea here is very similar to that in 1 Corinthians 5:3-4 (cf. also 1 Thess. 2:17).

Is Paul referring to some metaphysical, other-dimensional reality in which he could in his spirit transcend space and actually in some sense be

---

[440] Rienecker, 572.
[441] Friberg, 62.

present with these people? It seems unlikely that Paul is describing an "out of body" experience. Yet the Apostle seems (especially in 1 Cor. 5:3-4) to intend something more than a weak "my thoughts are with you." Perhaps O'Brien (following Best's lead) comes closest to the truth when he links this to their being made one Body in Christ[442], something actualized by the Spirit of God (cf. 1 Cor. 12:12-13; Eph 4:3-5). Thus in a true, though spiritual, sense, Paul is

> **Ministry Maxim**
>
> Because believers are bound together by the Spirit, we can find joy in those we've never personally met.

"with" them—not in an out-of-body state, but truly bound by one Spirit with them into one Body.

The Apostle now employs two present-tense participles to speak to his inward state as he contemplates the Colossians. The two participles are joined by the coordinating conjunction καὶ. The KJV holds forth this coordinate relationship most clearly: "joying and beholding" (χαίρων καὶ βλέπων). Perhaps this is the simplest and most straightforward way to understand the relationship.[443] However, many commentators along with most English translations, rather than holding the two participles in parallel relationship, believe it more fitting to view the second participle as indicating reason— the rejoicing is because he sees.[444] Most English translations, as here in the NASU, render the second participle as an infinitive which qualifies the first participle ("rejoicing to see") in an attempt to give the sense in English. The participles describe the circumstances which accompany Paul's spiritual presence with the Colossians.[445] Paul again is surely using "see" (βλέπων) in a metaphorical sense, not claiming that he possesses some kind of "spiritual sight" which allows him to peer in on the Colossians over the miles that separate them.

What the Apostle sees in the Colossians and which creates such joy within him is twofold. First it is "your good discipline" (ὑμῶν τὴν τάξιν). The personal pronoun is placed before the noun for emphasis—Paul is concerned about the Colossians personally.[446] The noun spoke of the ordered

---

[442] O'Brien, 98.

[443] Abbott, 243; Wright, 96.

[444] BAGD, 392, 873; Harris, 87; Lohse, 83-84; Moo, 174; O'Brien, 98-99.

[445] Harris, 87.

[446] Abbott, 243.

arrangement by which priests would serve their duty in the Temple service (Luke 1:8). It spoke then also of a "distinctive class characterized by fixed appointment and position *kind, type, order.*"[447] In this way it is used repeatedly in Hebrews to speak of "the order of Melchizedek" (Heb. 5:6, 10; 6:20; 7:11, 17) and once of "the order of Aaron" (Heb. 7:11). In Paul's only two uses of the word he seems to apply it to behavior (1 Cor. 14:40) or belief (Col. 2:5) which is appropriately regimented, well-regulated, and orderly. Some see here hints of military imagery—orderly ranks of soldiers.[448] Soldiers stood in a sharp, clear, regimented line, refusing to break rank with one another even in the face of an enemy onslaught. So too here the Colossians were standing shoulder-to-shoulder against the falsehood being marketed by the false teacher(s). Others, however, doubt this military background for the word.[449]

The second (καὶ, "and") quality which Paul sees and rejoices over is "the stability of your faith in Christ" (τὸ στερέωμα τῆς εἰς Χριστὸν πίστεως ὑμῶν). The noun "the stability" (τὸ στερέωμα) is used only here in the NT. It speaks of what is firm, hard, or solid.[450] Here too some see a military metaphor ("a solid front")[451] while others do not.[452] While both words can carry this military imagery, they are often used in a wider nontechnical sense, and it is the immediate context which is determinative. Given Paul's impending turn toward confronting the false teaching (2:8, 16-23) it is not unlikely that he has something of this military imagery in mind as he writes these words.

This solidity and firmness is what characterized their faith (τῆς ... πίστεως ὑμῶν, "your faith"). Though the noun is found only here in the NT, the cognate verb is used three times (Acts 3:7, 16; 16:5). In the first two instances it describes the feet and ankles of a lame man that are made firm. This literal usage is a good illustration of the figurative sense as attached to faith both here and in Acts 16:5. The genitive may be subjective—a firmness created by their faith. Or it may be possessive—a firmness that belongs to their faith.[453] In either case it is faith that found its

---

[447] Friberg, 374.

[448] Dunn, 135; Lightfoot, 174; Martin, 76-77; Rienecker, 572; Robertson, *Word Pictures*, 4:489.

[449] Abbott, 243; Eadie, 122, Hendriksen, 107; Lohse, 84; O'Brien, 99.

[450] Rienecker, 572.

[451] Dunn, 135; Martin, 76-77; Rienecker, 572; Robertson, *Word Pictures*, 4:489.

[452] Abbott, 243; Hendriksen, 107; Lohse, 84.

[453] Moo, 174.

object "in Christ" (εἰς Χριστὸν). Their faith was directed toward (εἰς, "in") Christ alone (cf. 1:15-20).[454] Herein is its solidity and firmness.

Paul's commendation of and confidence in the faith of the Colossians in this verse may seem to stand in opposition to the more general urgency with which he seems to deal with the false teaching throughout the letter. However, Paul has already praised the Colossian believers for their faith (1:3-8). He is delighted by what he knows of their faith, but continues to urge them ever forward in that faith in the face of a very real threat. As Wink points out, "The epistle is a vaccination against heresy, not an antibiotic for those already afflicted."[455]

Digging Deeper:

1. In what ways are believers today in danger of being deluded "with persuasive argument" (v. 4)?
2. Who is doing the deluding and persuading today?
3. Will the culprit always be aware that is what they are doing? Or can it be done unwittingly?
4. In what sense can believers "be with" other believers "in spirit," though separated by distance?
5. In practical terms, what does "good discipline and stability" of faith look like in God's people today?

2:6 Therefore as you have received Christ Jesus the Lord, so walk in Him,

Paul here transitions and begins a new section of his epistle (running through 2:15). The conjunction οὖν ("Therefore") signals a logical, inferential relationship. It builds on what has just been said, but takes it forward a new step. Indeed, verses 6-7 seem to gather up the whole of the introduction (1:3-2:5) and transition to the main body of the letter (2:6-4:6). More specifically in view of the "good discipline and stability"

---

[454] Lohse, 84; O'Brien, 99.
[455] Quoted by Moo, 175.

of their faith (v. 5), Paul now moves on to make an exhortation regarding their continued advance along those lines.

The main verb of this sentence, which runs through verse 7, is the imperative "walk" (περιπατεῖτε). This is the first imperative found in the letter and opens the way for a flurry of such commands in the main body of the letter (2:6-4:6).[456] The verb is one frequently used to view the unfolding of one's life step-by-step (i.e., how one conducts his life; cf. "live," NET, NIV, NRSV). Paul is especially fond of the word and has already thus used it in 1:10 and will again in 3:7 and 4:5. The present tense demands action (presumably already begun) in an ongoing and unending fashion into the future.

This walk is to be "as you have received Christ Jesus the Lord" ('Ὡς ... παρελάβετε τὸν Χριστὸν Ἰησοῦν τὸν κύριον). Paul uses Ὡς ("as") to signal that what follows is a comparison. Paul uses the verb παραλαμβάνω ("have received") most often to describe the reception of the gospel message itself (1 Cor. 11:23; 15:1, 3; Gal. 1:9, 12; 1 Thess. 2:13), but can also use it to refer to receiving exhortation about how to live out the gospel (1 Thess. 4:1) and "the tradition" (2 Thess. 3:6) associated with it. In Jewish circles it was used to describe the transmission of rabbinical traditions from teacher to disciple.

Only here does Paul speak about receiving "Christ Jesus" (τὸν Χριστὸν Ἰησοῦν) Himself. The aorist tense points to a definite act and views their reception of Christ as a crisis of faith when they turned from darkness to light. The word underscores the divine initiative in salvation—it is given by the Lord and then "received" by the individual. Apart from God's initiative there would be nothing to receive and no ability to receive on the part of the individual.

"Christ Jesus" (τὸν Χριστὸν Ἰησοῦν) and "the Lord" (τὸν κύριον) are marked out by a double accusative. What they received is a person: Christ Jesus, the Lord. Note that a single definite article governs both. He is first designated by His office as Messiah (τὸν Χριστὸν, note the definite article: "*the* Christ") and then by His personal name (Ἰησοῦν, "Jesus"). He is then set forth as to His station and supremacy as "the Lord" (τὸν κύριον, again, note the definite article: "*the* Lord").

---

[456] Moo, 175.

This particular formula is found nowhere else in the NT. It is not that what it teaches is novel, but that the unique expression itself is never fashioned this way again in the pages of the NT. Paul crafts this both to strike a blow against the false teacher(s) (emphasizing the historical person of Jesus, His divinely appointed office as Messiah, and His absolute supremacy and deity as "the Lord") and to once again set forth the proper Christocentric orientation of the Christian life which has been so richly introduced in the letter's

> **Ministry Maxim**
>
> One's introduction to Christ is the pattern for one's continuation in Christ.

extended introduction (e.g., 1:15-20, 27, 28; 2:2). Of course the Colossians did not receive Christ directly through the teaching of Paul, but through that of Epaphras (1:7; 2:1).

Perhaps by "as you have received Christ Jesus the Lord," Paul focuses on the message itself—the truth, the doctrine of the genuine gospel. In that case they must continue in the truth as it is in Jesus and not be turned aside to novelties and falsehoods by the false teacher(s). On the other hand, perhaps he refers to the way in which they received the Lord. That is clearly by faith (v. 5). It is through repentance and humility (1:13). It is in recognizing and acknowledging the Person of Jesus as God's appointed Messiah ("Christ"), the Savior. And it is by bowing to Him as "the Lord." This is not required in simply a one-time act, but as an ongoing frame of reference for all of life as it continues to unfold before us. This sets the trajectory and gait of believers for the rest of their journey.

This walk is said to be "in Him" (ἐν αὐτῷ). The phrase is actually positioned in front of the imperative, giving it special emphasis. The antecedent of the pronoun is clearly the theologically loaded designation "Christ Jesus the Lord." The preposition (ἐν, "in") probably marks out the sphere in which the believer's life is to be carried out.

This simple phrase (ἐν αὐτῷ) is used extensively in this letter to set forth dramatic and profound truths. It was "in Him" (lit; "by Him," NASU) that all things were created (1:16). It is "in Him" that all things hold together (1:17). The Father was pleased to have all His divine fullness dwell "in Him" (1:19). Indeed, it is "in Him" that "all the fullness of Deity dwells in bodily form" (2:9)! With the next swipe of his pen the Apostle will say it is "in

Him" that each child of God has "been made complete" (2:10). Satan and all demonic powers have been defeated "in Him" (2:15; lit.; "through Him," NASU). Now consider that we are able and responsible to make our way step by step through this life "in Him"! What is this journey to which we have been called? What honor! What responsibility! What possibilities!

2:7 having been firmly rooted and now being built up in Him and established in your faith, just as you were instructed, and overflowing with gratitude.

The sentence continues as four participles are used to modify the imperative "walk" (περιπατεῖτε, v. 6). These participles enlarge upon what the Apostle meant by his command (see Col. 1:10-12 where Paul followed this same verb with four participles). They likely function as adverbial participles of attendant circumstances—that is to say they describe not so much the means of the Christian's "walk," but typical characteristics of such a "walk."[457] Yet the influence of the imperative probably bleeds into the action of the participles, giving them thrust and power. As the Apostle sometimes does, he mixes his metaphors here, yet his intent is clear.

The first three participles introduce significant metaphors.[458] The first is a *horticultural* metaphor: "having been firmly rooted" (ἐρριζωμένοι). The word is found only here and in Ephesians 3:17 in the NT (where it combined with a word from the architectural world, as it is here; cf. also 1 Cor. 3:6, 9, 10). The word is also rich in imagery throughout its extrascriptural usages. It speaks of sending down roots, or in the passive as here, of being rooted or taking root. The passive voice probably points to God as the active agent in the action. The perfect tense points to action that has taken place in the past and which has brought about an abiding state in the present.

The prepositional phrase "in Him" (ἐν αὐτῷ) probably should be connected to both this participle and the next. In Ephesians 3:17 it is "in love" that one is to be "rooted and grounded." Here it is Christ Himself who is the "soil" in which they have been rooted. Recall the rich trove of truth here in Colossians conveyed through this simple prepositional phrase (ἐν αὐτῷ, see above under v. 6), then contemplate the imagery here again.

---

[457] Harris, 89.
[458] NET Bible.

Like a giant redwood, the believers in Colossae had their roots sunk deep into Christ—the embodiment of all God's deity, the great mystery of God—and were firmly planted there "in Him."

To this horticultural imagery Paul adds (καὶ, "and") a second, *architectural* metaphor: "being built up" (ἐποικοδομούμενοι). The word is a favorite of Paul (six of seven NT usages). In all his other usages he links it with building upon a foundation (1 Cor. 3:10 [twice], 12, 14; Eph. 2:20). Sometimes he speaks of that foundation as being "the apostles and prophets" with Christ as the cornerstone (Eph. 2:20), but more often as the foundation being Christ Jesus Himself (1 Cor. 3:10-14). Here it is the latter that is in mind, as signified by "in Him" (ἐν αὐτῷ). The present tense pictures an ongoing construction process in the believer's life. Having been firmly rooted (downward), now each one must continue to be built up (the prefix ἐπι- may indicate upward building) in Christ.[459] The passive voice points once again to God the great builder of all things as the active agent in the building process. Though the obedient cooperation of the believer is necessary, it is only in constant dependence upon God that their continued life is possible.

> **Ministry Maxim**
>
> Discontent and ingratitude make fertile soil for false teaching to put down roots.

To the first two metaphors Paul now adds (καὶ, "and") a third from the *legal* world: "established" (βεβαιούμενοι). The word could be used to describe what is legally guaranteed.[460] It thus sometimes had the sense of "guarantee" or "validate."[461] This background may still be evident in most NT usages where it means "to confirm." In Mark 16:20, for example, it speaks of miracles which confirm or validate (and thus "establish") the message preached by the Apostles. In Romans 15:8 we read that "Christ has become a servant to the circumcision on behalf of the truth of God to confirm [validate, and thus establish as true and viable] the promises given to the fathers." It was the visible and outward evidences of the Corinthians' faith that confirmed the testimony of Christ they proclaimed (1 Cor. 1:6). God would continue to produce this in and through them and thus confirm, establish,

---

[459] Harris, 90.
[460] Little Kittel, 103.
[461] Moo, 181.

and validate them as His own until the very end (1:8). It was through those who first heard Christ speak the message that it was confirmed and validated (and thus established as true) to those who later heard this same message (Heb. 2:3). Consider also the use of the cognate noun (Phil. 1:7; Heb. 6:16) and adjective (Heb. 2:2).

So in what sense does it here have the meaning "establish" or "strengthen"?[462] The present tense conveys the continual nature of the action intended. The passive voice once again implies divine involvement. This strengthening or establishing is "in your faith" (τῇ πίστει). The word could be understood in the subjective sense of personal trust. This seems to be the way the NASU understands the word (cf. also the NET, NLT). In this case the definite article is seen as possessive in meaning ("your").

It seems more likely, however, that here it carries the objective sense, referring to the body of truth/doctrine which makes up the gospel ("in the faith," ESV, NKJV, NIV, NRSV).[463] The definite article would thus be understood, not as indicative of possession, but as specifying the truth in mind. The dative could be understood either instrumentally ("by") or as a locative ("in").[464] Here the latter seems the more likely.

Thus the idea here is that of the Colossian believers being validated or confirmed (and thus "established") as truly "in the faith." How did this happen? Presumably as they matured and were built up in Christ, there were obvious changes to their lives and evident traces of their new character and of their obedience to a new Master, Christ. Through these transformational changes, God confirmed to the believers themselves and to others around them that they were truly "in the faith."

Now the Apostle adds, "just as you were instructed" (καθὼς ἐδιδάχθητε). Does this apply just to the third of these participial clauses or to all three? Either is possible, but it seems best here to read it with all three in mind. Epaphras was no doubt the one who had done the instructing (1:7). He surely taught them not simply the doctrines (the last of the three participial phrases), but how to "walk" in those doctrines (which brings in all three participial phrases).

---

[462] BAGD, 138.

[463] Rienecker, 573.

[464] Harris, 90.

The Apostle now adds the fourth participle, which does not convey as powerful a metaphor, but which is just as important: "overflowing with gratitude" (περισσεύοντες ἐν εὐχαριστίᾳ). The participle (περισσεύοντες, "overflowing") means to abound or overflow. Alternatively it may have the meaning of "excelling."[465] The present tense underscores the continual nature of the action. They are to abound, overflow, or excel "in thanksgiving" (ἐν εὐχαριστίᾳ). The noun and its associated word group carry the idea of not merely an attitude of gratitude, but an active expression of that attitude in the giving of thanks.[466] The preposition (ἐν, "in") may describe the sphere in which they are to "abound" or "overflow."

A thankful heart is taken up with what it has, not what it does not have. Falsehoods based on empty promises gain no hearing with the grateful person. Discontent and ingratitude make fertile soil for false teaching to put down roots. It is not without purpose that thankfulness is a centerpiece of this epistle (1:3, 12ff.; 2:7; 3:15, 16, 17; 4:2). Worship—both corporate and private—is a safeguard and weapon against error.

Some manuscripts add prepositional phrases here (either "in it" or "in him"). Both seem to be unnecessary additions to the original text.

Digging Deeper:

1. In what sense does our reception of Christ at the beginning of our Christian life point the way for our continued growth in the Christian life (v. 6)?
2. In what way can verses 6-7 become a road map for a healthy Christian life?
3. How does active gratitude protect us from vulnerability to falsehood?

---

[465] BAGD, 651.
[466] O'Brien, 108.

2:8 See to it that no one takes you captive through philosophy and empty deception, according to the tradition of men, according to the elementary principles of the world, rather than according to Christ.

Beginning here the Apostle attacks more directly the falsehoods being peddled in Colossae (2:8-23) before turning more positively to exhort the believers regarding how to live in the fullness of Christ (3:1ff.). Paul begins here a long and complex sentence that in the Greek text runs, at least in some editions, through verse 15.

The Apostle opens with a command to "See to it" (Βλέπετε). The first imperative of the letter demanded that we "walk" (v. 6) and to this is now added the command to "See"! Watching and walking are always good in combination! Two simple imperatives of discipleship—"come, follow Me" (Matt. 19:21) and "See to it that no one misleads you" (Matt 24:4)—are now applied to a specific people in a particular place with precise challenges.

The present active imperative used here places responsibility squarely upon the Colossian believers. It is a continuous watchfulness to which Paul calls them. The intent of the command might be brought out by any of several expressions in English such as "watch out," "beware," "look out," or "see to it," all capturing the urgency of Paul's command.

They are to see to it that "no one takes you captive" (μή τις ὑμᾶς ἔσται ὁ συλαγωγῶν). The construction Βλέπετε μή usually is followed by a subjunctive, but here we meet the future indicative (ἔσται). Kent remarks, "The difference may emphasize that the danger is viewed as real, not merely a hypothetical possibility."[467] The expression is somewhat awkward. The indefinite pronoun (τις, "one") is singular, indicating that Paul may have just one person in mind, perhaps some individual of charismatic personality that is the front man for falsehood in Colossae (cf. v. 16).[468] The use of the personal pronoun in the plural form ("you," ὑμᾶς) indicates that not one believer is exempt from the command.

---

[467] Kent, 85.

[468] "It appears to point to some particular person whom the apostle has in view but does not wish to name," Abbott, 246. See our Introduction under "Occasion: What Circumstances Gave Rise to the Writing of This Epistle?"

The identity of this deceiver is made known through the use of a participle with the definite article (ὁ συλαγωγῶν). He is the one "who takes you captive." The word is used only here in the NT. It is a compound word comprised of σύλη ("booty," "spoil") and ἄγω ("to carry"). It came to describe carrying off booty or spoils from battle or a raid. But it extended out over time to describe more generally being taken captive.[469] The idea here is that "of carrying someone away fr[om] the truth and into the slavery of error."[470] The singular forms of the participle and verb along with the singular indefinite pronoun ("one," τις) may further indicate that there was a definite individual who was at the head of this false teaching in Colossae.[471] The Colossian Christians would make a nice "prize" for the trophy case of some false teacher.

Paul now specifies the means (διά, "through") of this false teacher's trickery: "philosophy and empty deceit" (τῆς φιλοσοφίας καὶ κενῆς ἀπάτης). The word "philosophy" (φιλοσοφίας) is a compound whose parts mean "love of wisdom." It is found only here in the NT and clearly in this case with a negative connotation, though it is by itself a neutral word. It is not philosophy proper that Paul is denouncing here, but the specific form of error being peddled in Colossae at that time. That is spelled out more clearly in the remainder of this chapter, but includes claims to private and special insight into divine things, worship of angels, along with legalistic and ascetic practices (vv. 16, 18, 20-23). This syncretistic amalgam from various streams of thought and religion probably passed itself off as a "philosophy," and Paul may be using their very word to denounce them.[472]

Paul makes this first noun definite by use of the article. If this definite article is intended to govern both nouns, it is likely that the second noun and its adjective are intended as a hendiadys—meaning the second noun and adjective are intended to expand and expound upon the meaning of the first noun. This would make the conjunction (καί, "and") epexegetical (i.e., "the philosophy, which amounts to empty deceit"). In this case the whole

---

[469] Thayer, 594.

[470] BAGD, 776.

[471] "It points at some known person," Alford, 3:217; "There was some one outstanding leader who was doing most of the damage in leading the people astray," Robertson, *Word Pictures*, 4:490; contra, Moo, 185.

[472] Little Kittel, 1272.

phrase might be translated something like "empty, deceitful philosophy"[473] (cf. "hollow and deceptive philosophy," NIV). The noun "deceit" (ἀπάτης) describes deception with a hint of seduction involved (cf. "the deceitfulness of wealth," Matt. 13:22; Mark 4:19). It is deceit in order to lead away. This deceit is "empty" (κενῆς). The adjective can have the literal meaning of "empty-handed" (Mark 12:3; Luke 1:53; 20:10, 11). It also describes what is void of purpose or in vain (Acts 4:25; Phil. 2:16).[474] Thus the philosophy which claims to be *full* of insight and rich with reward is in fact a lie which is *empty, futile,* and *vain.* The deceit seduces with promises of great reward, but leads only to hollow disappointment.

> **Ministry Maxim**
>
> In any age and in any place the basic demands of discipleship are "follow Me" and "keep your eyes open"!

The Apostle now states the flavor of this "philosophy and empty deceit." He does so by three times using the preposition κατὰ ("according to"). The first two uses set forth the spirit of the false teacher's manipulation; the final occurrence makes clear what his efforts are not. First, it is "according to the tradition of men" (κατὰ τὴν παράδοσιν τῶν ἀνθρώπων). When Paul speaks of "the tradition" (τὴν παράδοσιν), he employs a word which he elsewhere uses of both Jewish tradition (Gal. 1:14) and the Christian faith (2 Thess. 2:15; 3:6). It can describe the humanly engineered traditions of Jewish thought as opposed to the Word of God itself (Mark 7:3, 5, 8, 9, 15). The word itself simply describes a giving up or giving over of something and comes to refer to instruction.[475]

In the present case what is passed on has its origin in "men" (τῶν ἀνθρώπων)—it is human and earthly as opposed to divine and heavenly. It identifies the falsehood being propagated in Colossae as a humanly engineered amalgam of ideas, probably picked up by bits and pieces from Jewish, Christian, and pagan religious thought.

Second, it is "according to the elementary principles of the world" (κατὰ τὰ στοιχεῖα τοῦ κόσμου). The word rendered here as "elementary principles" (τὰ στοιχεῖα) at its root describes "what belongs to a basic series

---

[473] NET Bible.
[474] Friberg, 228.
[475] Thayer, 481.

in any field of knowledge; in grammar, the ABCs; in speech, basic sounds; in physics, the four basic elements (earth, air, fire, water); in geometry, the axioms; in philosophy, the givens."[476] In the NT then it is used of the basic elements of physical creation (2 Peter 3:10, 12), elementary religious teachings (Gal. 4:3, 9), and the basics of God's Word (Heb. 5:12). Here it is qualified by the genitive "of the world" (τοῦ κόσμου). It is bound by an orientation limited to the horizontal plane. Paul will use the expression again in verse 20 and say that the believer has "died with Christ to the elementary principles of the world."

The remainder of this chapter seems to indicate that "the elementary principles" would include a combination of legalistic strictures (vv. 11-17), mystic musings about the worship of angels (vv. 18-19), and ascetic practices (vv. 20-23).

Many recent scholars conclude that the phrase refers to spiritual beings, though this meaning is not attested before the third century AD. Since in the ancient world different parts of the physical creation were often believed to have specific spirits associated with them, and since Paul repeatedly lays emphasis on Christ's victory over the spirit powers, and since there was a clear emphasis upon the worship of angels in the false teaching at Colossae (1:16, 20; 2:10, 15, 18), it seems likely that something of this was in Paul's mind as he wrote.[477]

As specific to the problems in Colossae, then, it seems to refer to "humanistic teachings common to Jewish and pagan religions, involving binding traditions, taboos, prohibitions, ordinances, ceremonies, etc., teachings involving either supernatural elemental or animating spirits."[478] Such a meaning, even in Paul's two usages of the word in Galatians (4:3, 9), seems likely given that their freedom in Christ is contrasted with "those which by nature are no gods" (4:8).

Finally, then, Paul adds (καὶ οὐ, "rather than"; lit., "and not") that this means the falsehoods are not "according to Christ" (κατὰ Χριστόν). Moo is right when he says, "In this short phrase the dominant theological teaching of the letter is brought to bear on the central purpose of the letter."[479]

---

[476] Friberg, 357.
[477] Moo, 187-192; O'Brien, 131-132.
[478] Friberg, 357.
[479] Moo, 193.

False teaching is by nature both overly simplistic and ever-increasingly complex. It must by nature evolve in increasing and unbearable complexity. Its internal inconsistencies require constant morphing and changing of its teachings so as to remain tenable on the surface. The Christian faith, however, consists of the "simplicity and purity of devotion to Christ," and it is away from this simple, restful trust that the evil one and those who serve him seek to lure us (2 Cor. 11:3).

2:9 For in Him all the fullness of Deity dwells in bodily form,

Paul now (through all of vv. 9-15) gives the reason (ὅτι, "For," causal) for the warning just sounded (v. 8). In contrast to "rather than according to Christ" (v. 8), Paul now sets forth what is true in Christ.[480] The familiar and meaning-packed expression "in Him" (ἐν αὐτῷ) follows next, being emphatic by being thrust forward (i.e., "in Him and in Him alone").[481] The personal pronoun (αὐτῷ, "Him") finds its antecedent in "Christ," the last word of the previous verse. Paul now builds upon the Christological focus so thoroughly laid down already in the letter (see especially 1:15-20).

What resides "in Him"? It is nothing less than "all the fullness of Deity" (πᾶν τὸ πλήρωμα τῆς θεότητος). The noun "Deity" (τῆς θεότητος) is used only here in the NT. It is used as an abstract noun for θεός ("God"). There is thus a distinction to be made between our word here (θεότης) and the one used in Romans 1:20 (θειότης, "divine nature"). Our word speaks of the divine essence as opposed to simply the attributes of deity. "They were no mere ways of divine glory which gilded Him lighting up His person for a season and w[ith] a splendor not His own; but He was and is absolute and perfect God."[482] The article makes definite that of which Paul is speaking (lit., "*the* Deity").

> **Ministry Maxim**
>
> A few, well-chosen words describe what can be said in human language about the mystery of the Incarnation—the more our words the more likely our error.

This noun and article are in the genitive, qualifying "the fullness" (τὸ πλήρωμα). This same noun has just been used in Colossians 1:19 where

---

480 Ibid.
481 Harris, 99; Johnson, "Beware of Philosophy," 308.
482 Rienecker, 573.

Paul says it was the Father's "good pleasure for all the fullness to dwell in Him." Paul more specifically designates just what this fullness is in our present passage. Once again the article makes definite that of which he speaks ("*the* fullness," emphasis added). It describes the sum total, fullness, or even the superabundance of something.[483] In this case it is the very essence of Deity which resides in its fullness in Jesus Christ.

But Paul's description of Christ is not yet complete, for he makes clear that it is "all" (πᾶν) the fullness of Deity which resides in Jesus Christ. When used with a singular noun that is accompanied by the definite article (as here) it conveys the meaning of "the whole" or "all" of that which it qualifies.[484] Thus it "means 'all the fullness' or 'the entire fullness,' no element of the fullness being excepted."[485] This does not, of course, imply that the Second Person of the Trinity is the only Person in the divine Godhead. It does not mean that the Father and the Spirit do not likewise partake in all the fullness of Deity. There is but one God. God exists eternally in three Persons—each of which share fully in the divine essence. A mystery indeed! Yet Paul's point here is to make certain that his readers understand that Jesus shares fully in that divine essence along with the Father and the Spirit as the one true God.

Yet even here, Paul's statement regarding Christ is not done, for he adds that this fullness is found in Christ "in bodily form" (σωματικῶς). Again this adverb is used only here in the NT (and not in the LXX). Though some want to make it mean "really" or "actually," it seems here to designate what is corporeal, tangible, touchable, and physical.[486] In this way, with a great economy of words, Paul emphasizes both the complete deity and genuine humanity of Jesus Christ. God Himself took to Himself a human body and lived a fully human life on this earth.

Thus notice the ever-expanding and all-encompassing scope of the Apostle's assertion: Jesus Christ possesses "Deity." Yet He possesses not just "Deity," but "*the fullness* of Deity." And it is not just "the fullness of Deity," but "*all* the fullness of Deity." Even this is not the end, for He possesses not just "all the fullness of Deity," but "all the fullness of Deity *in bodily form*"!

---

[483] BAGD, 672.
[484] Ibid., 630.
[485] Harris, 98.
[486] BAGD, 800.

This fullness of Deity "dwells" (κατοικεῖ) in Christ. While this verb appears forty-four times in the NT, only three of those uses are by Paul. Twice here in Colossians he employs it to speak of Deity dwelling in Christ (Col. 1:19; 2:9). The other is a reference to Christ dwelling in us (Eph. 3:17). Paul chose to use, not the simple verb, but its compounded form: κατά ("down") and οἰκέω ("to dwell"). The compound has "the added force of a permanent dwelling."[487] Thus Paul stresses that Deity "has its fixed abode" in Christ.[488] The present tense of the verb indicates that this is an ongoing state. From the moment of conception onward and forever, the fullness of Deity has dwelt continuously in the body of Jesus. Even after His death, resurrection, and glorification, Jesus Christ remains—continuously—the God-man, both fully God and fully man.

Thus with amazing brevity of language and succinctness of expression, the Apostle does away with many of the gravest errors regarding Christ to have arisen over the centuries.

2:10 and in Him you have been made complete, and He is the head over all rule and authority;

As breathtaking as is Paul's statement in verse 9, he is not finished. As defining as the statement of verse 9 is with regard to Christ, so is the statement of verse 10 with regard to what the follower of Christ is "in Him." The coordinating conjunction (καὶ, "and") holds the statements of verses 9 and 10 parallel to one another as independent clauses. This then presents a second part of the reason why the Colossians must beware (v. 8). The first reason is because of who Christ is; the second because of who we are "in Him."

If the verb is taken absolutely the present tense (ἐστὲ) might be rendered *"You are* in Him having been made complete."[489] As such it points to the ongoing and continuous nature of their position "in Him" (ἐν αὐτῷ). But the verb and participle probably should be understood as a periphrastic construction.[490] The plural form of the verb indicates that Paul is addressing the whole of the Colossian church. The familiar "in Him" (ἐν αὐτῷ) points

---

[487] Johnson, "Beware of Philosophy," 308.
[488] Lightfoot, 157, 179.
[489] Ibid., 180.
[490] Harris, 100; Moo, 195; Robertson, *Word Pictures*, 4:491.

again to our union with Christ. The clause is emphatic by being thrust to the front of the whole.

The fact that the Colossians are "in Him" is not the news here; this ground has been well established by the Apostle already. The revelation is that they "have been made complete" (πεπληρωμένοι). This is the verbal cognate of the noun "fullness" used in the previous verse (and in v. 19). The verb form is found also in Colossians 1:9, 25 and 4:17. It seems that in Colossians the noun is used to describe what it true of Christ; the verb what is true of the believer. In the previous verse the noun designated the completeness, totality, or superabundance of the Deity filling Christ. Here the verb describes the state of the believer. The perfect tense points to past action which has been completed and has now brought about an abiding state. The passive voice indicates that God is the active agent. Paul may well have chosen this word group (noun, 1:19; 2:9; verb, 1:9, 25; 2:10; 4:17) for this letter to counter the claims of the false teacher(s) who it seems likely was claiming to offer something fuller and richer than could be found in Christ.

But just what fills the believer? Though the construction (πληρόω + ἐν + the dative of whatever it is that fills) can mean "filled with," here it seems not to mean that we are filled with Christ, but rather it is "in Him" that we are then filled.[491] But filled with what? Perhaps Paul's point is not to point out just what we are filled with, but rather to indicate that because of our union with Christ—who is the fullness of God in human flesh—we have no lack of anything we need, we are brought to utter fullness in every circumstance and find thus God's purposes completed in and through and to us. "In Him they find their needs fully met."[492] To have specified that which fills us would have limited the breadth of the Apostle's statement. Speaking as he does, he broadens the sweep to include everything and anything necessary to being God's people and fulfilling His will in any given moment or circumstance. In union with Christ (who possesses all the fullness of the Godhead) I lack nothing. I possess all that I need and fulfill every requirement God might put upon me.

---

[491] BAGD, 671.
[492] Rienecker, 574.

This is a most sweeping statement. Indeed, this should take our breath away. Yet it is not a novel concept in the NT, but something emphasized

> **Ministry Maxim**
>
> Christology and Sanctification are directly linked—when I disparage Christ, I deprive myself.

repeatedly. "For of His fullness we have all received, and grace upon grace" (John 1:16). Paul prayed for the Ephesian believers "to know the love of Christ which surpasses knowledge, that you may be filled up to all the fullness of God" (Eph. 3:19). He said that we serve Christ's body "until we all attain to the unity of the faith, and of the knowledge of the Son of God, to a mature man, to the measure of the stature which belongs to the fullness of Christ" (Eph. 4:13). The church is Christ's "body, the fullness of Him who fills all in all" (Eph. 1:23).

No one and nothing can arise to prove otherwise, for "He is the head over all rule and authority" (ὅς ἐστιν ἡ κεφαλὴ πάσης ἀρχῆς καὶ ἐξουσίας). The relative pronoun (ὅς) finds its reference in Christ (ἐν αὐτῷ, "in Him" in v. 10a and v. 9 and from there back to Χριστόν, "Christ" in v. 8). The verb (ἐστιν, "is") is in the present tense, indicating what is the current and ongoing nature of things. Christ is "the head" (ἡ κεφαλὴ). Christ has already been called head of the body (1:18), the church, and will be again (2:19). See the discussion on 1:18 for fuller details on this word. It carries the notion of authority over that of which it is the head. In this case it is "over all rule and authority" (πάσης ἀρχῆς καὶ ἐξουσίας). The two nouns are used together again to speak of angelic or demonic beings in Colossians 1:16 and 2:15 (see comments on 1:16 for background on these words). The adjective (πάσης, "all"), when used with anarthrous nouns, means "every" or "all," as in "every kind of."[493] It is an all-encompassing statement, indicating that Christ is the head over *each* individually and *all* collectively. Christ is supreme over all spiritual beings by both creation (1:15-16) and conquest (2:15).[494]

---

[493] Harris, 31.
[494] Harris, 100.

Digging Deeper:

1. How are "philosophy and empty deception" being sold in the marketplace of ideas today? Can you cite modern examples?
2. How would you explain "the elementary principles of the world" to a fifth grader?
3. In what way are failures in our sanctification traceable to failures in our Christology? How do verses 9 and 10 demonstrate this?
4. In what way does "in Him you have been made complete" hold the foundation of freedom for those we counsel? How might you explain and demonstrate this to them?

2:11 and in Him you were also circumcised with a circumcision made without hands, in the removal of the body of the flesh by the circumcision of Christ;

We come now (vv. 11-15) to some of the most difficult and intricate reasoning anywhere in the NT. Much ink has been spilt in an attempt to untie the knots encountered here. We will move forward phrase by phrase to offer our best understanding of what the Apostle intended here.

Paul continues the theme of the believer being "in Him" ('Εν ᾧ) which has dominated his writing (vv. 6, 7, 9, 10). The expression again emphasizes what is true with regard to our union with Christ, which is the emphasis of verses 11 through 13. The same emphasis will continue in verses 12 and 13 by using συν– prefixed words.[495] The relative pronoun (ᾧ) clearly refers to Christ. Next we encounter the conjunction καὶ ("also"). It could be used as a simple connective, but it seems more likely to be used as an adverb ("also") here. This views what follows as what is "also" true of believers "in Him." It means something like "in addition to your completeness in him (v. 10a)."[496]

Paul says that in Christ "you were ... circumcised" (περιετμήθητε). The aorist tense looks back to an event that took place in the past—probably a reference to their conversion (not, or only indirectly, to their baptism as we shall see in due course). The passive voice views God as the active

---

[495] Dunn, 154.
[496] Harris, 101.

agent. Circumcision was widely practiced throughout the ancient world, but it had been owned particularly by the Jewish people since God gave this to Abraham as a sign of His covenant with him and his descendants (Gen. 17:1-14). Some view its mention here as evidence that the false teaching in Colossae was primarily Jewish in nature. Yet the practice is never directly addressed in this letter, as it is, for example, in Galatians. The notion of the believer being circumcised "in" or "with" Christ is without parallel in the NT (though cf. Phil. 3:3; Rom. 2:28-29).[497] O'Brien concludes, "We cannot say with certainty why Paul introduced the circumcision motif at this point."[498]

Paul goes on to explain that what he has in mind is "a circumcision made without hands" (περιτομῇ ἀχειροποιήτῳ). The adjective (ἀχειροποιήτῳ, translated "made without hands") is found only two other times in the NT (Mark 14:58; 2 Cor. 5:1). In both cases the strong negative expression ("made without hands") is used to convey a powerful positive idea ("made by God").[499] This notion is reinforced by the use of the passive voice verbs throughout the paragraph which point to God as the active agent.[500] This only makes sense when we remember that the Apostle is discussing what is true of us in union with Christ Himself. But just what does this mean? It is helpful to remember that such talk was not without precedence. Even in the OT God had begun to consistently set forth the primacy not of the physical act of circumcision in the flesh, but of the "circumcision of the heart" (Deut. 10:16; 30:6; Jer. 4:4; 6:10 ["their ear is uncircumcised," KJV]; 9:26; Ezek. 44:7, 9). It seems clear that the Apostle is calling upon such imagery at the present time. What had been demanded in the Old Covenant has now been accomplished through Christ for everyone in union with Him by grace through faith. In this it seems clear that by "a circumcision made without hands," Paul is referring, metaphorically, to the transition from our old, unregenerate existence to the new life Christ offers.[501] This is confirmed by verse 13 where "the uncircumcision of your flesh" is a metaphorical description of being "dead in your transgressions." Thus, stated positively

---

[497] Moo, 196.
[498] O'Brien, 115.
[499] Moo, 197; O'Brien, 115; Lohse, 102.
[500] O'Brien, 116.
[501] Moo, 198.

here in verse 11, to have experienced "a circumcision made without hands" is to have been born again into eternal life.[502]

To this Paul adds two phrases both beginning with the preposition ἐν. In each case the preposition might be used instrumentally ("by"), temporally ("when"), or epexegetically ("that is in").[503] In each case we will make that determination in the flow of our comments below. First is "in the removal of the body of the flesh" (ἐν τῇ ἀπεκδύσει τοῦ σώματος τῆς σαρκός). The noun translated "the removal" (τῇ ἀπεκδύσει) is found only here in the NT. In fact it appears this may be the first usage documented in any Greek literature. Its verbal cognate, however, is found in Colossians 2:15 and 3:9. The idea appears to be that of stripping off or thoroughly removing ones clothing.[504] The double prefix (ἐκ, "off from"; απο, intensive or perfective) denotes the thoroughness and completeness of the action.[505] As a noun ending in -σις it indicates action ("removal").

> **Ministry Maxim**
>
> Christ always works from the inside-out, from spiritual to physical, from heart to body—and in this way the outward becomes a picture of the inward.

But just what has been stripped off? And from whom has it been taken? The genitives that follow help us answer this question, but not without some necessary interpretation. Commentators have failed to agree on just what the expression "the body of the flesh" (τοῦ σώματος τῆς σαρκός) is meant to describe. Paul can use the noun "flesh" (σάρξ) to refer either to the physical body (e.g., Col. 1:22, 24; 2:1, 5) or to that part of even regenerate man that tends away from God (e.g., Rom. 8:4-13; Gal. 5:13-24). This means that there are two primary ways in which this expression is understood. First, it may be a metaphorical description of the violent death of Christ Himself ("the body of the flesh" thus referring to Jesus' own body). Second, it may refer to the stripping away of the old, unregenerate life when a person comes to faith in Christ (cf. NEB, NIV, NJB, GNB). In this case it would be equivalent to Paul's statement in Romans 6:6: "our old self was crucified with Him."

---

[502] Kent, 91-92.
[503] Harris, 101-102.
[504] BAGD, 83.
[505] Harris, 101.

In favor of the first view is the fact that the only other usage of the expression ("body of flesh") by the Apostle Paul is in 1:22 where it clearly refers to Christ's physical body. Some object that in that case the pronoun αὐτοῦ ("His") is used to specifically designate that it is Christ's body which is under consideration, whereas no such pronoun is found here.[506] Yet it seems unlikely that the only two times he uses the combination of these words (σῶμα, "body" and σάρξ, "flesh"), and then so closely placed together, that they would mean something different in each case. Furthermore, thus far in the letter all the references to "flesh" have referred to physical flesh (1:22, 24; 2:1, 5).[507] Another objection is that this smacks of dualism (seeing the physical body as sinful) which the Bible nowhere else embraces and which may stand in opposition to Paul's theology of the resurrection.

Yet it must be admitted that just because some might read it this way, does not mean that is what Paul intended by the expression. In this way we would understand the first genitive (τοῦ σώματος, "of the body") as objective, indicating what has been stripped off.[508] The second genitive (τῆς σαρκός, "of the flesh") could be epexegetical (further indicating what is meant by "the body," i.e., "that is the flesh"). But it seems more likely that it is used adjectivally, indicating the physicality of the body.[509] In this case the preposition (ἐν) seems to be either instrumental ("by") or temporal ("when"). Thus we were circumcised with a circumcision made without hands "by" (ἐν, instrumental) Christ's physical death on the cross or "when" (ἐν, temporal) Christ died on the cross.

In favor of the second view (the stripping away of the old, unregenerate life through faith in Christ) is the fact that the verbal cognate of the noun (ἀπέκδυσις, "removal") is used in 2:15 of the stripping away of "the old self." This rare noun is best understood by the usage of its cognate verbs, especially when so used in this same context. Furthermore it is significant that nowhere else in the NT is circumcision used as a metaphor for death. It is true that elsewhere in Colossians to this point σάρξ is used only of the physical flesh, but a transition to its use as a reference to the sinful self will be made soon enough. Indeed, that transition is made by verse 13, in which

---

[506] See O'Brien's refutation of these concerns, 117.
[507] Dunn, 157.
[508] Ibid., 101; O'Brien, 117.
[509] Harris, 101.

"the uncircumcision of your flesh" is a clear reference, not to their lack of physical circumcision, but to their sinfulness in their preconversion state. If the transition is made just two verses later, it seems less of a leap to see it being made here.

Also, to make "the removal of the body of the flesh" a reference to Christ is less likely grammatically, since it is more natural to understand the believer as the subject of the sentence. In this way "the body of the flesh" (τοῦ σώματος τῆς σαρκός) is equivalent to the "body of sin" (τὸ σῶμα τῆς ἁμαρτίας) in Romans 6:6. In both cases Paul's point is Christ's uniqueness as the only one who can free from the power of sin. In fact Paul will go to great lengths in the latter half of this chapter to demonstrate that what the false teacher(s) offers in this regard is useless (vv. 21-23). In this way the first genitive (τοῦ σώματος, "of the body") is understood as objective, identifying what is stripped off. The second genitive (τῆς σαρκός, "of the flesh") could be epexegetical (i.e., "of the body *which consists of* the flesh"), or, more likely, it functions as an adjective describing the quality of the body which is stripped off ("your fleshly body").[510]

In this reckoning the opening preposition (ἐν) could be rendered any one of three ways: temporally ("you were also circumcised with a circumcision made without hands *when* the body of your flesh was stripped away") or instrumentally ("you were also circumcised with a circumcision made without hands *by* the body of your flesh being stripped away) or epexegetically ("you were also circumcised with a circumcision made without hands *which consists of* the body of your flesh being stripped away). Perhaps the temporal is the most favorable option.

The decision with regard to this phrase ("in the removal of the body of the flesh") is difficult, and godly and wise scholars have landed on both sides. It is my opinion that the balance of the evidence favors the second view. In either case we have here a recognizable pattern found often in the Apostle Paul's writings: death (in this case referred to metaphorically as "circumcision"), burial (v. 12a), and resurrection (vv. 12b-13a; cf. Rom. 6:3-4; 1 Cor. 15:3-4).

The second phrase, which is parallel to the first, is: "by the circumcision of Christ" (ἐν τῇ περιτομῇ τοῦ Χριστοῦ). In this case the preposition (ἐν)

---

[510] Ibid.

seems to be used either epexegetically, so that "the circumcision of Christ" is simply a restatement or expansion upon what was intended by "the removal of the body of the flesh," or temporally, explaining when "the removal of the body of the flesh" took place ("when Christ was circumcised" [i.e., died on the cross]).

There are several ways to understand the genitive (τοῦ Χριστοῦ, "of Christ") here, the determination of which yields three basic interpretations of the phrase: subjective genitive ("circumcision performed by Christ"), objective ("circumcision performed on/experienced by Christ"), possessive ("Christ's circumcision," i.e., Christian circumcision).[511] The first would presumably refer to the circumcision of heart which Christ's death brings about in the case of each believer. The second could refer either to Jesus' physical circumcision on the eighth day in conformity with the Mosaic Law or to His death on the cross under the continuing metaphor of circumcision as death. The third option would view the "circumcision" as the rite of entrance into Christ's church.

If the previous phrase is understood as a reference to Christ's own death on the cross then it means "the circumcision of Christ" is simply another way of referring to "the death of Christ" (objective genitive).[512] If one concluded, as we tentatively have, that the previous phrase described the removal of the believer's "old self," then this phrase would be understood as a subjective genitive ("the circumcision which Christ performs")[513] or possessive ("Christ's circumcision").[514] The subjective genitive seems the more likely.

As we warned, things are getting complicated. Allow me, therefore, to simply offer a paraphrase of verse 11 as I believe we are to understand it: "In union with Christ in His death you also were circumcised in heart, by the Spirit, not by human hands in the flesh, by the stripping off of your old self by the spiritual circumcision which Christ performs on those in union with Him."

---

[511] Moo, 198.
[512] Dunn, 158; O'Brien, 117.
[513] Kent, 91.
[514] Moo, 200.

2:12 having been buried with Him in baptism, in which you were also raised up with Him through faith in the working of God, who raised Him from the dead.

Paul continues his thoughts with an aorist passive participle (συνταφέντες, "having been buried"). This verb is used only here and in Romans 6:4, the entire section of which offers a significant parallel to this passage. The participial form is perhaps best understood as indicating a temporal relationship (i.e., "you were circumcised … *when* you were buried with Him in baptism"). The aorist tense looks to a definite event in the past. The passive voice makes clear that someone else (God) has performed this work upon the believer. God buried the believer (whom he has already said died with Christ, v. 11) along "with him" (αὐτῷ). The Apostle is clearly continuing the discussion of the believer's union with Christ.

This coburial in some way took place "in baptism" (τῷ βαπτισμῷ). There is a debate as to the text here. The manuscript evidence is balanced between βαπτισμῷ ("washing," "dipping," used of Jewish purification rites in two of its three other NT uses[515]) and βαπτισματι, ("baptism"). The former is, because of frequency of use, considered the more difficult reading and thus more likely to have been "corrected" by scribes. Thus it is the probable reading.[516]

Many make baptism the primary point of this passage (i.e., baptism has replaced circumcision as the rite of initiation or entrance into the people of God). However, Paul's use of a participle at this point, rather than a finite verb, is instructive. He did not place the emphasis upon baptism, but upon death ("circumcision," v. 11) and resurrection (v. 12) with Christ. This is done via the use of finite verbs in both cases. Paul's comments regarding baptism, while certainly God-breathed (2 Tim. 3:16), were nevertheless secondary in the development of his thought here. To come away with a theology of baptism from this passage is to miss the Apostle's main point and to misconstrue his words. It seems that by use of the participle he was intending to refer to burial as the crowning event of death, as its crowning, concluding, and confirming end. Just as Jesus' burial confirmed that He

---

[515] Ibid., 201.
[516] Dunn, 145; Harris, 103-104; Moo, 202; O'Brien, 118.

had in fact died, so our coburial with Him indicates that we have indeed been fully identified with Him and that our "old self" is truly dead.

But, further, we must ask: To just what does this baptism point? To the physical, water baptism of the believer? Or does it point to the baptism by the Spirit (1 Cor. 12:13) to which the physical, water baptism rightly points? Paul has just made clear that the circumcision which conveys the element of death with Christ is "a circumcision made without hands" (v. 11). That is to say, he did not reference physical circumcision, but the spiritual circumcision of the heart to which physical circumcision ought rightly to have pointed. Thus it would be a strange twist for him now to change direction and refer to physical, water baptism in the next element of our union with Christ.

Surely Paul is referring here to that union with Christ effected by the Spirit wherein we are placed into the experiences of Christ (in this case His burial) when regenerated to eternal life.[517] This spiritual union is pointed to by the physical, water baptism of the believer. It is fair to say, however, that though Paul has the work of the Spirit in mind specifically, it would hardly have been separated entirely from the physical evidence of that inward work through water baptism. Of course this does not mean that water baptism effected the burial (nor yet the codeath of verse 11 or coresurrection of verse 12b), but rather that what was effected by the Spirit in regeneration is in some sense graphically and powerfully set forth in the believer's water baptism. This understanding is further supported by Everett Ferguson's work which demonstrated that the early church writers did not compare circumcision with baptism, but with the work of the Spirit.[518]

Paul's next phrase, "in which ... also" (ἐν ᾧ καὶ), has also elicited great debate. Should the relative pronoun (ᾧ) be understood as neuter ("which") or masculine ("whom")?[519] In favor of the masculine is the fact that the precise phrase (ἐν ᾧ καὶ) was just used in verse 11 and it is there clearly a reference to Christ. Throughout this section of the letter there is also the clear theme of union with Christ using expressions like "with Him" and "in Him" (vv. 9, 10, 11, 15) and verbs prefixed with συν-.[520] In favor of the

---

[517] Kent, 92.
[518] Cited by Moo, 202.
[519] Some translations simply avoid the decision by skipping over it (e.g., NIV, NLT, NRSV).
[520] Lohse, 92; O'Brien, 102, 119.

neuter is that the closest and most natural antecedent is found in "baptism" (βαπτισμῷ).[521] The decision between these two in some sense may be moot, for baptism only has meaning in relationship to what was effected (in the case of the Spirit's baptism) and pictured (in the case of water baptism) of the believer in union with Christ in His death, burial, and resurrection. The preposition (ἐν, "in") may point to the instrument by which this resurrection took place or it may be used simply to refer to the place/sphere in which it took place.[522]

It was in this baptism that Paul can say "you were ... raised up with Him" (συνηγέρθητε). The aorist tense looks to this as a definite act. The passive voice views God as the active agent in raising the believer from death with Christ. As stated earlier, the emphasis falls upon this finite verb, rather than the previous participle (συνταφέντες, "having been buried"). Paul speaks here of the believer's coresurrection with Christ as an accomplished fact (cf. Col. 3:1) whereas in Romans he speaks of it as a yet future (though possibly a logical, rather than temporal future) event (Rom. 6:5).

Commentators have made much of this, even to the point of insisting this proves Paul did not write Colossians. Yet in Romans 6 the Apostle goes on to demand that believers "consider yourselves ... alive to God in Christ Jesus" (v. 11). Paul is fully capable on a number of fronts of speaking in both the present and future tenses, the former a real, though partial, down payment of what will be gloriously and fully made known at Christ's return. We have been redeemed (Eph. 1:7), but we are yet to be redeemed (Eph. 1:14; 4:30). We are saved now (Rom. 8:24; Eph. 2:8), but we are yet to be saved (Rom. 5:9-10). So too we are raised up

> **Ministry Maxim**
>
> What the Spirit *effects*, the waters of baptism *reflect.*

with Christ to newness of life, yet the fullness of this—including our new bodies—awaits the return of Christ. We have the Spirit as a present foretaste and guarantee of all which will be most fully made ours in due time (Rom. 8:23; 2 Cor. 1:22; 5:5; Eph. 1:14). It is in this way that Paul will say in the next verse "He made you alive together with Him" and in 3:1 will say, "Since, then, you have been raised with Christ ..." (NIV).

---

[521] Harris, 104.
[522] Ibid.

This coresurrection took place not through baptism, but "through faith in the working of God" (διὰ τῆς πίστεως τῆς ἐνεργείας τοῦ θεοῦ). The preposition (διὰ, "through") designates the means by which this coresurrection took place.[523] That means is "faith" (πίστεως). This should be understood in the subjective sense of "trust." The object of this trusting faith is τῆς ἐνεργείας ("the working").[524] Moo says this is the only place in which Paul names "working" as the object of faith.[525] This noun was already employed in Colossians 1:29. It is always used in the NT of supernatural power, whether of Satan (2 Thess. 2:9) or of God (the other seven usages). Here it is God's divine power that is in view (τοῦ θεοῦ, "of God"). This is to be understood as a subjective genitive: the power exercised by God.[526] For it is He "who raised Him from the dead" (τοῦ ἐγείραντος αὐτὸν ἐκ νεκρῶν). The genitive aorist participle introduces what amounts to a relative clause describing God: "through faith in the working of God—the one who raised Him from the dead."[527]

Given the complexity and controversial nature of verses eleven and twelve, it behooves us to stop again and summarize, through an expanded paraphrase, what we have concluded with regard to their message. Paul has said that "in union with Christ in His death you also were circumcised in heart, by the Spirit, not by human hands in the flesh, by the stripping off of your old self by the spiritual circumcision which Christ performs on those in union with Him. When you were buried in baptism by the Spirit (to which your water baptism bears witness), you were also raised with Christ to new life through faith in the divine working of God—the one who raised Jesus Himself from the dead." This union with Christ, made actual through conversion, is now expanded upon as the Apostle continues.

---

[523] Ibid., 105.
[524] O'Brien, 121.
[525] Moo, 205.
[526] Harris, 105.
[527] Ibid.

2:13 When you were dead in your transgressions and the uncircumcision of your flesh, He made you alive together with Him, having forgiven us all our transgressions,

Paul continues (καὶ, "And," NASB) his thought, though now he intro-duces a significant shift of focus. This shift is seen in the pronoun (ὑμᾶς, "you," plural), which is thrust forward for emphasis. No longer is Paul thinking of believers from the perspective of their union with Christ in His death, burial, and resurrection. Rather, now they are viewed as, in their pre-Christian state, having been dead in their trespasses and sins, but now made alive by God with Christ.[528] The shift is seen also in that the subject shifts from "you" to "He."[529]

The main verb is "made … alive together with" (συνεζωοποίησεν). This is then qualified by two participial phrases, one preceding and the other following the main verb. The main verb is used only here and in Ephesians 2:5 in the NT. God is expressly the agent in Ephesians 2:4 and should be understood to be here as well.[530] The word is a compound: συν ("with") + ζωός ("alive") + ποιέω ("to make"). The word may have been coined by the Apostle himself.[531] This is the third verb in two verses to be prefixed with συν-; Paul has returned quickly to pressing the emphasis of our union "with" Christ. Again Paul is clear that it is "you" (ὑμᾶς, plural)[532] that were so raised "with Him" (σὺν αὐτῷ; i.e., Christ). The repetition of the preposition (σὺν, found also as the prefix to the compound verb) makes the notion doubly strong.

Now we come to the qualifying participial phrases. First, consider their preceding condition. This coresurrection in union with Christ took place "When you were dead in your transgressions and the uncircumcision of your flesh" (καὶ ὑμᾶς νεκροὺς ὄντας [ἐν] τοῖς παραπτώμασιν καὶ τῇ ἀκροβυστίᾳ τῆς σαρκὸς ὑμῶν). There was a time when the Colossian believers "were dead" (νεκροὺς ὄντας). The present participle (ὄντας) is translated as a past tense. It describes an ongoing state of being which,

---

[528] O'Brien, 121.
[529] Lohse, 106.
[530] Robertson, *Word Pictures*, 493.
[531] Ibid.
[532] This is surely the correct reading. Some manuscripts lack the pronoun, but that can be understood as an effort to avoid redundancy. Those which have added a first-person plural pronoun can be read as an attempt to conform it to the ἡμῖν ("us") which follows.

because of its relationship to the main verb ("He made ... alive together with") is clearly referring to a condition which predated their current new life with Christ. Thus the NASU translators render the participle temporally ("*When* you were dead," emphasis added), describing the circumstances in which they found themselves when God made them alive together with Christ. It could also be understood as indicating amplification ("you, who were dead in the sins ..."), concession ("although you were dead ... he made you alive together with"), or contrast ("you were dead ... but he made you alive together with ...").[533] It seems best, however, to go with the majority of commentators and translators and see it as temporal or as describing the circumstance in which they were found when God made them alive together with Christ.

The adjective (νεκρούς, "dead") is a favorite of Paul, one he uses often to underscore the spiritual deadness of those without Christ (e.g., Eph. 2:1, 5). Here in Colossians he has previously said that we "were formerly alienated and hostile in mind, engaged in evil deeds" (Col. 1:21). But here he presses the ultimate reality—our spiritual death.

This state of being then is described by two articular nouns in the dative case. First, "in your transgressions" (τοῖς παραπτώμασιν). The noun describes a false step or a misstep in regard to a standard.[534] "The word signifies the actual and numerous [plural] results and manifestations of our sinful nature."[535] The article is understood as possessive, thus the translation "your." It was our being "in" these "transgressions" which constituted our spiritual deadness toward God (Eph. 2:1, 5). Some manuscripts have ἐν ("in") here. The dative is sufficient to describe the notion of circumstances or sphere.[536] Yet if the preposition is original, then it may be used here not in its normal sense, but to indicate a causal relationship (i.e., "you were dead *because of* your transgressions ...").[537] Jesus "was delivered up because of our transgressions" (Rom. 4:25) and thus God is "not counting [our] trespasses against" us (2 Cor. 5:19). Rather, "we have redemption through His blood, the forgiveness of our trespasses" (Eph. 1:7).

---

[533] King, 158.
[534] Friberg, 298.
[535] Rienecker (citing Eadie), 522.
[536] Robertson, *Word Pictures*, 4:493.
[537] Harris, 106; Moo, 206.

To this Paul adds (καὶ, "and") the second articular noun, "the uncircumcision of your flesh" (τῇ ἀκροβυστίᾳ τῆς σαρκὸς ὑμῶν). The dative case affirms this as a parallel to the previous clause. Not only were the Colossians guilty of individual acts of sin (τοῖς παραπτώμασιν, "transgressions"), but they were in a state of "uncircumcision." Though in verse 11 Paul clearly used circumcision metaphorically, here it appears that he uses it literally.[538] The Colossians were Gentiles; they were uncircumcised in body. This was the traditional Jewish way of referring to non-Jews, those who resided outside of God's covenant.

> **Ministry Maxim**
>
> The unredeemed human heart's problem is both individual acts of sin and an abiding state of deadness.

By "flesh" (τῆς σαρκὸς) Paul means the physical body, not the sinful nature. In a moment Paul will transition from the second-person plural (ὑμᾶς, ὑμῶν, "you") to the first-person plural (ἡμῖν, "we"), indicating that he was counting himself among those whose transgressions had been forgiven and signaling that he was not guilty of Jewish arrogance. Presently he is simply stating the facts with regard to the Colossians. Prior to their conversion, the Colossians stood outside of God's covenant—a fact traditionally described by the fact that they were uncircumcised in their flesh. In this regard Ephesians 2:11-12 provide a good parallel.

Yet, while this is clearly referring to their lack of physical circumcision, it was not the physical flesh that was truly their problem. Their physical uncircumcision was an outward sign of their uncircumcised hearts toward the Lord.[539] Thus the intent is not entirely distant from that expressed in verse 11. Their hearts were uncircumcised toward the Lord (as witnessed by their uncircumcision in body). Apart from Christ everyone—Jew and Gentile alike—exists in a state of sin amid an ocean of sins. Our individual sins arose out of our old, unredeemed (i.e., uncircumcised) nature. Thus we were dead spiritually. It was for this very reason that God "made you alive together with Him" (συνεζωοποίησεν ὑμᾶς σὺν αὐτῷ).

And He did this (second qualifying participial phrase), "having forgiven us all our transgressions" (χαρισάμενος ἡμῖν πάντα τὰ παραπτώματα).

---

[538] Harris, 106; Wright, 109.
[539] Abbott, 253; O'Brien, 122-123.

Note the change from "you" (ὑμᾶς, ὑμῶν; second-person plurals, used three times) to the first-person plural "us" (ἡμῖν). Here God has dealt with the aforementioned "transgressions" (τὰ παραπτώματα). The definite article is understood as possessive ("our"). Indeed, He has decisively provided for "all" (πάντα) of them! This He has done by "having forgiven" (χαρισάμενος) us for them. The verb can have a fairly wide range of meaning, but at root has the notion of giving freely or graciously. It can, as here, be used of forgiving sin, whether by God (Eph. 4:32; Col. 2:13; 3:13) or by humans (Luke 7:42, 43; 2 Cor. 2:7, 10; 12:3; Eph. 4:32; Col. 3:13). It is used here with the sense of remit, forgive, or pardon.[540] The emphasis is placed upon the grace which motivates the forgiveness.[541]

2:14 having canceled out the certificate of debt consisting of decrees against us, which was hostile to us; and He has taken it out of the way, having nailed it to the cross.

Continuing to pile up the participles, the Apostle now enlarges upon this forgiveness of our transgressions (v. 13c). God forgave us, "having canceled out" (ἐξαλείψας) what separated us from Him. The aorist active participle describes simultaneous action; the forgiveness and the canceling out were accomplished in one divine motion.[542] And it was precisely by this act of cancellation that our forgiveness was effected.[543] The participle explains the forgiveness. The word is used by Paul only here (though cf. Acts 3:19; Rev. 3:5; 7:17; 21:4). The word is a compound comprised of ἐκ ("out of") and ἀλείφω ("anoint"). The preposition in compound denotes the completeness or perfection of the action.[544] The word basically meant to wipe away. Written records were expunged by being inundated with water (wiping them away) or through scraping. In this way it essentially describes what we would mean by erasing. Over time it came to mean "*remove, destroy, obliterate* ... in so far as the removal results fr[om] the blotting out of a written record."[545] This seems to be the intent here.

---

[540] BAGD, 876.
[541] Rienecker, 574.
[542] Harris, 107; Robertson, *Word Pictures*, 4:494.
[543] Abbott, 254; Moo, 208-209.
[544] Harris, 107; King, 164; Thayer, 221.
[545] BAGD, 272.

J. I. Packer writes, "The image expressed by the verb here and perhaps elsewhere is most probably smoothing the surface of a wax writing-tablet for re-use (cf. 'wiping the slate clean'). The bond in Col. 2:14 is our obligation as God's creatures to keep his law on pain of death—a bond which becomes an actual death warrant as soon as we sin."[546] By wiping clean this record God fulfills the word of the prophet: "I, even I, am the one who wipes out your transgressions for My own sake, / And I will not remember your sins" (Isa. 43:25).

What God "canceled out" is "the certificate of debt" (το ... χειρόγραφον). The noun is found only here in the NT. Strictly speaking, it refers to a hand-written document. It came to refer more specifically, however, to a promissory note, a record of indebtedness, or bond.[547] Such a "certificate of indebtedness"[548] is admission that money had been "lent to him by another, to be returned at an appointed time."[549] It functioned as an IOU personally signed by the debtor.[550] Thus, if one was in possession of such a note, it was testimony of another's indebtedness and obligation to the possessor of the note (cf. Philem. 18-19). And, as the Proverb says, "the borrower becomes the lender's slave" (Prov. 22:7b). The definite article makes it "*the* certificate" indicating our debt. This note pointed to our ultimate indebtedness to God. Some make a case that Paul is thinking of a Jewish notion in which God keeps a written record of all our transgressions and then bases His judgment upon what is recorded.[551] Whether or not this was in Paul's mind, the image is clear.

To this Paul added a prepositional phrase: "against us" (καθ᾽ ἡμῶν). Paul will repeat this emphasis in a moment even more explicitly, giving double emphasis to this sense of personal ownership. This prepositional phrase is tucked between the noun and its definite article in order to emphasize the quality of the certificate—it was an against-us kind of certificate of

> **Ministry Maxim**
>
> The record of your sins has been erased, removed, and crucified—be at rest!

---

[546] NIDNTT, 1:471.
[547] Friberg, 408.
[548] BAGD, 880.
[549] Thayer, 668.
[550] Rienecker, 574.
[551] Dunn, 164.

debt. Our signature was on the note, confirming that we owed an infinite debt to the holy God.

It is significant that though Paul had just singled out the Gentile character of the Colossians with the second-person plural pronoun (ὑμῶν, v. 13), he had immediately turned to the first-person plural pronoun to indicate that God had forgiven "us" (ἡμῖν, v. 13) all, including himself as a pious Jew. Here again he numbers himself as one of those who, for all of his persnickety religious observances, was found indebted to God for his failures to keep His Law (ἡμῶν, "us").

This certificate of debt was "consisting of decrees" (τοῖς δόγμασιν). Paul uses this noun in only one other place, and there it clearly refers to the Mosaic Law: "the Law of commandments contained in ordinances [ἐν δόγμασιν]" (Eph. 2:15; though see the cognate verb in Col. 2:20). It is reasonable to believe that he used it similarly here. The only other usages refer to decrees handed down by Caesar (Luke 2:1; Acts 17:7) or the Jerusalem Council (Acts 16:4). It thus describes orders handed from a higher authority to those obligated to comply with them. Because Paul uses the first-person plural pronoun (ἡμῶν, "us"), including both Jews and Gentiles, it seems likely to include the Mosaic Law which was given to the Jews, but also the law written upon the heart of the Gentiles as well (Rom. 1:18-19; 2:15). Friberg says "the certificate of debt" (τὸ … χειρόγραφον) is to be viewed "not as the law itself, but as the *record of charges* (for breaking God's law)."[552] And thus "decrees" (τοῖς δόγμασιν) "referred to a legal obligation which was a binding law or edict which was placed on a public place for all to see."[553]

The dative form could be descriptive, meaning this "certificate of debt" was a document containing or consisting of "decrees" that we had broken.[554] What we should have been and done is plain for all to see. What we are and the debt we owe for it is equally clear. Or the dative may be causal, making clear why the "certificate of debt" had a case against us.[555] Our obligations are listed on the written document, thus making plain the cause of our standing in the position of debtor.

---

[552] Friberg, 408; cf. Bruce, NIC, 109.
[553] Rienecker, 574.
[554] Ibid.
[555] O'Brien, 125.

It was this "which was hostile to us" (ὃ ἦν ὑπεναντίον ἡμῖν). What had been a terse prepositional phrase (καθ᾽ ἡμῶν, "against us") is now reinforced and expanded upon. Whereas the previous phrase set forth as a bare fact the opposition of the "certificate of debt," this "emphasizes the direct and active opposition of the signed statement of indebtedness."[556]

We must be completely clear—it was precisely *this* which God "canceled out" for each of us. The record of our failures against the law of God is erased, obliterated, wiped clean so that no evidence of its previous existence can be tracked down, brought up, or used against us. Glory to God!

As if the picture were not already glorious enough, the Apostle piles on the good news, adding (καὶ, "and") that "He has taken it out of the way" (αὐτὸ ἦρκεν ἐκ τοῦ μέσου). The neuter form of the pronoun (αὐτὸ, "it") refers to the "certificate of debt." This "He has taken" (ἦρκεν). The verb means not only to lift up, but to lift up and take away, to remove.[557] The subject is God the Father. The perfect tense views the action as completed in the past, leaving a settled condition that exists right up to the present.

Where has He taken this "certificate of debt"? He took it "out of the way" (ἐκ τοῦ μέσου). The adjective's basic use is to designate "the middle." Here the preposition (ἐκ, "out of") means that "the certificate of debt" which once stood between God and us has been taken out from between us. Where once there was a barrier of our own making between God and us, now there exists an open plain with His welcome invitation to come to Him through Christ. God not only obliterated our debt before Him, but He removed "the certificate of debt" which detailed that debt.[558]

How did God accomplish this removal? By "having nailed it to the cross" (προσηλώσας αὐτὸ τῷ σταυρῷ). Once again the neuter pronoun (αὐτὸ, "it") refers to "the certificate of debt." The verb (προσηλώσας, "having nailed") is used only here in the NT. The aorist tense looks to the time of Jesus' crucifixion and death on "the cross" (τῷ σταυρω). The participle indicates the means by which God took the "certificate of debt" out of the way.[559] Some have tried to connect Paul's thought here to the ancient custom of canceling out a written record of indebtedness by crossing it out with the

---

[556] Harris, 108.
[557] BAGD, 24.
[558] Lohse, 110.
[559] Harris, 109.

Greek letter composed of an X or to the cancellation of a bond by driving a nail through it. Both attempts seem to overreach Paul's intent.[560] His words are powerful enough as they stand. There may be, however, some value in seeing a connection with the Gospel accounts which describe the charge against Jesus being nailed to His cross ("THE KING OF THE JEWS," Mark 15:26, cf. Matt. 27:37; Luke 23:37-38; John 19:18-22). Just as the charge against Jesus was nailed to His cross, so the charges against us were nailed to His cross as well.[561]

It is worth making clear that it is not the Law *per se* that has been nailed to the cross and thus taken from between God and us.[562] Paul insists in other places that the Law has a valid and necessary function. The Law is a valid and accurate revelation of God's character and will. "So then, the Law is holy, and the commandment is holy and righteous and good" (Rom. 7:12). "But we know that the Law is good, if one uses it lawfully" (1 Tim. 1:8). That "good" function of the Law is that it reveals to us "the certificate of debt" that stands between God and us. The Law thus rightly reveals our just condemnation before God and prepares us for the good news of the cross and empty tomb. Indeed, what is removed is "the certificate of debt" which is the record of our failures to keep God's Law. It is gone, removed, obliterated, and expunged from existence. We are free from our sin debt before God!

2:15 When He had disarmed the rulers and authorities, He made a public display of them, having triumphed over them through Him.

Not only did God wipe out the written record of our indebtedness to Him and not only did he take this record entirely away from between Himself and us by nailing it to the cross, but in addition "He made a public display" (ἐδειγμάτισεν) of the demonic forces that used that record of indebtedness to accuse and enslave us. This verb is used only here and in Matthew 1:19, where we read that Joseph did not want to "disgrace" Mary publicly when he discovered her pregnancy. In that sense the word was used of exposing or making a public example of someone (cf. the cognate noun in Jude 7). Among the Jews such a penalty could have meant death. Interestingly the

---

[560] O'Brien, 126.
[561] Ibid.
[562] Dunn, 165-166.

same verb is found in a compound form (prefixed by παρα-) to describe those who "put [Christ] to open shame" (Heb. 6:6) by their falling away from faith in Him. Here the meaning may have the idea of "mock" or "expose."[563] In this setting it depicts Christ making "a public exhibition of the vanquished forces, not just by proclamation, but by public display, as in a triumphal process."[564]

This exposure was made "public" (ἐν παρρησίᾳ) or more literally "in openness." The noun describes "*outspokenness, frankness, plainness of speech, that conceals nothing and passes over nothing.*"[565] Thus it is sometimes rendered "boldness" or "confidence."[566] But this developed into "*openness to the public, before whom speaking and actions take place.*" This is the sense here.[567]

This God did "When He had disarmed the rulers and authorities" (ἀπεκδυσάμενος τὰς ἀρχὰς καὶ τὰς ἐξουσίας). The basic notion of the verb is that of stripping off clothing, a sense which is seen more clearly in Colossians 3:9, the only other NT usage (cf. the use of the cognate noun in 2:11). There the Colossians are said to have "laid aside the old self." This is possible precisely because of what God did here through Christ on the cross.

The NASU has understood the participial form as temporal ("*When He had disarmed*"). Though it could also be understood as indicating result ("*with the result that He has disarmed*"), the temporal usage seems the more likely. The aorist tense looks back to the definitive work of Christ accomplished on the cross. Our understanding of the middle voice is the key to understanding just what Paul intended here. If indeed it has the middle (reflexive) meaning, the verb then views Jesus as acting upon Himself to strip away these powers. This has the support of Colossians 3:9 where this is clearly the meaning. But if the middle is understood as having an active meaning, something which the Greek of the NT did with certain verbs[568], then the notion is that of God (retaining the subject of vv. 13, 14) stripping these powers of their power, authority, and weapons used against us

---

[563] BAGD, 172; NIDNTT, 3:570.
[564] Little Kittel, 142.
[565] BAGD, 630.
[566] Rienecker, 575.
[567] BAGD, 630.
[568] O'Brien, 127.

(not least of which was the "certificate of debt" detailing our failures to keep God's "decrees," v. 14). In this way God was "disarming" them (as most English versions render it). This latter understanding seems, though unique, to be what Paul intended here.[569]

The two plural nouns (τὰς ἀρχὰς καὶ τὰς ἐξουσίας, "the rulers and the authorities") point to demonic powers.[570] The two nouns appear together elsewhere in Paul where they in some cases clearly refer to angelic powers (Eph. 3:10; 6:12) and in others to earthly beings (Titus 3:1). In yet other instances angelic powers or both may be in mind (1 Cor. 15:24; Eph. 1:21; Col. 1:16; 2:10). Here the reference is clearly to malevolent spiritual powers, which sought to dissuade Jesus from His appointed mission and seek still to harass and accuse His followers. But Jesus, through perfect obedience all the way through the cross, stripped them away, undoing their influence and sealing their doom.

Indeed, God thus "made a public display" of them by "having triumphed over them" (θριαμβεύσας αὐτοὺς). The verb describes a specific scene familiar to those of the ancient near east. When a military commander or king had been engaged in a distant battle and returned home victorious, he would march through the city in grand style followed by his army and all the plunder he had claimed as well as those vanquished foes which remained alive. They were led in triumphal procession to display the victory of the conquering king.

The only other use of the verb is in 2 Corinthians 2:14, which is telling. There Paul pictures us who are followers of Christ, including the Apostle himself, as those being thus led in "triumphal procession." It is precisely in having been gladly conquered by Christ that we find new life. Yet it is in being conquered by Christ that Satan and his demonic powers find their ultimate undoing. The aorist tense looks back once again to the event of the cross. The participle could be temporal (God made a public display of them *when* He triumphed over them), or, more likely still, it could indicate the means by which this public triumph took place ("God made a public display of them *by* triumphing over them").[571] The pronoun (αὐτοὺς, "them") is

---

[569] Lohse, 111-112; Moo, 212-213; O'Brien, 127-128.
[570] BAGD, 112.
[571] Harris, 111.

masculine plural where one would have expected the feminine plural so as to conform to ἀρχὰς ("rulers") and ἐξουσίας ("authorities"). This is, however, "a case of 'construction according to the sense' ... showing that the powers and authorities are not abstract entities but personal beings."[572]

This triumph, the Apostle tells us, took place "through Him" (ἐν αὐτῷ). Grammatically the pronoun could point either to Christ Himself or to His cross. The NASU (cf. ESV) has chosen the former. Others designate it "the cross" explicitly (NET, NIV, NLT) or indirectly with "it" (KJV, NKJV, NRSV). The nearest antecedent is "the cross" (τῷ σταυρῷ) in verse 14. The sense of disgrace inherent in the "public display" and "having triumphed" is best understood as happening through the cross.[573] Yet because of our understanding of the middle voice in "He had disarmed" (ἀπεκδυσάμενος) and the fact that this retains God the Father as the active agent, it is best to read this as "in Him" (as a reference to Christ, who in His work on the cross and His resurrection triumphed over Satan and his demonic forces).

> **Ministry Maxim**
>
> The only answer the accuser can't outmaneuver is to point him to the cross.

This then signals that we have ended where we began. Paul began by telling us "in Him (ἐν αὐτῷ) you have been made complete" (v. 10). He has taken all the space between verse 10 and verse 15 to unpack just what that means, culminating here with the declaration that we have been freed from all evil powers "through Him" (ἐν αὐτῷ). In this case the preposition (ἐν, "through") indicates the means by which the "public display" was accomplished. Irony of ironies! The cross in which the evil powers thought they had defeated Christ was the cross through which He sealed their doom! It is through the cross that we who were doomed are set free!

---

[572] Ibid.
[573] NET Bible.

Digging Deeper:

1. How might you use verses 13 and 14 in counseling someone struggling with truly resting in God's forgiveness?
2. What is the connection between resting in God's forgiveness of our sins (v. 14) and understanding Christ's triumph over demonic spirits (v. 15)?
3. How should verse 15 inform our theology and practice of spiritual warfare?
4. See if you can explain to someone how union with Christ enables us to live victoriously over the world (vv. 8, 20), the flesh (v. 11), and the devil (v. 15).

2:16 Therefore no one is to act as your judge in regard to food or drink or in respect to a festival or a new moon or a Sabbath day—

In verse 8 Paul issued a warning which began to move more directly against the false teaching in Colossae: "See to it that no one takes you captive through philosophy and empty deception, according to the tradition of men, according to the elementary principles of the world, rather than according to Christ." Paul asserts his Christological answer to this false teaching in verses 9 and 10. In verses 11-15 Paul has expounded what it means that we "have been made complete" in Christ (v. 10). In so doing he has given us some of the most intricately woven theology found anywhere in the NT. In the fine weave of these statements we find marvelous and freeing truths, not the least of which are eternal life in Christ, forgiveness in Christ, and freedom in Christ from all opposing spiritual forces.

Now the Apostle moves to draw implications (οὖν, "Therefore") from this for the Colossians even as he more directly takes on the false teaching (vv. 16-23). In doing so he takes up again the basic outline he set forth in verse 8. In verse 8 the false teaching is denounced as human in origin ("according to the tradition of men") and here he states the same ("in accordance with the commandments and teachings of men," v. 22). In verse 8 the false teaching was "according to the elementary principles of the world," and the same is true here (v. 20). In verse 8 the basic failure of the false teaching was that it was "rather than according to Christ." Here it is that the false teacher(s) was "not holding fast to the head" (v. 19).[574]

Because of the false teacher(s) present in Colossae, Paul's instruction must be given from the negative perspective (Μὴ ... τις, "no one"). The indefinite pronoun (τις, "one") broadens out the scope to include anyone who might step in to play the judge over the Colossians in the matters enumerated. Yet it is in the singular form and may thus point to one particular leader or charismatic figure (cf. v. 8).[575] Arnold says, "The language of this passage (esp. the Gk. pronoun *tis*, 'a certain person'), may point to an influential teacher—perhaps a shaman-like figure—who is ringleader of this emerging faction."[576]

The prohibition is that no one be allowed to "act as ... judge" (κρινέτω). The present imperative with negation may be understood in the sense of stopping action which is already in progress. The false teacher(s) in Colossae had apparently already begun imposing his judgments on the believers with regard to the various observances Paul names. The verb has a broad spectrum of meaning, ranging from the positive (separate, distinguish), to the neutral (reach a decision, decide), to the negative (as here). Here κρινέτω has the sense of *"pass an unfavorable judgment upon, criticize, find fault with, condemn."*[577] The plural personal pronoun (ὑμᾶς, "your") is thrust forward for emphasis—"No one is to act as judge of you, you who are made complete in Christ."

The Apostle now enumerates five matters in which the Colossians are to stop allowing the false teacher(s) to pass judgment upon them. The first two are linked together (ἐν βρώσει καὶ ἐν πόσει, "in regard to food or drink"). It is more simply and literally, "in food and in drink." The preposition (ἐν, "in regard") designates the sphere in which the judgment is made. The preposition is repeated "to show that the dietary regulations concerning food and drink are being viewed separately."[578] The first noun is used only three other times by Paul (Rom. 14:17; 1 Cor. 8:4; 2 Cor. 9:10), two of

---

[574] Moo, 217.

[575] See our comments under v.8 above and also our introduction under "What Circumstances Gave Rise to the Writing of This Letter?"; Abbott (263) and O'Brien (138) both suggest the Apostle has specific "persons" in mind.

[576] Arnold, *Bible Backgrounds*, 3:388.

[577] BAGD, 452.

[578] Harris, 118.

which are in the context of the "weaker brother" vs. "stronger brother" debate (Rom. 14-15; 1 Cor. 8-9). These sections are a general and helpful exposition of the very problem being faced in Colossae. The second noun is found only one other time in Paul's writings, also in that same context (Rom. 14:17). Both nouns point to the acts of eating[579] and drinking.[580]

The OT contained many regulations regarding "clean" and "unclean" foods, which are probably the focal point of the matters related to food (e.g., Lev. 11:1-23; Deut. 14:3-21). It did not contain the same level of regulation with regard to drink (though cf. the regulations for ministering priests in Lev. 10:9 and the Nazirite vow in Num. 6:1-21). Obviously, however, the falsehood being spread in Colossae included dietary regulations. Perhaps the notion was that fasting and total abstinence were being pressed upon the believers as a necessary factor in discovering the insights the false teacher(s) was peddling (cf. "severe treatment of the body," v. 23; 1 Tim. 4:3). But as Paul says in using both nouns elsewhere: "the kingdom of God is not eating and drinking, but righteousness and peace and joy in the Holy Spirit" (Rom. 14:17). Jesus categorically "declared all foods 'clean'" (Mark 7:19). God reinforced this for Peter and the early church (Acts 10:15; 11:9).

> **Ministry Maxim**
>
> We are changed from the inside out—thus neither diet nor calendar determines the state of one's heart.

Paul strings together (using the connective conjunction ἤ, "or") three more areas in which he warns them against being judged. All three have a distinctive Jewish matter in mind. First is "in respect to a festival" (ἐν μέρει ἑορτῆς). The noun "respect" (μέρει) means basically "part" or "share," but finds its distinctive meaning from its context. Here it seems to mean something like "in the matter of" or "with regard to."[581] The prepositional phrase, like the one preceding, points to the sphere in which the judgment may take place. By "festival" (ἑορτῆς), Paul means the annual Jewish festivals such as Passover and Pentecost.[582] Then there is the matter of "a new moon" (νεομηνίας). The noun is found only here in the NT. It points to monthly

---

[579] BAGD, 148.
[580] Ibid., 694.
[581] Friberg, 259.
[582] Rienecker, 575.

religious observances regulated by the lunar cycles. Both Jews and Gentiles were known to make the first of the month a time of religious observance (Num. 10:10; 28:11-15).[583] Then also there was the matter of "a Sabbath day" (σαββάτων). Of the sixty-eight occurrences of the word in the NT, only two appear after the Gospels and Acts (1 Cor. 16:2; Col. 2:16). Here it points, of course, to the weekly religious observance of the Jews on the seventh day of each week. Though it is plural in form, this is because of its transliteration from Aramaic; it is singular in meaning.[584]

The Apostle categorically denies any calendar observances and dietary restrictions as obligatory for Christians. Each one may determine his practice in these matters according to his own conscience (Rom. 14:5-6). No one is to be allowed to pass judgment on another for his observance or nonobservance of such regulations (Rom. 14:3).

2:17 things which are a mere shadow of what is to come; but the substance belongs to Christ.

There are no clear linking words to signify the relation of this verse to the previous one. Yet the intent seems clear enough: the Colossian believers are to allow no one to judge them regarding these legalistic rituals *because* they are related to the former order, and the new age has now dawned in Christ.[585]

The neuter plural form of the relative pronoun (ἅ, "things which") points to the dietary and calendar regulations under consideration in verse 16. Such legalistic regulations "are a mere shadow" (ἐστιν σκιά). The present tense of the verb describes the ongoing nature of such rules. The noun "shadow" (σκιά) is used by Paul only here. It can be used literally (Mark 4:32; Acts 5:15) or figuratively, as here (Matt. 4:16; Luke 1:79).

The Apostle is taking up language that was familiar to first-century readers from Hellenistic philosophy where thinkers like Plato used the shadow/substance argument in their writings. The Hellenistic Jewish philosopher Philo also made use of this line of thought. But, as he often does, Paul turns this existing language to the service of the truth in Christ.

---

[583] BAGD, 535.
[584] Abbott, 264.
[585] Bruce, NIC, 115-116; Moo, 222; O'Brien, 139.

A shadow has no substance, but is only an indicator of something else which does possess mass and dimension. A shadow exists only when light is

Ministry Maxim
We are called to walk in the light, not settle down in a shadow.

cast upon something that has actual mass and sub-stance. So the regulations of the Law or any extended legalistic regulations others might add to it are not the substance of the reality God had planned for us all along. Rather they are only the fleeting evidence that such a reality exists and that God is seeking to reveal it to us. When the light moves from behind the reality to the other side of it, the shadow disappears.

The writer to the Hebrews likewise indicated that the regulations of the Mosaic Law were a mere shadow and thus fleeting (Heb. 8:5; 10:1). They were without substance and, with the advent of Christ, the light of revelation has shifted to this side of the Law (John 8:12; 9:5), rendering such regulations pointless.

Indeed, Paul says that such dietary and calendar regulations are only a shadowy indicator "of what is to come" (τῶν μελλόντων). The participle is used as a substantive to describe "the future."[586] It can "according to the context" describe "the more perfect state of things which will exist in the" age to come.[587] The present tense should be understood as speaking from the vantage point of the shadow, so it might be translated "the things that were to come" (NIV).[588] The Apostle reminds us that God has more for us and it lies ahead, not behind. The path of life is not backward, but forward.

The shadow is fleeting, airy, weightless; "but the substance belongs to Christ" (τὸ δὲ σῶμα τοῦ Χριστοῦ). Literally the expression is "but the body of Christ." The word "body" (σῶμα), however, when used in contrast to "shadow" (σκιά) takes on the notion of its opposite, thus describing not the physical body of Jesus, but the reality which is the opposite of "shadow."[589] Some have wanted to see a dual or even triple meaning here, relating this not only to the shadow-substance contrast, but to the church as the body of Christ (cf. v. 19) and/or the resurrection body of Christ.[590]

---

[586] BAGD, 501.

[587] Thayer, 396.

[588] Harris, 119; Moo, 223.

[589] BAGD, 799.

[590] O'Brien, 140-141.

Given the immediacy of the contrast within the verse, this seems an unnecessary reach.[591] The genitive (τοῦ Χριστοῦ, "of Christ") may be possessive: the reality that belongs "to Christ" (NASU)[592] or appositional: the reality "is Christ" (GNB, JB).[593] The reality has come and is present in the person of Jesus Christ.[594] "For in Him all the fullness of Deity dwells in bodily [adverbial form of the noun used here] form" (2:9). The substance is present among us, though its reality is still unfolding in its fullness and indeed will continue to do so throughout eternity.

Digging Deeper:

1. In what ways are issues of diet spiritualized and moralized in your church fellowship?
2. How should this relate to decisions regarding policies of abstinence from alcohol among members or leadership?
3. Does verse 16 set aside the fourth commandment?
4. Identify issues or practices within your church fellowship or your own life which are "shadows" elevated to the status of "substance."
5. What steps must be taken to correct this?

2:18 Let no one keep defrauding you of your prize by delighting in self-abasement and the worship of the angels, taking his stand on visions he has seen, inflated without cause by his fleshly mind,

The apostle issues a command to "Let no one keep defrauding you of your prize" (μηδεὶς ὑμᾶς καταβραβευέτω). The verb is a compound made up of κατά ("against") and βραβεύω ("to be umpire in the games"; used in the NT only in Col. 3:15). It meant to decide against someone as an umpire might do with the result that they are robbed of the prize for which they were competing.[595] It came to be used more generally of simply deciding against someone or condemning them.[596]

---

[591] Moo, 224; O'Brien, 141.
[592] Harris, 120.
[593] NET Bible.
[594] Bullinger, 872.
[595] BAGD, 409.
[596] Rienecker, 576.

The present imperative with the negation (μηδείς, "no one") could be understood as a demand that they stop action now in progress. This may then be a repeated and intensified form of the prohibition just issued in verse 16. The "prize" of which the Colossian believers are being robbed is the fullness of life in union with the incomparable Christ. Instead they are being taken back to ground from which they have already been delivered.

Paul follows up this command by a series of four present active participles (three in v. 18 and one in v. 19), each enlarging upon how the false teacher(s) in Colossae was going about his work of judgment against the believers. The first three are stated positively concerning what the false teacher(s) does. The fourth (v. 19) is stated negatively concerning that which he fails to do.

The first participial phrase is "by delighting in self-abasement and the worship of angels" (θέλων ἐν ταπεινοφροσύνῃ καὶ θρησκείᾳ τῶν ἀγγέλων). The verb usually means to will or to wish, but here it has the relatively rare sense of "take pleasure in."[597] It has been suggested that the verb followed by the preposition (ἐν, "in") means "being bent upon."[598] But the notion of "delighting in" or "taking pleasure in" something seems more likely.[599]

The object of the false teacher's delight is twofold. Both clauses are ruled by the single preposition (ἐν, "in"), indicating "the close conceptual link between" them.[600] First is "self-abasement" (ταπεινοφροσύνη). The word is used seven times in the NT. Five o f those are by Paul and three of those are here in Colossians. It can be used positively (Col. 3:12) to describe "a quality of voluntary submission and unselfishness humility, self-effacement," but here (and in v. 23) it is clearly used in a pejorative sense and means "a misdirected submission in cultic behavior *self-abasement, (false) humility, self-mortification.*"[601] Some believe the meaning ranges closer to the idea of "self-mortification" and is actually a reference to the practice of fasting as a

> **Ministry Maxim**
>
> No spiritual experience can outweigh what God's Word clearly says.

---

[597] BAGD, 355.
[598] Rienecker, 576.
[599] BAGD, 355; Dunn, 178; Lightfoot, 193-194; Moo, 224; O'Brien, 142.
[600] Harris, 121; cf. O'Brien, 142.
[601] Friberg, 375.

preparation to receive heavenly visions.[602] Others contend that the false teacher(s) viewed God as so lofty and removed from human affairs that He could be addressed only through angelic mediators. Thus through misdirected or feigned humility the false teacher(s) drew in the naive believers of Colossae.

As noted, the false teacher(s) also (καὶ, "and") took delight in "the worship of angels" (θρησκείᾳ τῶν ἀγγέλων). The noun θρησκείᾳ ("the worship") pictures worship expressed in active service to whatever god is being venerated. The being to whom the worship is addressed is identified by an objective genitive, in this case "of angels" (τῶν ἀγγέλων).[603] This is nothing but idolatry, a violation of the first commandment. True angels refuse worship, deferring it to God who alone is worthy (Rev. 22:8-9). The fallen angel, Lucifer, seeks worship for himself (Luke 4:7). Paul insists that worship of idols is actually worship of the demons that stand behind them (1 Cor. 10:20-21; cf. Rev. 9:20).

As noted, the false teacher(s) operating in Colossae was apparently setting forth a system in which God was pictured as so high and removed from humanity as to be unapproachable in any direct fashion. Thus a system or series of intermediaries were pictured as necessary mediators through which a worshipper would need to pass. The Mosaic Law was given through the mediation of angels (Gal. 3:19). But now Christ, who fulfills the Law, has come, and He alone is the mediator between God and man (1 Tim. 2:5). The old lie lives on in systems both blatantly pagan and pseudo-Christian wherever the believer's privilege of direct address to God through Jesus Christ is muted or misdirected.

The second participial phrase is "taking his stand on visions that he has seen" (ἃ ἑόρακεν ἐμβατεύων). A more literal rendering is "which he has seen upon entering."[604] The participle (ἐμβατεύων) is found only here in the NT and has given occasion to a great deal of discussion as to its meaning. Strictly speaking it means *"step in or on, stand on."*[605] What is obvious is that it is used figuratively here. But just what particular nuance is intended? It may mean simply "to enter into" or "to penetrate," thus describing the

---

[602] O'Brien, 142.

[603] BAGD, 363; Moo, 229.

[604] O'Brien, 143.

[605] Friberg, 145.

worshipper's step into ecstatic, heavenly experiences via their visions (KJV, NKJV).[606] Some suggest that it means to enter into a subject, to go into great detail about some matter. In this case it might mean *"entering at length upon the tale of what he has seen* in a vision" (ESV, NET, NIV, NRSV).[607] It may also have the sense of *"take one's stand on, base one's authority on* (what one has seen or claims to have seen in ecstasy)."[608] The word has been discovered in some writings from the second century where it is used as a religious technical term, referring to "the second step of an initiate into a mystery religion as he entered an inner sanctuary" and thus meant to *"enter* into mysteries."[609] But it is probably unwise to read this technical meaning back into the first century.

The object of such trust or talk is "what he has seen" (ἃ ἑόρακεν). The perfect tense points to an abiding state—such a one has seen something so overwhelming that the vision is burned into his memory, never to be forgotten. It seems to describe an experience so powerful as to dominate one's thinking ever after. The false teacher(s) seems to have been taken up with an ecstatic experience(s) which dominated his talk and which he believed authenticated the claims of his teaching. Some manuscripts insert here a negation (μή). These variations are to be regarded as later scribal additions to the text and thus not genuine.[610]

The third participial phrase is "inflated without cause by his fleshly mind" (εἰκῇ φυσιούμενος ὑπὸ τοῦ νοὸς τῆς σαρκὸς αὐτοῦ). The verb occurs seven times in the NT, all by Paul. Six of those references occur in 1 Corinthians (4:6, 18, 19; 5:2; 8:1; 13:4), signaling that they may have had a particular issue at this point. It comes from φῦσα ("a pair of bellows") and literally means "to puff up" or to "inflate."[611] It came to be used metaphorically of pride and arrogance, as it is here.

Here the inflation is "without cause" (εἰκῇ). There is no corresponding reason for his pride. Instead it is "by his fleshly mind" (ὑπὸ τοῦ νοὸς τῆς

---

[606] Francis, "Humility and Angelic Worship in Col 2:18" (*Conflict*, 163-95) and "The Background of EMBATE☐EIN (Col 2:18) in Legal Papyri and Oracle Inscriptions" (*Conflict*, 197-207) cited in O'Brien, 144-145; Rinecker, 576.
[607] BAGD, 254.
[608] Friberg, 145.
[609] Ibid.
[610] O'Brien, 144.
[611] Thayer, 660.

σαρκὸς αὐτοῦ) that he thinks such high thoughts of himself. The preposition (ὑπὸ) with the genitive indicates the agent or cause by which this individual becomes puffed up.[612] This is self-inflation. The air to puff up his ego arises from within his own self. He is, to borrow the old phrase, "blowing his own horn," and that for no valid reason.

With "fleshly" (τῆς σαρκὸς) Paul uses the word that he began using quite literally of human flesh (Col. 1:22, 24; 2:1, 5) but has already transitioned to using in the sense of man's inward, sinful bent (2:11, 13). It is in this latter sense that he employs it here (cf. Col. 2:23). To form his closing expression Paul strings together a series of three genitives: "of the mind" (τοῦ νοὸς), "of the flesh" (τῆς σαρκὸς), "of him" (αὐτοῦ). Note that the pronoun is singular (αὐτοῦ), signaling again that perhaps Paul has one singular leader in mind.

This verse is important in understanding more exactly the nature of the false teaching in Colossae. It seems clear that what was being peddled was a syncretistic amalgam of Judaism (v. 16) and other religious notions, probably drawn from the Greek mystery religions (v. 18).

2:19 and not holding fast to the head, from whom the entire body, being supplied and held together by the joints and ligaments, grows with a growth which is from God.

The fourth in a series of four participles following on the prohibition of verse 18 ("Let no one keep on defrauding you") is added (καὶ, "and"): "not holding fast to the head" (οὐ κρατῶν τὴν κεφαλήν). The imagery is not new in this epistle, for Paul has already introduced Jesus as "head of the body, the church" (Col. 1:18). He does now further develop the imagery regarding the organic connection of Christ and His redeemed people. He designates Christ not only head of His body (1:18), but "head over all rule and authority" (2:10). Thus for the false teacher(s) to be "not holding fast to the head" (2:19) places him under His feet, subdued as a foe, rather than as part of His body (1 Cor. 15:25-27; Eph. 1:22). For the noun (τὴν κεφαλήν, "the head") see our comments under 1:18.

---

[612] BAGD, 843.

The basic notion of the verb κρατῶν ("holding fast") is to be strong or to possess power.[613] It can be used of arresting a person (Matt. 14:3; 21:46) or of seizing him by force (Matt. 12:11; 18:28).[614] Here it has the notion of holding fast to someone with strength and to "hence remain closely united to" him.[615] This the false teacher(s) does "not" (οὐ) do. In using οὐ rather than μή, Paul bluntly denies as fact (rather than just the notion of) the false teacher(s) clinging to Christ as head. Having no connection to the head of the body, this individual has no life or communication from the head.

Do not lose sight of the exalted view of Christ already set forth in this letter (1:15ff.). Having relegated Christ to a diminished standing as one among (though perhaps even first among) a series of intermediaries between God and man, he has made Him to be something less than the exalted "head" of His body and "head over all things" (Eph. 1:22). Surely this individual pictured himself as a part of Christ's body, in vital relationship to Christ.[616] Yet Paul deals a devastating blow in suggesting he has no living relationship at all with the preeminent Christ. As such he may have become the Colossian version of the problem Paul predicted for Ephesus: "from among your own selves men will arise, speaking perverse things, to draw away the disciples after them" (Acts 20:30).

In earlier letters Paul had spoken of the church as Christ's body, but there dwelt more upon the interrelationship of the members (Rom. 12:4-5; 1 Cor. 12:12-31). Here in Colossians (1:24; 2:19; 3:15; and in Ephesians 1:22-23; 4:4, 12, 16; 5:23, 30), Paul develops more of the relationship of the whole of the body to Christ Himself as head. He does so in this instance by saying that it is the head "from whom the entire body ... grows" (ἐξ οὗ πᾶν τὸ σῶμα ... αὔξει). It is out "from" (ἐξ) the person of Christ[617] that our life arises. This is true for "the entire body" (πᾶν τὸ σῶμα) of Christ. The adjective (πᾶν, "entire") denotes the whole of the noun which it qualifies. There is no part of Christ's body that He does not rule and to which He does not extend life.

---

[613] Friberg, 236.

[614] O'Brien, 146.

[615] BAGD, 448.

[616] O'Brien, 146.

[617] οὗ, "whom"; a masculine singular relative pronoun is used, rather than the feminine to match τὴν κεφαλήν, because it refers to Christ.

Paul has already used the verb (αὔξει, "grows") to describe the growth and advance of the gospel itself (Col. 1:6) and of the Colossian believers' growth in the knowledge of God (1:10). Here the present tense emphasizes the continual outflow of life from the head and thus the growth that results in His body (cf. its use in similar contexts in Eph. 2:21; 4:15). From this life the false teacher(s) and his disciples have severed themselves by their diminished view of Christ.

This ("from whom the entire body ... grows") is qualified in two ways. First, using the noun form of the verb, Paul indicates that the body grows "with a growth which is from God" (τὴν αὔξησιν τοῦ θεοῦ). The genitive (τοῦ θεοῦ, "of God") obviously is subjective (growth which God grants) rather than objective (growth which God experiences), for God, being perfect, immutable, and infinite, cannot grow or change. What could be more inviting than the knowledge that the body, literally, "grows with the growth of God"? Christ confers upon His body, the church, His very own life! Indeed, as Paul will soon enough say, it is "Christ, who is our life" (Col. 3:4).

This is divine, eternal life coming out from (ἐξ) Christ Himself, as the head of His body, yet it is "being supplied and held together" (ἐπιχορηγούμενον καὶ συμβιβαζόμενον) by what each member of the body contributes, for the supply and linkage are "by the joints and ligaments" (διὰ τῶν ἁφῶν καὶ συνδέσμων). The two participles describe both a supply line and a means of binding support. First is "being supplied" (ἐπιχορηγούμενον). The word is a compound comprised of ἐπι ("upon") and χορηγέω ("provide," "supply"). The root verb was used to describe the leading of a public chorus or drama or to foot the bill for one. Thus it came to mean "*furnish, supply, provide (abundantly).*"[618] The preposition in compound indicates the direction of the action. The passive form is frequently rendered "be supported" or "receive help."[619] Christ works through the members of His body to supply life to the whole of that body and each of its other members.

> **Ministry Maxim**
>
> Our failure in horizontal relationships is a sign of a failure in our vertical relationship with the Christ.

---

[618] Friberg, 169.
[619] BAGD, 305.

Second (καὶ, "and") is the participle rendered "held together" (συμβιβαζόμενον). Paul has already used this verb in verse 2 where he prayed that they may be encouraged "having been knit together [συμβιβασθέντες] in love." As we noted there, this is the causal form of συμβαίνω ("to bring together"). In the passive voice, as here, it means "to be united together." The root verb (βιβάζω) was used, among other things, to describe the most intimate human union.[620] The word is similarly employed in Ephesians 4:16 (where vv. 15-16 serve as a parallel to this passage) to describe the body held together by its various sinews. Both participles are in the present tense pointing to the continual, unceasing nature of Christ's supply and support of His body. Christ continually works through the individual members of His body not only to supply His life to that body, but to make it an upright, moving, unified whole, able as one body to perform His will and to work together.

Indeed, this takes place "by the joints and ligaments" (διὰ τῶν ἁφῶν καὶ συνδέσμων). The preposition (διὰ) plus the genitive points to the channels by which the supply and support of the body comes from Christ its head and could be rendered "through." The means are described as two-fold. First, there are "the joints" (τῶν ἁφῶν). This noun is used only here and in Ephesians 4:16, the close parallel to this passage. Strictly speaking it means *"fastening"* or *"connection."*[621] It became a technical term in the realm of medicine and referred to the points of the body where limbs are joined one to another.[622] The single definite article governs both nouns.

Second, there are the "ligaments" (συνδέσμων). This noun refers to *"that which binds together."* It could be used in nonbiblical Greek to describe the fasteners that hold different ships together. But here it refers to the sinews that join the various parts of the body together, thus "ligaments."[623] Paul will use the word again in Colossians 3:19 to refer to love as "the perfect bond of unity" (σύνδεσμος). In Ephesians 4:3 Paul uses the word to exhort the Christians to preserve the unity of the Spirit "in the bond [τῷ συνδέσμῳ] of peace" (cf. its only other NT usage in Acts 8:23).

---

[620] Thayer, 595.
[621] Friberg, 83.
[622] Lightfoot, 197.
[623] BAGD, 785.

It is not merely the individual members that serve as the supply line from the head to His body, but their joining points—relationships—which must be characterized by both love and peace if the supply and support of the head is to bring life to His body. Both nouns are in the plural, reminding us of the many members of the body ruled by the singular head, Christ (cf. 1 Cor. 12:12-31).

This verse provides a beautiful picture of the church, though the Apostle strains the metaphor of the body to do so. The source (ἐξ) of life is Christ, the head. What is supplied by the head is "the growth of God." The means (διὰ) by which this life and growth move from the head to the members of His body are "the joints and ligaments" (which is to say the relationships characterized by love and peace). All this the false teacher(s) and his disciples miss out on by having jettisoned Christ as the supreme Lord of all, relegating Him to merely one place—even if first place—in a line of mediators between God and man. From this it may be confidently inferred that once severed from the head, the flow of life ceases and the relationships between individuals begin to break down, being characterized by disunity and selfishness.

Digging Deeper:

1. How are Christians today tempted to put their trust in mystical spiritual experiences rather than the truth of the Word of God?
2. What are the inherent dangers of founding one's spiritual life upon experience rather than objective truth?
3. What does verse 19 teach us about the necessity of living in active Christian community if spiritual maturity is our goal?

2:20 If you have died with Christ to the elementary principles of the world, why, as if you were living in the world, do you submit yourself to decrees, such as,

This new sentence runs through verse 23 in the Greek text. The heart of the sentence is the question "why ... do you submit yourself to decrees"? (τί ... δογματίζεσθε). The verb is used only here in the NT. In the active voice it means "*to decree, command, enjoin, lay down an ordinance.*"[624] The form could be either middle or passive. In either case the meaning is not significantly different. If passive, it means to submit one-self to such decrees laid down by others.[625] If middle, "why are you allowing yourselves to be subjected to authorita-tive decrees?"[626] The root of the word is δόγμα ("decree," "ordinance"). Paul has already demanded that Christ, through the cross, has "canceled out the certificate of debt consisting of decrees [τοῖς δόγμασιν]" (Col. 2:14). The particular decrees the Apostle has in mind here are those laid down by the false teacher(s) in Colossae and detailed in 2:16ff.[627] The present tense indicates that they were under a clear and present danger from the false teacher(s).

> **Ministry Maxim**
>
> Do not submit again to that to which you have died.

This then is qualified by two clauses which work one against the other. First is "If you have died with Christ to the elementary principles of the world" (Εἰ ἀπεθάνετε σὺν Χριστῷ ἀπὸ τῶν στοιχείων τοῦ κόσμου). The conditional particle (Εἰ, "if") with the aorist indicative verb (ἀπεθάνετε, "you have died") depicts a condition in which the outcome is determined. Paul contends that there is no doubt—the Colossian believers "have died with Christ" (cf. NIV's "*Since* you died with Christ," emphasis added). Paul again will say as much in 3:3. This death took place in union "with Christ" (σὺν Χριστῷ) and is pictured in one's burial "with Him in baptism" (Col. 2:12; cf. also the imagery of circumcision in 2:11). Compare the preposition (σὺν) with verses 12 and 13 where the same preposition is found repeatedly in compound and standing alone.

Paul says elsewhere that the believer has died to sin (Rom. 6:2-8, 11), the Law (Rom. 7:4-6; Gal. 2:19), and, as here, "to the elementary principles of the world" (ἀπὸ τῶν στοιχείων τοῦ κόσμου). This latter expression Paul has already used in verse 8. See there for a fuller description of its meaning. It appears in this context to point to the amalgam of humanly generated religious teaching which syncretistically combined ideas from Judaism and paganism and in some way or another, given its propensity toward the

---

[624] Thayer, 154.
[625] Friberg, 119.
[626] Rienecker, 577.
[627] Robertson, *Word Pictures*, 4:498.

worship of angels (v. 18), included some involvement with supernatural beings. Christ utterly defeated these beings through His death on the cross (v. 15). The Apostle is adamant that in union with Christ, the true follower of Jesus has also died to such "self-made religion" (v. 23).

Indeed, he does not say simply that they died "to" these things, but, more literally, "from" (ἀπὸ) these things. The preposition with the genitive denotes separation from something—in this case "the elementary principles of the world."[628] This is strengthened when we realize that the preposition is actually repeated from the prefix of the verb (ἀπεθάνετε, "died"), a compound comprised of ἀπὸ ("from") and θνῄσκω ("to die").[629] Since they have been utterly separated "from" these "elementary principles of the world" through union with Christ in His death, how can they "submit to [its] decrees"?

The second qualifying clause of "why ... do you submit yourself to its decrees" is "as if you were living in the world" (ὡς ζῶντες ἐν κόσμῳ). Their incongruous decision to submit to the pronouncements and decrees of such a cultish sect made it appear "as if you were living in the world." In one sense we all are. True—we still physically exist in this world. Yet Paul will soon enough assert that our "life is hidden with Christ in God" (3:3). He can tell the Philippians that "our citizenship is in heaven" (Phil. 3:20a). You must "keep seeking the things above" and "[set] your mind on the things above, not on the things that are on earth" (Col. 3:1b-2). Though physically we do still live in this world, the locus of our life is outside of this physical world and is defined by spiritual realities that are identified by what is true of us as we stand in union with Christ.

2:21 "Do not handle, do not taste, do not touch!"

Paul now gives three examples of the kind of "decrees" (v. 20) the false teacher(s) in Colossae was handing down. Each of the three phrases consist of an aorist subjunctive verb with the negative particle μή, thus forming a prohibition. The first two are in the middle voice, denoting the subject taking action upon or within himself. The abrupt, staccato expressions make it probable that Paul implies a mocking tone. It is not so much that he is

---

[628] BAGD, 86.
[629] Harris, 127.

quoting directly from the false teacher(s), but that he is paraphrasing in a derisive tone the general nature of the kind of things he teaches.[630]

The middle word (γεύσῃ, "taste") means simply to taste or eat food or drink. The first (ἄψῃ, "handle") and third (θίγῃς, "touch") words are nearly synonymous—indeed in some contexts they appear to have no difference in meaning (e.g., Exod. 19:12). Yet many conclude that the first (ἄπτω) is a slightly stronger word than the last (θιγγάνω). The first has the sense of touching with "the idea of voluntary or conscious effort, 'to take hold of.'"[631] Some have tried to imply certain objects such as women (making it refer to sexual contact, cf. 1 Cor. 7:1) or food. But without an object specified, this constrains the words too narrowly in this context. The latter is a somewhat colorless word which implies a more casual, even passing contact.[632] In this way many commentators identify a descending movement toward an anticlimax: Do not take hold of! Do not taste! Do not even touch![633] On the face of it such an order moves from full engagement to slightest encounter, but from a moral-awareness level it moves from least sensitive ("Do not handle") to hypersensitive ("Do not touch!").

> **Ministry Maxim**
>
> Mockery at times can be an acceptable polemic against falsehood.

2:22 (which all refer to things destined to perish with use) — in accordance with the commandments and teachings of men?

The relative plural pronoun (ἅ, "which") finds its antecedent in the implicit objects of the three examples of the "decrees" (v. 21) handed down by the false teacher(s). Those implicit objects are food and drink of various kinds.[634] Whatever their individual nature or form, "all" (πάντα) of them are included in the description that follows.

The present-tense verb (ἐστιν) points to the ongoing nature of food and drink. The singular form is unexpected when a plurality of rules is in view, and thus a plural pronoun has been used (ἅ, "which"). They are "all" (πάντα)

---

[630] Moo, 235.
[631] Lightfoot, 201.
[632] Harris, 129.
[633] Abbott, 273; BAGD, 102-103; Harris, 129; Johnson, "Human Taboos and Divine Redemption," 208; O'Brien, 150; Wright, 126; contra, Moo, 235-236.
[634] King, 205.

dealt with as a single entity (food or drink) irrespective of the plurality of their individual characteristics.

By the very nature of things, food and drink are "destined to perish with use" (εἰς φθορὰν τῇ ἀποχρήσει). More literally it might read, "unto destruction in the using." The preposition (εἰς, "to") is used here with "the vocation, use, or end indicated" and may be translated "for."[635] Food and drink "perish" (φθορὰν) and cease to exist in their original form as we eat or drink them. The word, depending upon its context, means ruin, destruction, dissolution, deterioration, corruption.[636]

Ministry Maxim
Never hang matters of eternal weight upon temporal hooks.

The reason for the destruction is not inherently communicated by the word itself, but is indicated by those words connected with it in each given context.[637] In this case the destruction comes simply "with use" (τῇ ἀποχρήσει). The noun is a compound comprised of ἀπό ("from") and χρῆσις ("usage"). The preposition when used in a compound word is perfective and thus the word means "completely using up."[638] The Apostle here echoes Jesus' instruction in Matthew 15:17 and Mark 7:19.

It is irrational to base one's eternal, spiritual destiny upon the use of things that are inherently so temporal. Food and drink were designed by God as "consumables," things provided to assist us along our earthly, temporal sojourn on this earth (Mark 7:18-19). They exist for this temporary function. They cease to exist when that fleeting, momentary, time-bound purpose is fulfilled in our eating or drinking of them. Paul says elsewhere, "we look not at the things which are seen, but at the things which are not seen; for the things which are seen are temporal, but the things which are not seen are eternal" (2 Cor. 4:18). The false teacher(s) has inexplicably made eternal things dependent upon temporal, earthbound things. "Food is for the stomach and the stomach is for food, but God will do away with both of them" (1 Cor. 6:13a).

It seems that we can misuse food and drink in one of two ways. On the one hand, as here, one may overestimate their importance, wielding ascetic

---

[635] BAGD, 229.
[636] Ibid., 858.
[637] Ibid.
[638] Rienecker, 577.

laws toward them and, by such obsessing, end up making eternal things rest upon temporal, earthly things. On the other hand, one may make food and drink of no import whatsoever, indulging at will and may thus inadvertently end up as those whose "god is their appetite" (Phil. 3:19).

This first portion of verse 22 refers to the implied objects of the prohibitions of verse 21 and is thus parenthetical, as the NASU appropriately marks out by use of parentheses.[639] The remainder of verse 22 seems then to return to the main thrust of the sentence as a whole (vv. 20-22). After having died with Christ and been made citizens of the heavenly kingdom, living by such decrees amounts to living "in accordance with the commandments and teachings of men" (κατὰ τὰ ἐντάλματα καὶ διδασκαλίας τῶν ἀνθρώπων). The preposition may have the sense of "in compliance with."[640]

The two nouns are closely related to one another, sharing a common preposition and definite article (though they differ in gender). The coordinating conjunction (καὶ, "and") holds them in a roughly parallel relationship. The first (ἐντάλματα, "commandments") refers to "what has been ordered" and thus refers to a *commandment, precept, ordinance*."[641] It is used only here by Paul and only two other times in the NT (Matt. 15:9; Mark 7:7). The second (διδασκαλίας, "teachings") is used twenty-two times in the NT; nineteen of those are by Paul and fifteen of those are in the Pastoral Epistles (1 Tim. 1:10; 4:1, 6, 13, 16; 5:17; 6:1, 3; 2 Tim. 3:10, 16; 4:3; Titus 1:9; 2:1, 7, 10). The noun may refer to either the act of teaching or to what is taught ("doctrine").[642] It is in the former sense that it is used here.

If there is a distinction to be made between the two nouns, the "commandments" may be a more specific outgrowth or example of the "teachings."[643] Both are "of men" (τῶν ἀνθρώπων). The noun "commandments" (ἐντάλματα) is always used with this noun in the genitive (Matt. 15:9; Mark 7:7). The genitive is either subjective (that which is given by humans) or adjectival (human commandments and teachings).[644] Paul is echoing his own point already made in 2:8 (cf. Titus 1:14). And once again, as in the first

---

[639] Harris, 130.
[640] Ibid.
[641] Friberg, 152.
[642] BAGD, 191.
[643] King, 207.
[644] Harris, 130.

clause of this verse, Paul appears to echo Jesus' own instruction (Matt. 15:9; Mark 7:7) which in turn echoes Isaiah (Isa. 29:13).

Digging Deeper:

1. In just what sense can it be said that "you have died with Christ"?
2. In what way can it be said that we "have died with Christ" and yet still are "living in the world"?
3. Identify specific ways in which the legalistic laws of verse 21 might be found in your church today.
4. Is it possible to avoid all use of "commandments and teachings of men"?
5. We must make applications of the principles of God's Word for our corporate life together in local churches, so how do we avoid developing our own "commandments and teachings of men"?

2:23 These are matters which have, to be sure, the appearance of wisdom in self-made religion and self-abasement and severe treatment of the body, but are of no value against fleshly indulgence.

This closing verse of the chapter (and of the larger section of thought) is notoriously difficult. The combination of rare words and difficult syntax has created a plethora of interpretational challenges. We shall seek a clear line of thought, leaving to others the duty of providing a thorough survey of the nearly endless possibilities.[645]

The opening words "These are" (ἅτινά ἐστιν) reveal a parallel with the opening of verse 22 (ἅ ἐστιν). The relative pronoun (ἅτινά, "These ... matters") is plural in form and finds its antecedent in the laws articulated in verse 21. The pronoun, says Thayer, "refers to a single person or thing, but

---

[645] For thorough overviews of the possibilities consult Lohse, 124-127; Moo, 238-242; O'Brien, 151-155.

so that regard is had to a general notion or class to which this individual person or thing belongs, and thus it indicates quality: *one who, such a one as, of such a nature that.*[646] By using this pronoun, Paul is identifying specifically the three laws set out in verse 21, but is also broadening the reference to include all such man-made religious rules (cf. "*Such* regulations," NIV). The previous relative pronoun ἅ ("which," v. 22) "makes an objective statement about the regulations" of verse 21 while here ἅτινά ("These matters") "characterizes and condemns not only the particular precepts of verse 21 but also others falling within the same category."[647]

Though the pronoun is plural, it is paired with a verb in the singular form (ἐστιν, "are"). The word "the appearance" is a translation of λόγον. Instead of the simpler and natural translation "word," here it has the sense of "anything reported in speech" and thus means "*to have the* (unmerited) *reputation of* any excellence."[648] Such laws "have" (ἔχοντα) this. The present tense, like the previous verb, points to the ongoing nature of things. The plural form agrees with ἅτινά and admits the multiplicity of such rules and the things said about them. The two verbs (ἐστιν ... ἔχοντα) may form a periphrastic present.[649]

The affirming particle μέν ("to be sure") usually is followed up by δέ, which reveals the opposite side of the matter (i.e., "on the one hand ... but on the other hand"). Some see the countering negative aspect coming in an unorthodox fashion at the end of the sentence (οὐκ ἐν τιμῇ τινι πρὸς πλησμονὴν τῆς σαρκός; thus the NASU'S addition of "but are"; cf. also ESV, NIV, NKJV, NRSV).[650] Others believe the contrasting state of things is implied by the nature of the context.[651] The reputation regards the supposed "wisdom" (σοφίας) of the false teacher's way that has been under consideration throughout this second chapter and will

> **Ministry Maxim**
>
> Pragmatism has a legitimate place in the Christian life. So in your strategy against sin, ask: "How's that working for me?"

---

[646] Thayer, 457.
[647] O'Brien, 152.
[648] Thayer, 381.
[649] Robertson, *Word Pictures*, 4:499.
[650] Harris, 131.
[651] BAGD, 503.

be summarized briefly in a moment. Paul has already designated the false teacher's product as a "philosophy" (v. 8; φιλοσοφίας, a compound word whose parts mean "love of wisdom"). But Paul insists that "all the treasures of wisdom [τῆς σοφίας] and knowledge" are found in Christ (2:3).[652]

The reported value of such ascetic laws (v. 21) is now set forth in three parallel dative nouns which follow the preposition ἐν ("in"). The preposition may be instrumental ("through," "with"), locative ("in the sphere of"), or causal ("by reason of," "as a consequence of").[653] The last seems the most likely. The coordinating conjunction καὶ ("and") appears twice (though the second instance is disputed as to its genuineness) to hold these three in parallel relationship.

The first of these is "self-made religion" (ἐθελοθρησκίᾳ). The word occurs only here in the NT. It may have been coined by Paul for this specific occasion. It appears to be a compound made up of ἐθέλω ("to will") and θρησκεία ("religion"/"worship"; cf. v. 18) and describes "worship which one devises and prescribes for himself."[654] Vincent says, "The idea of *pretence* seems to be involved here along with that of *self-chosen* worship."[655] It is not entirely clear whether their worship was directed to God or to angels (v. 18). "The apostle regards this worship as freely chosen but wrong!"[656]

The second is "self-abasement" (ταπεινοφροσύνη). Elsewhere in the NT (e.g., Col. 3:12) the word is used in a positive sense, but here (as in v. 18, see our comments there) Paul uses it in a negative sense to describe self-imposed ascetic practices.

The third is "severe treatment of the body" (ἀφειδίᾳ σώματος). Once again we encounter a word used only here in the NT. The first word is in the dative form as were the previous two. It is a compound comprised of the α-privative ("not") and φείδομαι ("sparing"). It means "*severe* (lit., *unsparing*) *treatment*" of the body (the genitive σώματος denoting the object).[657] It is thus a further reference to the self-inflicted flagellations and pains of asceticism. If the second καὶ is not genuine, then ἀφειδίᾳ

---

[652] Moo, 240.
[653] Harris, 132.
[654] Thayer, 168.
[655] Vincent, *Word Studies*, 3:500.
[656] O'Brien, 153.
[657] BAGD, 124.

σώματος ("severe treatment of the body") may be epexegetical ("self-mortification, that is, severe treatment of the body").[658]

Such actions, though impressive on a human level, are "of no value" (οὐκ ἐν τιμῇ τινι). This forms the second half of the previous μὲν ("to be sure") clause. The noun (τιμῇ), instead of the more usual idea of "honor," has here the sense of "value."[659] The idea of "benefit" or "usefulness" may be appropriate here.[660] Despite appearances ("the appearance of wisdom"), such ascetic laws and practices possess no value when pitted "against fleshly indulgence" (πρὸς πλησμονὴν τῆς σαρκός). Though not its usual meaning, the preposition πρὸς may denote a hostile relationship ("against") when used with a negative concept (such as we have in the rest of the clause here).[661] The noun (πλησμονὴν, "indulgence") is used only here in the NT. When it is used in a positive sense, it can mean something like satiety, satisfaction, or gratification. But σάρξ is most assuredly used here in a negative sense. Whereas σῶμα ("body") points to the physical body, σάρξ ("flesh") points here to that fallen part of man that tends naturally away from the things of God (following on its use in v. 18). Thus the noun is negative in connotation and "indulgence" is an appropriate rendering.[662] The genitive (τῆς σαρκός, "fleshly") is understood by the translators as adjectival ("sensual indulgence," NIV). It could also be understood as an objective genitive ("indulgence of the flesh," ESV).[663]

Digging Deeper:

1. Ask someone you trust this question: In what ways do you think I may be guilty of "self-made religion"?

2. Paul appeals to the pragmatism of things that simply don't "work" in dealing with temptation—so when is it safe for us to appeal to pragmatism and when is it not?

---

[658] Harris, 132.

[659] BAGD, 817.

[660] Friberg, 380.

[661] BAGD, 710; O'Brien observes that the noun πλησμονή ("indulgence") can be used in a positive sense ("satisfaction") and then contends that πρὸς points to the aim or goal of the false teacher(s): they aimed for "satisfaction," "But all that was satisfied was 'the flesh' (τῆς σαρκός). Their energetic religious endeavors could not hold the flesh in check. Quite the reverse. These man-made regulations actually pandered to the flesh." (155).

[662] BAGD, 673.

[663] Ibid.

COLOSSIANS 3

3:1 Therefore if you have been raised up with Christ, keep seeking the things above, where Christ is, seated at the right hand of God.

While the inferential conjunction (οὖν, "Therefore") clearly links what follows with something that has come before, the Apostle seems to be making a new start here. Chapters one and two have largely established personal connections (1:1-12, 24-29) and laid down doctrinal foundations (1:13-23; 2:1-23), while exposing the false teacher(s) of Colossae. Chapters three and four will be far less direct regarding the falsehood being taught and will draw out applications of these doctrines (3:1-4:6) and give way to personal explanations and greetings (4:7-18). In this it is not unlike the epistle to the Ephesians. Colossians 3:1-4 are transitional verses, harkening clearly to themes already developed and opening the way for instruction yet to come.

> **Ministry Maxim**
>
> Believe Bible information; practice Bible imperatives—and never confuse the two.

To what precisely does οὖν ("Therefore") look back? Given what follows in the rest of the verse, it appears that the truths of 2:12 and 13 provide the most obvious connection. There Paul speaks of the believers being "raised up with Him [Christ] through faith in the working of God, who raised Him from the dead" and that "He [the Father] made you alive together with Him [Christ]." This is a real union with Christ that is entered through faith and is witnessed to in the believer's baptism (v. 12).

The surety of these facts and experiences is in Paul's mind here as he says, "if you have been raised up with Christ" (Εἰ ... συνηγέρθητε τῷ Χριστῷ). The condition is of the first class (Εἰ + aorist indicative), meaning that the matter is not in question, but considered assured in its fulfillment (thus the NIV: "*Since*, then, you have been raised with Christ," emphasis added; cf. NLT). The precise verb that Paul employs makes this connection clear in that it is used only three times in the NT, once in 2:12 (see comments there; cf. also Eph. 2:6). It is a compound comprised of σύν ("with") and ἐγείρω ("to raise"). The aorist tense looks to this as a definite act. The passive voice views God as the active agent in raising the believer from death with Christ. The word then depicts God the Father as raising the believer (through faith, 2:12) in union with Christ in His resurrection. This is a fact for the believer. It is not an experience to be scrambled after through zealous effort or the fulfillment of religious rites. It is a settled fact accomplished by God through Christ. It is a work accomplished by God and actualized through the vehicle of the believer's resting faith, reposed upon the finished work of the crucified and risen Lord Jesus Christ. This is not an experience to seek, but a fact in which to rest. The phrase "if you have been raised up with Christ" (Εἰ ... συνηγέρθητε τῷ Χριστῷ) is set in parallel to "If you have died with Christ" (Εἰ ἀπεθάνετε σὺν Χριστῷ, 2:20a). The one introduces a section speaking of one's cocrucifixion with Christ (2:20-23), the other speaking of one's coresurrection with Christ (3:1-4).[664]

This being the fact, the Apostle commands "keep seeking the things above" (τὰ ἄνω ζητεῖτε). The command "keep seeking" (ζητεῖτε) is a present-tense imperative, underscoring that the action must be taken repeatedly, continuously, and as a matter of habit. The word carries the idea of aiming for and striving after.[665] It may have here the notion of "try to obtain" or "desire to possess."[666] What is to be thus sought are "the things above" (τὰ ἄνω). An adverb (ἄνω, "above"), when accompanied by a neuter article (τὰ), can function as a substantive.[667] This is just such a case. Paul will use the precise expression again in the next verse. But to what does it point? Surely it refers to the heavenly realms and its realities. It looks to the place

---

[664] Harris, 136.
[665] Thayer, 272.
[666] BAGD, 339.
[667] Harris, 137.

of God's abode. The adverb was used by Jesus to say, "You are from below, I am from above; you are of this world, I am not of this world" (John 8:23). Paul employs it to speak of "the Jerusalem above" (Gal. 4:26) and of the believer's "upward call of God in Christ Jesus" (Phil. 3:14). Paul told those same believers "our citizenship is in heaven, from which also we eagerly wait for a Savior, the Lord Jesus Christ" (Phil. 3:20). To the Colossians he has already spoken of "the hope laid up for you in heaven" (Col. 1:5). Seek and keep seeking "the things above" for that is where "your life is hidden with Christ in God" (3:3)!

Paul further qualifies just where he is referencing by saying it is "where Christ is" (οὖ ὁ Χριστός ἐστιν). True to form, Paul makes our pursuit a Christocentric one. Our quest is not simply for a "place," but a person. We seek Him, rather than subscribing to legalistic rules (2:16-17), spiritual elitism (2:18-19), or ascetic rigors (2:20-23), because it is He "in whom are hidden all the treasures of wisdom and knowledge" (Col. 2:3). There Christ "is" (ἐστιν)—a present tense, ongoing existence in real time. Many commentators agree that the NIV wrongly removes the comma ("where Christ is seated at the right hand of God"), failing to distinguish the verb as independent rather than part of a periphrastic expression.[668] The comma "places the emphasis where it belongs, on the simple fact of where Christ *is* rather than on what he is doing."[669]

Indeed, we seek that place where Christ is "seated at the right hand of God" (ἐν δεξιᾷ τοῦ θεοῦ καθήμενος). This fact finds its roots in Psalm 110:1, which Christ insisted was fulfilled in Himself (Matt. 22:41-46; Mark 12:35-37; Luke 20:41-44). It is marked as a place of both authority and intimacy. It is a place of authority in that there Christ is "far above all rule and authority and power and dominion, and every name that is named not only in this age, but also in the one to come" (Eph. 2:21; cf. Col. 1:16; 2:15). There God the Father has "put all things in subjection under His feet" and it is there that He "gave Him as head over all things to the church" (Eph. 2:22; cf. Col. 1:18). Peter tells us that Jesus "is at the right hand of God, having gone into heaven, after angels and authorities and powers had been subjected to Him" (1 Peter 3:22). This is the very place Christ took His seat after

---

[668] E.g., Moo, 247; O'Brien, 161; Wright, 131.
[669] Moo, 247.

"having offered one sacrifice for sins for all time" (Heb. 10:12). It is also a place of intimacy, for there Christ takes up the care and concern of His own, presenting those needs to the Father in ongoing intercession (Rom. 8:34; 1 Tim. 2:5; Heb. 7:25; 1 John 2:1-2).

3:2 Set your mind on the things above, not on the things that are on earth.

Paul repeats "the things above" (τὰ ἄνω) verbatim from verse one. Now he connects it to one of his favorite verbs (φρονεῖτε, "Set your mind"). Paul makes use of it in twenty-three of its twenty-six NT usages (ten of those in Philippians). It describes the realm of the mind: to think, to have an attitude, to form an opinion. Paul's frequent use of the word underscores the high place he affords the Christian mind. The present-tense imperative calls for continual, habitual action ("Keep thinking," NET). We are to "seek" the things above (v. 1) and "set" our thoughts upon them (v. 2). "You must not only *seek* heaven; you must also *think* heaven."[670] We are responsible for both the *posture* ("Set," v. 2) and the *pursuit* ("keep seeking," v. 1) of our minds.

This is to be done rather than (μὴ, "not") thinking about "the things that are on earth" (τὰ ἐπὶ τῆς γῆς). This stands as the polar opposite of "the things above" (vv. 1, 2). This is the realm where "fleshly indulgence" (2:23) takes place. This is the place where the false teacher(s) centers his counsel and teaching as he prescribes "severe treatment of the body" (2:23). While the believer resides "on the earth" (ἐπὶ τῆς γῆς), his home and the center and source of his life is from above (3:3, 4). The believer has "been firmly rooted" and is now "being built up in" Christ (2:7). Jesus is the locus of the believer's life and existence. The believer has died to the "elementary principles of the world" (2:8, 20). Indeed, the believer has died with Christ and is raised up with Him to a new life (2:13; 3:1). It is in Christ that the believer "has been made complete" (2:10). The ascetic, legalistic rules of the false teacher(s) regarding diet, drink, and days (2:16) serve as "a mere shadow of what is to come" whereas "the substance belongs to Christ" (2:17). The believer is one who is "holding fast to the head," Christ Himself (2:19a). To move a boulder requires a solid, stable point of leverage outside

---

[670] Lightfoot, 207.

the rock itself. To achieve real life-change requires a leverage point outside of ourselves and outside of this world—"the things that are on earth" can only be moved by leveraging against them "the things above." This is done via the believer's mind (see Appendix D).

The little phrase τὰ ἐπὶ τῆς γῆς ("the things that are on earth") becomes quite significant for Paul. Christ has created all things "on earth" (ἐπὶ τῆς γῆς; Col. 1:16). God's purpose is to sum up all things—including those "things upon the earth"—in Christ (Eph. 1:10). To this end God, through Christ, has reconciled to Himself all things "upon the earth" (Col. 1:20). Yet we are to put to death our members "which are on the earth" (τὰ ἐπὶ τῆς γῆς; 3:5, NRSV). Part of how we carry this out is by not setting our minds upon these things (3:2).

> **Ministry Maxim**
>
> The "things that are on earth" only change when we leverage our minds in faith against "the things above."

Paul sets heavenly realities ("the things above") in contrast to earthly realities ("the things that are on the earth"). In doing so he tells us that reality upon earth is defined by the reality of heaven, not the other way around. Spiritual truth defines tangible reality. We are on dangerous ground when we weigh spiritual matters by what appears to be the facts based on limited, earthly evidence. He who sees only the earthly sees only partial reality; he misses the most vital pieces of evidence for interpreting reality in its fullness.

3:3 For you have died and your life is hidden with Christ in God.

Paul now states the grounds (γὰρ, "For") for seeking "the things above" and setting our hearts upon them (vv. 1-2). The Apostle gives a twofold reason for these exhortations. First, Paul asserts simply that "you have died" (ἀπεθάνετε). This echoes Paul's earlier statement in Colossians 2:20, employing the same verb. There Paul's statement was a part of a conditional statement assumed to be fact. That assumption is proven valid as here he speaks of this death as an accomplished fact for the believer. The aorist tense describes a completed act. It is not an experience to seek, but a fact to be reckoned on by faith. As he stated in Colossians 2:20, so he asserts again—this death took place in union "with Christ" (σὺν τῷ Χριστῷ). Previously this death was said to be pictured in one's burial "with Him in baptism" (Col. 2:12; cf. the imagery of circumcision in 2:11). We should compare this declaration ("with [σὺν] Christ") with verses 12 and 13 where the preposition (σὺν) is found repeatedly both in compound and standing independently. Paul says elsewhere that the believer has died to sin (Rom. 6:2-8, 11), to the Law (Rom. 7:4-6; Gal. 2:19), and "to the elementary principles of the world" (Col. 2:20).

The second reason for Paul's previous exhortations is now added (καὶ, "and"). Alternatively, the conjunction may be understood to denote the result of their death with Christ.[671] That reason or result is that "your life is hidden" (ἡ ζωὴ ὑμῶν κέκρυπται). The expression "your life" (ἡ ζωὴ ὑμῶν) surely refers not to our earthly, human, physical life on this earth, but to the eternal life we have in Christ. Indeed, the precise phrase (ἡ ζωὴ ὑμῶν, "your life") appears again in verse four where we are told that Christ "is your life" (ἡ ζωὴ ὑμῶν, ESV). Thus Paul says both that our life is hidden *with* Christ and *is* Christ. The perfect tense of the verb (κέκρυπται, "is hidden") underscores the completed nature of the action with a resulting state of being. The passive voice makes clear that this standing was not self-produced, but is brought about by God's gracious hand. The aorist tense of "have died" makes that a singular event. The perfect emphasizes the enduring, present reality of believers in the present. "The 'death' is fact *accomplished*, the resulting 'life' is fact *continuing*."[672]

> **Ministry Maxim**
>
> Relax—your life in Christ is tucked away secretly and securely "in God"!

Our life is thus hidden "with Christ" (σὺν τῷ Χριστῷ) and "in God" (ἐν τῷ θεῷ). The preposition σὺν ("with") signals a symbiotic relationship between Christ's risen, heavenly life and the spiritual life of the believer.[673] God the Father has in fact "raised us up with [Christ], and seated us with Him in the heavenly places in Christ Jesus" (Eph. 2:6). We are thus in union with Christ, and our essence, our very life, is tucked away secretly and securely "in God" (ἐν τῷ θεῷ)—beyond the prying eyes of voyeurs and the accusing threats of opponents.

---

[671] Harris, 139.
[672] H. C. G. Moule, quoted by Johnson, "Human Taboos and Divine Redemption," 212.
[673] Harris, 139.

3:4 When Christ, who is our life, is revealed, then you also will be revealed with Him in glory.

Paul continues to make all things orbit around Christ, now referring to Him "who is our life" (ἡ ζωὴ ὑμῶν; lit., "the life of you"). There is a debate as to whether the pronoun should be second-person plural (ὑμῶν, "your," ESV, NET, NIV, NRSV) or first-person plural (ἡμῶν, "our," KJV, NASU). It is possible that a scribe changed to the second-person plural to make it conform to verse 3, but the external evidence seems to support this reading. The first-person plural may have arisen as an attempt to "universalize" the truth asserted since Christ is the life of every believer.[674] Whereas verse 3 says our life was hidden "*with* Christ," Paul here declares that Christ "*is* our life." The deep nexus of Christ and our new life is represented by placing ἡ ζωὴ ὑμῶν (lit., "the life of you") in apposition to ὁ Χριστός ("Christ"). Indeed, note the chiasmus employed by the Apostle in verses 3b-4a:

ἡ ζωὴ ὑμῶν ("your life")
  τῷ Χριστῷ ("Christ")
  ὁ Χριστός ("Christ")
ἡ ζωὴ ὑμῶν ("who is our life")[675]

As remarkable as this statement is, Paul has elsewhere expressed it with equal clarity (Gal. 2:20; Phil. 1:21), as did Jesus before him (John 14:6).

Paul has been emphasizing our present union with Christ in His death (v. 3a), resurrection (v. 1a), life (vv. 3b, 4a), and glory (v. 4b).[676] Yet the bulk of this verse speaks of future events. He speaks of "When Christ ... is revealed" (ὅταν ὁ Χριστὸς φανερωθῇ). Though the epistles normally drop the definite article when Χριστὸς is employed as a proper name, this is now the fourth time in 3:1-4 that it appears with the definite article (ὁ Χριστός).[677] The conjunction (ὅταν, "When") is used to designate an indefinite time (i.e., "Whenever"). When used with the aorist subjunctive, as here, it indicates action which precedes the action of the main clause ("you also will be revealed").[678] Christ will be revealed and then we "will be

---

[674] NET Bible.
[675] Harris, 136.
[676] Ibid.
[677] Ibid., 139-140.
[678] Friberg, 286.

revealed with Him." The verb (φανερωθῇ, "is revealed") is used frequently throughout the NT and depicts the act of making visible what has heretofore been unseen.[679] In this letter Paul uses it to describe the revelation inherent in the gospel (1:26) and also to solicit prayer that he might make "the mystery" of the gospel plain in his preaching (Col. 4:4). Here the same verb is used to refer both to the second coming of Christ and to the revelation of believers in their new glorified state at that time. The aorist tense sees this as a singular event. The subjunctive mood places its reality in dependence upon other factors. Elsewhere the verb is used to describe the first advent of Christ (Heb. 9:26; 1 Peter 1:20; 1 John 1:2; 3:5, 8) and is also used, as here, of Christ's second advent (1 Peter 5:4; 1 John 2:28; 3:2).

> **Ministry Maxim**
>
> The world won't understand who you really are until they behold Jesus is in His glory.

Whenever that takes place, "then you also will be revealed with Him" (τότε καὶ ὑμεῖς σὺν αὐτῷ φανερωθήσεσθε). First Christ's unveiling at His return, "then" (τότε; an "adverb of subsequent time"[680] that is correlated with ὅταν) our glorified state "also" (καὶ) will be made known. Once again our experience is inextricably bound up "with Him" (σὺν αὐτῷ). Again note the frequent use of σὺν, either in compound (2:12; 3:1) or independently (2:13, 20; 3:3) to describe our union with Christ. The future tense of the identical verb used to describe Christ's unveiling is now employed to speak of our unveiling. All our hope watches in confident anticipation of His revelation. Our hope is inextricably bound to Christ. For all the mystery, what we do know is that our manifestation at the time of Christ's coming will be "in glory" (ἐν δόξῃ). At His return Jesus "will transform the body of our humble state into conformity with the body of His glory, by the exertion of the power that He has even to subject all things to Himself" (Phil. 3:21). We are to live a life worthy of God "in order that the name of our Lord Jesus may be glorified in you, and you in Him, according to the grace of our God and the Lord Jesus Christ." (2 Thess. 1:12). Christ's present indwelling of the believer is his "hope of glory" (Col. 1:27). We wait for a time when the dead in Christ will be "raised in glory" (1 Cor. 15:43).

---

[679] Mounce, 439.
[680] Friberg, 383.

Digging Deeper:

1. In practical terms, what does it mean to seek and to set your mind on things above? Is there a distinction to be made between the two?

2. What does it mean when we say that we can only see change in the "things that are on earth" when we leverage our minds in faith against "the things above"? What does that look like in moments of trial or temptation?

3. How would you answer the person who says that "Set your mind on the things above" (v. 2) is a call to deny reality and live in a pretend world?

4. If "you have died with Christ" (v. 3), why doesn't it feel like it? What does this tell us about the nature of this death?

3:5 Therefore consider the members of your earthly body as dead to immorality, impurity, passion, evil desire, and greed, which amounts to idolatry.

Paul builds logically (οὖν, "Therefore") upon what he has said in verses 1-4. The believer has been placed in union with Christ in His death (v. 3; cf. 2:12, 20), resurrection (v. 1), and ascension (vv. 1b, 3), "Therefore" he should take the action prescribed here. That action is to "consider ... as dead" (Νεκρώσατε). This clearly builds on Paul's previous statement of fact: "you have died" (v. 3a). The verb here is used only two other times in the NT, both of which describe Abraham's body "as good as dead" when God fulfilled His promise to give him a son (Rom. 4:19; Heb. 11:12). It means simply "put to death" or "kill" (cf. ESV, KJV, NIV, NRSV). The aorist imperative demands that decisive action be taken immediately and without delay. The NASU uniquely makes this a mental exercise ("*consider* ... as dead," emphasis added). It is not less than that, but it certainly is more than a simple trick of the mind. That being said, the Apostle probably has something in mind very similar to "consider [λογίζεσθε] yourselves to be dead to sin" (Rom. 6:11). Romans 6 states the matter as a fact: "our old self was crucified with Him" (v. 6). In Galatians it is phrased similarly: "Now those who belong to Christ Jesus have crucified the flesh with its passions and desires" (Gal. 5:24). This states the matter as a fact to be believed and reckoned on. Yet Paul also makes this a matter of our action, for he says "present yourselves to God as those *alive from the dead*" (Rom. 6:13, emphasis added). And it is "by the Spirit [that] you are putting to death the deeds of the body" (Rom. 8:13). Scripture's back-and-forth between a description of accomplished fact and a call to action is a command, as some have well said, to "Be what you are!"

Here Paul says that each one is to put to death "the members of your earthly body" (τὰ μέλη τὰ ἐπὶ τῆς γῆς). The foundational part of this clause is "the members" (τὰ μέλη). Paul frequently uses the same expression in his description of the body of Christ (1 Cor. 6:16; 12:12, 18, 25, 26). The other two uses of the exact expression are in Romans 6:13 and 19 which is similar to our context here. Thus, though there is nothing in the Greek text here corresponding to the NASU's "body," it may represent an appropriate understanding of the Apostle's intent. Here the definite article may be understood as possessive and thus is rendered "your." Yet it is doubtful that the Apostle means the literal members of one's body (e.g., arms, legs, eyes). It refers rather to the kinds of sins that are committed by the "members" of one's body. O'Brien seems to have captured the idea when he says, "Here the practices and attitudes to which the readers' bodily activity and strength had been devoted in the old life is in view."[681] The rest of the clause (τὰ ἐπὶ τῆς γῆς) may be understood as an adjectival phrase describing "the members"—"your members, that is to say the upon-the-earth [members]."[682] This precise phrase is used three other times by Paul. The first two times refer to God's intent to sum up all thing in Christ, whether things in heaven or "things on the earth" (τὰ ἐπὶ τῆς γῆς; Eph. 1:10; Col. 1:20). The other occurrence is in Colossians 3:2 where he said, "Set your mind on the things above, not on *the things that are on earth* [τὰ ἐπὶ τῆς γῆς]." We died and our "life is now hidden with Christ in God" (v. 3). We eagerly look to heaven for the revelation of Christ "who is our life," and anticipate the consummation of our greatest hopes at that time (v. 4). We are to seek and set our minds upon "the things above"

---

[681] O'Brien, 178.
[682] Harris, 145.

(vv. 1, 2). Thus all "the things that are on earth" have nothing to offer us. They are connected with our old, hell-bound life. They offer temporary titillation, but cannot offer hope or ongoing life. Thus whatever is in "the members" of our earthly bodies that is connected to these time-bound, temporary matters, we put to death, considering them worthless to us and to our ultimate desire and destiny.

Just what does this mean in practical terms? This putting to death involves both a negative and a positive action (see Appendix D). Negatively, it means that we resist all such temptations and impulses as Paul will begin to describe in the latter part of this verse. We, to use his words from Romans 13:14, "do not think about how to gratify the desires of the sinful nature" (NIV). But a wholly negative approach to the matter may leave one obsessed with the very temptations and impulses which he is trying to "put to death." There also must be a corresponding and dominant focus which is positive. This is found precisely in what the Apostle has already prescribed: that we *seek* and *set* our minds upon "the things above" (3:1, 2). We must resist temptation as it presents itself. But ever and always we must seek and set our minds positively on Christ as the locus of our life and hope. This is the path to victory. This negative and positive approach is fleshed out as the chapter continues to unfold. Negatively we are commanded to "put ... away" (v. 8) and "put off" (v. 9). This explains and expands upon what Paul means by "put to death" in verse 5. Yet we are also, positively, to "put on" (vv. 10, 12, 14).

The Apostle now lists five of the impulses and vices which we must put to death (in v. 8 he will add five additional vices; in v. 12 he will add five contrasting virtues). The believer is able to take these actions because of the fivefold grace bestowed upon him by virtue of being in union with Christ: he died with Christ (v. 3a), he has risen with Christ (v. 1a), he is seated with Christ (v. 1b; cf. Eph. 2:6), he is hidden with Christ (v. 3b), and he will be revealed with Christ (v. 4).

The five terms we meet here in verse 5 are common to other vice lists in Paul's writings, though they are not all used together in any other place. All but the first appear in Romans 1; three of the five appear in Galatians 5. Each is in the accusative case, being either accusatives of reference (i.e., "put to death the members in reference to ... ")[683] or in apposition to "the members" (τὰ μέλη).[684]

The first here is "immorality" (πορνείαν). The word refers to "every kind of unlawful sexual intercourse."[685]

To this is added "impurity" (ἀκαθαρσίαν). In the LXX the word is used in the familiar cultic sense of ritual uncleanness. In the NT it can continue to carry this connotation, but widens out to include uncleanness in a moral sense. It is often connected with sexual sin.[686] It is a broader word than the previous one, but it "denotes immoral sexual conduct."[687] It is paired with the previous word frequently (2 Cor. 12:21; Gal. 5:19; Eph. 5:3, 11).

Then comes "passion" (πάθος). It designates "a strong emotion of desire or craving,"[688] a "drive or force which does not rest until it is satisfied."[689] It is used elsewhere in the NT only in Romans 1:26 and 1 Thessalonians 4:5, both of which confirm that a sexual connotation may be implied here as well.

Next is "evil desire" (ἐπιθυμίαν κακήν). The word "desire" (ἐπιθυμίαν) points to any strong and overwhelming desire, but here clearly it is "evil" (κακήν) desire that is in mind. It can refer to everything from the desire to be told what one wants to hear (2 Tim. 4:3) to illicit sexual desire (1 Thess. 4:5). False teachers thrive on those who never rise above their bondage to such impulses (2 Tim. 3:6).

To these Paul adds (καὶ, "and") "greed" (τὴν πλεονεξίαν). The καὶ may, alternatively, note emphasis, "especially."[690] The word literally refers to "a desire to have more." It can be variously rendered as greediness, insatiableness, avarice, and covetousness.[691] After a string of four anarthrous nouns, Paul now employs the definite article. Harris says that the article may be used here because: 1) only this word is described as "idolatry"; 2) the following clause serves to make the word definite; 3) the Apostle may have in view

---

[683] Rienecker, 578.

[684] Harris, 146; Moo, 256; O'Brien, 176.

[685] BAGD, 693.

[686] Mounce, 756.

[687] O'Brien, 181.

[688] Friberg, 291.

[689] Rienecker, 578.

[690] Lightfoot, 210; Vincent, *Word Studies*, 3:502.

[691] BAGD, 667.

some specific, concrete expressions of covetousness; and 4) it singles out a "covetousness" that is known to all his readers.[692]

To this final, climactic word Paul adds a relative clause: "which amounts to idolatry" (ἥτις ἐστὶν εἰδωλολατρία). The relative pronoun (ἥτις, "which") may emphasize a particular characteristic quality[693] ("which, by its very nature")[694] or it may have a causal sense ("for").[695] The present tense verb (ἐστὶν, "is") emphasizes the ongoing nature of "greed." It is ever and always "idolatry" (εἰδωλολατρία).

> **Ministry Maxim**
>
> Efforts to stop manifesting sin will prove futile if we fail to address the motivation to sin.

The latter term (τὴν πλεονεξίαν, "greed") may seem out of place after four nouns that all relate to sexual sins. But this disassociation is probably only apparent. The word group can be associated with sexual sin as well (cf. the cognate πλεονεκτέω in 1 Thess. 4:6), and Plato and Aristotle both used this noun of sexual sin.[696] Furthermore, sexual sin is viewed elsewhere in the NT as a form of idolatry (Rom. 1:23-27). Sexual sin—like so many other forms of vice—is subject to the law of diminishing returns. What once titillated and thrilled has now become less exciting. "More!" is required in terms of experience and expression in order to maintain the initial level of excitement. Thus "greed" is an apt description of sexual lust. And the all-consuming desire for "more" in terms of sexual experience begins to dominate one's every waking moment, consuming every thought, every look, and every relationship. Sex has become lord of every moment and as such is aptly designated as idolatry.

Thus by using these five nouns, the Apostle may be developing a theme, rather than simply stringing random nouns together. He seems to be moving from the more specific expressions of sexual sin in the direction of less specific expression and on to the core inner impulses that drive such sexual deviance. O'Brien calls it "a movement from the outward manifestations of sin to the inward cravings of the heart, the acts of immorality and

---

[692] Harris, 146-147.
[693] BAGD, 587.
[694] Harris, 147.
[695] Lightfoot, 210.
[696] O'Brien, 182.

uncleanness to their inner springs."[697] Paul begins at the broad end of the problem with manifold individual expressions of sexual sin ("sexual immorality") and moves toward the narrows of the single impulse from which they arise ("greed").

We must "put to death" (ESV) all such impulses and actions (See Appendix D). We must do so with each expression of sin and with the root disposition that gives rise to it. Strategically speaking, however, we will never win the battle simply by addressing the "acts" or expressions of sexual sin (the initial nouns in the list). We must discontinue these, but we must strategically go to the root of such acts and there deal death to those impulses and desires, and the lies which feed them (cf. v.2). James is right; "each one is tempted when he is carried away and enticed by his own lust. Then when lust has conceived, it gives birth to sin; and when sin is accomplished, it brings forth death" (1:14-15).

3:6 For it is because of these things that the wrath of God will come upon the sons of disobedience,

In a sentence running through verse 7, the Apostle now gives a reason for the jarring imperative of verse 5. The preposition (δι', "For") with the accusative can mean "of the reason or cause on account of which anything is or is done, or ought to be done; *on account of, because of*."[698] The plural relative pronoun (ἅ, "these things") looks back to the five vices in Paul's list in the previous verse.

The powerful motivating force is "the wrath of God will come" (ἔρχεται ἡ ὀργὴ τοῦ θεοῦ). The precise phrase "the wrath of God" (ἡ ὀργὴ τοῦ θεοῦ) is found in Ephesians 3:6 following a similar vice list (v. 5). The only other place the precise expression is used is in John 3:36: "He who believes in the Son has eternal life; but he who does not obey the Son will not see life, but the wrath of God [ἡ ὀργὴ τοῦ θεοῦ] abides on him." God's wrath, of course, is spoken of more broadly in the NT. Paul lays special emphasis on it in his letter to the Romans. He is "The God who inflicts wrath" (3:5). And God's wrath presently abides on the unbelieving (John 3:36); indeed they are storing up God's wrath against them by their unbelief (Rom. 2:5).

---

[697] Ibid., 178.
[698] Thayer, 134.

And yet God's wrath is in some way currently falling from heaven against unrighteousness (Rom. 1:18). At least one expression of this would be through the secondary means of the government's power to punish evildoers (Rom. 13:4). Yet God is patient in the expression of His wrath (Rom. 9:22).

Here we are told that the outpouring of God's wrath "will come" (ἔρχεται). The verb is present tense and thus might be better rendered "is coming" (ESV, NET, NIV, NKJV, NLT, NRSV). The middle voice pictures God acting upon Himself to express His wrath, moving Himself in the current expression of His wrath, and moving toward its fullest and unrestrained outpouring. This, says Paul, is good reason to take the radical step of putting to death the vices and impulses within us as listed in the previous verse.

There is significant question as to the genuineness of the rest of this verse: "upon the sons of disobedience" (ἐπὶ τοὺς υἱοὺς τῆς ἀπειθείας). Several important manuscripts do not contain these words. Other significant manuscripts do contain them. Some English versions do not include them (ESV, NASB, NIV, TNIV). They do appear to be genuine in the parallel statement in Ephesians 5:6. So it is easy to see how a scribe may have attempted to conform our present verse to that one. Yet others argue that the shorter text is the less likely to be genuine. A decision either way is difficult, coming down to a judgment call by the interpreter. It is probably best to note the presence of the words in some fashion, either to include them in the text with a footnote explaining their questioned authenticity or not include them in the text but with a footnote to draw attention to their presence in some important manuscripts.

> **Ministry Maxim**
>
> God's wrath against sins and those who commit them is a good and proper motive for holy living.

The expression itself ("the sons of disobedience") is a "Semitic idiom that means 'people characterized by disobedience.'"[699] That the wrath of God is described as coming "upon" (ἐπὶ) indicates that the judgment falls from above, from a higher plane of authority—that is to say, it is indeed divine. Those who live out their lives on the purely horizontal plane, seldom if ever lifting their eyes to include the higher perspective of divine realities, exist for the purely selfish ("greed") and sensuous ("evil desire," "passion,"

---

[699] NET Bible.

"impurity," and "sexual immorality"). They assume there is no one "above" them—who created them, who owns them, who is ruling them—no one to whom they must answer. One day they will be utterly shocked to discover divine, inescapable, eternal wrath descending upon them and holding them accountable for a lifetime of misdirected desires and actions.

3:7 and in them you also once walked, when you were living in them.

The opening "and" has no corresponding conjunction in the Greek text. The NASU translators make it an interpretive addition in an attempt to render the original text in good English. The phrase ἐν οἷς ("in them") could find its antecedent in "the sons of disobedience" (v. 6), if that is genuine. It seems more likely that it refers back to the list of five vices in verse 5. The preposition (ἐν, "in") pictures the sphere of the Colossian believers' pre-Christian lives. It stands in stark contrast to their present life "in" Christ, an emphasis found so frequently in Colossians (e.g., 1:2, 28; 2:3, 6, 7, 9, 10, 11-13, 15) and elsewhere in Paul's writings. The καὶ in most English translations either isn't translated at all (NIV, NLT), or the translators see it as adding emphasis, using words such as "also" (NASU, NET, NRSV), "too" (ESV), and "yourselves" (NKJV). It is our opinion that it should be translated and that it serves to bring emphasis, thus a rendering such as "also" is appropriate. That Paul is speaking here of the Colossian believers is made clear by his use of the plural form of the personal pronoun (ὑμεῖς, "you").

The verb (περιεπατήσατέ, "once walked") is a common one, used almost one hundred times in the NT. It means simply "to walk." But it is often used by Paul, as he does here (cf. also 1:10; 2:6; 4:5), in a figurative sense to describe the unfolding of one's life one step at a time. Thus some translations render it "lived" (e.g., NET). The aorist tense looks at their past lives as a singular event, each one viewed as a whole. This way of life was true of them "once" (ποτε), though, apparently, no longer because of the liberty from sin they had found through repentance and faith in Jesus Christ.

> **Ministry Maxim**
>
> The sins we once walked and lived in are no longer obligatory for us.

Paul is thinking back to the time "when you were living in them" (ὅτε ἐζῆτε ἐν τούτοις). The subordinating conjunction ὅτε carries a temporal connotation ("when") so that it specifies the time of the verb's action ("walked"). That was a time when they "you were living" (ἐζῆτε) in those vices of verse 5. The imperfect tense views their former life as simply unfolding unendingly. It was an ongoing, repeated set of experiences that made up a certain quality of life. The second-person plural reminds the Colossian believers that this was the case in each and every one of their lives. Again, as in the opening of the verse, Paul pictures the sphere of their pre-Christian lives (ἐν τούτοις, "in them"). The demonstrative plural pronoun (τούτοις, "them") looks back, as did the previous relative pronoun (οἷς, "them"), to the vices listed in verse 5. In the sphere of these sins and impulses the Colossians—and we—had both "walked" and "lived" before we met Christ.

Digging Deeper:

1. If we "have died" with Christ (v. 2), what then are we to "Put to death" (v. 5)? Is this a call to kill what is already dead?
2. If we once (past tense) walked in and lived in (v. 7) these various vices (v. 5), how can we now in the present need to put them to death (v. 5, ESV)?
3. Using the illustrations in Appendix D, explain to someone the inside-out nature of sexual sin.
4. Discuss with them a corresponding strategy to live free from sexual idolatry. Discuss how you can help one another live free in this regard.

3:8 But now you also, put them all aside: anger, wrath, malice, slander, and abusive speech from your mouth.

With a mild adversative (δέ, "But") Paul makes a turn from what used to be true of the Colossian believers (v. 7) to what must "now" (νυνὶ) be true of them. The adverb νυνὶ ("now") is in direct contrast with ποτε ("once") of verse 7.[700] Instead of the indulgence they once practiced, now they are to "put ... aside" (ἀπόθεσθε). The word simply means "to put off" or "to put aside," as one would do with clothing (cf. Acts 7:58). It is found only

---

[700] Robertson, *Word Pictures*, 4:501.

in the middle/passive voice in the NT. It comes then to mean to give up or renounce.[701] Paul employs it similarly in his other uses (Rom. 13:12; Eph. 4:22, 25). To "put ... aside" is another way of describing what Paul meant by "Put to death" (v. 5, ESV, NIV) of verse 5. In fact Paul will employ another verb in verse 9 to communicate the same basic idea: "laid aside" (ἀπεκδύομαι). Here the aorist imperative matches the same form in "Put to death" (ESV) of verse 5. The Apostle makes this a matter of urgent, immediate obedience. Paul makes the personal nature of compliance emphatic (καὶ ὑμεῖς, "you also"). The expression may mean either "you also" as with all other Christians[702] or "you yourselves."[703]

The call is to put aside "them all" (τὰ πάντα). Does this expression serve as "a summation of what precedes"[704] (the vice list of v. 5) or does it anticipate the list of vices that is to follow in verse 8?[705] Most likely it serves in an all-inclusive manner, indicating all that relates to "the old self" (v. 9)—including all the items in these two vice lists[706] and whatever else may be added to them. All these must be "put ... aside" as worn-out clothing from a previous life.

Now, as in verse 5, Paul strings together another series of five nouns to form a second list of vices. Whereas verse 5 dealt with sexual sins, here the focus is upon social sins.

First is "anger" (ὀργήν). The word is a powerful one. Thayer says it derives from ὀργάω which means "to teem, denoting an internal motion, especially that of plants and fruits swelling with juice."[707] Unresolved conflicts fester and eventuate in bitterness. The churning resentment eventually erupts upon the surface and destroys those in its path. What is holy in God ("the wrath [ἡ ὀργὴ] of God," v. 6) is unholy and destructive in man (v. 8).

> **Ministry Maxim**
>
> Mastery of our mouths begins with mastery of our hearts.

---

[701] Thayer, 69.
[702] Abbott, 282.
[703] Moo, 262.
[704] BAGD, 633.
[705] O'Brien, 187.
[706] Alford, 3:233; Kent, 128; Wright, 136.
[707] Thayer, 452.

Second is "wrath" (θυμόν). This often appears in Paul's vice lists (2 Cor. 12:20; Gal. 5:20; Eph. 4:31). The previous word describes a settled wrath, but in contrast this word "is used of *anger* that boils up and subsides again."[708] Thus it describes *active* anger or wrath. It can be thus variously translated as "angry tempers" (2 Cor. 12:20) and "outbursts of anger" (Gal. 5:20).

Third is "malice" (κακίαν). Paul can use it more generally simply of "evil" (1 Cor. 14:20), but often also in the more specialized sense, as here, of "malice" (Rom. 1:29; 1 Cor. 5:8; Eph. 4:31; Titus 3:3). In this latter sense it describes "maliciousness or inward viciousness of disposition."[709]

Fourth is "slander" (βλασφημίαν). We derive our word "blasphemy" from this word, and it can have that connotation when used of speech directed against God (e.g., John 10:33). When directed at persons, however, it can also refer to "slander" or more generally to "abusive language" (1 Tim. 6:4). The adjective and verb forms are used in both the sense of blasphemy against God (1 Tim. 1:13, 20; 6:1; Titus 2:5) and speech against humans (2 Tim. 3:2; Titus 3:2).

And finally Paul cites "abusive speech" (αἰσχρολογίαν). The word is used only here in the NT. The word comes from αἰσχρολόγος which in turn was formed from αἰσχρός ("disgraceful") and λέγω ("word").[710] Lightfoot contends that the dual elements of "filthiness" and "evil-speaking" are contained in the word.[711] It is "*evil speech* in the sense of *obscene speech*."[712] This is to be kept "from your mouth" (ἐκ τοῦ στόματος ὑμῶν) or more literally "out from the mouth of you" (cf. v. 5 where the final vice in the list was similarly qualified by an adjectival phrase). It is possible that this clause governs both of the last two words, since they both have to do most directly with sins of the tongue.

In the previous list of vices (v. 5), Paul began with the manifestation of the evil and worked backward toward its root motivation (see discussion on v. 5 and Appendix D). Here, however, he moves in the opposite direction— beginning with the root motivation ("anger") and moving outward in ever

---

[708] Friberg, 200, emphasis original; cf. Thayer, 293.
[709] Robertson, *Word Pictures*, 4:332.
[710] Thayer, 17.
[711] Lightfoot, 212.
[712] BAGD, 25.

increasingly demonstrative expressions of that anger (concluding with "abusive speech"). Thus we may trace the progressive nature of these sins. It begins with an inward "anger," which, if unchecked, moves forward into a flash of anger ("wrath"). Such "wrath," if not "put ... aside" quickly, festers and becomes increasingly intent on actually harming the other person ("malice"), an impulse which may express itself in "slander" or "abusive speech."

Many a married couple, if they are willing, can trace this pattern through some of their worst moments together. Jesus was correct in His analysis of the order: "the mouth speaks out of that which fills the heart" (Matt. 12:34b; cf. 15:18-19). Again, as in verse 5 (though here it is developed in reverse order), the implication is that victory is found in dealing with the root motivation, not at the level of fruit bearing.

If, then, we have accurately perceived the root-to-fruit pattern of the vice lists in verses 5 and 8, that means that Paul is identifying two key root sins here: "greed" (v. 5) and "anger" (v. 8). What are "greed" and "anger" except selfishness—self-orientation toward what another has ("greed") or does ("anger")? This serves only to underscore the essential nature of a Christ-focused, heaven-directed orientation for our thinking as set forth in verses 1-4. The key to deliverance from the power of these sin vortexes is found at the root of our thoughts and interpretations of life and its relationships: "Set your mind on the things above, not on the things that are on earth" (v. 2)!

3:9 Do not lie to one another, since you laid aside the old self with its evil practices,

The Apostle now commands: "Do not lie" (μὴ ψεύδεσθε). The present-tense imperative with the negation (μὴ, "not") forms this into a prohibition—either demanding that action now in progress be dropped or forbidding any such deception in any form or at any time. A prepositional phrase narrows the focus of the prohibition: "to one another" (εἰς ἀλλήλους). The reciprocal pronoun underscores the relational nature of the concern and probably refers to the circle of relationships among believers, though Paul clearly would not condone lying to nonbelievers. In the absolute sense of the word, lying is a sin of the tongue and might be grouped with the five vices listed in verse 8. Yet the word describes not only verbal utterances of falsehood, but also deceptive actions (Acts 5:3, 5). Thus Paul may have in mind not simply lying words, but the lying lifestyle of one who claims the name of Christ but continues to live after the old, sinful nature. Such a one may be "living a lie." This Christians must not do. When he demands "Do not lie to [εἰς] one another" the preposition may indicate direction ("to one another" as in most English versions)[713] or opposition (*"tell lies against someone,* i.e., to his detriment"[714]). The former seems the more likely of the two.

Paul now gives support for this prohibition (and probably all the prohibitions and commands of vv. 5-9a[715]) in the form of two parallel participial phrases, the first here in verse 9 and the second making up verse 10. The first picks up on the imagery of taking off one's old clothing (v. 8), though using a different word: "since you have laid aside" (ἀπεκδυσάμενοι). This word is used elsewhere in the NT only in Colossians 2:15: "When He had disarmed [ἀπεκδυσάμενος] the rulers and authorities ..." (though the cognate noun is found in 2:11). The basic notion of the verb is that of stripping off clothing. This is a stronger term than that of verse 8 (ἀπόθεσθε, "put ... aside") and indicates something even more fundamental, something foundational that makes that action possible.[716]

What Paul demands here is possible precisely because of what God did through Christ on the cross (2:15). Because Christ disrobed (and thus disarmed) the demonic powers that once sought to hold us in bondage to sin (2:11) and through Him we have "laid aside" the old life of slavery (3:9b), we are able to lay aside falsehoods (3:9a). Here the aorist tense views the action as decisive. The middle may have its standard reflexive sense of taking action upon oneself, but we understood the middle form of Colossians 2:15 to have an active meaning (see discussion there) so it may have that same sense here as well. But just when did this action take place? Is this synonymous with salvation? Or is this an event of one's sanctification subsequent to salvation? Given the

> **Ministry Maxim**
>
> Any ability to change our ways is a result of Christ having changed our identity.

corresponding expression of the next verse ("and have put on the new self") it seems best to understand this as descriptive of the change wrought by

---

[713] Harris, 150.
[714] BAGD, 229, 891.
[715] Moo, 265.
[716] Bruce, NIC, 146.

repentance and faith at the time of salvation and witnessed to in one's baptism. Subsequently the believer must "Put to death" (v. 5, ESV) the sin that continues to cling to him in this life (in a quest to become in experience what he is by gracious declaration of God). The participial form is to be understood as indicating the grounds upon which the imperative is expected to be obeyed ("*since* you laid aside," as with most English translations: e.g., ESV, NET, NKJV, NIV, NRSV).[717] In view of the fact that we have, through repentance and faith, taken off and cast aside the old life and have "put on the new self" (v. 10), we ought no longer to live a double life, lying to our brothers and sisters in Christ.

That which is laid aside is "the old self" (τὸν παλαιὸν ἄνθρωπον) or, more literally, "the old man" (NET, NKJV). The precise phrase is used elsewhere only in Ephesians 4:22, and that in a similar context. But nearly the same expression is used in Romans 6:6 which will aid us in understanding just what Paul is referencing here. There he speaks of both "our old self" (ὁ παλαιὸς ἡμῶν ἄνθρωπος) and our "body of sin" (τὸ σῶμα τῆς ἁμαρτίας). The first, he says, "has been crucified" (συνεσταυρώθη). The second "might be done away with" (καταργηθῇ). From Paul's discussion it seems best to understand "our old self" to refer to our old, unregenerate person, prior to conversion.[718] This "old self" has now ceased to exist, for I have been made a new person in Christ (2 Cor. 5:17). Yet my "body of sin" continues to harass me, though its power has been broken. It continues to shout, to demand, and to woo me toward sin, but it can no longer *compel* me to sin. The translation of the particular verb in Romans 6:6 is somewhat unfortunate (καταργηθῇ, "might be done away with"). The idea might be better expressed as "rendered powerless," as opposed to ceasing to exist.[719] Thus, when Paul says here, "you laid aside the old self," he is speaking of the change wrought in regeneration at the time of conversion. It is through repentance and faith in Jesus Christ that a person lays aside their former life and receives new life in Jesus Christ, becoming an entirely new person. This is a truth which has both individual and corporate aspects to it.[720]

---

[717] King, 245; as opposed to vesting imperatival meaning to the participle to conform it to Eph. 4:22 as some do (e.g., Lightfoot, 212-213).

[718] BAGD, 605.

[719] Stott, 44-45.

[720] O'Brien, 190.

Individually, my preconversion, unregenerate life has ended, and I have been born again to new life in Christ, having been given an entirely new existence. Corporately, I have ceased to exist "in Adam" and now exist "in Christ" (1 Cor. 15:22). In this latter sense I belong now to a new humanity.

In such a state one then is able to lay aside "the old self" along "with its evil practices" (σὺν ταῖς πράξεσιν αὐτοῦ). It is precisely because the "old self" has ceased to exist through cocrucifixion with Christ on the cross and because we have been brought into union with Christ our head that we are able now in the present to set aside the "evil practices" that once characterized our life without Christ. Our word *praxis* is brought over directly from πρᾶξις, which variously describes an activity, function, way of acting, etc. Here in the plural it refers to evil or disgraceful deeds (cf. Rom. 8:13).[721] Presumably this term gathers up all the vices listed in verses 5, 8, and 9 along with any others that might be added to them. Once again Paul is stressing that we must become in practice what we are by profession of faith.

3:10 and have put on the new self who is being renewed to a true knowledge according to the image of the One who created him —

Paul now adds (καὶ, "and") the second participial clause, providing the second ground upon which the imperatives (vv. 5-9a) are based. Corresponding to the first participle ("since you laid aside the old self," v. 9) Paul tells us we "have put on the new self" (ἐνδυσάμενοι τὸν νέον). Once again the tense is aorist and the voice middle—with the same emphases as the previous participle (see v. 9). The verb will be used again in verse 12 where it is clear that what is "put on" are new virtues and actions. Paul has emphasized the change of position and identity with regard to "the old man" (v. 9) and now he intends the same here with regard to "the new self." This is a change both of regeneration to new life with a new heart individually and of transfer from being counted "in Adam" to being established "in Christ" corporately.[722] The articular adjective "new self" (τὸν νέον) employs a word that "denotes the new primarily in reference to time, the young, recent."[723] The adjective should be read with an understood ἄνθρωπον, transferred over from verse 9.

---

[721] BAGD, 697-698.
[722] O'Brien, 190-191.
[723] NIDNTT, 2:669-670; Rienecker, 579; Thayer, 318.

While such a change will be manifested clearly in one's outward behavior (vv. 9, 12), it is fundamentally an inward change, for such a one is he "who is being renewed to a true knowledge" (τὸν ἀνακαινούμενον εἰς ἐπίγνωσιν). The participle seems to explain or expound upon what has just been said ("which," ESV, NIV) rather than being understood as substantival ("who," NASU, NKJV). The participle itself is a compound word comprised of "again" (ἀνά) and "make new" (καινόω). The word is used only here and in 2 Corinthians 4:16: "though our outer man is decaying, yet our inner man *is being renewed* day by day" (emphasis added). The present tense underscores the continual nature of the process (cf. Rom. 12:2; 2 Cor. 3:18). The passive voice emphasizes that the accomplishment of this renewal is the doing of another—God Himself.

The second component of the compound (καινόω) is from a word group that denotes newness with regard to quality.[724] It is possible that the two adjectives for "new" used here are simply used for variety's sake and are synonymous in meaning. If there is any implied difference in meaning, perhaps it is being emphasized that in time (νέος) and space God has made us new by the regeneration of the Holy Spirit. We are, by His grace, not what we once were in Adam. Yet He is ever and always working to make what He has effected in us true of us in every dimension of our being. He is thus always making us anew, actualizing a new (καινός) quality of life here and now. In this there is constant hope, for we are not what we shall yet be in Christ by God's grace.

This ongoing transformation is "to a true knowledge" (εἰς ἐπίγνωσιν). This is now the fourth time in this letter that Paul has used the noun ἐπίγνωσις (1:9, 10; 2:2; 3:10), and he employs the cognate verb in 1:6. It is a compound word (ἐπί, "upon" and γνῶσις, "knowledge") which intensifies the root and points to fullness, depth, and completeness of knowledge. He has been using the word in a thrust against the false teacher(s) in Colossae. He was emphasizing his knowledge of things spiritual (2:4, 8, 18), but Paul makes clear that in Christ "are hidden all the treasures of wisdom and knowledge" (Col. 2:3). In the earlier usages Paul prays or longs for the realization of this knowledge in the Colossian believers' lives. In 1:9 the knowledge Paul desired for the Colossian believers was "of His will," in 1:10 it was "of God," and in 2:2 it

---

[724] NIDNTT, 2:669-670; Rienecker, 579; Thayer, 318.

was knowledge "of God's mystery," a "mystery" which is "Christ Himself." The preposition is directional—God is ever moving us "into" this full, true, complete knowledge that is found in Christ alone.

This renewal is not nebulous or without form. It has a pattern, a goal, a destination. It is "according to the image of the One who created him" (κατ' εἰκόνα τοῦ κτίσαντος αὐτόν). The word translated "the image" (εἰκόνα) immediately reminds one of Genesis 1:26-27: "Then God said, 'Let Us make man in Our image, according to Our likeness ...' God created man in His own image, in the image of God He created him; male and female He created them." Yet here in Colossians the word was used by Paul earlier to say that Christ "is the image [εἰκὼν] of the invisible God" (1:15a). As we pointed out in our comments on that verse, this is a theologically rich and significant word as it relates to one's Christology. The same word that in 1:15 stresses not just similarity but shared essence is now used of the pattern after which the believer is being remade. While Christ is the image of God (1:15), we have been and are being remade "according to" (κατ') the image of Christ (3:10).

This is holy ground, and we must take off our theological sandals and walk softly. This does not say that we are the "image" of Christ as He is the "image" of God, but that we are being remade "according to" (κατ', "*in accordance with, just as, similar(ly) to*"[725]) His "image." It is not that the believer ever shares in the divine essence itself, yet the union of the believer with Christ is indeed real. So real is it that Paul has been able to speak of "Christ, who is our life" (3:4). "For in Christ all the fullness of the Deity lives in bodily form, and you have been given fullness in Christ" (Col. 2:9-10a). Peter asserts that we "may become partakers of the divine nature" (2 Peter 1:4). To be sure—and to emphasize once again—we do not

> **Ministry Maxim**
>
> Our life and goal and pattern are Christ Himself— and nothing less.

and never will share in Christ's divinity or Godhood. Yet the writers of Scripture speak of the union of the believer with Christ in the most intimate of ways. Paul speaks elsewhere of the body of Christ coming to a place where we attain "to the measure of the stature which belongs to the fullness of Christ" (Eph. 4:13) and that together we may actually become "the

---

[725] BAGD, 407.

fullness of Him who fills all in all" (1:23). This is a mystery whose subtle nuances are difficult to draw out in detail (and which we attempt at our own peril), but whose parameters are clearly drawn (and which we ignore to our own spiritual detriment).

The image after which we are being remade is "of the One who created him" (τοῦ κτίσαντος αὐτόν). Here in Colossians it is Christ who is pictured as the Creator. He is "the firstborn over all creation. For by Him all things were created" (1:15b-16a). The personal pronoun (αὐτόν, "him") finds its antecedent in "the new self" (τὸν νέον [ἄνθρωπον]).[726] Since inwardly we are being remade after Christ's image (v. 10b), we ought then to put on new outward actions to reflect this inward change (vv. 8-9). This inward-to-outward movement of logic confirms our understanding of the vice lists in verses 5 and 8 where we saw Paul logically moving from inward impulse to outward action in his description of sin and in implicitly outlining a strategy for overcoming these sins.

3:11 a renewal in which there is no distinction between Greek and Jew, circumcised and uncircumcised, barbarian, Scythian, slave and freeman, but Christ is all, and in all.

The adverb ὅπου ("in which") is used as a subordinating conjunction in relative clauses.[727] In this instance its antecedent is "the new self" (τὸν νέον, v. 10). In what follows it is clear that Paul now has the corporate nature of "the new self" in view more than the individual. Thayer says that here it means "in which state (viz. of the renewed man)."[728] Robertson says that here it "is almost personal."[729] The next phrase (οὐκ ἔνι, "there is no") is used six times in four passages in the NT (1 Cor. 6:5; Gal. 3:28 [3x]; Col. 3:11; James 1:17). Robertson says it "means 'there is not' rather than 'there cannot be,' a statement of a fact rather than a possibility."[730] Its use in

> **Ministry Maxim**
>
> The grace of God given indiscriminately to us in Christ behooves us to share it indiscriminately among ourselves.

---

[726] Harris, 153.
[727] Friberg, 283.
[728] Thayer, 450.
[729] Robertson, *Grammar*, 712.
[730] Robertson, *Word Pictures*, 4:299.

Galatians 3:28 is similar to how Paul uses it here—to indicate distinctions between classes of people which are no longer valid within the circle of the gospel. The negation (οὐκ, "no") "denies the thing itself (or to speak technically, denies simply, absolutely, categorically, directly, objectively)."[731] The word ἔνι is variously explained either as an original and strengthened form of the preposition ἐν ("in") combined with the verb ἐστιν, whose presence is presumed, or as an abbreviated form of a verb which comes ultimately from ἔνειμι ("be, exist").[732]

Paul now designates different racial, religious, cultural, and social distinctions that, while found on earth among the unredeemed, are obliterated and cease to exist in "the new self" re-created by Christ. He first gives two pairs that contrast ethnicities, then names two groups individually, and then closes with another contrasting pair.

First is the pair "Greek and Jew" (Ἕλλην καὶ Ἰουδαῖος). Eleven of the thirteen times Paul uses the noun "Greek" (Ἕλλην), he combines it, as he does here, with the word "Jew" (Ἰουδαῖος). It refers not simply to people of Greek culture or language, but more broadly to pagan or heathen peoples generally.[733] This is in distinction from the "Jew" as determined by birth, race, or religion.[734]

The next pair is "circumcised and uncircumcised" (περιτομὴ καὶ ἀκροβυστία), which is the same distinction simply considered now by that characteristic mark (or its absence) which set the Jew apart from the Gentile (cf. Col. 4:11). Paul may have repeated himself in this way for sake of emphasis simply because the false teacher(s) in Colossae seemed to have had a significant Jewish bent to his teaching and may have been championing physical circumcision as necessary for saving faith. Paul has already made use of the word for "circumcision" in 2:11. It was when you were "dead in your transgressions and the uncircumcision of your flesh" (2:13) that God made you alive together with Christ.

Then there is "barbarian" (βάρβαρος). The word referred to those who spoke in *stammering, stuttering* expressions, *"uttering unintelligible sounds"* and who were thus considered of "strange speech or foreign

---

[731] Thayer, 408.
[732] Moo, 270.
[733] BAGD, 252.
[734] Ibid., 379.

language (i.e., non-Greek in language and culture in the NT)."[735] The word itself had an "onomatopoetic repetition" to its intonation—with the sound *bar-bar*.[736] Then comes "Scythian" (Σκύθης). The Scythians were inhabitants of what is today southern Russia. "By the more civilized nations of antiquity the Scythians were regarded as the wildest of all barbarians."[737] They were "the barbarian or savage 'par excellence'."[738]

Finally there is the pair "slave" (δοῦλος) and "freeman" (ἐλεύθερος), which mark out both sides of the social scale of bondage to servitude on the one hand and self-directed autonomy on the other.

The false teacher(s) was preaching a "gospel" that divides—some are "in" and others are "out." Some are "in the know" and others are not. The gospel of Jesus Christ unites. It overcomes social, racial, religious, and cultural distinctions to make all believers stand on the level ground of grace before God "in Christ." The grace of God coming down to man is given without regard to such distinctions. That grace which operates on a vertical axis from God to man then goes horizontal between the recipients of such grace, and those same distinctions fade away in the fellowship of those who make up the "new self."

In strong contrast to such distinctions (ἀλλά, "but"), Paul makes the amazing assertion that "Christ is all, and in all" (πάντα καὶ ἐν πᾶσιν Χριστός). He closes with a phrase which is void of a verb, but is all the more powerful for its succinctness. Most English translations appropriately add the verb "is" for our understanding. The proper noun (Χριστός, "Christ") is placed at the end of the sentence for emphasis. Christ is said to be "all and in all" (πάντα καὶ ἐν πᾶσιν). Just what is meant by saying Christ is "all" (πάντα)? The neuter plural form serves to encompass all things. Robertson says that πάντα is used as a predicate for Χριστός and thus stands "for the totality of things."[739] Christ created all things (1:16a). Christ sustains all things (1:17b). Christ is supreme over all things (1:17a). Christ is "all" (πάντα). This is not a pantheistic statement, but a way of saying that the sum and substance of everything is Christ. He is the singular point of their

---

[735] Friberg, 87.
[736] Robertson, *Word Pictures*, 4:503.
[737] Thayer, 580.
[738] BAGD, 758.
[739] Robertson, *Grammar*, 657.

origin. He is the one necessity for their continuance. All things exist for Him (1:16b). It is then both logical and appropriate to speak of Christ as "all." In the application of God's grace, then, Christ engulfs all racial, religious, and cultural differences with His indiscriminate grace. "Christ is all" anyone needs to become a fully welcomed and functioning participant in the "new self." Nothing added. Nothing needed. "Christ is all."

Paul speaks here of this as an established fact. Yet he speaks elsewhere of it as a fact (in the universal, all-inclusive sense) yet to be established. "When all things are subjected to Him, then the Son Himself also will be subjected to the One who subjected all things to Him, so that God may be all in all [πάντα ἐν πᾶσιν]" (1 Cor. 15:58). Indeed, even here in Colossians he does so: "He is also head of the body, the church; and He is the beginning, the firstborn from the dead, so that He Himself will come to have first place in everything [ἐν πᾶσιν]" (1:18). What Christ is now, He is by divine and redemptive right. Yet this is not currently seen and acknowledged by all. At His return, however, all will see what has always been true of Him—"Christ is all in all"!

As sweeping as is the first part of this statement, this is not all that Paul asserts. He adds (καὶ, "and") that Christ is "in all" (ἐν πᾶσιν). The adjective (πᾶσιν, "all") by form may be either neuter ("in all things") or masculine plural ("in all [redeemed] people"). The first would be a pantheistic statement, something Paul would not make. Surely then it is the latter, and Paul is emphasizing that Christ now indwells His people through His Spirit (John 14:16-18). He has made His people His temple, both individually (1 Cor. 6:19) and corporately (1 Cor. 3:16). Elsewhere Paul speaks of God as the "Father of all who is over all and through all and in all [ἐν πᾶσιν]" (Eph. 4:6). Now the fullness of God (Christ) has come to fill us full of Himself (Col. 2:9-10) and to be in us and to us and for us all that we should be. Indeed, our calling is to be "His body, the fullness of Him who fills all in all [πάντα ἐν πᾶσιν]" (Eph. 1:23)! This will not be fulfilled by straining effort to achieve such a standing. It is achieved by Christ as He indwells His people who in restful faith simply find Him to be their all in all. This cannot be restricted by any distinction found among mankind—be it cultural, racial, religious, or social. "Christ is all and in all"!

Digging Deeper:

1. Though different in nature, in what ways do the social sins of v. 8 follow the same developmental pattern of the sexual sins of v. 5?
2. How does the root-to-fruit orientation of such relationally destructive sins explain their origin? Help define the path to triumph over them?
3. Where do you see discriminations made relationally among others? How do these deny the grace of God and destroy the fellowship and witness of God's people (v. 11)?
4. What should "Christ is all and in all" mean practically for you and for your local church collectively?

3:12 So, as those who have been chosen of God, holy and beloved, put on a heart of compassion, kindness, humility, gentleness and patience;

Paul now draws a logical inference (οὖν, "So") from what he has just explained. He takes up the same verb (Ενδύσασθε, "put on") he used in verse 10. Previously he stated that believers "have put on" (ἐνδυσάμενοι) the "new self." Now, in keeping with that new reality and identification, we are exhorted to "put on" the graces that match our standing. We are to become in experience what we have been declared to be in fact. The aorist imperative indicates that the necessary action is urgently needed and demands that it be undertaken at once. The middle voice pictures the subjects as responsible to take this action upon themselves.

In verses 5 and 8 the Apostle chose in each instance to name five vices to be "put aside." Now he identifies five graces which are to be "put on." But before he identifies what these are, he uses a subordinate clause to explain how it is he is able to expect obedience to this imperative. We are to undertake this action "as those who have been chosen by God" (ὡς ἐκλεκτοὶ τοῦ θεοῦ). Such an imperative is not laid upon us in our humanness and finite strength, but "as" (ὡς) we are under the electing love of God. The conjunction ὡς ("as") "introduces the characteristic quality of a pers[on] ..."[740] Here we

---

[740] BAGD, 898.

are considered as we are, to use Paul's oft-employed expression, "in Christ." The adjective is used as a substantive (ἐκλεκτοὶ, "those who have been chosen," emphasis added). It refers to "those whom God has chosen fr[om] the generality of mankind and drawn to himself."[741] This selection was made "by God" (τοῦ θεοῦ). The eternal God, before time began, laid His electing, choosing love upon those He selected. It is only in this way that His grace came to us and we believed unto eternal life. It is precisely because of this that we are therefore deemed by Him to be "holy and beloved" (ἅγιοι καὶ ἠγαπημένοι). God alone is "holy" (ἅγιοι) by nature. Yet because of His grace made possible through the sacrificial death of Jesus, God Himself will present us before Himself as "holy [ἁγίους] and blameless and beyond reproach" (1:22). Because of this He can rightly call us "saints" (1:2, 4, 12, 26). To this adjective Paul adds (καί, "and") a participle: "beloved" (ἠγαπημένοι). The perfect tense indicates that they became thus "beloved" at a point in time in the past and continue in this abiding state at the present moment. The passive voice reveals that this was accomplished by God's electing love. God simply chose to set His love upon the elect from the creation of the world. The Apostle is not indiscriminately laying moral imperatives upon people and expecting them to fulfill them in their own strength. Rather it is precisely because of this gracious favor of God that we are able to "put on" these various graces. Gospel imperatives are possible precisely because of gospel grace.

> **Ministry Maxim**
>
> Gospel imperatives are possible precisely because of gospel grace.

From this fount of grace the believer is to "put on" five graces. Paul has listed five vices to be put off in verses 5 and 8, and now he maintains the symmetry by calling for five virtues to be put on. By another calculation one might conclude that Paul actually enumerated six vices and virtues in each case, or, perhaps even more accurately, he used a "five plus one" configuration, enumerating five vices or virtues and then providing a concluding explanatory or summarizing element: "immorality, impurity, passion, evil desire, and greed" plus "idolatry" (v. 5); "anger, wrath, malice, slander, and abusive speech" plus "Do not lie" (vv. 8-9a); and "a heart of compassion, kindness, humility, gentleness and patience" plus "love" (vv. 12, 14a).

---

[741] Ibid., 242.

By whatever enumeration, the present virtues stand in contrast to the socially destructive vices of verse 8 and mark those qualities which make actual the unity in the midst of diversity that characterizes the body of Christ. All five are qualities found first in God or Christ: "compassion" (Rom. 12:1; 2 Cor. 1:3; Phil. 2:1), "kindness" (Rom. 2:4; 11:22; Eph. 2:7; Titus 3:4), "humility" (Phil. 2:3, 5), "gentleness" (2 Cor. 10:1), and "patience" (Rom. 2:4; 9:22; 1 Tim. 1:16; 1 Peter 3:20; 2 Peter 3:15). Three of the five ("kindness," "gentleness," and "patience") are specifically listed as the fruit of the Spirit (Gal. 5:22-23). As the vices of verses 5 and 8 traced a trajectory from root to fruit, so also among these virtues. But in this case there appears to be an alternating, back-and-forth emphasis from one inward virtue to an outward evidence that grows from it, to another inward virtue to another outward expression of that inward transformation, and so forth.[742]

The first grace to be "put on" is "a heart of compassion" (σπλάγχνα οἰκτιρμοῦ). The first word, when used literally, refers to one's "bowels" or the inward parts located in the belly (Acts 1:18). Thus the KJV's "bowels of mercies." Metaphorically, however, it referred to the seat of one's deepest emotions and for that reason is often rendered in English as "heart." Paul uses the word in eight of its eleven NT appearances. Interestingly, four of those are in his correspondence with those in Colossae (Col. 3:12; Philem. 7, 12, 20).

The second word (οἰκτιρμοῦ, "of compassion") is described as "a motivating emotion" such as pity, compassion, mercy, etc.[743] Moving out from this inward disposition, the other graces are enumerated.

The next word is "kindness" (χρηστότητα). It is used only by Paul in the NT. It refers to goodness, kindness, and generosity, either of man (2 Cor. 6:6; Gal. 5:22; Col. 3:12) or of God (Rom. 2:4; 11:22; Eph. 2:7).[744] Naturally man has no such "kindness" in himself (Rom. 3:12). It can only describe him as God produces this "kindness" in him (Gal. 5:22). This seems to be an outward expression of the "heart of compassion" which has been put on first.

After this comes "humility" (ταπεινοφροσύνην). This again is an inward virtue. Paul uses the word five times, three of which appear here in

---

[742] Piper, 55-58.
[743] Friberg, 279.
[744] BAGD, 886.

Colossians (2:18, 23; 3:12). The word is generally used in a positive sense, as it is here, to describe "a quality of voluntary submission and unselfishness *humility, self-effacement*."[745] But in both Colossians 2:18 and 23 it was clearly used in a pejorative sense, meaning "a misdirected submission in cultic behavior *self-abasement, (false) humility, self-mortification*."[746] In those cases it described the misguided practices taught by the false teacher(s) at work in Colossae. But clearly in this case, Paul has in view the possibility of a right, godly, Spirit-produced practice of humility.

Such "humility" enables us to deal with others in "gentleness" (πραΰτητα). It points to a humble and gentle attitude which bears up under offense with patient submissiveness and without a move toward revenge.[747] Such "gentleness" is a fruit of the Spirit's work in an individual's life (Gal. 5:23). Paul uses it in regard to confrontation or discipline (2 Cor. 4:21; 10:1; Gal. 6:1) or in general instructions about avoiding difficulties in relationships (Eph. 4:2; Col. 3:12; Titus 3:2). It is usually set as the opposite of harsh, divisive, defiant, brusque attitudes and actions. It speaks of humility, courtesy, considerateness, and meekness, in the sense not of weakness, but of power under control.[748]

Finally, there is "patience" (μακροθυμίαν). The word is used by Paul in ten of its fourteen NT appearances. It is often used of human patience (2 Cor. 6:6; Eph. 4:2; Col. 3:12; 2 Tim. 3:10; 4:2), but also of God's (Rom. 2:4; 9:22; 1 Tim. 1:16). Such patience—as with the other graces—is produced in us only by the indwelling Holy Spirit (Gal. 5:22). The word generally refers to a long-suffering endurance in the face of indignities and injuries by others.

Thus we see the three inward virtues that deal with the whole of our lives: "a heart of compassion" (how we view others and their circumstances), "humility" (our orientation toward self), and "patience" (how we deal with difficult circumstances and the people who become caught up in them with us). And each will have its outward evidence: "a heart of compassion" becomes "kindness," "humility" acts in "gentleness," and "patience" is going to evidence itself in the two actions set before us in verse 13.

---

[745] Friberg, 375.
[746] Ibid., 375.
[747] Rienecker, 485.
[748] BAGD, 699.

3:13 bearing with one another, and forgiving each other, whoever has a complaint against anyone; just as the Lord forgave you, so also should you.

The Apostle now takes up two participles to reveal the way (or at least one way) in which the five graces of verse 12 are to be "put on."[749] Sometimes these are cited as examples of participles with imperatival force, but Wallace believes this is doubtful.[750]

The first participle is "bearing with" (ἀνεχόμενοι). The present tense marks this as a constant necessity in relationships. The word means to endure, to bear with, or to put up with difficult people or circumstances.[751] This action is to be taken reciprocally upon "one another" (ἀλλήλων).

A second participle is now added (καὶ, "and"): "forgiving" (χαριζόμενοι). Again the present tense pictures this as a repeated, regular feature necessary to make relationships within the body of Christ work. The word means to give freely or graciously as a favor and then by extension to forgive or pardon.[752] This action is to be taken upon "each other" (ἑαυτοῖς), the reflexive pronoun being used for the reciprocal pronoun.[753] The reflexive pronoun pictures action "of each one toward all,—yea even to themselves included, Christians being members of one another."[754]

These two actions, then, are the way we demonstrate "a heart of compassion, kindness, humility, gentleness and patience" (v. 12) toward one another. The object of forbearing and forgiveness are not the same, however. Indeed, they may be extended to one and the same person, but that within the person which requires forbearance and forgiveness are not the same. As someone has well said, we forebear *silliness* (or at least what seems so to us), we forgive *sin*.[755]

This must be the response of "whoever has a complaint against anyone" (ἐάν τις πρός τινα ἔχῃ μομφήν). The use of the conditional particle (ἐάν) and the subjunctive mood of the verb (ἔχῃ, "has") forms a third-class

---

[749] NET Bible; Rienecker, 580.
[750] Wallace, 652.
[751] BAGD, 65.
[752] Ibid., 876.
[753] Ibid., 212.
[754] Rienecker, 580.
[755] Piper, 53. (Actually John Piper calls it "strangeness" and "sin.")

condition which pictures the condition as uncertain of fulfillment, but still likely (e.g., "if one has a complaint," ESV). The unfortunate fact is that wherever followers of Christ live together complaints arise one against another. Paul is a realist and here outlines the prescription for such occasions. The issue is individual and personal—both pronouns being singular. Indeed, the Greek text pictures the reality by setting the two indefinite pronouns in careful juxtaposition over against one another: τις πρός τινα (lit., "someone to someone"). In such a pair someone "has" (ἔχη)—

> **Ministry Maxim**
>
> Forbearance and forgiveness are the proving grounds of faith.

present tense—"a complaint" (μομφήν) against the other. The noun is used only here in the NT. The verb from which this noun arises refers most commonly to errors of omission, meaning "to find *fault* with." Thus the noun is probably pointing to "a *debt*, which needs to be remitted."[756] Far too often in the body of Christ someone concludes that some brother or sister "owes" them something for a wrong done. And far too often they are out to extract payment from that person. In such cases, the Apostle says, forbearance and forgiveness from "a heart of compassion, kindness, humility, gentleness and patience" (v. 12) are the order of the day.

And this cannot be merely granted in some grudging way. Both the "ground and motivation"[757] of such grace are set forth when Paul adds: "just as the Lord forgave you, so also should you" (cf. Eph. 4:32). The comparative conjunction (καθώς, "just as") provides the hinge point of similarity between our forgiveness and that of Christ. The standard is "the Lord forgave you" (ὁ κύριος ἐχαρίσατο ὑμῖν). By "the Lord" (ὁ κύριος), Paul probably intends Jesus Christ rather than God the Father. There are some variants here in various manuscripts. Some have "Christ" (Χριστός) instead of "Lord" (κύριος), but that may be read as an attempt to clarify just who was intended by the original "Lord."[758] Other variants include "God" (θεός) or "God in Christ" (θεὸς ἐν Χριστῷ), but they are even less likely to be original. He "forgave" (ἐχαρίσατο) is an aorist tense simply noting the doing of the deed. Paul repeats the same verb used earlier in the verse, here

---

[756] Lightfoot, 220; cf. Little Kittel, 580.
[757] O'Brien, 202.
[758] Harris, 163.

however describing the forgiveness of the Lord toward us (cf. 2:13). This He did for "you" (ὑμῖν), a plural pronoun acknowledging Christ's death for each one of us, but picturing us as a redeemed company.

With this beautiful picture of redeeming grace in view, the Apostle now says, literally, "so also you" (οὕτως καὶ ὑμεῖς). The adverb (οὕτως, "so") correlates this statement regarding us to the preceding statement regarding Christ. What is true of Christ toward us should "also" (καὶ) be true of us toward one another. The pronoun is again plural (ὑμεῖς, "you"), laying the responsibility upon each one of us, but picturing us as a whole body practicing such grace among ourselves. Obviously none of us can give ourselves with the same redemptive effect as Christ gave Himself. His work is done "once for all" (Rom. 6:10; Heb. 7:27; 9:12; 10:10). He alone is the sin bearer. Yet precisely because of what He has done for us, we can (and must) in like fashion extend grace to one another, not holding our offenses against one another. Reflection on the relationship of Paul's instruction here and Jesus' teaching in Matthew 18:23-35 will prove instructive.

3:14 Beyond all these things put on love, which is the perfect bond of unity.

Paul has one more notion to add before he closes the sentence: "Beyond all these things" (ἐπὶ πᾶσιν δὲ τούτοις). The conjunction δὲ extends the thought Paul is on (vv. 12-13). The remainder of the clause means something like "to all these."[759] By "these" (τούτοις) Paul is referring to the graces set forth in verses 12 and 13. This is clear because the imperative "put on" (Ἐνδύσασθε) from verse 12 should be supplied here. The precise emphasis of ἐπὶ has been debated. It could mean "over" (as in the final piece of clothing placed over all the other garments/virtues; cf. NIV); "in addition to" (as in "love" being counted as just one more virtue to be "put on"; cf. NET); or "above (all)" (thus marking "love" as the superlative or crowning virtue in the list; cf. ESV).[760]

> **Ministry Maxim**
>
> Love is the relational glue that holds the body of Christ together as one.

---

[759] BAGD, 287.
[760] Harris, 163.

That additional virtue is to be "love" (τὴν ἀγάπην). It is in the accusative case, matching the five virtues of verse 12. Here, however, the noun is accompanied by the definite article, while those virtues were anarthrous. This touch underscores the elevated estimate of this final virtue. It is *"the love"* above all loves which is in view—the love extended to us by God through the incarnate Christ and now extended through us to others by the indwelling Christ. Indeed, it is this "which is the perfect bond of unity" (ὅ ἐστιν σύνδεσμος τῆς τελειότητος). The relative pronoun (ὅ, "which") is in the singular and points back to "love" (τὴν ἀγάπην). The verb (ἐστιν, "is") is in the present tense underscoring the abiding, ongoing nature of "love." The noun (σύνδεσμος, "bond of unity") refers to *"that which binds together."*[761] It could be used in nonbiblical Greek to describe the fasteners that hold different ships together. In Ephesians 4:3 Paul used it to exhort the Christians to preserve the unity of the Spirit "in the bond [τῷ συνδέσμῳ] of peace." Paul used it in Colossians 2:19 in a metaphorical reference to the "ligaments" which hold the body of Christ together in unity (cf. its only other NT usage in Acts 8:23).

The relationships of believers within the body of Christ must operate in "love" if they are to maintain the unity of the Spirit. What is bound together could be either the previously listed virtues of verses 12 and 13[762] or the believers who are to practice them.[763] The former seems the more likely, given the nature of the imagery used. In that case "love" could be seen either as the final layer of clothing (virtue) "put on," as a necklace or broach which caps off the clothing, or as a sash or girdle which physically binds all the virtues together.

Paul adds a genitive noun to round out the meaning (τῆς τελειότητος, lit., "of perfection"). The noun speaks of a state of completion or perfection.[764] But how are we to understand the genitive? It is unlikely to be a subjective genitive: "the bond produced by perfection." It could possibly be a genitive of apposition: "the bond that consists of perfection."[765] It might be a "descriptive gen[itive] indicating the bond which signifies or indicates

---

[761] Thayer, 601.
[762] Harris, 164; Moo, 281.
[763] NIDNTT, 3:592; Lohse, 148-149; O'Brien, 203-204.
[764] Friberg, 377.
[765] Robertson, *Word Pictures*, 4:504.

perfection."[766] Thus this makes it "the *bond that unites* all the virtues (which otherwise have no unity) *in perfect harmony* or *the bond of perfect unity* for the church."[767] Or it could be an objective genitive: "the bond which brings about perfection" or "the bond that perfects."[768] In this case it would be the "new self" as a corporate whole, not simply the individual believer, which is brought to "perfection."[769]

Digging Deeper:

1. The Apostle bases his imperatives upon gospel grace (v. 12). How should this affect the way we preach Christian obedience? How might this save us from mere moralistic preaching?

2. How do forbearance and forgiveness serve as the proving grounds of our faith?

3. How does the phrase "just as the Lord forgave you" inform our understanding of the forgiveness required of us? In what way has the Lord forgiven us?

4. Why is "love" held back as the crowning virtue of the list (v. 14)?

3:15 Let the peace of Christ rule in your hearts, to which indeed you were called in one body; and be thankful.

The Apostle has been establishing personal connections (1:1-12, 24-29) and laying doctrinal foundations (1:13-23; 2:1-23) even while exposing the false teacher(s). He has transitioned to providing specific application of these truths (3:1ff.). Most of his attention recently has been given to the "put off/put on" demands of the gospel as the path to sanctification (3:5-14). This has been applied both to sexual idolatry (v. 5) and social destruction (v. 8). Since verse 8 the focus has been largely upon the social/interpersonal aspects of our sanctification. In a few moments Paul will turn more pointedly to specific relationships (3:18-4:1) and give instructions with regard to how this grace applies to each of these. But how are we, then, to understand

---

[766] Rienecker, 581.
[767] BAGD, 785.
[768] Harris, 164-165; Lohse, 136, 148-149; Moo, 282; O'Brien, 203-204.
[769] Moo, 282.

the purpose of verses 15-17? Understanding what has gone before in verses 5-14, it seems the Apostle now provides broadly stated guidelines for living together as God's people within the local fellowship of Christ's church. This prepares the way for his more specific instructions related to how this grace should show up in our homes (3:18-4:1). Thus Paul moves from an inter-personal emphasis (vv. 8-14) to the texture of the corporate life of God's people (vv. 15-17) and then on to the quality of relationships within our homes (3:18-4:1).

The Apostle now adds another command, though the updated NASU does not translate the conjunction καὶ (cf. "And," NASB). The command is to "Let the peace of Christ rule" (ἡ εἰρήνη τοῦ Χριστοῦ βραβευέτω).[770] The present imperative demands that action be taken repeatedly, habitually, and as a pattern of life. The verb is used only here in the NT, but it is widely attested in the secular Greek of the day. It meant to be a judge or umpire in the athletic games. More generally it means to preside, to direct, to control.[771] The same verb is compounded with κατά in Colossians 2:19 (see comments there).

We are to give these broad powers to "the peace of Christ" (ἡ εἰρήνη τοῦ Χριστοῦ). The genitive could be objective: the peace which Christ possesses. But surely it is a subjective genitive: the peace which Christ gives, the peace which comes from Christ,[772] or "the peace brought by Christ."[773] Robertson suggests a combination of the two, saying it is the peace that Christ "has and gives."[774] The peace which Christ brings and gives to us is first redemptive and vertical—establishing peace with God (Col. 1:20). From that restored relationship, Christ then brings to each of us peace within our hearts (the peace of God) and peace within our circle of relationships.

The arena of this peace's reign is "in your hearts" (ἐν ταῖς καρδίαις ὑμῶν). The heart is the core of one's being—the place from which intellect, volition, and emotion arise. In and from this locus, peace is to be permitted sovereignty. The preposition (ἐν, "in") identifies the location of peace's

---

[770] A few Greek manuscripts have the peace "of God" (θεοῦ) rather than the peace "of Christ" (Χριστοῦ), but the only English translation to follow the former is the KJV.

[771] Friberg, 93.

[772] Thayer, 182.

[773] BAGD, 227.

[774] Robertson, *Grammar*, 499.

rule, but it could mean either "in" or "among." The former would point to a personal experience; the latter to a communal experience. Which is intended here? Though the verb (βραβευέτω, "Let … rule") is singular, this phrase is in the plural. Each individual believer is responsible to make certain that Christ's peace reigns *in* his heart and *from* his heart in his relationships with others. This would seem to underscore the more inclusive sense of the phrase "the peace of Christ"—it is something each one must receive, experience, and appropriate, but it is something that is also then experienced collectively as God's people.

This is not simply a wise idea passed on by the good Apostle. Rather this is that "to which indeed you were called" (εἰς ἣν καὶ ἐκλήθητε). The preposition is used spatially meaning it is "into" such "peace" that we were called. The relative pronoun (ἣν, "which") is feminine singular to match it with its antecedent "the peace" (ἡ εἰρήνη) of Christ. The καὶ is left untranslated by some English versions (e.g., NIV). Among those who translate the word into English, it is either rendered as giving emphasis ("indeed," e.g., ESV, NASU, NRSV; "in fact," NET) or marking an addition ("also," e.g., NKJV).

To this peace "you were called" (ἐκλήθητε). Paul has just referred to the Colossians as "those who have been chosen by God" (v. 12). Here the aorist tense looks upon the event of God's call extended to each believer. The passive voice pictures God's initiative in calling each believer. God's call to Himself through Christ is a call to be at peace (with Him) and to live at peace (with ourselves and others). This was a call "in one body" (ἐν ἑνὶ σώματι). This could be understood in any number of ways, but it probably should be understood simply as attendant circumstances,[775] "the oneness of the body being the sphere and element in which that peace of Christ was to be carried on and realized."[776] Each one is called individually, but God is calling more than one; all of them together discover that they have been called into one unified body.

Paul now adds (καὶ, "and") a second imperative: "be thankful" (εὐχάριστοι γίνεσθε). The verb (γίνεσθε, "be," lit., "become") may be surprising. It may simply be a matter of style (since the second plural

---

[775] Alford, 3:237; Eadie, 249-250; Harris, 166.
[776] Alford, 3:237.

imperative of εἰμί is not found in the NT),[777] or it may be that it "draws attention to the 'constant striving after this exalted aim as something not yet attained.'"[778] The present imperative demands repeated habitual action. Gratitude is to become the default setting of our hearts and minds. The adjective (εὐχάριστοι, "thankful") is used only here in the NT, though thanksgiving is a major theme in Colossians (1:3, 12; 2:7; 3:16, 17; 4:2). The present word designates the compulsion of one who is grateful to another for a favor bestowed.[779] Here then it views the believer's gratitude in response to God's grace extended into his life. The emphasis may be not simply upon thanksgiving, but upon thanksgiving *expressed*.[780] In the midst of all the hard work of horizontal relationships

> **Ministry Maxim**
>
> Gratitude toward God makes peace toward others possible.

(vv. 8-14), in which the believer must constantly be extending grace, the well of God's unceasing grace must constantly be bubbling up within him, manifesting itself vertically in gratitude to God. Apart from this ever-present, always-flowing supply of God's grace and our resultant gratitude, we will soon run dry of grace to extend to the next person, and our relationships will no longer be marked by the touch of God.

3:16 Let the word of Christ richly dwell within you, with all wisdom teaching and admonishing one another with psalms and hymns and spiritual songs, singing with thankfulness in your hearts to God.

How may we ever keep the well of God's grace bubbling up within us? How are we to cultivate a habitual gratitude (v. 15)? The Apostle steers us directly into the path of an answer with his next imperative: "Let the word of Christ richly dwell within you" (Ὁ λόγος τοῦ Χριστοῦ ἐνοικείτω ἐν ὑμῖν πλουσίως). Though we have no transitional conjunction or particle here, this is an obvious parallel to the opening expression of the previous verse (ἡ εἰρήνη τοῦ Χριστοῦ βραβευέτω ἐν ταῖς καρδίαις ὑμῶν, "let the peace of Christ rule in your hearts"). The expression "The word of Christ"

---

[777] Harris, 166.
[778] O'Brien, 206.
[779] Rienecker, 581.
[780] O'Brien, 205.

('Ο λόγος τοῦ Χριστοῦ) is found only here in the NT. The "word of the Lord" (1 Thess. 1:8; 4:15; 2 Thess. 3:1) or the "word of God" (e.g., Rom. 9:6; 1 Cor. 14:36; Eph. 6:17) are more common. This has given rise to some Greek manuscripts with these expressions here. But both externally and internally the evidence supports the reading "the word of Christ" ('Ο λόγος τοῦ Χριστοῦ).[781] This is in keeping with the Christological focus of the letter. Elsewhere in Colossians we encounter the afflictions "of Christ" (1:24), the circumcision "of Christ" (2:11), the substance (lit., body) "of Christ" (2:17), the peace "of Christ" (3:15), and the mystery "of Christ" (4:3). The genitive ("of Christ") here could be subjective ("the word which Christ speaks")[782] or objective ("the word that speaks about Christ").[783] Probably the latter is closer to Paul's intent, but perhaps he provides an intentional ambiguity—it is the message Christ gave, which expounds and explains who He is, that has its core and center in Him.[784] This would be another way of referring to the gospel message itself, as expounded from the Scriptures—primarily at that time the OT (he does, after all, refer to Him as "Christ" or "Messiah[785]"), but also to include the NT (cf. Rom. 16:25-27).

This "word of Christ" we are commanded to "Let … dwell" (ἐνοικείτω) in us. The present imperative form, as with the command of verse 15, demands that action be taken repeatedly, as a habit of life. The word simply means to dwell or live in. But here surely it means to dwell personally and powerfully, pulling in some of the idea of the parallel verb from verse 15 ("Let … rule"). It is used five times in the NT, all by Paul and all metaphorically. It describes God (2 Cor. 6:16) by the Holy Spirit residing in the believer (Rom. 8:11; 2 Tim. 1:14). It also, closer to our usage here, can describe faith dwelling in the believer (2 Tim. 1:5). Here the word of Christ is to dwell "in you" (ἐν ὑμῖν). Continuing the idea of their corporate experience and life (from v. 15), the plural form means "in your assembly"[786] not simply in each one of you personally. Certainly for this to be true of all of them together, it must be true of each one individually, but the point is that if "the peace of Christ"

[781] NET Bible.
[782] Bruce, NIC, 157; Lightfoot, 222.
[783] O'Brien, 206; Moo, 285-286.
[784] Dunn, 236.
[785] Moo, 286.
[786] Thayer, 217.

is to rule their relationships (v. 15), then "the word of Christ" must dwell in their midst (v. 16). Personal opinion must bow to Christ's word. Personal feelings must yield to what Christ says. Individual ideas must bow to Christ's determinations through His word. When this happens, then peace will rule in our relationships.

Paul emphasizes even further the nature of this indwelling by saying it must be "richly" (πλουσίως) undertaken. The adverb is used four times in the NT, three of those by Paul (Col. 3:16; 1 Tim. 6:17; Titus 3:6; 2 Peter 1:11). It is related to the more frequently used noun πλούσιος ("rich"). The adverb thus has the sense of richly, abundantly, and lavishly. When God's people live together in fellowship and gather together for worship, "the word of Christ" must have a prominent and primary place. Christ dwells among His people where His word is anticipated, sought out, welcomed, and allowed to rule. Christ's own indwelling is enabled through His word preached and taught in the power of the Holy Spirit.

Paul follows up with two participles: "teaching and admonishing" (διδάσκοντες καὶ νουθετοῦντες). Some contend that these participles receive imperatival weight from the previous imperative ("Let ... dwell," cf. NRSV),[787] yet this seems doubtful[788] It is best to find their meaning in subordinate relationship to that imperative. Just what is that relationship? They could indicate the means by which we are to let the word of Christ dwell in us richly,[789] or the mode in which this dwelling becomes reality,[790] or the result of letting that word so dwell within us.[791] There is a lack of agreement regarding the function of these participles. All in all the best option seems to view them as expressing either means or mode, the difference in meaning being negligible.

These two actions have already been used to describe Paul's personal ministry in 1:28, though in reverse order. Now they are to characterize what the local believers are to practice with "one another" (ἑαυτούς). The plural form of the reflexive pronoun can function also in a reciprocal manner and pictures the back-and-forth nature of the fellowship intended.[792]

---

[787] Lightfoot, 222; Lohse, 150; Robertson, *Word Pictures*, 4:505.
[788] Wallace, 652.
[789] Harris, 168.
[790] Moo, 228; O'Brien, 207.
[791] Alford, 3:238; Wright, 144.
[792] Robertson, *Grammar*, 690.

In speaking of "teaching" (διδάσκοντες), Paul uses a word which is used at times to speak of official teaching of doctrine within the church, and the scope of those who are to undertake this ministry is limited (1 Tim. 2:12). But here the word is clearly broadened to include all members of the body of Christ.

The word "admonishing" (νουθετοῦντες) comes from νουθετης, which in turn comes from νοῦς ("mind") and τίθημι; ("to place/put"). Thus the literal sense of the word is "to put in mind."[793] It means to admonish, to warn, or to instruct in the sense of "giving instructions in regard to belief or behavior."[794] For both words see our comments at 1:28. Being coordinate (καὶ, "and") with one another, they present a positive ("teaching") and more negative ("admonishing") side to the total ministry of the word among the believers.

As one can quickly see, this ministry must be undertaken "in all wisdom" (ἐν πάσῃ σοφίᾳ). This is the third time this precise phrase has been used in Colossians (1:9, 28; 3:16). Most telling is its use in 1:28 where it similarly tells us the manner in which Paul undertook these same two ministries. Wisdom is a significant theme in this letter (1:9, 28; 2:3, 23; 3:16; 4:5), playing a more prominent role than it does in Ephesians (1:8, 17; 3:10). This may be due to a special emphasis on wisdom by the false teacher(s) in Colossae (2:23). Paul has in view "all" (πάσῃ) or every form or expression of God's wisdom.

Next we meet the clause "with psalms and hymns and spiritual songs" (ψαλμοῖς ὕμνοις ᾠδαῖς πνευματικαῖς). To what is this connected? Does this rightly modify what precedes ("teaching and admonishing") or does it modify what follows ("singing")? The former is represented in the NASU and NKJV; the latter in the ESV, NET, NIV, and NRSV. If the former, then "psalms and hymns and spiritual songs" would identify the means by which the "teaching and admonishing" take place (thus the NASU's "with").[795] If it is the latter, then "psalms and hymns and spiritual songs" identify what is sung[796] or the

> **Ministry Maxim**
>
> A people in whom the Word of God dwells is a people in whom the Spirit of God dwells.

---

[793] Thayer, 429.
[794] Friberg, 273.
[795] Alford, 3:237; Fee, 652-653; Lenski, 177; Moo, 287; O'Brien, 208.
[796] Eadie, 252; Wright, 145.

instrument for expressing their praise ("singing with thankfulness in your hearts to God").[797] Commentators are divided; a decision is not easy. The scales, however, seem to be tipped by holding it next to the parallel passage from Ephesians (5:19). There the threefold descriptions of songs are unambiguously connected to "speaking to one another." So here it seems best to understand "psalms, hymns and spiritual songs" as modifying "teaching and admonishing" and thus indicating *a* (not *the* exclusive) means by which that takes place. To this reasoning Moo adds two other arguments: First, that this understanding addresses the fact that there is no "and" before the third participle ("singing"). Second, this makes for a balance between the two clauses.[798]

It may seem awkward that one's singing can at one and the same time be both "to God" and "to one another." Yet this is an idea familiar to us from the OT.[799] This is instructive to us for our gathered worship. Our singing is not simply to warm individual hearts, but to testify to, instruct, and edify the larger body. Though we may have sung the words to the current song many times and though we may all be speaking the same words, this is nevertheless a God-ordained means of instruction and edification for the whole. We may be instructed by a worship leader to simply "sing to God" and not worry about the person next to you and what they think of your voice, but the fact is that we are to consider the person next to us and to realize that while we are addressing our praise to God, we are speaking truth into our brother's or sister's heart.

Now just what does Paul mean by "with psalms and hymns and spiritual songs" (ψαλμοῖς ὕμνοις ᾠδαῖς πνευματικαῖς)? A great deal of scholarship has gone into trying to differentiate between the three nouns, but a consensus remains elusive. All three appear again in Ephesians 5:19. Gregory of Nyssa (*In Psalm.* 2, 3) made "psalm" a song produced by the playing of an instrument, the "song" a melody sung with the voice, and "hymn" a song of praise to God for His gracious acts and gifts.[800] The noun "psalms" (ψαλμοῖς) can certainly be used to refer to what is found in the OT book of Psalms (Luke 20:42; 24:44; Acts 1:20; 13:33). Paul lists it alongside "a

---

[797] Bruce, NIC, 158; Harris, 169; Hendriksen, 161.
[798] Moo, 287.
[799] Fee, 652.
[800] Lohse, 151.

teaching" and "a revelation" as something a believer may come to the gathered worship of believers to share (1 Cor. 14:26). It would seem then to be either an actual psalm from the book of Psalms, sung in worship to God and for the edification of the believers, or a contemporary song composed along those same lines and used for the same purposes. There may be an emphasis here on the fact that this was singing with musical accompaniment,[801] though the exclusivity of this meaning is not to be pressed.[802]

The noun "hymns" (ὕμνοις) is used only here and Ephesians 5:19, though its cognate is used four times (Matt. 26:30; Mark 14:26; Acts 16:25; Heb. 2:12). The word describes a song composed and sung in praise of God. The NT may contain examples or fragments of such hymns composed with specifically Christian meaning (e.g., Phil. 2:6-11; Col. 1:15-20; 1 Tim. 3:16).

The noun "songs" (ᾠδαῖς) is used again by Paul only in Ephesians 5:19. Beyond this is it used four times by John in Revelation, twice referring to "a new song" (Rev. 14:3) and the other two times referring to "the song of Moses" and "the song of the Lamb" (Rev. 15:3). It is the general word for "song" in the Greek language. There is debate about whether the adjective (πνευματικαῖς, "spiritual") modifies just this last noun[803] or all three nouns.[804] In favor of taking it with just the final noun is the fact that it agrees with it in gender (feminine), while the previous two nouns are masculine. Though this does not absolutely disqualify the former sense, it does point to the latter. Also, given the general nature of the noun (ᾠδαῖς, "songs"), it seems more likely that Paul would want to qualify it.

But just what does Paul mean by "spiritual" (πνευματικαῖς)? The word is used in the NT with reference to what is caused by, filled with or pertaining or corresponding to the Holy Spirit.[805] Beyond this, commentators have offered various meanings such as: "prompted by the Spirit," "spiritual," or simply "sacred" as opposed to secular.[806] Perhaps it is best to realize that the same expression appears in the parallel passage in Ephesians 5:19. There it follows upon Paul's command to "be filled with the Spirit"

---

[801] Lightfoot, 223; Lohse, 151; Rienecker, 581.
[802] Bruce, NIC, 159.
[803] Fee, 653-654; Moo, 290; Wright, 145.
[804] Lohse, 151; O'Brien, 210.
[805] BAGD, 678-679.
[806] Harris, 169.

(Eph. 5:18b). The notion there is not one of quantity, but of control (cf. the illustration of not being drunk on wine, 5:18a). Thus we should simply conclude that Paul is describing songs that are offered in praise under the control of the Holy Spirit. To offer any conclusion more specific than this runs the risk of speculation or bending Scripture to support partisan causes.

Most commentators agree that it is unwise to attempt too narrow a demarcation between these three nouns. Precise classification of song types was probably not the Apostle's intent. Perhaps Paul was not enumerating three strict classifications of musical worship, but simply piling up the nouns to make his point—that in our gathered worship we must be "teaching and admonishing" one another so that the word of Christ has central place in our worship and is made to dwell richly in our hearts. Wright says, "Together these three terms indicate a variety and richness of Christian singing which should [not] be stereotyped into one mould ..."[807]

These three, though probably modifying "teaching and admonishing," naturally suggest Paul's third participle: "singing" (ᾄδοντες). This too, like the previous participles, is present active in form. Just how does this participle relate to the two that have gone before? Some see all three as coordinate, and thus the NIV supplies "and," though it is not present in the original text. It seems best, however, to understand this entire participial clause as subordinate to the previous one—indicating "the attitude or disposition which is to accompany the previously mentioned instruction and admonition."[808] This then yields a syntactical relationship something like this:

> Let the word of Christ richly dwell within you,
> > teaching and admonishing one another in all wisdom with
> > psalms, hymns, and spiritual songs,
> > > singing within thankfulness in your hearts to God.[809]

Our singing, then, is to be carried out "with thankfulness" (ἐν [τῇ] χάριτι). The manuscripts are divided over the authenticity of the definite article (τῇ, "the"), and a final resolution on this matter is yet to be reached. The noun is the common word for "grace," and some have taken the word in that sense here (KJV, NET). The word, as the NASU translation dem-

---

[807] Wright, 145.
[808] O'Brien, 210.
[809] Moo, 288.

onstrates, can mean "thankfulness" (or "gratitude," NIV, NRSV) for such divine grace.[810] Given the emphasis upon thankfulness in Colossians as a whole (1:3, 12; 2:7; 4:2) and in this immediate context (3:15, 17), perhaps we should understand it in this way here as well.[811]

This gratitude is to be "in your hearts" (ἐν ταῖς καρδίαις ὑμῶν). This does not refer to some kind of "silent singing." Rather the word "heart" (καρδία) refers to the essential core of one's being, including the intellect, emotion, and volition. This means the indwelling word we share among ourselves by teaching and admonishing one another with psalms, hymns, and spiritual songs should have its effect first within us and then all our responses to one another should arise from an inside-out orientation. We do not derive our heart's condition from outward circumstances and relationships. Rather we allow the word of Christ to richly dwell within us and then govern our outward relationships and interactions from this inward state of heart. From a heart truly grateful for the ongoing grace of God received by His Spirit's work through Christ's word, we sing. All of this—singing with thankfulness in our hearts—is to be directed "to God" (τῷ θεῷ). We live with one another in this word-reigning, grace-receiving, edification-dealing way on a horizontal level because there is all the while a vertical relationship with God that is governing all our earthly relationships.

This verse finds a close parallel in Ephesians 5:18-20. The parallel is significant when we note that the key concept here ("Let the word of Christ dwell in you richly") has become in Ephesians "Be filled with the Spirit" (5:18). Just how should this difference be understood? Do they describe the same reality—being filled by the Spirit is synonymous with letting the word of Christ dwell in you richly? Is the one dependent upon the other—one is filled with the Spirit by letting the word of Christ dwell in him richly? Are they describing two realities that are somehow loosely connected—you cannot be filled with the Spirit without letting the word of Christ dwell in you richly and you cannot let the word of Christ dwell in you richly without being filled with the Spirit? The Holy Spirit's role is to bring glory to Christ (John 14:14-15). He serves as the Illuminator who enables one to understand Christ's word. Thus being "filled with the Spirit" and letting "the word

---

[810] BAGD, 878.
[811] O'Brien, 210.

of Christ richly dwell within you" can never be separated from one another, though their precise relationship cannot be reduced to a formulaic equation.

God's intent is that we live together in peace-ruling (v. 15a), thanks-expressing (v. 15b), word-indwelling (v. 16a), and praise-singing (v. 16b) assemblies.

3:17 Whatever you do in word or deed, do all in the name of the Lord Jesus, giving thanks through Him to God the Father.

This sentence opens with καὶ ("and"), though the NASU has dropped it (cf. NASB). This appears to make this statement coordinate with verse 16, but what Paul says now seems to serve a summarizing effect for the whole of verses 12 through 16. The Apostle now casts a net as broadly as he can, using words to bring everything possible under this closing exhortation. The English word "Whatever" actually represents four in the Greek (πᾶν ὅ τι ἐάν). The word πᾶν has here the broadly inclusive sense of "*everything (anything) whatsoever.*"[812] The words ὅ τι are the uncompounded form of the relative pronoun ὅστις, which means "whatever."[813] The combination of πᾶν ὅ τι is a strengthened effort as saying "whatever"[814] or "whatsoever."[815] Then the addition of ἐάν achieves an even further heightened indefiniteness beyond just ὅ τι.[816] The effect is a clear attempt to make a statement so broadly inclusive as to gather up all possible scenarios. Clearly God intends that worship should touch all of life and all of life should become worship.

That which is so broadly considered is whatsoever "you do" (ποιῆτε). The subjunctive mood is used to further cast this in the realm of the possible or hypothetical. The present tense points to whatever the present moment may at any given time find one engaged in. This includes what one does both "in word or deed" (ἐν λόγῳ ἢ ἐν ἔργῳ).

The first noun (λόγῳ) is used in its most general sense of "word." The second noun (ἔργῳ) means here simply "deed" or "action" in contrast to "word."[817] The singular forms look to each and every individual act or word

---

[812] Thayer, 492.
[813] Harris, 171.
[814] BAGD, 632.
[815] Thayer, 492.
[816] BAGD, 586; Harris, 171.
[817] BAGD, 307.

and bring them under the microscope. Anything whatsoever that one may either say or do, whatever word or work you may find yourself occupied with at any given moment—this is the Apostle's net cast as broadly and as inclusively as possible. This entire opening phrase (πᾶν ὅ τι ἐὰν ποιῆτε ἐν λόγῳ ἢ ἐν ἔργῳ, "Whatever you do in word or deed") is classified as a nominative absolute—an independent phrase which is thrust to the fore of the sentence for emphasis.[818]

Having thus gathered up all possible endeavors any one of us might at any given time engage in, the Apostle now says we must "do all in the name of the Lord Jesus Christ" (πάντα ἐν ὀνόματι κυρίου Ἰησοῦ). The imperative "do" is supplied in English, though it is not present in the Greek text. Yet clearly some such word is expected to be supplied mentally by the reader. Reading an imperative such as "do" seems the safest assumption given the previous subjunctive (ποιῆτε, "do"). The "all" (πάντα) is shorthand for the fuller earlier attempt at gathering all possible scenarios together (πᾶν ὅ τι ἐὰν).

We are to do "all" the "whatsoever"(s) "in the name of the Lord Jesus" (ἐν ὀνόματι κυρίου Ἰησοῦ). The historical person of "Jesus" (Ἰησοῦ) is "Lord" (κυρίου) over all our individual words and works in each and every moment of life. But just what is meant by "in the name of" (ἐν ὀνόματι)? Given the broad and inclusive nature of the wording of this sentence, it probably has the widest sense possible. To do something "in the name of the Lord Jesus" is then to do it in dependence upon Him, relying upon His strength and power. It is to do whatever we do, or say whatever we say for the furtherance of His established purposes. It is also to do it for His glory, that He might be the One noticed and remembered in our words and actions. To be such, each and every thing we say and do must be in conformity with the character and revealed will of Jesus. We should so act and speak that it would be as if Jesus Himself were performing the act or speaking the word. Indeed, we must speak and act in conscious awareness of our union with Christ, cognizant of being "in Christ" (Col. 1:28) and Christ being in us (1:27). In this sense it is what Paul described of his own life: "it is no longer I who live, but Christ lives in me; and the life which I now live in the flesh I live by faith in the Son of God, who loved me and gave Himself up for me" (Gal. 2:20).

---

[818] Abbott, 292; Harris, 170; Kent, 140; Moo, 291; O'Brien, 211.

And all of this is to be done, "giving thanks through Him to God the Father" (εὐχαριστοῦντες τῷ θεῷ πατρὶ δι' αὐτοῦ). This is the cognate verb to the adjective just used in verse 15 to speak of thankfulness. See there for comments on the meaning of this word group. As we have seen, thankfulness is a major theme of this letter (1:3, 12; 2:7; 3:15, 16, 17; 4:2). Here the

> **Ministry Maxim**
>
> It is a glad thing to live under Jesus' Lordship.

present tense emphasizes ongoing, regular action. The participial form modifies the assumed imperative "do" and is used to express attendant circumstances—in the unfolding of our daily lives, thanksgiving should ever and always be permeating the atmosphere of all our words and works. This gratitude is directed "to God the Father" (τῷ θεῷ πατρὶ). A few manuscripts add καὶ ("and") before πατρὶ ("Father"). This may have been an attempt by scribes to conform it to passages such as 1 Corinthians 15:24, Ephesians 5:20, and Philippians 4:20.[819] Among English translations only the King James Version adopts the reading ("to God *and* the Father," emphasis added). Our thanksgiving "to God the Father" is to be offered "through Him" (δι' αὐτοῦ), clearly referring to "the Lord Jesus," and viewing Him in His role as our mediator at God's right hand.

Digging Deeper:

1. Think of one relationship you're struggling with right now and describe what it would mean to allow the peace of Christ to rule in your two hearts (v. 15).
2. Why is gratitude an indispensible component to the unity of the local church (v. 15)?
3. Why do you think gratitude is explicitly tied to the peace of Christ (v. 15), the word of Christ (v. 16), and the name of Christ (v. 17)?
4. What is the role of Scripture in the worship of a local church (v. 16)? How ought this be evidenced in your worship services?
5. What is the interconnection between the Lordship of Christ and the gratitude of our hearts (v. 17)?

---

[819] Harris, 171.

3:18 Wives, be subject to your husbands, as is fitting in the Lord.

The Apostle has explained how the believer's union with Christ (1:1-2:23) becomes a living experience (3:1-14) and how this is revealed generally in the corporate fellowship of God's people (3:15-17). Paul now shifts his thoughts more specifically to how the reality of our union with Christ is seen in the various kinds of relationships believers live in (3:18-4:1). One should compare Paul's statements here with their close parallel in Ephesians 5:22-6:9. We have here three groupings of relationship pairs, each one beginning with the subordinate in the relationship (wives, children, slaves) and then addressing the one in authority (husbands, fathers, masters). In each case Paul makes compliance a matter of Christian duty ("in the Lord," v. 18; "this is well-pleasing to the Lord," v. 20; "fearing the Lord," v. 22; "as for the Lord," v. 23; "from the Lord you will receive the reward," v. 24a; "It is the Lord Christ whom you serve," v. 24b; "you too have a Master in heaven," 4:1).

> **Ministry Maxim**
>
> What is "fitting" for the believer is determined not by popular culture, but by Christ.

Paul begins with "Wives" (Αἱ γυναῖκες). The word can refer to women generally, but here it seems to mark off "wives" specifically. Note the use of the definite article (Αἱ) to designate the wives as a distinct grouping under present consideration.[820] The nominative form serves the role of the vocative in this direct address.[821]

Wives are to "be subject" (ὑποτάσσεσθε). The verb is a compound arising from "under" (ὑπό) and "appoint" or "order" (τάσσω). It is a word that bespeaks authority and submission. It was a military word which described the ranks of soldiers arranging themselves under the leadership of their commander. Here the decision as to whether it is middle or passive voice is difficult. If passive, it may have a reflexive sense to it, and thus in either case it shows that it is a voluntary and personal choice of the wife.[822] The present tense reveals that the wife is to choose this as an abiding attitude, not simply when such feelings may arise. Such submission is to be the ongoing pattern of a wife's relationship to her husband. And of course

---

[820] Robertson, *Word Pictures*, 4:506.
[821] Harris, 178.
[822] Ibid.

the imperative mood makes this obligatory. She is to willingly obey this injunction of God. A broader look at the NT reveals that such submission to authority is required not only of wives, but of all. All people are subject to the governing authorities (Rom. 13:1-5; Titus 3:1). Believers are subject to one another (Eph. 5:21). Children are subject to their parents (Luke 2:51). Slaves are subject to masters (Titus 2:9). The church is subject to Christ (Eph. 5:24). All things are subject to Christ (1 Cor. 15:27-28; Eph. 1:22; Phil. 3:21). Indeed, no one is exempt from submission to authority. In this case the submission is of the wives "to your husbands" (τοῖς ἀνδράσιν). As with the previous noun, this word can be used generally, in this case to describe males. Here, however, it is clear that it is "husbands" who are in view. The definite article (τοῖς) is translated as a possessive ("your").

The imperative of a wife's submission to her husband is sounded throughout the NT (Eph. 5:22-24; Titus 2:4-5; 1 Peter 3:1-6). This is troublesome to many in our contemporary culture with its egalitarian impulses. Some have sought to alleviate their concerns by looking to the parallel passage in Ephesians 5 and citing verse 21: "be subject to one another in the fear of Christ." They contend that this verse, coming immediately before the instructions for a wife to submit to her husband (v. 22), reveals the Apostle's true intent. He does not, they say, envision a male-led relationship, but a mutually submissive one. And this is correct, if we allow the rest of Ephesians 5 to inform what Paul meant by his words in verse 21. In what sense is submission a responsibility of both husband and wife? The text seems to make clear the answer. The husband submits himself to his wife by lovingly, selflessly taking the initiative in putting her needs before his own (Eph. 5:25-32). This is Christlike leadership. But let's be clear—it is leadership. Robertson quips that while the NT pictures the husband as the head of the home, it does so assuming "the husband has a head and a wise one."[823] The wife subjects herself to her husband by way of submissive respect (Eph. 5:33). This affirms that both husband and wife submit to one another, but it rightly distinguishes the *way* in which each does so according to the wise order established by God.

Such subjection by the wife is to take place "as is fitting in the Lord" (ὡς ἀνῆκεν ἐν κυρίῳ). The comparative particle ὡς ("as") indicates

---

[823] Robertson, *Word Pictures*, 4:506.

"the manner in which someth[ing] proceeds" and can be rendered "in such a way." The verb describes what is proper or fitting.[824] It is used only three times in the NT, all by Paul (Eph. 5:4; Col. 3:18; Philem. 8). Here the tense has a present-tense meaning to express "necessity, obligation, or duty."[825] It may express the notion that this is behavior which has been and continues to be "fitting."[826] This obligation is not the Apostle's way of asking believers to simply conform to current cultural customs. Rather he is reiterating what God had established long before. Paul elsewhere makes clear that God has established from creation a hierarchical order which is reflected in marriage (1 Cor. 11:3, 7-9) and that He has maintained this in the new order established by Christ (Eph. 5:23-24).[827] Thus Paul can also say here that this necessity and obligation is pressed upon us "in the Lord" (ἐν κυρίω). By "Lord" (κυρίω) Paul is referring to Jesus. This is in keeping with his Christological focus throughout this letter. Paul consistently grounds these relational instructions in our relationship to the person of Christ (vv. 18, 20, 22, 23, 24). Our vertical relationship to Christ rules our horizontal relationships within society. Christ, not current, popular culture, defines what is "fitting" and proper in our relationships.

3:19 Husbands, love your wives and do not be embittered against them.

Paul now turns to the "Husbands" (Οἱ ἄνδρες). As in the previous verse, the noun can refer to men generally or to husbands more narrowly. Here also the latter is clearly intended. The presence of the definite article sets them apart and considers them as a class. As in verse 18 the nominative form again serves the role of a vocative for purposes of direct address.

Two requirements are laid upon husbands. The first is to "love your wives" (ἀγαπᾶτε τὰς γυναῖκας). The present imperative (ἀγαπᾶτε, "love") demands action that is habitual and regular. The word group connected with the verb "love" has been infused by the writers of the NT with significant Christian meaning. It should not pass without notice that the only other place the verb is used here in Colossians is in a description of God's love

---

[824] BAGD, 66.
[825] Rienecker, 582.
[826] Harris, 179; Moo, 302.
[827] O'Brien, 222.

toward us (3:12). In light of this divine love set upon us, we are to "put on love" (v. 14) toward one another.[828] That this "love" has uniquely Christian content is seen in the parallel passage where Christ's love for the church is the standard of measure for the husband's love of his wife (Eph. 5:25).

This "love," having been applied to relationships more generally (v. 14), now is made specific to the relationship of husbands toward "your wives" (τὰς γυναῖκας). The same noun occurred in verse 18. The definite article can be rendered "your," as in the previous verse. As already noted, Paul just used the same verb in a participial form in verse 12 to insist that every believer is "beloved" of God through His electing ("chosen of God") grace. Paul went on to demonstrate that in this grace God not

> **Ministry Maxim**
>
> Being loved precedes and enables being loving.

only loves the sinner, but sets him apart to Himself as "holy." From the secure base of God's enduring, covenant love, Paul issued moral imperatives (vv. 12-13). It is this same foundation of God's love to the husband that frees him to selflessly love his wife in a singular, unique relationship.

The second (καί, "and") command is "do not be embittered against them" (μὴ πικραίνεσθε πρὸς αὐτάς). The verb is used only here by Paul and elsewhere in the NT only in Revelation (8:11; 10:9, 10). In Revelation it is used literally of something that goes into the stomach and brings bitterness and a violent response. It speaks of that which is "sharp, harsh, and bitter."[829] Here it is used metaphorically and points toward anger, resentment, and bitterness of spirit.[830] The present imperative with the negation (μὴ) "forbids a habitual action."[831] In the passive, as here, it means to "become bitter" or to have become "embittered."[832] This must not happen "against them" (πρὸς αὐτάς). The preposition (πρὸς) speaks "of the goal or limit toward which a movement is directed."[833] The "them" (αὐτάς) is clearly a reference to "wives."

What exactly is forbidden here? Is the husband forbidden to become bitter toward his wife (KJV, NASU, NET)? Or is he forbidden to treat her

---

[828] Moo, 303.
[829] Rienecker, 582.
[830] Friberg, 312
[831] Rienecker, 582.
[832] BAGD, 657.
[833] Thayer, 541.

harshly or bitterly (ESV, NIV, NRSV)? The answer is probably "yes." Paul forbids the husband to develop an inward bitterness toward the wife which will give vent to harsh and bitter words and actions toward her.

What would cause a man to be thus "embittered against" his wife and thus "be harsh with" her (NIV)? The emotional void left in the absence of a secure, singular, covenant love will incite the wife to feel insecure and uncertain. This insecurity and uncertainty regarding their relationship tends to create in the wife that which produces bitterness in the husband—qualities such as possessiveness, clinginess, complaining, and nagging.

Digging Deeper:

1. Ultimately how does a believer in Jesus Christ determine what is "fitting" in his or her relationships (v. 18)?
2. How does the magnitude of the grace described throughout the earlier part of this letter inform our understanding of what Paul means by "in the Lord" (v. 18)?
3. How do Paul's previous statements regarding God's love (3:12, 14) inform our understanding of his call for husbands to "love your wives" (v. 19)?
4. What might incite a man to be "embittered" toward his wife (v. 19)? In this, does the Apostle have in view something that arises from inside the husband or out of his wife?

3:20 Children, be obedient to your parents in all things, for this is well-pleasing to the Lord.

As in the last two verses, the presence of the definite article sets the children apart and considers them as a class. As also in verses 18 and 19, the nominative again serves the role of a vocative for purposes of direct address. With the "Children" (Τὰ τέκνα), the Apostle begins a new couplet. He singles out "Fathers" (v. 21) to be paired with "Children" but makes no mention of mothers and their role.

In beginning with the "Children," he again initiates the pair by mention of the deferential one in the relationship. The noun "Children" (Τὰ τέκνα) refers to offspring without regard to their sex, designating them simply according to their origin. There is no hint here of the age of the one under consideration, though it would seem children still under the protection and provision of their parents are in view.

The duty laid upon the children is to "be obedient" (ὑπακούετε). The word means simply "to obey," "to follow," and "to be subject to."[834] The present imperative demands this become an ongoing disposition of life (cf. Eph. 6:1). The same imperative will be laid upon slaves in verse 22. With regard to children the command is limited in its application: "to your parents" (τοῖς γονεῦσιν). The definite article is understood as possessive ("your"). Paul only uses this noun five times in his writings, but two of those describe disobedience to parents as characteristic of the last days (Rom. 1:30; 2 Tim. 3:2). While only the father is instructed in verse 21, both parents are under consideration here. This clearly implies that both mother and father are expected to be giving directives to the children.

The extent of the children's obligation to obedience is cast in the broadest possible terms: "in all things" (κατὰ πάντα). The preposition (κατὰ) is used here to denote relationship to something and should be rendered as "with respect to" or "in relation to." Thus here with the neuter plural adjective (πάντα) it has the connotation of "in all respects."[835] In a day and age when abuse is so prevalent, wisdom urges us to clarify that this does not remove all limitations. A child is not being obligated to carry out a parent's sinful wishes. But, having said that, it should be noted that the first place a child learns to relate to authority is in the home. If parents fail to instill the lessons of submission to and appreciation of legitimate authorities, society as a whole will never be able to right the ship. Such a child will meet with difficulty at every turn.

> **Ministry Maxim**
>
> A parent's affirmation may be unattainable, but the Lord's is not.

The reason for such obedience is "for this is well-pleasing to the Lord" (τοῦτο γὰρ εὐάρεστόν ἐστιν ἐν κυρίῳ). Justification for the child's obedience is cast similarly to that of the wife's submission to her husband ("as is fitting in the Lord," v. 18). The use of the conjunction (γὰρ, "for")

---

[834] BAGD, 837.
[835] Ibid., 407.

signals the foundational rationale for the directive just given. By "this" (τοῦ το) Paul means the broad-ranging obedience just called for. The adjective "well-pleasing" (εὐάρεστόν) is used by Paul eight of its nine times in the NT (Rom. 12:1, 2; 14:18; 2 Cor. 5:9; Eph. 5:10; Phil. 4:18; Col. 3:20; Titus 2:9; Heb. 13:21). The word describes what is acceptable or pleasing and always in reference to God (except perhaps Titus 2:9). Here that divine orientation is signaled by the expression ἐν κυρίῳ ("to the Lord"). The use of the preposition with the dative form of the noun indicates "a close personal relationship with Christ.[836] The believer's union with Christ, so richly spoken of throughout this book, is the foundation upon which the actions are seen to rest and thus "the expression is equivalent in meaning to *by virtue of spiritual fellowship or union with Christ.*"[837]

What are we to make of the fact that the Apostle grounds the motive for the obedience of children to their parents in the intimacy of their relationship to Christ and their longing to please Him rather than the intimacy of their relationship to their father or mother and the innate desire to please them? At least this much: a child's feelings of love may vary from moment to moment and their desire to please their parents may flee when a difficult directive is given, but their love for Christ should remain steady in their hearts at all times. Then also it is a sad fact that some parents are never pleased, no matter how well the child behaves. A parent's affirmation may be an unattainable goal, while the Lord's is not. Even if a parent is not pleased with a child, God may be. The authority of a parent is a delegated authority, handed down in measured form by God Himself. It is a good and wonderful thing when a parent is pleased with his child's obedience and affirms her in it. But that is a secondary standard. The primary standard lies with God Himself from whom the authority to exercise parental authority arose in the first place.

3:21 Fathers, do not exasperate your children, so that they will not lose heart.

Having issued the command for children to obey both parents (v. 20), Paul now turns to the "Fathers" (Οἱ πατέρες) alone. Some believe that the noun

---

[836] Ibid., 260.
[837] Thayer, 211.

is used in a reference more broadly to parents,[838] or to both parents, but especially to fathers.[839] But Paul has a perfectly good noun for parents (γονεύς) at his disposal and has shown he can use it (v. 20). It seems best to read this in its normal sense of "Fathers." Once again the nominative form serves the role of the vocative, and the definite article singles out "Fathers" as a group.

The prohibition is "do not exasperate your children" (μὴ ἐρεθίζετε τὰ τέκνα ὑμῶν). The verb is used only one other time in the NT, where it is used in a positive sense (2 Cor. 9:2). The root (ἐρέθω) means "to excite."[840] Here the meaning is clearly negative and means to "irritate," "embitter,"[841] "make resentful" or "rouse to anger."[842] The present imperative with the negation (μὴ) often signals that action now in progress is to be discontinued.[843] This may not imply that Paul had knowledge of such action by fathers in the Colossian church, but rather that it is not uncommon for fathers to fall into this kind of pattern of relating to their children. The Roman principle of *patria potestas* meant that fathers possessed unfettered authority and power in dealing with their children.[844] Without censure the father was free to deal with his children in any manner he wished. The gospel has reminded him that God has established boundaries for the use of the authority delegated to him by heaven.

The Apostle does not state just how it is a father can produce such provocation in his children. Common sense tells us that it could be through overly strict control of the child, elevated expectations that are not appropriate to the child's age, unjust rules and responsibilities laid upon the child, comparisons to their siblings, abuse of any type, severe or unjust discipline, and a lack of fatherly love and nurture. Surely there are many other ways. Children easily feel they cannot please their fathers and quickly give up trying, choosing rather to silently, but bitterly, conform to expectations, counting the days or years until they can be free of his tyranny or able to openly rebel.

---

[838] E.g., BAGD, 635.
[839] O'Brien, 225.
[840] Thayer, 249.
[841] BAGD, 308.
[842] Friberg, 171.
[843] Wallace, 724-725.
[844] Moo, 306; O,Brien, 225.

The reason for this command is "so that they will not lose heart" (ἵνα μὴ ἀθυμῶσιν). The conjunction (ἵνα) is used to express the reason for the

<table>
<tr><td>

Ministry Maxim

A child unable to please his father soon becomes a child unwilling to try.

</td><td>

command. The verb is used only here in the NT. It is related to the word ἄθυμος which is θυμός, ("spirit," "courage") affixed with the negating α-prefix. It means to have no spirit or courage, thus *"to be disheartened, dispirited, broken in spirit."*[845] To thus "be discouraged" or "lose heart"[846] is to lose the will to live and to give up

</td></tr>
</table>

attempts at success. The subjunctive mood of the verb depicts the action as objectively possible, but the reality depends upon external circumstances—in this case the father's behavior.

Digging Deeper:

1. Does anything limit the "in all things" of God's call for obedience from children (v. 20)? In answering this, how do you know you're not projecting your thoughts upon God's Word?
2. Who is easier or harder to please: God the Father or your earthly father (v. 20)? Why?
3. Enumerate ways earthly fathers can "exasperate" their children (v. 21).

**3:22 Slaves, in all things obey those who are your masters
on earth, not with external service, as those who merely
please men, but with sincerity of heart, fearing the Lord.**

Whereas his comments to wives, husbands, children, and fathers have been brief and to the point (vv. 18-21), Paul now speaks at length to "Slaves" (Οἱ δοῦλοι). Once again the nominative form functions as a vocative in address. The definite article addresses the group as a class. What accounts for the more extended treatment of the responsibility of slaves? It may be

---

[845] Thayer, 14.
[846] BAGD, 21.

that the church in Colossae was made up of a significant proportion of slaves. It may also have been an indirect way of dealing with a thorny issue which the book of Philemon clues us into. Assuming that the people and problem recounted in that letter were from Colossae, the theft, escape, and flight of the slave Onesimus and the subsequent upheaval it created among the congregation, which included his master Philemon, may be the reason for Paul's disproportionately extended comments to slaves here. He was seeking to bring calm to a congregation divided by this recent event. It may have been that Onesimus was among those returning to Colossae with both letters in hand (4:8-9).

The question comes, then, regarding how this ought to be applied—if at all—in our present context where, thankfully, slavery has been rendered illegal. It is helpful to realize that the situation for slaves of the first century was not identical to what slaves faced in the early centuries of settling North America. Still, the slave of Paul's day faced a daunting task and a grim future. How are the authoritative instructions directed toward those in that unique setting to be made applicable today with the authority of the Lord? Certainly there are many differences between the first century slave's experience and that of the modern employee, yet—having rightly identified those—the basic principles of labor and one's attitude about that labor are transferable to those who make up today's workforce. Thus the common homiletical decision to apply these verses to employees (and 4:1 to employers) is a wise one, though the exegete will need to practice caution in so doing.

The command is that slaves "obey" (ὑπακούετε). This is precisely the same command given to children with regard to their fathers (v. 20). See the comments on the word there. Again the present imperative demands that the obedience be typical, regular, and habitual. This obedience is cast in the broadest and most inclusive terms: "in all things" (κατὰ πάντα). Again this is the precise stricture placed upon the children in relationship to their fathers (v. 20). As there the preposition (κατὰ) is used here to denote relationship to something and should be rendered as "with respect to" or "in relation to." Thus here with the neuter plural adjective (πάντα), it has the connotation of "in all respects."[847]

---

[847] Ibid., 407.

The Apostle calls Christian slaves to render such obedience to "those who are your masters on earth" (τοῖς κατὰ σάρκα κυρίοις). The attributive position of the prepositional phrase marks the kind of masters that are being identified. A more literal rendering might be: "the according-to-the-flesh masters." This implies that they have a Master who is Lord of their lives in the ultimate sense, without limit and boundary. Paul will soon enough remind the masters that they "too have a Master in heaven" (4:1). In this Paul strikes a wise and winsome blow against the institution of slavery, without venturing a frontal assault on it. His immediate concern is not the overthrow of the social structure, but the salvation and sanctification of individuals and the progress of the gospel. The definite article (τοῖς) is understood as possessive ("your"), signaling that Paul is not speaking about the subservience of the slave to any and all, but to those who have an earthly claim upon them as masters.

The rest of the sentence defines the kind of obedience Paul is calling for, both negatively and positively. Negatively Paul instructs believing slaves to obey their masters "not with external service" (μὴ ἐν ὀφθαλμοδουλίᾳ). The noun (ὀφθαλμοδουλίᾳ) is used in the NT only here and in Paul's instructions to slaves in Ephesians 6:6. It has not been attested by earlier writers, but shows up in later ecclesiastical writers. It may thus have been a word of Paul's invention. It referred apparently to service performed diligently when the master was present and watchful, but which became slothful when he was absent. It is "service rendered without dedication or a sense of inner obligation but mainly to attract attention."[848] Such service is rendered only for visual appeal to others, "not for its own sake nor to please God or one's own conscience."[849]

> **Ministry Maxim**
>
> There may be many earthly "masters," but there is only one supreme "Lord."

Such obedience would mark them "as those who merely please men" (ὡς ἀνθρωπάρεσκοι). Here again the noun appears only here and in Ephesians 6:6. This noun is found in the LXX, but not elsewhere outside of

---

[848] Friberg, 289.
[849] BAGD, 599.

Paul's two usages. This describes one who seeks merely to please men "at the sacrifice of principle."[850] As such they would be mere "people-pleasers" (ESV).

Negatively stated, this is how slaves are not to render their service. Positively, and in strong contrast (ἀλλ᾽, "but"), the Christian slave's obedience must be "with sincerity of heart, fearing the Lord" (ἐν ἁπλότητι καρδίας φοβούμενοι τὸν κύριον). Compare this with the similar counsel to slaves in Ephesians 6:5. Here the noun "simplicity" (ἁπλότητι) has at its root the idea of singleness[851]—in this case singleness of focus and motive in one's deepest part. It comes then to include the ideas of sincerity, uprightness, and frankness[852] as opposed to pretense.[853] The genuineness of such a motive is underscored since this is to arise from the depths "of the heart" (καρδίας).

Alongside of this is the participial clause "fearing the Lord" (φοβούμενοι τὸν κύριον). The participle clause may indicate either the manner in which the slave's service is to be rendered or perhaps the cause which motivates his service.[854] The present tense emphasizes the ongoing nature of the action. The middle voice brings out the inward nature of the action. The fear of the Lord is the fundamental stance one takes before and in relationship to the Lord. It occurs when a person rightly apprehends who God is and who they are (and are not) before Him. The Christian slave is to ever live in the awareness of the presence of the Lord and His claim upon his every thought, word, motive, and action.

Indeed, the repetition of the word "Lord" at the end of this sentence brings out a powerful point— there may be earthly "masters" (κυρίοις), but there is only one "Lord" (τὸν κύριον). The power and authority of the one is only "on earth" (τοῖς κατὰ σάρκα). The other's is over all things in heaven and earth and under the earth. He is the "Lord" (τὸν κύριον) of even the "masters" (κυρίοις; lit., "lords"). As already noted, Paul will remind the masters: "you too have a Master in heaven" (4:1). Here again is a presentation of truth that will serve to transform not just individual hearts, but, over time, the very fabric of society.

---

[850] Ibid., 67.
[851] Moo, 310; O'Brien, 227; Thayer, 57.
[852] BAGD, 85.
[853] Thayer, 57.
[854] Harris, 183; Moo, 310-311.

3:23 Whatever you do, do your work heartily, as for the Lord rather than for men,

The Apostle's command is to "do your work" (ἐργάζεσθε). The present-tense imperative demands action that is continuous and habitual. This is to be the custom of the slave's life. The middle voice is deponent—having an active meaning. The word means simply "to do," "to accomplish," or "to carry out."[855] Paul has just used the cognate noun of this verb and also the verb which immediately follows here (ποιῆτε, "do") in verse 17, which serves as a more general application of the basic principle here applied specifically to slaves.

Paul now qualifies this imperative in a number of ways. First he speaks of the scope of its application, telling us this applies in "Whatever you do" (ὃ ἐὰν ποιῆτε). The expression ὃ ἐὰν ("Whatever") combined with the subjunctive verb is broad, intentionally generalizing the consideration as much as possible. Some suggest it may be best to render this clause "Whatever you are doing."[856] Thus slaves are commanded to accept the work assignments given to them by their masters—whatever they may be.

Furthermore slaves are to do their work "heartily," or more literally, "out from [their] soul" (ἐκ ψυχῆς). The noun is pliable and is used with many nuances of meaning, but generally it represents the immaterial nature of man. It is that part of humans which includes the intellect, emotion, and will. In English it might be best represented by the heart (cf. ἐν ἁπλότητι καρδίας "with sincerity of heart," v. 22)—thus you are to be doing your work "with all your heart" (NIV) or, as here in the NASU, "heartily." One's outward labors are to find their point of origin from within oneself. Our work arises "out from" (ἐκ) what we are on the inside. Our work is defined not by outward circumstance, but by inward character.

Indeed, deep inside we are to know that whatever our outward duties require, we do them "as for the Lord" (ὡς τῷ κυρίῳ). The conjunction ὡς is used here to introduce "the characteristic quality of a pers[on], thing, or action ... referred to in the context."[857] That governing person is designated here with the noun and its definite article in the dative case: "for the Lord"

---

[855] BAGD, 307.
[856] Harris, 184; NET Bible.
[857] BAGD, 898.

(τῷ κυρίῳ). Perhaps rather than "for," the dative might best be rendered by "to." Thus whatever we are given to do on earth by our earthly masters, we are to do it "to" the Lord. We may be undertaking our present task "for" our earthly master and because of his orders, but we can actually do it "to" the Lord as an offering of worship arising from the depths of our hearts.

Ministry Maxim
My work is defined not by outward circumstance, but by my inward character.

This, of course, stands in contrast (καὶ οὐκ, "rather than"; lit., "and not") to doing something simply "for men" (ἀνθρώποις). By this Paul might mean the approval of a slave's master or the earthly reward such a human being might render to you for work well done. Our motives and ambitions are to rise higher. Indeed, this is a liberating mind-set. If in our hearts we are able to transform any earthly duty—no matter how lowly, demeaning, or distasteful—into an act of worship rendered out from our hearts and up to God, then we are able to find joy in our work (whatever it may be or require) and a level of effectiveness that is impossible on the merely human plane.

3:24 knowing that from the Lord you will receive the reward of the inheritance. It is the Lord Christ whom you serve.

We are now confronted with a participial phrase which further expands upon how you are to "do your work" (v. 23). Work is to be undertaken with a certain mind-set (εἰδότες, "knowing"). The perfect tense has a present-tense meaning and thus describes what is to be an unceasing line of thought, regardless of the assignment laid upon the slave. The participle should probably be understood causally ("since you know," NIV, NRSV), expressing the underlying reason for the command of verse 23.[858] The line of thought we are to labor from is "that from the Lord you will receive" (ὅτι ἀπὸ κυρίου ἀπολήμψεσθε) your compensation. Rather than looking to an earthly master or to terrestrial circumstances for one's remuneration, this teaches the slave to look beyond the immediate, beyond the master-slave relationship, even past this life—and to look to "the Lord" (κυρίου), referring to Jesus, for what he needs and desires.

---

[858] Harris, 184; Moo, 312.

The verb is a compound comprised of ἀπό ("from") and λαμβάνω ("receive"). The first element doubles up the emphasis of the preposition which was used independently two words earlier (ἀπό, "from"). Indeed, the preposition in compound may mark "that the recompense comes immediately from Christ, its possessor."[859] But the future tense directs one's hopes forward, beyond the immediate. The middle voice may point to an inward, personal reward rather than an external, monetary, or circumstantial compensation.

Indeed, what the slave can expect from the Lord is "the reward of the inheritance" (τὴν ἀνταπόδοσιν τῆς κληρονομίας). Paul employs a double compound word in the noun "the reward" (τὴν ἀνταπόδοσιν). This is its only appearance in the NT. It is made up of "something given" (δόσις), "back" (ἀπὸ), and "in return" (ἀντί).[860] The preposition (ἀντί) when used in a compound may underscore the full or complete nature of the return being made.[861] This marks the third use of ἀπὸ in this clause, either in compound or standing alone. The word appears in the LXX where it is used almost exclusively in a negative sense to speak of retribution or judgment (though it is used in a positive sense in Psa. 18:12; 102:2; 130:2).[862]

The next noun (τῆς κληρονομίας, "the inheritance") is a genitive used in apposition to the first noun—it points thus to "the reward" which consists of "the inheritance" (cf. Col. 1:12). Paul uses this word four other times (Gal. 3:18; Eph. 1:14, 18; 5:5) as another way to describe salvation itself.[863] This is made the more emphatic in that both nouns are accompanied by their definite articles, pointing to a particular and unique reward which consists of a particular and unique inheritance. In view of the fact that slaves were legally prohibited from receiving an earthly inheritance, the word here has special import and power.[864]

To this Paul adds simply, as an independent statement: "It is the Lord Christ whom you serve" (τῷ κυρίῳ Χριστῷ δουλεύετε). Paul makes explicit that the one whom he had meant by "Lord" (κυρίου) earlier in

---

[859] Eadie, 265.
[860] Harris, 185.
[861] Hendriksen, 174.
[862] Moo, 312.
[863] BAGD, 435.
[864] Abbott, 295.

the verse was and is, indeed, "Christ" (Χριστῷ) Jesus Himself. The entire phrase is placed before the verb to make emphatic the contrast between "the Lord [τῷ κυρίῳ] Christ" and earthly "masters" (κυρίοις, v. 22). This precise combination and order (τῷ κυρίῳ Χριστῷ, "the Lord Christ") is found only here and in Romans 16:18 in the NT.

This much is abundantly clear, but how is one to understand the form δουλεύετε ("serve")? This same form can serve either as a present imperative or a present indicative. Most English versions take it, as does the NASU, as the indicative. It thus is read as making a statement or a declaration. This would serve the purpose of underscoring that believing slaves, while having earthly, human masters, in fact are really ultimately serving "the Lord Christ." As an imperative it would be commanding slaves to always do their work as service unto the Lord and not just to their earthly

Ministry Maxim
Labor that seeks *only* a paycheck is never worthy of the Lord.

masters. The NET Bible thus translates: "Serve the Lord Christ" (cf. also NEB). Commentators tend to favor the imperative[865] while translators tend to favor the indicative (e.g., ESV, KJV, NKJV, NASU, NIV, NRSV).

Arguments in favor of the indicative include: (1) an indicative form here would serve to explain what has just been stated in the first part of the verse (often inserting "For," cf. KJV, NKJV); and (2) if the form were an imperative we should expect ὡς τῷ κυρίῳ, as in Ephesians 6:7 (rather than τῷ κυρίῳ Χριστῷ).[866]

Arguments in favor of reading the form as an imperative include: (1) an imperative here would pick up on the imperative with which the sentence began (ἐργάζεσθε, "do your work") in verse 23, thus forming an inclusion; (2) an imperative here would make understanding γὰρ ("For") in the next verse clearer; (3) the form τῷ κυρίῳ Χριστῷ following an imperative finds a parallel in Romans 12:11, where τῷ κυρίῳ is combined with an imperatival participle; and (4) although understanding this as inferential (*"Therefore* serve the Lord Christ") works with the first part of the verse perfectly well, as well as if we understood it as causal (*"For* it is the Lord

---

[865] E.g., Abbott, 295; Harris, 186; Lohse, 161; Moo, 313; Moule, 131; O'Brien, 229.
[866] Lightfoot, 227.

Christ you serve"),[867] none of the other imperatives in this paragraph are introduced by a conjunction (vv. 18, 19, 20, 21, 22; 4:1), and thus the fact that one is missing here points toward understanding it as imperative here as well.[868] Ultimately it seems the arguments favor understanding the verb as an imperative.

3:25 For he who does wrong will receive the consequences of the wrong which he has done, and that without partiality.

Now we meet a conjunction (γὰρ, "For") which explicitly signals the grounds for the preceding instructions. A participle (ὁ ... ἀδικῶν, "he who does wrong") is used to identify the subject. The word particularly views doing of wrong as a violation of a law, whether it is human or divine.[869]

One who acts thus "will receive" (κομίσεται). The verb in the active voice simply means "to bring" (Luke 7:37), but in the middle voice, as we have it here, it means to "carry off," "get (for oneself)", or "receive."[870] It is used of receiving wages, a return on an investment (Matt. 25:27), and the fulfillment of a promise (Heb. 10:36; 11:39). It is also used of recompense or reward—either positively (Eph. 6:8; 1 Peter 5:4) or negatively (Col. 3:25) or both (2 Cor. 5:10). The future tense of the verb simply sets the action out beyond the act of lawbreaking without setting a definite time.

In this case what a wrongdoer receives is "the consequences of the wrong which he has done" (ὃ ἠδίκησεν). This is a somewhat interpretive and wordy rendering. It might be translated more literally, "what he has done wrong." The relative pronoun (ὃ) is singular and means "what" or perhaps "that which." The verb is the same one just employed to describe the subject of the sentence. Now the aorist singular form pictures the individual act of sin. God knows each thought, word, and deed. Each will be repaid. And that which such a one gets is their act of wrongdoing. If they look at sin and say, "I want that!" that is just exactly what they get ... and nothing more. That is their reward. Their reward is the act of sin and whatever pleasure it may temporarily give. They enjoy the "passing pleasures of sin" (Heb. 11: 25), but then they are gone. They enjoy the momentary pleasure.

---

[867] Harris, 186.
[868] Moo, 313.
[869] BAGD, 17.
[870] Ibid., 442-443.

Nothing more, except the compounding "consequences of the wrong which they have done."

As Ravi Zacharias has well said, "The difference between illegitimate and legitimate pleasure is this: For legitimate pleasure, the price is paid before it is enjoyed. For illegitimate pleasure, the price is paid after it is enjoyed."[871] Indeed, the one who does right receives an eternal reward—filled with divine pleasures that will never end (v. 24)!

Paul adds (καὶ, "and") that this divine retribution will be administered "without partiality" (οὐκ ἔστιν προσωπολημψία). The noun (προσωπολημψία, "partiality") is a compound comprised of "a face" (πρόσωπον) and "to receive" (λαμβάνω). It is used four times in the NT, three of those by Paul (Rom. 2:11; Eph. 6:9; Col. 3:25; James 2:1). It points to favoritism or prejudice. Thayer describes it as "the fault of one who when called on to requite or to give judgment has respect to the outward circumstances of men and not to their intrinsic merits, and so prefers, as the more worthy, one who is rich, high-born, or powerful, to another who is destitute of such gifts."[872] Paul always uses it with reference to what is not true of God.

> **Ministry Maxim**
>
> A sinner's reward is his sin—and nothing more.

But to whom does Paul address this—the slave, the master, or both? Commentators have long been divided on this matter. The context and comparisons with other "household codes" in the NT seem to demand that it be understood as spoken to the slaves. Certainly, however, the principles enunciated apply equally to masters. The last clause is addressed to slaves, but with their masters (and any earthly preferential treatment they may enjoy) in view (the parallel clause is addressed specifically to the masters in Eph. 6:9).

It seems likely that the situation with Onesimus, the thieving, runaway slave who apparently is returning with the carrier of this very letter (4:9), is behind these instructions. While Paul addresses slaves in his letter to the Ephesians (6:5-8), he seems to give more attention to them here,

---

[871] Zacharias, Ravi, "Pleasure at a Price," *A Slice of Infinity*, March 30, 2000. http://www.rzim.org/slice/slicearticleprint.aspx?aid=9044.

[872] Thayer, 551.

proportionally speaking. The Apostle is walking a careful line. He steers clear of undermining the lawful rights of Philemon, Onesimus's owner under the civil law, yet he seeks to bring the principles and power of the gospel to bear upon their circumstances and relationship. Indeed, the very verb twice used here (ἀδικέω) is employed by him to describe what Onesimus did to Philemon ("he has wronged you," Philem. 18). He seeks to undermine anarchy by reminding slaves of the fact that ultimately they serve the Lord Jesus Christ Himself and will stand before Him for review, but he seems to encourage them with the knowledge that they will be joined there by their masters and that together they will face a bar of justice which sees through all earthly distinctions.

Clearly contextual matters indicate that the chapter should have included what is chapter 4 verse 1, for it rounds out the Apostle's household code by addressing the "Masters" of slaves.

Digging Deeper:

1. What differences exist between first-century slavery and twenty-first-century employment which guard us from misapplying the Apostle's words here (vv. 22-25)?

2. Write down two principles from these verses which, if rightly applied, would change the way you work. Explain those to someone else and describe the changes you plan to make.

3. In these "household codes" (3:18-4:1), why do you think Paul always begins with the party typically considered subservient?

COLOSSIANS 4

4:1 Masters, grant to your slaves justice and fairness, knowing that you too have a Master in heaven.

The Apostle now rounds out and completes his household code (3:18-4:1) by addressing the "Masters" (Οἱ κύριοι) of the slaves that have been under consideration in 3:22-25. As he has done in 3:18, 19, 20, 21 and 22, Paul uses here the nominative form as a vocative-like address, and he employs the definite article to mark out the "Masters" as a distinct class. This being true, there is probably also, however, a sense in which Philemon himself would have been under the spotlight as this letter was read to the congregation. With the drama of his slave Onesimus's thievery and flight as a matter of record and with his return as a "faithful and beloved brother" (4:9), the center of attention would have fallen upon Philemon. His response to Paul's instructions regarding Onesimus would have likely set the course for any other slave owner's within the congregation at Colossae.

> **Ministry Maxim**
>
> Every earthly "master" does well to remember he is Someone's "slave."

The verb (παρέχεσθε, "grant") is a compound word made up of "beside" (παρά) and "to hold" (ἔχω). The middle voice may have the sense of granting something to someone,[873] it may point to the inward nature of the action and thus signal

---

[873] BAGD, 626.

required initiative on the part of the masters,[874] or it may indicate reciprocating action on the part of the masters ("exhibit on your part").[875] The present imperative demands action that is regular, consistent, and habitual. This should be the very nature of the relationship between master and slave. This is not simply counsel for a present crisis, but standing instruction for all master/slave relationships.

What is to be thus given is "justice and fairness" (τὸ δίκαιον καὶ τὴν ἰσότητα). The first word, an adjective used as an abstract noun (τὸ δίκαιον, "justice"), has a wide range of meaning, depending upon its context. Paul uses here the neuter form to generalize the concept, and it "denotes that which is obligatory in view of certain requirements of justice."[876] So often, as here, the context makes clear that the rightness of particular actions and attitudes is defined by who God is and how He acts (e.g., Acts 4:19; Eph. 6:1). To this Paul adds (καὶ, "and") a second word, now employing a noun (τὴν ἰσότητα, "fairness"). The word is used elsewhere in the NT only in 2 Corinthians 8:13 and 14 where it is translated "equality." The repetition of the definite article with this second word may indicate that Paul has in mind not so much the abstract principle of fairness, but individual, specific, concrete acts of equality.[877] Alford believes that the former word may point to instances where what "justice" requires is clear and the latter word "to matters not admitting of the application of strict rules—a large and liberal interpretation of justice in ordinary matters."[878] Of course, those to whom these things are to be granted are "your slaves" (τοῖς δούλοις). The definite article (τοῖς) is understood to convey possession ("your").

Paul uses a participial phrase to express the motivation for such action on the part of the masters: "knowing that you too have a Master in heaven" (εἰδότες ὅτι καὶ ὑμεῖς ἔχετε κύριον ἐν οὐρανῷ). The participle (εἰδότες, "knowing") is used in a causal sense ("because you know that," NIV). The verb is in the perfect tense but has a present-tense meaning. It has just been used (3:24) to provide a foundation for a Christian slave's conduct and so now is used here again to do the same with regard to that slave's master. For

---

[874] Harris, 187.
[875] Lightfoot, 228.
[876] BAGD, 196.
[877] Harris, 188.
[878] Alford, 3:241; cf. O'Brien, 232.

all the emotional fireworks that might surround a master/slave relationship, a common commitment to "knowing" the reality of things rightly will serve both parties well.[879]

As different as their daily experience of life was, the Apostle demands that the Christian masters in the church have a complete awareness of the fact that they share something in common with their slaves (τι καὶ ὑμεῖς ἔχετε, "you also have"). The present tense of the verb underscores that this is not a passing fact, but an abiding, constant one.

What they share in common with their slaves is "a Master in heaven" (κύριον ἐν οὐρανῷ). It is not that slaves have virtually no autonomy and that masters have complete autonomy. It is that both stand under a common master—and a heavenly one at that. The noun κύριος ("Master") has served a dual and important role throughout Paul's instruction to slaves and masters (3:22-4:1). It appears now for the seventh time. On the one hand Paul uses it to describe earthly, human slave "masters" (3:22a; 4:1a), but on the other hand he uses it repeatedly as a reference to Jesus Christ their common "Lord" (3:22b, 23, 24 [twice]) or "Master" (4:1b). Paul's use of the term here likely brings over something of the point made primarily to slaves in 3:25—that every earthly "master" too will stand before his "Master in heaven" and "will receive the consequences of [that] … which he has done, and that without partiality." Indeed, every earthly "master" must remember that he is ultimately a "slave" to a higher "Master."[880] "For he who was called in the Lord while a slave, is the Lord's freedman; likewise he who was called while free, is Christ's slave" (1 Cor. 7:22).

Digging Deeper:

1. To whom do the words of verse 1 rightly and authoritatively apply in our twenty-first-century world? Why? How do you know?

2. What do "justice and fairness" look like in your workplace? How might employer and employees differ in their opinions?

3. How does Christ's lordship ("a Master") inform how you wield authority in your workplace or home?

---

[879] O'Brien, 233.
[880] Moo, 316.

4:2 Devote yourselves to prayer, keeping alert in it with an attitude of thanksgiving;

The Apostle now breaks from the household codes that have occupied his attention (3:18-4:1) and moves to the matters of prayer (4:2-4) and witness (4:5-6). This will serve to bring the main body of his letter to a close (3:1-4:6), having focused positively on the correct understanding of the Christian life.

The call is to "Devote yourselves to prayer" (Τῇ προσευχῇ προσκαρτερεῖ τε). The command to "Devote" (προσκαρτερεῖτε) is in the present tense, demanding an ongoing, steady, habitual practice. Paul uses the same verb to describe our practice in prayer in Romans 12:12 ("devoted to prayer"). So too Luke employs the word to describe the practice of the early church with regard to prayer (Acts 1:14; 2:42, 46; 6:4). Six of the word's ten NT usages are related to prayer. It is a compound word comprised of πρός ("with") and καρτερός ("strong," "steadfast").[881] When it is accompanied by a noun in the dative case, as it is here (Τῇ προσευχῇ, "prayer"), it has the sense of *"busy oneself with, be busily engaged in, be devoted to"*[882] or *"to give constant attention to a thing."*[883]

This is to be the believer's stance toward "prayer" (Τῇ προσευχῇ). This is the most frequently used noun in the NT to designate prayer. It is also the most general word for prayer, but it often has the more specific sense of petition. That this might be the flavor of the word here is signaled by the fact that Paul immediately calls for "thanksgiving" to be included in this prayer (v. 2b), thus distinguishing between the two, and then cites specific requests that the Colossians ought to take up in "prayer" on behalf of him and his ministry team (vv. 3-4).[884]

Just what are we to make of the presence of the definite article? It is possible that it points to some specific "prayer" that Paul has in mind. The noun is found again with the definite article in Acts 2:42 to describe what all the believers devoted themselves to. It seems that the earliest believers may have continued the Jewish practice of keeping set, rhythmic hours for prayer,

---

[881] Thayer, 547.
[882] BAGD, 715.
[883] Thayer, 547.
[884] O'Brien, 237.

although now those prayers were in Jesus' name and were empowered by the Holy Spirit. Some such regime, habit, or discipline of prayer may well be what is in mind here as well.

The command is now modified by a participle. This devotion to prayer is to take place while "keeping alert" (γρηγοροῦντες). The participle can be understood to have the force of a command (KJV),[885] but it seems more likely that it is subordinate to the previous imperative, describing what should take place in prayer.[886] The word, most literally, means to be awake or stay awake. Figuratively, as here, it means to be on the alert or to be watchful. Along this line we might say, "Keep your eyes open!"[887] In the Gospels it is used either in eschatological warning to "be alert" for the coming of Christ (Matt. 24:42, 43; 25:13; Mark 13:34, 35, 37; Luke 12:37) or in Christ's call to the disciples to pray with Him in the garden (Matt. 26:38, 40, 41; Mark 14:34, 37, 38). Paul uses it with regard to the vigilance of church leadership in watching over the flock under their charge (Acts 20:31), as a call to alertness in the last days (1 Thess. 5:6, 10), and more generally in a call to all believers (1 Cor. 16:13).

Here the call is to keep alert in relationship to prayer (ἐν αὐτῇ, "in it"). But just what does this prepositional phrase mean? Does this mean to be alert to anything that might steal you away from such disciplined prayer? Or does it describe the nature of one's praying (i.e., with alertness)? Or does it mean that prayer is the means by which one stays awake with regard to dangers that might come upon the believer?[888] Perhaps to decide is to overanalyze. The Apostle would likely reply with a "yes." All this is involved in "keeping alert in" prayer.

> **Ministry Maxim**
>
> Gratitude is more than good manners; it is essential to my spiritual survival.

The participle ("keeping alert") is further qualified by a second prepositional phrase (ἐν εὐχαριστίᾳ) which the NASU has somewhat expansively rendered "with an attitude of thanksgiving." More simply and literally it might be rendered "in thanksgiving." The only other place in the NT where the precise expression is found is in Colossians 2:7, where it is rendered

---

[885] Harris, 192; Lohse, 164.
[886] Moo, 320.
[887] BAGD, 167.
[888] Lohse, 164.

"with gratitude." The noun and its associated word group carry the idea of not merely "an attitude of" gratitude, but an active expression of that attitude in the giving of thanks.[889]

There is a question regarding how to render the preposition (ἐν) in this case. Nearly all English versions translate it as "with," while the immediately preceding phrase finds the same preposition translated as "in." Martha King cites six different nuances of meaning that may be found in the preposition here: (1) it indicates the circumstance of praying, give thanks while praying; (2) it indicates a circumstance of being watchful in prayer while, at the same time, being thankful; (3) it indicates the circumstance of both persevering in prayer and being watchful; (4) it indicates the manner of being watchful; (5) it indicates the result of being watchful; and (6) it indicates the reason for being watchful.[890] What is certain is that thankfulness is a core theme of this epistle (1:3, 12ff.; 2:7; 3:15, 16, 17; 4:2) and prayer and thanksgiving can never be separated (1:3).

4:3 praying at the same time for us as well, that God will open up to us a door for the word, so that we may speak forth the mystery of Christ, for which I have also been imprisoned;

Paul now uses a second participial phrase to modify further the command of verse 2 ("Devote"). In doing so he uses the verbal form of the noun rendered "prayer" in verse 2 (προσευχόμενοι, "praying"). The present tense emphasizes the habitual, continual nature of the prayer being enjoined. The participle probably in this case takes on an imperatival form from the preceding command (v. 2). The adverb ἅμα is used to describe "the coincidence of two actions in time" and is thus rendered "at the same time."[891]

During their times of prayer (v. 2), Paul is asking/commanding them to make intercession "for us as well" (καὶ περὶ ἡμῶν). That for which they are to pray is indicated by the plural personal pronoun (ἡμῶν, "us") and includes most obviously Paul and Timothy (1:1) and perhaps others such as Epaphras (4:12-13). The preposition περὶ ("for") is to be understood not merely as "concerning," but as "on behalf of."[892] In all their praying for

---

[889] O'Brien, 108.
[890] King, 312.
[891] BAGD, 42.
[892] Harris, 193.

themselves and others, Paul wants the Colossian believers to pray for them also (καὶ, "as well").

The content of their prayers is spelled out: "that God will open to us a door for the word" (ἵνα ὁ θεὸς ἀνοίξῃ ἡμῖν θύραν τοῦ λόγου). The ἵνα does not introduce a purpose clause, but indicates the content of the prayers being requested.[893] That which is requested is something "God" (ὁ θεὸς) must do; thus it is a supernatural work. Indeed, it is that He "will open to us a door for the word" (ἀνοίξῃ ἡμῖν θύραν τοῦ λόγου). The aorist tense of the verb (ἀνοίξῃ, "will open") describes a decisive act which God will perform. The subjunctive mood views the action as possible, but dependent upon God's response to the prayers being requested.

What is to be opened is "a door for the word" (θύραν τοῦ λόγου). This is a metaphorical way of speaking of an opportunity (θύραν, "a door") to speak the message of the gospel (τοῦ λόγου, "the word"). The genitive is objective, meaning either "a door for our message" or "a door for preaching."[894] But just what does this mean? Paul was in prison as he penned this letter (4:3b). So does he mean being released from prison? Or is he asking them to pray for "an open door" to speak the gospel even while he is in prison? Minimally it is the latter; ideally it is the former.

An open door does not imply the absence of opposition (1 Cor. 16:9). But every opportunity is not necessarily God's open door (2 Cor. 2:12). Paul was looking not for an easy life, but for circumstances which would permit, even if with some difficulty, the fulfillment of his calling. If, as it seems probable, Paul's imprisonment here is the same as that described in Acts 28:16-31, he was under house arrest and able to receive guests. In this way God proved faithful in answering prayers to open "a door for the word" when the Apostle was in prison. As he would confidently assert from his much more restrictive and final imprisonment, "I suffer hardship even to imprisonment as a criminal; but the word of God is not imprisoned." (2 Tim. 2:9)

The motive for such prayer is "so that we may speak forth the mystery of Christ" (λαλῆσαι τὸ μυστήριον τοῦ Χριστοῦ). The infinitive (λαλῆσαι, "we may speak") may be used to indicate either purpose or result ("so

---

[893] Eadie, 275; Harris, 193; O'Brien, 238.
[894] Harris, 194; Robertson, *Word Pictures*, 4:509.

that"), more likely the former. The aorist tense may point to speaking which is effective.[895] It is to be the intent of the prayer that they may speak "the mystery of Christ" (τὸ μυστήριον τοῦ Χριστοῦ). The genitive (τοῦ Χριστοῦ, "of Christ") is probably to be understood as epexegetical, meaning that Christ is Himself the mystery (1:26-27; 2:2).[896] See our commentary on 1:26-27 and 2:2 for more on the meaning of this expression.

> **Ministry Maxim**
>
> Don't presume doors will open to speak of Christ; pray them open.

It is this mystery, says Paul, "for which I have also been imprisoned" (δι᾽ ὃ καὶ δέδεμαι). The preposition (δι᾽, "for" with the accusative ὃ) identifies the grounds ("because of" or "on account of") for Paul's request of prayer. The relative pronoun (ὃ, "which") refers back to the mystery (to which its number and gender are matched). The use of καὶ may be emphatic ("because of which I am, *in fact*, in prison"), may strengthen the relative pronoun ("because of this *very* mystery"),[897] or it may indicate an addition ("also").[898]

The verb (δέδεμαι, "I ... have been imprisoned") can refer to the actual binding of a person or animal or, metaphorically, to being imprisoned. The perfect tense lays emphasis upon Paul's present circumstances in light of his having been bound in the past. The passive voice pictures others acting upon Paul with force. Whether Paul at that very moment had chains upon his hands and feet or whether he was simply held in confinement by Roman decree, he was bound in regard to the most precious thing in his life— making known the mystery of Christ.

4:4 that I may make it clear in the way I ought to speak.

Paul now moves to finish the sentence by the use of a prepositional phrase (ἵνα, "that"). This could be viewed as indicating purpose, but the use of the preposition seems to be similar to the way it was used in verse 3. It thus indicates here a second part of the content of the prayer. Not only should they pray that God will open a door for Paul to speak the word of the gospel

---

[895] King, 315.

[896] Harris, 194; Moo, 323; Robertson calls it a "genitive of apposition," *Word Pictures*, 4:509.

[897] Harris, 195.

[898] King, 317.

(v. 3), but they should also pray, says Paul, "that I may make it clear" (ἵνα φανερώσω αὐτό). The verb (φανερώσω, "I may make … clear") describes making something visible or manifest. The prayer is that when Paul speaks "the mystery of Christ" (v. 3) that somehow, through the vehicle of his words, a manifestation, an unveiling would take place in the hearts and minds of the listeners. The preacher's words must show or reveal something … or more accurately Someone, Christ Himself, who is the mystery (v. 3).

Is, then, Paul asking primarily for something to be done in himself (as the preacher), in the hearers (as he speaks), or in both? The answer surely is "both"! The words of the preacher, by the working of the Holy Spirit, must become the means by which light comes to the heart of the hearers so that they see Christ as they had not seen Him before. The aorist tense looks to an actual event—Paul wants concrete opportunities to proclaim Christ and that in those moments Christ would be manifested to the hearts and minds of those to whom he speaks. The subjunctive mood indicates that the reality of this actually taking place depends upon some external conditions, in this case upon the Colossian believers' follow-through in praying as Paul requests and then also upon God answering those prayers. The personal pronoun (αὐτό, "it") finds its antecedent in "the mystery of Christ" (v. 3).

Such a proclamation, says Paul, is merely "in the way I ought to speak" (ὡς δεῖ με λαλῆσαι). The comparative form (ὡς, "in the way"; normally, "as" or "like") holds side-by-side what he asks them to pray will be and what indeed "ought" (δεῖ) to be. The word describes compulsion, necessity, or obligation. Preaching where this kind of a revelation does not take place simply falls short of its intended purpose. Clarity is indispensible because of the incomparable value of the One being proclaimed. Christ simply *must* be made clear every time we open our mouths to speak of Him! This is not merely an obligation Paul lays upon others, but which he took upon himself personally (με, "I") as he ventured "to speak" (λαλῆ σαι). The aorist tense of the infinitive again looks at concrete acts of speaking about Christ.

> **Ministry Maxim**
>
> Clarity in preaching is not optional, but obligatory.

Digging Deeper:

1. What is it about prayer that requires devotion?
2. See if you can explain to someone the interrelationship of gratitude and spiritual alertness.
3. What are the distinguishing marks of an open door for the gospel?
4. What has to happen in the speaker and what has to happen in the hearer for the gospel to be made clear? Why is God necessary to each of these?

4:5 Conduct yourselves with wisdom toward outsiders, making the most of the opportunity.

The Apostle now transitions from prayer concerning our witness to those outside the faith (vv. 2-4) to actual ministry to them (vv. 5-6). The command "conduct yourself" (περιπατεῖτε) is more literally "walk." The word is used regularly to describe metaphorically the conduct and course of one's life (Col. 1:10; 2:6; 3:7). In this it reflects earlier Hebrew thought (e.g., Prov. 2:20; 4:12; 6:22). Thus the command is to let your life unfold, take place, and be characterized "toward outsiders" (πρὸς τοὺς ἔξω) in a certain manner. The expression τοὺς ἔξω ("outsiders") is found also in 1 Thessalonians 4:12 and 1 Corinthians 5:12-13. It "is equivalent to the rabbinical term denoting those who belong to another religious group and is used here to denote those who are 'non-Christians.'"[899] The adverb with the definite article is used as a substantive.[900]

All our relationships with those outside the faith are to be "with wisdom" ('Εν σοφίᾳ). The preposition ('Εν) introduces the manner in which our walk is to take place. The noun (σοφίᾳ) has been used to form a rich vein of truth in this letter. Paul has told the Colossians that he prays that they might "be filled with the knowledge of His will in all spiritual wisdom" (1:9). Paul himself proclaims Christ, "admonishing every man and teaching every man with all wisdom" (1:28). It is in Christ that are "hidden all

---

[899] Rienecker, 583.
[900] BAGD, 279.

the treasures of wisdom and knowledge" (2:3). The Colossians themselves are to teach and admonish one another "with all wisdom" (3:16). The false teacher(s), however, has only "the appearance of wisdom" (2:23). Implicit, then, is the understanding that it is divine wisdom they need and that only God can supply this wisdom. The references that open (1:9) and close the letter (4:5) form an inclusio which, like bookends, holds together the rich emphasis on wisdom throughout the letter.[901]

The imperative ("Conduct yourselves") is further qualified by "making the most of the opportunity" (τὸν καιρὸν ἐξαγοραζόμενοι). The expression is more literally "the time redeeming." The verb is used only four times in the NT, all by Paul. He employs it twice in the active voice to speak of Christ redeeming sinners (Gal. 3:13; 4:5). Here and in Ephesians 5:16 it is in the middle voice. The verb is a compound made up of ἐκ ("from" or "out of") and ἀγοράζω ("to buy"). In this case the preposition probably intensifies the meaning of the verb, meaning to "buy up intensively" or "to snap up every opportunity."[902] The participle, under the influence of the preceding imperative,

> **Ministry Maxim**
>
> Each day
> and every
> encounter hold
> opportunities
> which will not be
> repeated.

may be read as a command;[903] it may describe circumstances attendant to the fulfilling of the imperative;[904] or it may be instrumental, describing the means by which one shows wisdom (i.e., by buying up the time).[905] The middle voice emphasizes that the Colossian believers are to redeem the time "for themselves."[906]

It is "the opportunity" (τὸν καιρὸν) which must be thus purchased or redeemed. As has already been noted, it more literally means "the time." Two Greek words are used for time. To put it rather simplistically, the noun χρόνος refers to time by the calendar while the noun καιρός, which is used here, refers to time by its significance.[907] The former tends to refer to a specific time. The latter refers to a season of time. This present evil season

---

[901] Dunn, 265.
[902] NIDNTT, 1:268.
[903] Harris, 196; Lohse, 168.
[904] Moo, 327.
[905] O'Brien, 241.
[906] Harris, 196; Moo. 328; Wallace, 421.
[907] Mounce, 732-733.

of time which stands between the advents of Christ must be bought up and redeemed by the believer so as to serve the purposes of God. "[Z]eal and well-doing are as it were the purchase-money by which we make the time our own."[908] This has particular emphasis, in this context, on the proclamation of the gospel to the unbelieving. "So then, *while we have opportunity, let us do good to all people*" (Gal. 6:10a, emphasis added). Jesus said, "We must work the works of Him who sent Me as long as it is day; night is coming when no one can work" (John 9:4; cf. Eccl. 9:10).

4:6 Let your speech always be with grace, as though seasoned with salt, so that you will know how you should respond to each person.

The sentence is missing a main verb, which must be supplied by the translator. Virtually all English versions supply a hortatory call ("Let ... be"). Literally rendered the main clause reads "The word of you always in grace."

The noun (ὁ λόγος) has a variety of connotations depending upon the context, and "speech" here seems a good rendering of the author's intent. The definite article sets it apart as a particular kind of "speech," in this case the interaction one has with unbelieving people (v. 5). Paul uses the noun in Colossians to describe both overt gospel proclamation (1:5, 25; 4:3) and more general conversation (3:17). It would include, then, not only our specific times of sharing the gospel, but also our daily, more routine interactions with the unbelieving, but watching, world. This is "your" (ὑμῶν) speech. You cannot control someone else's mouth. Fact is, ultimately you can't even control your own (James 3:2)! It must be brought under the control of the Holy Spirit (Gal. 5:22-23).

One's speech must "always be with grace" (πάντοτε ἐν χάριτι). The adverb (πάντοτε, "always") emphasizes the constant vigilance we must exercise over our conversation with the unbelieving. Every word matters; every interaction is essential. That our words should be "with grace" (ἐν χάριτι) means that they are permeated with, empowered by, and engulfed in the "grace" that the Holy Spirit brings when He is in control. The noun (χάριτι, "grace") can refer to divine grace or human graciousness.

---

[908] Thayer, 220.

Here it probably has the sense of "graciousness" or "attractiveness" which is a result of God's grace in and though the believer.[909]

Just what this means is now illustrated by a metaphor: "seasoned with salt" (ἄλατι ἠρτυμένος). Jesus used the noun (ἄλατι, "salt") to describe a disciple's role in the world (Matt. 5:13; Mark 9:50; Luke 14:34). In the ancient world, "salt" could be used either as a seasoning for food or as fertilizer for the ground. As such it became illustrative of the qualities of an ideal disciple of Jesus Christ. The participle "seasoned" (ἠρτυμένος) indicates that Paul is using it with the connotation of a food seasoning here. The verb means to prepare or to make ready. Thus in this context it conveys the idea of making our speech something palatable and thus beneficial to the nonbelieving. It speaks of speech which "is winsome or witty" and which thus is made "interesting and fruitful."[910] It is not the pleasure of the unbelieving which is in view, but their profit spiritually. Such speech preempts unnecessary objections. This kind of speech provokes interest by wise engagement and phraseology. The perfect tense is used to describe the character or "state" of such speech.[911] The passive voice emphasizes that our speech is not self-governing, but under our control—as we in turn are under the control of the Holy Spirit.

> **Ministry Maxim**
>
> Holy Spirit dependence, not cookie-cutter methods, is the key to personal evangelism.

Paul is not advocating "cleverness of speech," for "the cross of Christ should not be made void" (1 Cor. 1:17). Clearly "the word of the cross is to those who are perishing foolishness" (v. 18). God still says:

> "I will destroy the wisdom of the wise, / And the cleverness of the clever I will set aside." Where is the wise man? Where is the scribe? Where is the debater of this age? Has not God made foolish the wisdom of the world? For since in the wisdom of God the world through its wisdom did not come to know God, God was well-pleased through the foolishness of the message preached to save those who believe. For indeed Jews ask for signs, and Greeks search for wisdom; but we preach Christ crucified, to Jews a stumbling

---

[909] BAGD, 877.
[910] Ibid., 35, 111; cf. Lightfoot, 230-231.
[911] Moo, 331.

block, and to Gentiles foolishness, but to those who are the called, both Jews and Greeks, Christ the power of God and the wisdom of God. Because the foolishness of God is wiser than men, and the weakness of God is stronger than men. (vv. 19-25)

While Paul is not calling for clever rhetoric, he is demanding a wise use of words (v. 5). The two are not necessarily the same. Only a fool uses words that he knows to be inflammatory or that he believes are likely to be misunderstood by the one to whom he is speaking.

The goal is "so that you will know how you should respond to each person" (εἰδέναι πῶς δεῖ ὑμᾶς ἑνὶ ἑκάστῳ ἀποκρίνεσθαι). The infinitive (εἰδέναι, "know") should be understood as expressing either purpose[912] or result,[913] as most English translations recognize. The perfect tense of the verb is defective and is expressed here with a future tense ("will ... know"). What is to be known is how to "respond" (ἀποκρίνεσθαι). The verb is used 229 times in the Gospels and Acts and only two times elsewhere in the NT—here and in Revelation 7:13. Thus we have before us the only use of the verb in all the NT epistles. It is deponent—middle voice in form, but active in meaning. It means to answer a question posed to you. It is one's reply in a conversation. In this case, it has specifically to do with conversations with unbelievers regarding faith in the Lord Jesus Christ. There is a way which we "should" (δεῖ) reply in such cases (cf. 1 Peter 3:15). The word was just used in verse 4 to describe the way Paul believes he should speak the gospel message—which, by the way, is clearly. There is a sense of obligation or necessity about the kind of reply made in conversations with the unbelieving. And this is not wisdom and grace considered merely in a general way toward the unbelieving. Rather the obligation is specific to "each one" (ἑνὶ ἑκάστῳ) you may encounter. The emphasis is not on "everyone" you may meet, but upon "each separate person."[914]

Paul is not calling for a cookie-cutter approach to evangelism. He is calling for real-time, Spirit-born wisdom and grace to be applied in the specifics of each encounter with each person. The emphasis here is not on learning a method of gospel presentation, but upon personal dependence

---

[912] Harris, 197; Moo, 331.
[913] Alford, 3:243; Wright, 153.
[914] Harris, 198.

upon the Holy Spirit to produce in one's heart and mind the wisdom and grace essential to making the most effective use of each and every encounter with an unbeliever. It considers people as individuals, not as a category (unbelievers). It recognizes that we must listen carefully to each person God sovereignly puts before us. It also reminds us that each encounter demands fresh grace coming down from God, flowing through us and on to the person.

Digging Deeper:

1. Having prayed for opportunity to speak the gospel (v. 3) and for clarity in speaking it (v. 4), what precisely does "wisdom toward outsiders" (v. 5) look like in your current relationships with unbelievers?

2. In what way have you had an "opportunity" with the unbelieving this week? In what way did you "buy it up"?

3. How can canned gospel presentations help us in evangelism? How can they hinder us? What does verse 6 have to say to this?

4:7 As to all my affairs, Tychicus, our beloved brother and faithful servant and fellow bond-servant in the Lord, will bring you information.

The Apostle now moves to close the letter, providing various greetings and instructions either about or to various individuals. He will spend twelve verses doing so (vv. 7-18). The length of this section is disproportionately longer than the matching section in Ephesians, which runs a total of four verses (Eph. 5:21-24). In two epistles that are so closely matched as to content and structure, one has to wonder why this is so. The notion that Ephesians is a cyclical letter intended not simply for the specific church in Ephesus, but for it along with other churches in the Lycus Valley, may provide a partial explanation. Why include many personal greetings when it is a letter intended to be read at a variety of churches, some of which will not be home to those greeted. It might be argued that it was in Ephesus that Paul personally knew so many from his extended time of ministry there (Acts 19:10). But rather than providing reason to send the greetings, it might be viewed as a reason for withholding them—they already knew him and he did not need to try and reinforce the contents of the letter by indirectly reminding them of his relationship to them. It may also be that since Paul had never visited Colossae, he felt the need to make mention of those individuals he did know and who were known and appreciated by the Colossian Christians—thus strengthening his case with the church.

The first to be mentioned is "Tychicus" (Τύχικος). Tychicus probably carried Paul's letter to the Ephesians and was to inform them about Paul's circumstances (Eph. 6:21-22). Since the two letters seem to have been penned at approximately the same time, it seems likely that he was also the primary bearer of the letter to the Colossians and perhaps a letter to the church in Laodicea as well (Col. 4:16). He had been with Paul during the Apostle's emotionally charged meeting with the Ephesian elders along his journey to Jerusalem (Acts 20:4). He was thus well-known to the Ephesian church by the time Paul wrote 2 Timothy and the Apostle sent him to them again (2 Tim. 4:12). Acts 20:4 identifies Tychicus as one who was "of Asia" (v. 4), meaning he may have been well-known to the Christians in Colossae as well. Perhaps this is why he was entrusted with the responsibility of returning the newly converted runaway slave Onesimus to his master and the church in Colossae (Col. 4:9). He thus may also have been made the courier of Paul's letter to Philemon. Obviously then, Tychicus was a veteran of Paul's first Roman imprisonment. He appears to have been in the running to fulfill a similar role of service in Titus's regard, for he similarly wrote to him saying, "When I send Artemas or Tychicus to you, make every effort to come to me at Nicopolis, for I have decided to spend the winter there" (Titus 3:12).

Clearly Tychicus was a man of outstanding character, loyalty, and faithfulness. It is little wonder that Paul, nearing the end of his life, chose him to relieve Timothy in Ephesus so he could travel to Rome to be with the Apostle (2 Tim. 4:12). In all likelihood, he was tapped to carry the letter of 2 Timothy on his way. This would make him the possible courier of as many as four NT letters written by the Apostle Paul (Ephesians, Colossians, Philemon, 2 Timothy) and possibly also one that has not been preserved for us (letter to the Laodiceans, Col. 4:16).

Here Paul uses three descriptive expressions to tell us more directly what he thinks of Tychicus. He is "our beloved brother" (ὑμῖν ὁ ἀγαπητὸς ἀδελφὸς). The definite article (ὁ) governs all three expressions (agreeing in number and gender with each) and indicates that just one person is being described. Paul uses the same expression to describe him in Ephesians 6:21. He will also give the label to the once runaway slave and now new convert, Onesimus (Col. 4:9). The adjective "beloved" (ἀγαπητὸς) emphasizes the intimate connection that had arisen not only between Tychicus and Paul, but between Tychicus and the believers in Colossae. Paul uses the adjective four times in this letter. It designates Epaphras as their "beloved fellow bond-servant" (1:7), Onesimus (4:9) and Tychicus (4:7) each as a "beloved brother," and Luke as "the beloved physician" (4:14). The term "brother" (ἀδελφὸς) includes Tychicus in the circle of the believing, as it does Timothy (1:1) and all the disciples in Colossae (1:2).

> **Ministry Maxim**
>
> Deep relationships are forged through joint identification and shared service, with the result being deep affection.

He is also dubbed a "faithful servant" (πιστὸς διάκονος). This expression is also used to describe Tychicus in Ephesians 6:21. Paul uses the same two words in slightly different form and construction to speak of Epaphras as "a faithful servant of Christ on our behalf" (πιστὸς ὑπὲρ ὑμῶν διάκονος τοῦ Χριστοῦ) in Colossians 1:7. In designating Tychicus as "faithful" (πιστὸς) Paul demonstrates that he both believes in Christ and allows that trust to control his service for Christ, with the greater emphasis here upon the latter. It may be that "faithful" (πιστὸς) is meant to qualify not only "servant" (διάκονος), but also "fellow bond-servant" (συνδούλου), which follows. The word "servant" (διάκονος) points simply to one who voluntarily serves or ministers to or for another. The service of Tychicus was not grudging, but glad and willing. The word can refer to the office of deacon (1 Tim. 3:8), but here it is not confined to that specialized meaning.

Tychicus is also described as a "fellow bond-servant in the Lord" (σύνδουλος ἐν κυρίῳ). The noun rendered "fellow bond-servant" (συνδούλου) is a compound word, consisting of σύν ("with") and δοῦλος ("bond-servant"). Paul often speaks of co-workers with words compounded with σύν-, but his only other use of this word is found in Colossians 1:7 where it designates Epaphras. Paul does, however, use the root word (δοῦλος, "bond-servant") thirty-two times. This uncompounded word describes a slave (Col. 3:22; 4:1), not simply a servant (as with διάκονος, just above). Such a one serves at and according to the will of another. Paul frequently chose this word to describe himself (e.g., Rom. 1:1; Gal. 1:10; Phil. 1:1; Titus 1:1). The prefix (σύν) indicates that Epaphras and Tychicus had each joined Paul in abandoning their will to the will of God and had, with Paul, taken up the Great Commission of Christ as their marching orders.

This, says the Apostle, is true "in the Lord" (ἐν κυρίῳ). This may qualify only this third descriptive expression,[915] the last two,[916] or all three.[917] The precise phrase is attached to the previous two descriptors when they appear in Ephesians 6:21. The preposition describes the facts as they are "in the Lord." Because Tychicus had by divine grace and through faith been brought into union with Christ, he had become Paul's "fellow bond-servant." Their common faith in Christ brought them not only into union with Him, but also with one another as servants of the Lord. Paul uses the expression to speak of the responsibilities laid upon wives (3:18) and children (3:20) "in the Lord," as he does also with the ministry of Archippus (4:17).

Tychicus, says Paul, "will bring you information" (γνωρίσει). Paul has spoken a good deal in terms related to knowledge: "to make known" (1:27, same word used here), "wisdom" (1:28), "full assurance of under-standing" (2:2), "knowledge" (2:2), "wisdom" (2:3), "knowledge" (2:3), and "delude" (2:4).[918] This probably related to the false teaching in Colossae which he was seeking to expose and counter. Here at the end of the letter he reuses one of those terms, but it seems here not to be charged with the previous polemical concerns. The future tense of the verb anticipates the events that will unfold after the arrival of Tychicus. The information he shares will be "As to all my affairs" (Τὰ κατ' ἐμὲ πάντα). The expression would very woodenly be rendered, "The things about me all." If we drop the final word (πάντα) the remaining phrase is used two other times by Paul, both in letters similarly sent from this imprisonment (Eph. 6:21; Phil. 1:12). This information would include matters of a more personal nature, matters with which he did not wish to clutter this letter—including his condition

---

[915] Eadie, 285.
[916] Abbott, 298; Harris, 201; Moo, 335.
[917] Lohse, 171; O'Brien, 247.
[918] Moo, 148.

while currently imprisoned, his health, and other details of his welfare. The Colossians, as all other believers, would have been gravely concerned about the Apostle Paul's well-being while in prison, and he wants them to be fully informed and reassured.

Is a subtle progression of relationship hinted at in the Apostle's description of Tychicus? A relationship begins by joint identification (*"fellow* bond-servant"), grows through shared service (*"faithful* servant"), and is cemented in relational bonds of affection (*"beloved* brother," emphases added). We join one another that we might serve beside one another with the result that we grow to love one another.

4:8 For I have sent him to you for this very purpose, that you may know about our circumstances and that he may encourage your hearts;

The sentence begun in verse 7 continues in the Greek text through verse 9. Paul connects to what he's already said in verse 7 by simply using the relative pronoun ὃν ("him," more literally "whom"), which finds its antecedent in Tychicus of the previous verse. When Paul says "I have sent" (ἔπεμψα) him, he uses an aorist tense. This is an example of the epistolary aorist.[919] At the time of writing Paul had not yet sent Tychicus, but from the perspective of the readers when they later received the letter, it would have been a past event.

Paul says that he has sent Tychicus "to you" (πρὸς ὑμᾶς) as the bearer of this letter. As has already been noted, Tychicus—and along with him Onesimus (v. 9)—probably carried not only this letter to the Colossians, but also Ephesians, Philemon, and perhaps the letter to the Laodiceans (v. 16). So while it is true that Paul was sending Tychicus to the Colossians, he was likely also on a wider circuit of visits to other churches of Asia Minor on behalf of the Apostle Paul. His assignment in Colossae was "for this very purpose" (εἰς αὐτὸ τοῦτο). In this case εἰς is used to express purpose.[920] The entire phrase is one Paul uses on other occasions when he wants to underscore his purpose (Rom. 9:17; 13:6; 2 Cor. 5:5; Eph. 6:22).

---

[919] Robertson, *Word Pictures*, 4:510.
[920] BAGD, 229.

Here Paul uses it to point back to his words in verse 7: "As to all my affairs, Tychicus ... will bring you information."

Paul uses what would appear to be an additional purpose clause (ἵνα plus subjunctive verb, "that"), but it may be best understood as further elaborating on and explaining the purpose he spoke of in the first half of the verse.[921] The purpose in sending Tychicus is twofold. First, it is that "you may know about our circumstances" (γνῶτε τὰ περὶ ἡμῶν). Precisely the same phrase is used in Ephesians 6:22. The verb (γνῶτε, "you may know") here has the sense of "learn (of), ascertain, find out."[922] These circumstances included the Apostle's conditions in prison. Surely the Colossians, and many other followers of Christ at the time, were exceedingly concerned about the state of affairs for the great Apostle. Second (καί, "and"), Paul's purpose for sending Tychicus was that "he may encourage your hearts" (παρακαλέσῃ τὰς καρδίας ὑμῶν). Again the precise phrase appears in Ephesians 6:22. The verb (παρακαλέσῃ, "he may encourage") here means to comfort, encourage, or cheer up.[923] This is to happen with reference to their "hearts" (τὰς καρδίας)—the place that is the seat of all their thinking, choosing, and feeling. This latter purpose is very much like Paul's personal ministry purpose as expressed in Colossians 2:2. It is possible that this is seen as happening not only as Tychicus reports about Paul's personal affairs, but also as he reads and interprets this letter to the Colossian believers.[924]

> **Ministry Maxim**
>
> Sometimes information and encouragement go hand in hand— often people need to *know* in order to *hope*.

There are some textual matters of concern here. Some manuscripts do not have τά ("the things"). Some manuscripts have "*he* might know" rather than "*you* might know." And some have "*your* circumstances" instead of "*our* circumstances." The KJV/NKJV follow these variants, and the latter renders it "that he may know your circumstances and comfort your hearts." However, the text as we have it here seems to be supported by both the external and internal evidence.[925]

---

[921] Harris, 201.
[922] BAGD, 161.
[923] Ibid., 617.
[924] O'Brien, 248; Moo, 336.
[925] Harris, 202; Moo, 335-336; O'Brien, 245.

4:9 and with him Onesimus, our faithful and beloved brother, who is one of your number. They will inform you about the whole situation here.

The sentence begun in verse 7 concludes here in the ninth verse. The verse begins simply and literally "with Onesimus" (σὺν Ὀνησίμῳ). It connects back to the verb "I have sent" in verse 8 and indicates that Tychicus is not traveling alone, but that by the Apostle's intention he has been given this traveling partner. It is in the letter to Philemon that we become more familiar with Onesimus. There we discover him to be a slave of Philemon (Philem. 16), apparently a semiwealthy believer in whose home the church in Colossae met (vv. 1-2). Onesimus, however, appears to have first robbed his employer (v. 18) and then sought to escape by fleeing to Rome. It was there that Onesimus must have come into contact with Paul and was won to faith in Christ (v. 10). As a matter of his discipleship, Onesimus had some things to make right in Colossae. Thus the Apostle has sent him with Tychicus to restore what he has stolen and to take his place in Philemon's household once more.

Note the way the Apostle refers to Onesimus here. He is a "faithful and beloved brother" (τῷ πιστῷ καὶ ἀγαπητῷ ἀδελφῷ). The translators of the NASU understand the definite article as possessive (τῷ, "our"). The adjective "faithful" (πιστῷ) in this case means "trustworthy, faithful, dependable, inspiring trust or faith"[926] rather than "believing" (as in, "he is now your Christian brother"). It could be used "of persons who show themselves faithful in the transaction of business, the execution of commands,

> **Ministry Maxim**
>
> People are not necessarily who they once were and must not be related to for what they once did.

or the discharge of official duties."[927] It is the same word used to describe all the Colossian believers in Paul's salutation to the letter (Col. 1:2) and to designate Epaphras (1:7) and Tychicus (4:7) as servants of the Lord.

---

[926] BAGD, 664.
[927] Thayer, 514.

To this he adds (καὶ, "and") that Onesimus is "beloved" (ἀγαπητῷ). Again, this is a descriptor of both Epaphras (1:7) and Tychicus (4:7). It is also used of both Philemon (Philem. 1) and Onesimus (16).

Both of these qualities are true of Onesimus as a "brother" (τῷ .... ἀδελφῷ). Paul uses this noun often as a way of referring to those who share common faith in Christ Jesus. He uses it in Colossians of Timothy (Col. 1:1), of all the believers in Colossae (1:2) and Laodicea (4:15), and of Tychicus (4:7). He uses it also to describe both Philemon (Philem. vv. 1, 7, 20) and his runaway slave now returned home, Onesimus (v. 16).

Additionally Paul says Onesimus is he "who is one of your number" (ὅς ἐστιν ἐξ ὑμῶν). It might more literally be rendered "who is out of you." This surely means that Onesimus was one from their community (a citizen of Colossae and one familiar to the church, being the slave of the owner of the home where they meet). But perhaps the Apostle also intended a bit of double entendre—Onesimus was also now out of their congregation (as a fellow believer in Jesus Christ). Paul uses a similar expression of Epaphras in verse 12 ("one of your number," ὁ ἐξ ὑμῶν).

"They will inform you about the whole situation here" (πάντα ὑμῖν γνωρίσουσιν τὰ ὧδε). Paul shifts from the singular to the plural with the verb "They will inform" (γνωρίσουσιν).[928] This serves to make Onesimus an integral part of a team (along with Tychicus) that is to report information which the Colossian believers will find vital. This may be a subtle means of elevating Onesimus from simply a runaway slave or even a now-*converted* runaway slave into a useful servant of the gospel and one possessing information which the Colossians will wish very much to hear. In short, the Colossians *need* him now as Paul's emissary. The verb is the same one used in verse 7 to describe Tychicus's role in updating the Colossians. Paul speaks more broadly ("the whole situation here," πάντα ... τὰ ὧδε) than he has in verse 7 ("As to all my affairs," Τὰ κατ' ἐμὲ πάντα) or verse 8 ("our circumstances," τὰ περὶ ἡμῶν).[929] Those previous expressions were more specifically related to Paul's personal condition and situation. This expression will also include news about how it was Onesimus came into contact with Paul, how he was won to faith in Christ, the state of affairs in the church in Rome, etc.

---

[928] O'Brien, 284.
[929] Harris, 202-203.

4:10 Aristarchus, my fellow prisoner, sends you his greetings; and also Barnabas's cousin Mark (about whom you received instructions; if he comes to you, welcome him);

The Apostle now sends greetings from six individuals—half of whom are Jewish (Aristarchus, Mark, and Jesus who is called Justus, vv. 10-11) and half of whom are Gentile (Epaphras, Luke, and Demas, vv. 12-14). This is a more extensive list than is usual for Paul's letters, being surpassed only by Romans 16. Perhaps this is because Paul had never visited Colossae personally and he is striving to establish connectedness with the congregation.

"Aristarchus" (Ἀρίσταρχος) was from Macedonia—specifically from Thessalonica (Acts 20:4)—and had been a member of the team accompanying Paul back to Jerusalem with the offering from Gentile believers. He was present with Paul when the notorious riot broke out in Ephesus. Indeed he had been personally accosted in that mêlée (Acts 19:29). He was still a part of the team traveling with Paul when later a plot of the Jews was formed against him in Greece and they had to take evasive measures (Acts 20:4). He was also among Paul's companions on his fateful voyage as a prisoner to Rome (Acts 27:2) and thus faced the fierce storm that nearly cost all of them their lives. Lightfoot conjectures that Aristarchus left the journey to Rome at Myra, but later rejoined Paul in Rome.[930] The Apostle also includes greetings from Aristarchus in the letter to Philemon (Philem. 24).

This was clearly a man who had stood with the Apostle Paul through thick and thin. Indeed, he is even now, says Paul, "my fellow prisoner" (ὁ συναιχμάλωτός μου). The same expression is used of Epaphras in Philemon 23. The uncompounded form (αἰχμάλωτος) means most literally "prisoner of war," but the compounded form can be used in a general sense.[931] Precisely what this means, however, is not clear. It could simply mean that they accompanied him to Rome in his imprisonment and have stayed on in the city, frequently visiting him and tending to his needs while he was imprisoned. Or it could mean that they voluntarily submitted to imprisonment with him, refusing to leave him even for a moment while he was incarcerated. Or it could be used metaphorically of his being a glad

---

[930] Lightfoot, 234.
[931] Rienecker, 584.

captive of Jesus Christ. Whatever the case, Aristarchus was obviously a man of utter devotion and faithfulness.

Aristarchus, says Paul, "sends you his greetings" ('Ασπάζεται ὑμᾶς). As he does here, Paul often uses the indicative of this verb to convey personal greetings or those of others who are with him (e.g., Rom. 16:21-23; 1 Cor. 16:19-20; 2 Cor. 13:12; Phil. 4:21-22; Col. 4:10, 12, 14; Titus 3:15). Paul also often uses this verb in the imperative at the close of his letters to command the recipients to "Greet" others in the body of Christ (e.g., Col. 4:15).

Paul adds (καὶ, "and") greetings from "Barnabas's cousin Mark" (Μᾶρκος ὁ ἀνεψιὸς Βαρναβᾶ). Mark had been chosen to travel with Paul and Barnabas on their first missionary journey (Acts 13:5). Yet not long after, he deserted Paul and Barnabas and returned to Jerusalem (13:13). At the beginning of the second missionary journey, Barnabas's insistence in bringing him along again led to a division between himself and Paul (15:37-39). Whether this was because of Barnabas's heart as an encourager (4:36) or because Mark was his "cousin" (ὁ ἀνεψιὸς), we do not know. The reference to Mark here is the first surviving mention the Apostle Paul has made of him in the twelve years since their falling out.[932] As we can see here, Mark was with Paul in his first imprisonment. Over a decade later, during Paul's second imprisonment, the Apostle longs for his ministry (2 Tim. 4:11). Clearly Paul's opinion of him changed and he speaks of him positively (cf. also Philem. 24). Mark appears to have undertaken ministry in Rome, for he is mentioned also by Peter, writing from there (1 Peter 5:13). It is likely that Mark wrote the Gospel bearing his name from the city of Rome.

> **Ministry Maxim**
>
> Grace *required* may become grace *extended* by the comparison of two cases that at first don't seem similar at all.

Why is Mark identified as "Barnabas's cousin" (ἀνεψιός means "cousin," not nephew as in KJV's "sister's son"[933])? It may have been that, while the Christians in Colossae did not personally know Mark, they did know Barnabas—or at least his reputation. Or it could have been that Mark was

---

[932] Lightfoot, 234.
[933] Moo, 338.

such a common name that Paul only used the additional designation to make clear just which Mark he was referring to.

The Apostle adds a parenthetical comment to these greetings: "(about whom you received instructions; if he comes to you, welcome him)," (περὶ οὗ ἐλάβετε ἐντολάς, ἐὰν ἔλθῃ πρὸς ὑμᾶς, δέξασθε αὐτόν). Just when or how or from whom the Colossians had "received instructions" concerning Mark is unclear. What is clear is that Paul does not want his first verdict on Mark (Acts 15:37-39) to be the final word on him. Perhaps the Apostle sent word not only to the Colossian believers, but to the followers of Christ throughout Asia Minor regarding warmly receiving Mark into their midst. The noun "instructions" (ἐντολάς) describes a "prescribed rule in accordance with which a thing is done."[934] The conditional clause ("if he comes to you," ἐὰν ἔλθῃ πρὸς ὑμᾶς) is of the third class—pointing to the uncertainty of the conditions set forth. Paul does not know if Mark will come to them (though it seems somewhat likely),[935] but, if indeed he does, he wants their response to be correct. In such a case they are to "welcome him" (δέξασθε αὐτόν). The verb is deponent (middle voice with active meaning) and is used to describe welcoming someone gladly and hospitably into one's home.[936]

Did Paul make mention of Mark to provide a subtle prototype of how they should welcome Onesimus? Both men had a blot on their record. Both were now being set before the congregation as worthy of their welcome, love, and grace.

4:11 and also Jesus who is called Justus; these are the only fellow workers for the kingdom of God who are from the circumcision, and they have proved to be an encouragement to me.

Additional (καὶ, "and") greetings are sent from "Jesus who is called Justus" (Ἰησοῦς ὁ λεγόμενος Ἰοῦστος). We know nothing more of this individual than what we find here. "Jesus" (Ἰησοῦς) appears to have been his given, Jewish name. It was common practice in the first century for Jewish men to also take a Hellenistic Roman name as well, often similar to their given

---

[934] Thayer, 218.
[935] Harris, 207.
[936] BAGD, 177.

name. He may also have chosen another name because his name was identical with our Lord's. Thus, says Paul, he "is called" (ὁ λεγόμενος) by another name. The participle is present tense, underscoring that this is the name he routinely is known by. The passive voice emphasizes that this is what others call him. The definite article and the participial form are used as a substantive ("who is called"). Just why "Justus" (᾽Ιοῦστος) became the name he was known by is not clear. He appears to be distinct from "Joseph called Barsabbas (who was also called Justus)" (Acts 1:23) and the Corinthian proselyte "Titius Justus" (Acts 18:7). It was a common name and was the Latin equivalent of the Greek *Dikaios* and the Hebrew *Zadok*.[937] It has been conjectured that this "Jesus" may be mentioned again in Philemon 23,[938] but it is unlikely that the familiar combination Χριστῷ ᾽Ιησοῦ ("Jesus Christ") would be thus divided.

> **Ministry Maxim**
>
> Your ministry *with* someone may also be a ministry *to* them—doubling the return on your labors.

The next line has proven a challenge for interpreters: "these are the only fellow workers for the kingdom of God who are from the circumcision" (οἱ ὄντες ἐκ περιτομῆς, οὗτοι μόνοι συνεργοὶ εἰς τὴν βασιλείαν τοῦ θεοῦ). Grammatically it could indicate either that the only fellow workers with Paul are the three already named (Aristarchus, Mark, and Jesus who is called Justus, vv. 10-11) or that the only *Jewish* fellow workers with Paul are the three named here.[939] Verses 12 through 14 seem to indicate that Epaphras, Luke, and Demas are also laboring with Paul, though they are Gentiles. Thus it seems more likely that Paul's intent was to say that the three already named (vv. 10-11) are the only Jewish converts who are currently laboring with him in Rome. Most English translations follow this understanding.

Let's examine this line following the order of the Greek text. First and literally we face "the ones being of the circumcision" (οἱ ὄντες ἐκ περιτομῆς). The articular participle (οἱ ὄντες) is present tense underscoring their ongoing nature. The preposition (ἐκ, "of") indicates the

---

[937] Lightfoot, 236; Robertson, *Word Pictures*, 4:511,

[938] BAGD, 374.

[939] To these Douglas Moo adds a third option: that Paul is contrasting the three Jewish men mentioned with other Jews in his area. He defends this view as the most likely, cf. 340-341.

direction from which something comes;[940] that point of origin is "the circumcision" (περιτομῆς). The term is used simply to designate them as "of the Jews."[941] By this Paul means that they are Christian Jews. Some, however, believe that it may be a designation differentiating between strict, Hebraic Jews who follow Christ and the more open, Hellenistic Jewish followers of Christ.[942] Then comes "these only" (οὗτοι μόνοι). Because of the placement of this phrase it can be read as connected to what goes before (i.e., these are the only ones from among the Jews) or with what follows (i.e., these are my only fellow workers). As indicated above, given the context (vv. 12-14), it seems best to understand it as narrowing the number of Jewish fellow workers with Paul. Finally and still literally we face "fellow workers for the kingdom of God" (συνεργοὶ εἰς τὴν βασιλείαν τοῦ θεοῦ). The noun "fellow workers" (συνεργοὶ) is one Paul uses twelve times in his letters (used elsewhere only in 3 John 8). It is another of the compound words beginning with σύν ("with") of which Paul is so fond. Such compounds appear twelve times in Colossians. He has now used eight different such compounds: "fellow bond-slave" (σύνδουλος, 1:7; 4:7), "understanding" (σύνεσις, 1:9; 2:2), "hold together" (συνίστημι, 1:17), "buried with" (συνθάπτω, 2:12), "raised up with" (συνεγείρω, 2:12; 3:1), "ligaments"/"bond of unity" (σύνδεσμος, 2:19; 3:14), "fellow prisoner" (συναιχμάλωτος, 4:10), and here, "fellow worker" (συνεργός). Our present word is used also in Philemon to describe Philemon himself (Philem. 1) as well as Mark, Aristarchus, Demas, and Luke (v. 24). The labor they together expend is "for the kingdom of God" (εἰς τὴν βασιλείαν τοῦ θεοῦ). The preposition (εἰς, "for") probably points toward purpose—the purpose of their labors is to spread "the kingdom of God."[943] The rule of God over an ever-expanding number of people was their goal. The "kingdom of God" was obviously a present reality to Paul and his colaborers. They lived in it themselves and sought to bring others under God's reign as well.

What is quite clear, says Paul, is that "they have proved to be an encouragement to me" (οἵτινες ἐγενήθησάν μοι παρηγορία). The nominative plural of the relative pronoun (οἵτινες) points to the three men just named:

---

[940] BAGD, 234-235.
[941] Ibid., 653.
[942] cf. the discussion in Moo, 342 and O'Brien, 251-252.
[943] King, 336.

Aristarchus, Mark, and Justus (vv. 10-11). The verb is deponent (middle form with active meaning) and in Hellenistic Greek meant simply "I became" or "I was."[944] The noun (παρηγορία, "an encouragement") appears only here in the NT. The term, along with others which arise from it, was used as medical terminology, often in the sense of "assuaging" or "alleviating." From this arose the more common emphasis of comfort or consolation.[945] Thus the word has been found on gravestones and in a letter of condolence with this sense of comfort.[946] Paul's construction here lays special emphasis upon this final word in the sentence.[947]

4:12 Epaphras, who is one of your number, a bondslave of Jesus Christ, sends you his greetings, always laboring earnestly for you in his prayers, that you may stand perfect and fully assured in all the will of God.

We have already met "Epaphras" (Ἐπαφρᾶς) in Colossians 1:7. See our comments there for a fuller description of this man. Paul clearly considered Epaphras as a trustworthy "fellow bond-servant" (συνδούλου, 1:7). He had likely evangelized in and around Colossae during Paul's ministry in Ephesus. He may have been responsible for not only the founding of the Colossian church, but also for the churches in other cities of the Lycus valley, such as Laodicea and Hierapolis (4:13).

Paul calls Epaphras "one of your number" (ὁ ἐξ ὑμῶν, lit., "one out of you"), probably indicating he had been originally a citizen of Colossae, whether as a native born or one transplanted there. He just described Onesimus in similar terms in verse 9 ("who is one of your number," ὅς ἐστιν ἐξ ὑμῶν).

In Philemon 23 the Apostle calls Epaphras "my fellow prisoner in Christ Jesus." He is here designated "a bondslave of Jesus Christ" (δοῦλος Χριστοῦ [Ἰησοῦ]). Paul has used the noun "bondslave" (δοῦλος) to designate those literally in the bonds of slavery (Col. 3:11, 22; 4:1). Metaphorically it can describe an unredeemed person's bondage to sin (Rom. 6:17). Yet Paul often used the term to designate himself as a "bond-servant" of Christ (Rom. 1:1;

---

[944] Harris, 208.
[945] Lightfoot, 237.
[946] Reinecker, 584.
[947] Harris, 208.

Gal. 1:10; Titus 1:1), and in Philippians 1:1 he so designated both himself and Timothy. As noted, it is the root of the compound word used to describe Epaphras in Colossians 1:7 (συνδούλου, "fellow bond-servant").

Christ Himself took "the form of a bond-servant" (Phil. 2:7) and thus it is the proper station of every follower of His (Rom. 6:16; 1 Cor. 7:22; Gal. 1:10; Eph. 6:6). At times it is even appropriate to call yourself a "bond-servant" of others to whom you are bound by Christ's call (2 Cor. 4:5). It originally designated the bottom rung of servitude, but then came to describe one who simply yields himself to another's will.[948] There is some doubt as to whether the original text should be simply "of Christ" (e.g., KJV, NKJV) or "of Christ Jesus" (e.g., ESV, NIV) or "of Jesus Christ" (only the NASU follows this reading). The manuscript support for the various readings makes it difficult to decide, and ultimately the meaning is not changed. Like those already mentioned in verses 10 and 11, Epaphras, says Paul, "sends you his greetings" (ἀσπάζεται ὑμᾶς). This phrase actually begins the sentence and throws emphasis upon it.

This man, the Apostle tells the Colossians, is "always laboring earnestly for you in his prayers" (πάντοτε ἀγωνιζόμενος ὑπὲρ ὑμῶν ἐν ταῖς προσευχαῖς). Epaphras, says Paul, is "laboring earnestly" (ἀγωνιζόμενος). The verb, when used literally, can describe either competing for a prize in an athletic contest (1 Cor. 9:25) or engaging another in a battle with weapons (John 18:36). When it is used figuratively, it often has the sense of contending or struggling with great effort against difficulties or dangers generally (Col. 1:29; 1 Tim. 4:10) or of striving after something with strenuous zeal (Luke 13:24; Col. 4:12).[949] Paul uses it to summarize the entire nature of his battle in this life: "I have fought the good fight" (2 Tim. 4:7). The present tense stresses the continual nature of the action. The middle voice is deponent, having an active meaning. Paul has used this verb to describe his own efforts in ministry (Col. 1:29). But there he makes clear that the effort goes beyond his own strength and that he labors "according to His power, which mightily works within me." This too is Epaphras's pattern in ministry, indeed it is "always" (πάντοτε) his way—meaning not constant, unceasing

---

[948] Vine, 141.
[949] Thayer, 10.

intercession, but regular and repeated prayer. And this is particularly on behalf of the Colossian believers (ὑπὲρ ὑμῶν, "you").

Epaphras had been physically removed from their locale, but his labor never ceased, for he continued on "in his prayers" (ἐν ταῖς προσευχαῖς). Prayer is the arena (ἐν, "in") of his agonizing outlay of effort on their behalf. The word used is the most frequently used noun in the NT to describe prayer. It is also the most general word for prayer, but it often has the more specific sense of petition. This is probably the general intent of Paul's use of it here. The definite article is understood by the translators as possessive (ταῖς, "his").

The purpose (ἵνα plus the subjunctive verb, "that") of this intense prayer life is that the Colossian believers might "stand" (σταθῆτε). The verb can mean simply the physical act of standing upright (e.g., Matt. 12:47), but also shades over to the notion of resolute faith which finds victory in life's battles (cf. Eph. 6:11, 13, 14). The passive voice of this verb has an intransitive meaning and thus is not emphasizing "made to stand [by God]," but more simply just "to stand."[950] Surely it will be God who enables them to stand, but the verb alone does not make that point.

This "stand" is now described in a twofold way. First, Epaphras prays they will stand "perfect" (τέλειοι). The word

> **Ministry Maxim**
>
> The price tag on making mature, focused disciples of Christ is the agonizing labor of prayer.

generally describes something that has attained its appointed purpose or end. It is thus complete or perfect. Here it may point to that which is *fully developed* in a moral sense."[951] Paul has already said that this is the end goal of all his own labors as a servant of Christ (1:28) and now he indicates that Epaphras also adds his prayer labors to this pursuit. See our comments on 1:28 for the background this word may have played in the mystery religions of the day.

Second, the Apostle adds (καί, "and") that Epaphras prays that in their "stand" they will be "fully assured in all the will of God" (πεπληροφορημένοι ἐν παντὶ θελήματι τοῦ θεοῦ). The verb (πεπληροφορημένοι, "fully assured") is a compound which is ultimately comprised of πλήρης ("filled"/"full")

---

[950] Moo, 344.
[951] BAGD, 809.

and φέρω ("to bear"). So by simple addition of its parts it might mean "to bear full" or "to make full."[952] It is used six times in the NT, five of those by the Apostle Paul (Luke 1:1; Rom. 4:21; 14:5; Col. 4:12; 2 Tim. 4:5, 17). When it is used of persons it can mean "filled with something," which in this case would be those things which comprise the will of God.[953] But in the passive voice, as it is here, it is more likely to mean "fully convinced, assured, certain."[954] It appears to have this meaning in Romans 4:21 and 14:5. This seems the more probable meaning here. It is "to be assured through rich, gratifying insight into all spiritual matters ... understanding which not only penetrates the mind but also fills the heart w[ith] satisfying conviction."[955]

The arena (ἐν, "in") of this stand of mature, inward conviction is "in all the will of God" (ἐν παντὶ θελήματι τοῦ θεοῦ). Paul is fully convinced that he is an apostle by the will of God (Col. 1:1), and Epaphras wants each believer in Colossae to share the same depth of conviction about God's will for their life. Paul elsewhere makes clear that God's will is that we remain sanctified in sexual matters (1 Thess. 4:3), be thankful (1 Thess. 5:18), and be delivered out of this present evil age (Gal. 1:4). We are each to live so as to prove God's will "good and acceptable and perfect" (Rom. 12:2). Indeed, we are to do the will of God from the heart (Eph. 6:6), which is precisely Epaphras's prayer for the believers in Colossae.

4:13 For I testify for him that he has a deep concern for you and for those who are in Laodicea and Hierapolis.

The Apostle now underscores his statements about Epaphras and his intense prayer support for the Colossian believers (v. 12) by offering his own testimony. The conjunction γὰρ ("For") indicates that Paul is now confirming what he has just stated concerning Epaphras.[956] By saying "I testify" (μαρτυρῶ), Paul means he is about to bear witness personally to the authenticity of his claims about Epaphras (αὐτῷ, "for him"). The content of that testimony is introduced by ὅτι ("that").[957]

---

[952] Thayer, 517.
[953] BAGD, 670.
[954] Ibid.
[955] Rienecker, 585.
[956] Abbott, 302; Eadie, 293.
[957] Harris, 210.

Paul can vouch that "he has a deep concern for you" (ἔχει πολὺν πόνον ὑπὲρ ὑμῶν). The present tense of the verb points out that this concern is Epaphras's abiding disposition toward the Colossian believers. The word

> **Ministry Maxim**
>
> Ministry = pain:
> other-oriented,
> God-exalting,
> soul-sapping pain.

translated "concern" (πόνον) is used only three other times in the NT, all of which are translated as "pain" (Rev. 16:10, 11; 21:4). Here the word points to hard labor or toil.[958] "It is labor such as does not stop short of demanding the soul strength of a man; and this exerted to the uttermost, if he is to accomplish the task which is set before him."[959] Paul intensifies the word further by adding πολὺν ("deep"). It underscores the degree of his painful toil: *"much, great, strong, severe, hard, deep, profound."*[960] And all of this, says Paul, is on behalf of (ὑπὲρ) the Colossian believers.

We do well to consider the depth of this man's concern for the church and its individual members. It will repay us richly to reflect that it was his prayer life on their behalf which reached such extremities of both physical labor and emotional pain. Surely Epaphras knew better than any other the conditions within those churches and the actual threat of the heresy that was spreading among them. He had fought for the truth while among the believers, and now removed physically from them, he continues the battle on their behalf through prayer.

But Epaphras's concern is not exclusively for the believers in Colossae; it is also (καὶ, "and") "for those who are in Laodicea and Hierapolis" (τῶν ἐν Λαοδικείᾳ καὶ τῶν ἐν Ἱεραπόλει). The disciple had learned well from the Apostle, for he too knew "the daily pressure ... of concern for all the churches" (2 Cor. 11:28). The twice-employed combination of the definite article (τῶν), plus the preposition (ἐν), plus that dative form of the noun (Λαοδικείᾳ or Ἱεραπόλει) means "those in—" or "the people at—."[961] Both Laodicea (cf. Col. 2:1; 4:15) and Hierapolis were neighboring cities in the Lycus Valley. The former was about twelve miles from Colossae and the latter about fifteen.[962] They all alike were key cities, located along important

---

[958] BAGD, 691.
[959] Reinecker, 585.
[960] BAGD, 688.
[961] Harris, 211.
[962] Moo, 346.

Roman roads and characterized by their industry and importance for commerce.[963] It seems likely that Epaphras was the one who, during Paul's tenure of ministry in Ephesus (Acts 19:10, 26), was responsible for the evangelization in all three of these towns, and thus his pastoral concern for all the Christ followers there continued to run deep.

4:14 Luke, the beloved physician, sends you his greetings, and also Demas.

Paul uses the same verb form as in verses 10 and 12 to convey the "greetings" (ἀσπάζεται) of two more companions.

Luke (Λουκᾶς) was likely a Gentile who had come to faith in Christ through the witness of the Apostle. He was often a travel companion of the Apostle Paul on his missionary journeys (note the "we" sections of Acts; e.g., 16:10ff.). He was obviously with Paul in this his first Roman imprisonment (Col. 4:14; Philem. 24). He was a "physician" (ὁ ἰατρὸς) which was undoubtedly of great help to Paul personally and in ministry. He was a learned man, capable of careful research and writing (Luke 1:1-4; Acts 1:1). He was a trusted and loyal friend and colaborer of the Apostle. Luke never mentions himself in either his writing of the Gospel of Luke or in Acts. He seems to have been the epitome of a faithful, loyal friend and coworker. At the close of his life the Apostle can confess that "Only Luke is with me" (2 Tim. 4:11).

Luke is to Paul not simply a "physician," but "the beloved physician" (ὁ ἰατρὸς ὁ ἀγαπητὸς). The adjective "beloved" (ὁ ἀγαπητὸς) already has been used in this letter to distinguish Epaphras (1:7), Tychicus (4:7), and Onesimus (4:9). Of the six (or seven, depending upon the variant in Luke 8:43) times that the noun "physician" is used in the NT, this is the only occasion when it is accompanied by the definite article—marking out Luke for special note as "*the* physician" (ὁ ἰατρὸς), indeed "*the* beloved" (ὁ ἀγαπητὸς) one (emphases added). Just why Luke is described in this way is not certain. Some speculate that Luke served as

> **Ministry Maxim**
>
> To love is to risk—if you await guarantees that people will not disappoint you, you will never enjoy any relationship.

---

[963] Bruce, NIC, 6-8; Moo, 346.

Paul's personal physician in many of his travels and now in his imprisonment, but this is speculation. It is possible that he is thus identified in order to distinguish him from someone else by the same name. It seems best to conclude that Luke had simply endeared himself both to Paul and to the many that they together ministered to, and that he had become renowned as a worthy ministry partner of the Apostle.

Paul refers to Demas (Δημᾶς) as one of "my fellow workers" in Philemon 24. He seems, then, to have been a man who had come to faith in Christ, advanced in the things of God to a level where he was recognized as having gifts for ministry, and then was chosen to travel and minister with Paul on his missionary journeys. He may have hailed from Thessalonica since he is mentioned next to Aristarchus (Philem. 24), who was from that city (Acts 20:4; 27:2). This may explain why in Paul's second Roman imprisonment, as the Apostle's martyrdom approached, Demas left and was said to have "gone to Thessalonica" (2 Tim. 4:10). He would have been running for home. The church in Thessalonica was one of the most dear to Paul's heart (1 Thess. 2:7-8, 17-20; 3:9-10) and if Demas was an official representative of that congregation, it would have meant that he was likely very close to the Apostle himself. Sadly, in the end, the Apostle's final testimony concerning Demas is that "having loved this present world, [he] has deserted me" (2 Tim. 4:10). But as things stands here at the time of the composition of this letter to the Colossians, Demas appears to have been a colaborer in good standing whose greetings were conveyed through the Apostle to this church.

Whether either Luke or Demas had visited the Colossian church is unknown, but clearly their names must have been known among the believers there.

In this verse we meet two who will prove to be the epitome of both faithfulness ("Luke") and faithlessness ("Demas"). To love is to risk—if you await guarantees that people will not disappoint you, you will never enjoy any relationship. In the choice to trust and enter into relationship with a person in the present moment, all we have is their testimony and their track record of faith. The future and their faithfulness is embraced one step, one moment at a time.

4:15 Greet the brethren who are in Laodicea and also Nympha and the church that is in her house.

Paul now turns from sending greetings from ministry associates (vv. 10-14) and sends his personal greetings to be conveyed by the Colossian believers to others (v. 15). In doing so he uses the same verb (vv. 10, 12, 14), though he switches from the indicative to the imperative ('Ασπάσασθε, "Greet"). Those to whom they are to convey these greetings are "the brethren who are in Laodicea" (τοὺς ἐν Λαοδικείᾳ ἀδελφοὺς). The neighboring city of Laodicea has already been mentioned in 2:1 and 4:13; see our comments there. The prepositional phrase (ἐν Λαοδικείᾳ, "in Laodicea") is tucked between the plural noun and its definite article and thus functions as an attributive adjective (lit., "the in Laodicea brothers").

The Apostle's greetings are "also" (καὶ) to go to "Nympha and the church that is in her house" (Νύμφαν καὶ τὴν κατ᾽ οἶκον αὐτῆς ἐκκλησίαν). This is the only mention of this individual (Νύμφαν, "Nympha") in the NT. The manuscript evidence is divided over whether this is a feminine or masculine noun, the difference being indicated only by accent marks which were not included in the earliest manuscripts. The copyists who considered this a reference to a man used the pronoun αὐτοῦ ("his") in the next phrase (cf. KJV), while those who viewed it as a reference to a woman used αὐτῆς ("her," so most English versions). Some other manuscripts have opted for αὐτῶν ("their"), indicating either their uncertainty about how to

> **Ministry Maxim**
>
> True fellowship requires both personal ("Nympha") and corporate ("the brethren," "the church that is in her house") relationships.

understand the personal name or their conviction that the reference to the ownership of the home was understood more generally. The more difficult reading is αὐτῆς ("her"), and thus we understand this as a reference to a female who is otherwise unknown to us.[964] We can surmise that she was perhaps a widow and of sufficient wealth to own a home sizeable enough to host the gatherings of a house church, and that she was of sufficient generosity to make it available for the Lord's work.

---

[964] NET Bible.

But the greetings are not just to Nympha, but are also (καὶ, "and") to be sent to "the church that is in her house" (τὴν κατ' οἶκον αὐτῆς ἐκκλησίαν). We again, as above, have a prepositional phrase tucked between the noun and its definite article (lit., "the at [the] house of her church").

Because church buildings devoted to the worship and service of God and the gathering of His people were unknown in this early stage of the church's development, believers gathered for their meetings in the homes of those among them. The fact that Paul mentions both "the brethren who are in Laodicea" and then "the church that is in [Nympha's] house" may mean that the former is a reference to all the believers in Laodicea and the latter to only those believers who gather together for worship in Nympha's house—implying that there was more than one house church in Laodicea. This is a possibility since there appears also to have been a church in Colossae that met in the home of Philemon (Philem. 2). Alternatively, the latter might be a reference to a congregation that met outside of Laodicea, for example in Hierapolis (cf. v. 13).[965] In addition to this reference, the NT speaks of or alludes to house churches in the homes of Gaius (in Corinth, Rom. 16:3, 5), Aquila and Priscilla (in Ephesus, 1 Cor. 16:19, and in Rome, Rom. 16:3, 5), Lydia (in Philippi, Acts 16:15, 40), Philemon (in Colossae, Philem. 2), Mary (in Jerusalem, Acts 12:12), and Jason (in Thessalonica, Acts 17:5-6).[966]

4:16 When this letter is read among you, have it also read in the church of the Laodiceans; and you, for your part read my letter that is coming from Laodicea.

The opening conjunction (καὶ), which is left untranslated here (though cf. "And," NASB), transitions from Paul's greetings (v. 15) to further instructions he wishes to leave with the church (vv. 16-17).

Paul was concerned that the Scripture get fully exposed to every believer in the area and that every believer in Christ get full exposure to all the Scripture possible. By saying "When this letter is read among you" (ὅταν ἀναγνωσθῇ παρ' ὑμῖν ἡ ἐπιστολή,), Paul reveals his expectation that this present letter would be read aloud to the gathered church (cf. 1 Thess. 5:27).

---

[965] Harris, 212.
[966] Ibid., 246.

Such a precious epistle would not be handed around to travel from house to house so each individual might read it personally. The document had to be guarded, and the message, being for the collective church as a whole, should be heard in that context.

But Paul's desire went even further: "have it read in the church of the Laodiceans" (ποιήσατε ἵνα καὶ ἐν τῇ Λαοδικέων ἐκκλησίᾳ ἀναγνωσθῇ). What was good for the Colossians would be good for the Laodiceans. One may wonder why the instruction was not given that it be read also by the believers in Hierapolis (v. 13). Indeed, for that matter, why were greetings not sent to those of Hierapolis (v. 15; assuming our understanding that Nympha's house was in Laodicea not Hierapolis)? Only speculation can answer, but perhaps the false teaching present in Colossae had made it only so far as Laodicea and not to Hierapolis, and thus the contents of this letter, specially aimed as they were to those wrestling with the false teacher(s), were not to be sent there. This may be even more plausible since Paul goes on to say, "and you, for your part read my letter that is coming from Laodicea" (καὶ τὴν ἐκ Λαοδικείας ἵνα καὶ ὑμεῖς ἀναγνῶτε). It has been speculated that the "letter that is coming from Laodicea" is none other than what our Bibles contain as the letter to the Ephesians. This views the letter to the Ephesians as a circular letter intended for all the congregations of Asia Minor. If this were the case and if the false teaching had not yet reached Hierapolis, then, given the close similarities between Colossians and Ephesians, Paul may have considered that letter as sufficient for the needs of those in Hierapolis.

> **Ministry Maxim**
>
> All Scripture to every believer—this is God's intent and the passionate pursuit of His servants.

This reconstruction of course is entirely speculative and must be afforded only the confidence that speculation deserves. The most likely scenario is simply that we have lost the letter to the Laodiceans and that God did not see fit to include it in the canon of Scripture.

If the "letter to the Laodiceans" was not the same as our Ephesians, then the question arises as to just what happened to this letter. Why is it not known to us? Why did God not see fit to include it in the canon of Scripture? These are questions for which a fully satisfying answer is not possible. Apparently Paul also wrote a third letter to the believers in Corinth which, like the letter to the Laodiceans, has not survived and which we may assume God in His wisdom determined not to include in the canon of Scripture (1 Cor. 5:9). What is clear is that the Apostle wanted his words to reach every believer and that every believer have all the Scriptures. May our hearts be as his.

4:17 Say to Archippus, "Take heed to the ministry which you have received in the Lord, that you may fulfill it."

We know nothing about Archippus except what we find here and in Philemon 2, where he is also mentioned. In the latter passage he is called "our fellow soldier" (τῷ συστρατιώτῃ ἡμῶν), employing a noun used elsewhere only of Epaphroditus (Phil. 2:25). It is clear that Paul counts him within the circle of his trusted ministry associates, one enlisted in the same force, battling side-by-side with all true soldiers of the Lord (cf. 2 Tim. 2:3). In the letter to Philemon, Archippus is mentioned in connection with Philemon and Apphia (his wife) in such a way that it appears Archippus may be a member of their household, perhaps their son. Apparently one of the house churches in Colossae met in their home (Philem. 2). Tradition says that Archippus went on to become bishop of Laodicea and was martyred for his faith in that region, but the historicity of this account is questionable. Knox theorizes that Archippus was the actual owner of the runaway slave Onesimus and that "the ministry" he is to "fulfill" is the acceptance of his slave back, now as a brother.[967] This appears an unlikely scenario.

Archippus is to be told to "Take heed" (Βλέπε). The verb means simply "to see," but here in the imperative mood it commands action and orders Archippus to direct his attention to something, to consider or note something. The present tense demands that this action be taken in an unending, continuous fashion. An alternate translation may be "take care."[968]

That to which he is to give such attention is "the ministry which you have received in the Lord" (τὴν διακονίαν ἣν παρέλαβες ἐν κυρίῳ). The noun "ministry" (διακονίαν) is a broad word that gathers up all the diverse elements of what may be required of one who serves God. The definite article (τὴν) plus the note that this is a ministry "which you have received in the Lord" make clear that it is a particular ministry role or task

---

[967] Knox, 49-51.
[968] BAGD, 143.

laid upon Archippus by God. Just what that charge is is not certain, but given the way Paul singles Archippus out and the way he is described in Philemon, it surely had to do with some spiritual leadership role in the church at Colossae.

Epaphras had probably served as the founder of the church in Colossae, but he is now with the Apostle Paul (Col. 1:7; 4:2). It is not unlikely, then, that Archippus was given charge of the spiritual oversight of the congregation.

Archippus, and with him all who are called to the ministry, "have received" (παρέλαβες) that charge. Paul uses the verb one other time in Colossians, when he says "as you have received Christ Jesus the Lord" (2:6). It is clear that all believers receive Jesus as their Lord (or they are not believers at all) and some within that circle of faith also "receive" a charge by the Lord to specific ministry responsibility (4:17). Archippus may have most immediately "received" this ministry charge at the hands of the Apostle Paul, but ultimately he understood that it was a divine commission laid upon him, for it was "in the Lord" (ἐν κυρίῳ) that he received it. The precise phrase was used to tell wives to "be subject to [their] husbands, as is fitting in the Lord [ἐν κυρίῳ]" (Col. 3:18). Similarly, children are told to obey their parents "for this is well-pleasing to the Lord [ἐν κυρίῳ]" (v. 20). Just as the various members of the family have their responsibilities "in the Lord" (ἐν κυρίῳ), so too those who are called to the pastoral care of the flock. There are specific good works "which God prepared beforehand so that we would walk in them" (Eph. 2:10). Note how the Apostle Paul exhorted Timothy, "fulfill your ministry" (2 Tim. 4:5). As I have said elsewhere, "Ministry requires *this* of some and *that* of others, but we each must know what it is God has called us to do and must keep our hand to the plow until our fields of service have been plowed, planted, prayed over and readied for harvest."[969]

> **Ministry Maxim**
>
> The congregation helps its pastor most when it urges his faithfulness to God's call, not to their personal preferences.

The purpose (ἵνα) for the command and Archippus's obedience to it is "that you may fulfill it" (ἵνα αὐτὴν πληροῖς). Clearly the "it" (αὐτὴν) referred to is "the ministry which you have received in the Lord." The verb

---

[969] Kitchen, *The Pastoral Epistles for Pastors*, 440.

Paul uses here (πληροῖς, "may fulfill") is from a word family that has played an important role in this letter, and he employs it here for the last time.

The false teacher(s) seems to have claimed that only in the path of his instruction is spiritual "fullness" truly found. Paul argues in this letter that such fullness is found only in Christ and is only true for the one who is placed by God in union with Him. The Apostle uses the cognate noun to assert that "it was the Father's good pleasure for all the fullness [τὸ πλήρωμα] to dwell in" Christ (1:19). Indeed, he says, "For in Him all the fullness [τὸ πλήρωμα] of Deity dwells in bodily form" (2:9). Thus Paul used the verb to say that it is only in Christ that "you have been made complete [πεπληρωμένοι]" (2:10). To this end, Paul prayed that the Colossian believers "may be filled [πληρωθῆτε] with the knowledge of His will in all spiritual wisdom and understanding" (1:9). And perhaps closest to his charge here to Archippus, Paul himself claimed that his own charge from God was to "fully carry out [πληρῶσαι] the preaching of the word of God" (1:25). The Apostle also uses this word family in compound form. Paul labors that they might experience "the full assurance [πληροφορίας] of understanding, resulting in a true knowledge of God's mystery, that is, Christ Himself" (2:2), and Epaphras wrestles for them in prayer that they might be "fully assured [πεπληροφορημένοι] in all the will of God" (4:12).

Thus we might conclude here concerning Paul's charge to Archippus that *given Christ's full deity and full sacrifice on his behalf and given the ongoing labors in prayer and ministry of Paul and Epaphras to see all the Colossian believers experience the fullness of divine life in union with Christ, then Archippus must likewise draw upon the fullness of Christ's indwelling life in order to fully discharge all the duties of this divine service which he has received from the Lord.*

It is of some note, then, that the Apostle begins the sentence by ordering the church as a whole (εἴπατε, "Say") to command one of its servants (their acting pastor?): "Take heed to the ministry"! Clearly Paul is giving apostolic backing to the congregation which says to its pastor, "Do not shrink back in fulfilling God's call upon your life and the ministry He has charged you with among us!" Paul's charge to the congregation is in the aorist imperative form—demanding the action to be taken urgently and immediately. The congregation's command to Archippus (Βλέπε, "Take heed") is in the present imperative form—demanding ongoing, continuous, habitual fulfillment of the command. The pastor is not relieved of his responsibilities if the congregation does not encourage him in them, but blessed is the one who sees the congregation standing with the Lord, exhorting and encouraging him to full faithfulness in his divine commission.

This of course implies that Archippus and the congregation knew precisely what ministry the Lord had laid upon him and that in some fashion they therefore knew when he would have fully discharged it. The local church owes it to their pastor and all other ministry servants to help them define before the Lord their ministry responsibilities. In so doing they give both the servant and themselves a means by which to measure his faithfulness in ministry.

This implies a threefold relationship in a pastor's local church ministry. There is of course *his relationship to God*—for God has called him and the ministry that he undertakes is "received in the Lord." The pastor is called by God. He will stand before the bar of the individual congregant's judgment as he/she weighs his effectiveness and faithfulness in ministry, but he must always keep in the fore of his mind and heart that he stands ultimately only before the Lord who called him. There is then *his relationship to the congregation* as a whole, for the Apostle charges them to "Say to [their pastor], 'Take heed to the ministry ...'" The congregation does the pastor no favors by their flattery. Their great service to him is to exhort and encourage him in his faithfulness to His divine Master. Finally, there is *the pastor's relationship to himself*, for only he can and must "Take heed to the ministry [he has] received in the Lord." No one else can ultimately be responsible for the pastor's faithful discharge of his calling. The Lord calls and fills and enables. The congregation exhorts and encourages. The pastor, then, must be ever watchful over himself and the ministry God lays upon him. His great pursuit is to be found faithful—as had Epaphras (1:7), Tychicus (4:7), and Onesimus (4:9).

4:18 I, Paul, write this greeting with my own hand. Remember my imprisonment. Grace be with you.

The Apostle closes his letter with three clipped statements. First he says, "I, Paul, write this greeting with my own hand" (Ὁ ἀσπασμὸς τῇ ἐμῇ χειρὶ Παύλου). The original text contains no verb. It might be more literally rendered: "The greeting, by/with my hand, Paul." The noun "greeting" ('Ο ἀσπασμὸς) is cognate to the verb used already in verses 10, 12, 14 and 15. It is similarly used by Paul in 1 Corinthians 16:21 and 2 Thessalonians 3:17. The definite article might be rendered as a demonstrative pronoun (thus the NASU's "this"). The possessive pronoun (ἐμῇ, "my own") is emphatic. It is in the attributive position, tucked as it is between the noun and its definite article (τῇ ... χειρὶ). It thus makes clear the personal touch of the Apostle's "hand" (χειρὶ).[970] The dative case of the noun is used to indicate instrumentality—Paul affixed his signature with his own hand.[971] Even if Paul used an amanuensis to take down the letter as he spoke it (cf. Rom. 16:22), at the conclusion of the letter he would have taken pen in hand to add his own signature as an authenticating sign of its origin. This seems to have been Paul's practice at other times (1 Cor. 16:21; Gal. 6:11; 2 Thess. 3:17; cf. Philem. 19). Who the amanuensis may have been is a matter of speculation. A. T. Robertson comments: "The chain ... clanked afresh as Paul took the pen to sign the salutation."[972]

The second closing statement Paul makes is, "Remember my imprisonment" (μνημονεύετέ μου τῶν δεσμῶν). The present-tense imperative (μνημονεύετέ, "Remember") demands action be taken repeatedly or regularly. It required the Colossian believers "to think of and feel for" Paul.[973] It may have the further notion of "mention or remembering in prayer."[974] What is thus to be brought to mind is "my imprisonment" (μου τῶν δεσμῶν). The word "imprisonment" (τῶν δεσμῶν) refers literally to bonds, chains, or fetters (e.g., Luke 8:29; Acts 16:26). By metonymy it can then be used to speak of imprisonment generally (e.g., Phil. 1:7; Col. 4:18).[975] Paul adds the personal pronoun (μου, "my") to make emphatic that this is his very own experience.[976]

Finally, the Apostle closes this letter with the words "Grace be with you" (ἡ χάρις μεθ' ὑμῶν). As he does in all his letters, he closes with an expression of his desire that grace be granted to his readers. He uses this

---

[970] BAGD, 255.
[971] Harris, 215.
[972] Robertson, *Word Pictures*, 4:513.
[973] Thayer, 416.
[974] BAGD, 525; O'Brien, 260.
[975] Friberg, 106.
[976] King, 351.

precise expression to close both 1 Timothy (6:21) and 2 Timothy (4:22). The verb ("be") must be supplied by the reader. Note the use of the definite article with "grace" (ἡ χάρις). "It is no ordinary grace that Paul seeks ... but the unique and only grace—the grace of all grace—that comes exclusively from God the Father through Jesus Christ by the power of the Spirit."[977] The Apostle opened the letter with "grace" (1:2), and now he closes the letter with the blessing of grace extended. The use of the plural pronoun (ὑμῶν, "you") may be a subtle reminder to the gathered believers in Colossae that while each one must experience God's grace personally, God intends the fullness of His grace to be known and enjoyed in the context of Christian community.

> **Ministry Maxim**
>
> When it all begins and when it's all been said and done, grace is the great need of us all.

Some manuscripts contain a final "amen" (ἀμήν; cf. KJV and NKJV), but this seems clearly to have been an additional affirmation provided by the scribes who took care in transcribing the text from one manuscript to another.

Digging Deeper:

1. Considering what we know of the people Paul names in these closing verses and considering how he speaks of and to them, what do we learn about how we ought to speak of and to those who fill our ministry lives?
2. What do these verses tell us about how to handle the heartaches and hurts of our relationships?
3. What do these verses tell us about how to handle the opportunities and responsibilities of our ministries?

---

[977] Kitchen, *The Pastoral Epistles for Pastors*, 473.

PHILEMON

INTRODUCTION TO PHILEMON

Philemon is the shortest of the Apostle Paul's thirteen NT letters. It may also be the most personally revealing. This potent little letter provides us an intimate glimpse at the Apostle's pastoral finesse as he works with specific individuals to apply the grace of the Lord Jesus Christ to their relationships.

Before we immerse ourselves in the text of Philemon, we must test the waters to understand that into which we'll be diving. This introduction, like the one to Colossians, will pursue answers to five questions:

1. Who wrote this epistle?
2. To whom was this epistle written?
3. What circumstances gave rise to the writing of this epistle?
4. Why did Paul write Philemon?
5. What does Philemon teach us?[978]

Authorship: Who Wrote This Epistle?

The letter claims to have been written by the Apostle Paul (vv. 1, 9, 19). This witness has been accepted almost universally throughout church history. Early church witnesses such as Ignatius, Tertullian, Origen, Eusebius, and Marcion all attributed the letter to the Apostle Paul. Even when the critical schools of the nineteenth century began to sow seeds of doubt concerning the Pauline authorship of many of his NT letters, few ventured to question

---

[978] For those wishing a fuller, more technical introduction to Philemon I recommend Moo (361-378) and Dunn (299-309).

his authorship of Philemon. Those who deny Pauline authorship may, as O'Brien puts it, "rightly be consigned to the eccentricities of NT scholarship."[979] Indeed, Harris can say, "Hardly any modern commentator doubts that Paul wrote Philemon."[980]

As with the letter to the Colossians, we must ask: Does the expression ("and Timothy," v. 1) indicate that Timothy had a hand in either the composition or recording of this letter? The expression could indicate that Timothy served as an amanuensis, recording the words as Paul dictated them. It is also possible that Paul may have provided the gist of his thoughts, leaving to Timothy the task of fleshing out a draft of the letter which the Apostle would later review and revise. Whatever the case, in the end and as with Colossians, the Apostle laid claim to the letter and was responsible for its contents.

As to the location from which the letter was written, see the introduction to Colossians.

Recipients: To Whom Was This Epistle Written?

Paul writes this letter to four addressees (vv. 1b-2). First, and primarily, he designates it "To Philemon" (v. 1b) and he clearly is the focus the letter. Philemon appears to have been a resident of the city of Colossae (Col. 4:9). To Paul and Timothy he is "our beloved brother and fellow worker" (v. 1b), designating him as a fellow believer and gospel worker. In Colossians the Apostle used "beloved" of Epaphras ("beloved fellow bond-servant," 1:7), Tychicus ("beloved brother," 4:7), Onesimus ("beloved brother," 4:9), and Luke ("the beloved physician," 4:14). Philemon, then, stands in elite company. Interestingly, Paul also uses the same adjective (ἀγαπητός, "beloved") to describe Onesimus (v. 16), creating an intriguing dynamic between Christian slave owner and his newly converted slave. Paul also calls Philemon a "fellow worker" (v. 1), a noun the Apostle uses twelve times in his letters. He uses it in Colossians 4:11 to refer to Aristarchus, Mark, and "Jesus who is called Justus." He will use it again here in Philemon to describe Mark, Aristarchus, Demas, and Luke (v. 24). Philemon was, apparently, active in serving the Lord, at least in the church at Colossae and perhaps further afield.

---

[979] O'Brien, 269.
[980] Harris, 241.

In addition to Philemon, Paul addressed the letter to two other individuals and one group (v. 2). The letter also is addressed "to Apphia." Most believe Apphia was Philemon's wife.[981] Paul calls her simply "our sister," indicating that she shared their faith in Christ. By this designation Paul emphasizes her shared relationship with him and other believers, not her marital status to Philemon.

Then also the letter is addressed "to Archippus." The consensus seems to be that Archippus was the son of Philemon and Apphia.[982] What is explicit is that Paul calls him "our fellow soldier." The only other time Paul uses this word is in reference to Epaphroditus (Phil. 2:25). In the course of fulfilling his assignment, Epaphroditus had fallen ill and nearly died (v. 27). If this is any indication, the designation "fellow soldier" had a strong connotation of selflessness and sacrifice for the cause of Christ. It is clear, then, that Paul considered Archippus one of his trusted ministry associates, enlisted in the same force, battling side-by-side with all true soldiers of the Lord (cf. 2 Tim. 2:3). It may be that Archippus was the leader of the church in Colossae. Paul commanded the Colossian believers, "Say to Archippus, 'Take heed to the ministry which you have received in the Lord, that you may fulfill it'" (Col. 4:17). The fact that Paul singles him out in this way makes it possible that he had a role of spiritual leadership in the church at Colossae. Epaphras had founded the church in Colossae, but he was presently with the Apostle Paul (Col. 1:7; 4:2; Philem. 23). It is reasonable to conclude, therefore, that Archippus had been given charge of the congregation in Colossae.

Clearly the church in Colossae (or at least one house church) met in the home of Philemon and Apphia, for Paul adds: "and to the church in your house." In saying it was "your" (σου) house, the Apostle uses the singular form, a reference to Philemon alone. As one would anticipate in a patriarchal society, Philemon was viewed as the head of the family and was considered the owner of the home.

The letter appears to be intended primarily for Philemon, a fact attested by the singular forms throughout the body of the letter. However, it appears

---

[981] E.g., BAGD, 103; Bruce, NIC, 206; Harris, 245; Lightfoot, 304, 306; Lohse, 190; Moo, 383; O'Brien, 273.

[982] E.g., Bruce, NIC, 206; Lightfoot, 306-307; Moo, 383; O'Brien, 273.

Paul also wants the larger church body to hear his counsel contained herein because he employs the plural form of the second-person personal pronoun in verse 3 ("grace to *you*"), verse 22 ("I hope that through your prayers I shall be given to *you*"), and verse 25 ("The grace of the Lord Jesus Christ be with *your* spirit").[983] This is a strong confirmation that the Apostle, while addressing Philemon personally, desired the accountability the entire church family could bring to the situation.[984]

Though it cannot be confirmed, tradition tells us that Philemon, Apphia, Archippus, and Onesimus all were martyred for their faith in Jesus Christ.[985]

Occasion: What Circumstances Gave Rise to the Writing of This Epistle?

The Circumstances of the Recipients

Philemon was a follower of Christ who lived in the city of Colossae (Col. 4:9). He was wealthy enough to own a home suitable as a meeting place for the church (Philem. 1-2). He was also a slave owner (vv. 11, 16: cf. Col. 4:1, 9). One of those slaves, named Onesimus, apparently stole something from him (Philem. 18) and then ran (vv. 15-16). In that flight it appears that Onesimus made his way to Rome (in an attempt to blend into the crowds of the capital city?) and there providentially came into contact with the Apostle Paul. Though Paul apparently had not visited Colossae (Col. 2:1), surely Onesimus knew of the Apostle, having been in and around the home of Philemon during the times believers gathered for worship. In Rome the Apostle preached the gospel to the runaway slave, whose heart was opened by God, and he believed (Philem. 10, 16). How long the run-away-slave-now-Christian-brother remained with the Apostle Paul is not clear. Yet apparently it was long enough for Onesimus to enter into service for the Lord and His Apostle (vv. 11-13). Paul had come to love Onesimus deeply (vv. 12, 16). However long it was, Onesimus became convinced of his need for reconciliation with his owner-now-brother-in-the-Lord, Philemon. Thus Onesimus is returning (v. 12) with Paul's envoy Tychicus (Col. 4:7-9;

---

[983] Emphases added; Moo, 383.
[984] Contra, Lightfoot, 279; O'Brien, 267-268.
[985] Lightfoot, 308, 314.

cf. Eph. 6:21-22), and together they will explain everything (Col. 4:7-9). Paul may hint that he wishes for Philemon to release Onesimus to travel and minister with him (vv. 14, 20-21).

The Circumstances of the Author

For several reasons it appears probable that Paul wrote this letter at the same general time as Colossians. In both letters:

- Paul is in prison as he writes (Col. 4:3, 10, 18; Philem. 9-10, 13).
- Those sending greetings include Aristarchus, Mark, Epaphras, Luke, and Demas (Col. 4:10-14; Philem. 23-24).
- Timothy is associated with Paul, on both occasions being designated "our brother" (Col. 1:1; Philem. 1).
- Archippus plays a key role (Col. 4:17; Philem. 2).
- The return of Onesimus with Tychicus to Colossae is a common detail (Col. 4:9; Philem. 12).[986]

These details, shared commonly between the two letters, make it probable that they both were written at approximately the same time, by the same author, and from similar circumstances. See then the introduction to Colossians for further detail about Paul's circumstances at the time of writing.

The Apostle probably sent this letter at the same time as the letter to the Colossians (and probably Ephesians as well; perhaps also the letter to the Laodiceans, Col. 4:16). He sent them via the hand of Tychicus, who was accompanying Onesimus in his return to his master at his home in that city (Col. 4:7-9; Philem. 12; cf. Eph. 6:21). The letter to Philemon was thus probably written about the same time as Colossians and Ephesians, sometime between AD 60 and 62. Once again, see the introduction to Colossians for further detail.

Purpose: Why Did Paul Write Philemon?

The Apostle, writing at approximately the same time he penned the longer letter to the Colossians, authors this more personal letter for the purpose of effecting reconciliation between the believing slave owner, Philemon,

---

[986] Harris, 3-4.

and his runaway, but newly converted, slave, Onesimus. Paul spends more time on the topic of the responsibilities of slaves and masters in Colossians (74 words in the Greek text of Col. 3:22-4:1) than he does upon the relationships of wives/husbands and children/fathers combined (42 words in the Greek text of 3:18-21).[987] Perhaps a significant percentage of the church in Colossae was made up of slaves. It is not difficult to imagine the wisdom necessary to counsel all the parties through this reconciliation, one which would set a tone for the relationships between other believing slaves and their masters. Paul's words in Colossians 3:22-4:1 may have been intended as a general instruction for the tensions and questions this situation surely stirred up within the congregation in Colossae. But in the present letter the Apostle speaks more directly to Philemon (yet allowing the church as a whole to listen in, Philem. 2, 3, 22, 25), offering a revealing look into the Apostle's manner and method of dealing personally with others in challenging situations.

Theology: What Does Philemon Teach Us?

The Apostle Paul's letter to Philemon delivers a powerful message disproportionate to its diminutive size. The concerns of the letter are weighty; the implications of the counsel far-reaching. The texture of the letter is highly personal. Herein we observe the Apostle's Spirit-inspired wisdom, tact, and finesse in working through delicate matters in an emotionally charged set of circumstances. Every line makes us recognize that the transforming power of God's grace must be realized. We do well to linger long over this little letter, for here the river of wisdom may not run long, but it runs exceedingly deep. Explore its depths and your ministry will be better for your time and travel in its currents.

Nearly every verse of the letter drips with wisdom and pastoral savvy as the Apostle Paul shepherds Philemon through dark passages where ungodly motives, actions, and words might overtake him. Allow me to string together some of the pastoral gems along the way, leaving you to prayerfully embrace the text of Scripture at each point and to explore the commentary for detail as to what it means and how it may apply to your ministry.

---

[987] Compare Ephesians: wives/husbands and children/fathers = 241 words (5:22-6:4); slaves/masters = 87 words (6:5-9).

- Though the letter is brief, key words and themes by their repetition signal what the Apostle is after: love (vv. 5, 7, 9), hearts (vv. 7, 12, 20), refreshing (vv. 7, 20), brother (vv. 1, 7, 16, 20).
- As Paul seeks reconciliation between Philemon and Onesimus, note the way he balances the issues of apostolic authority and personal relationship (vv. 7-9, 14, 17, 19, 20). Even when Paul contemplates issuing commands, he grounds his appeal upon their shared union "in Christ" (v. 8) rather than upon his standing as an Apostle.
- Note the way Paul emphasizes his present circumstances as a prisoner for the Lord (vv. 1, 9, 10, 13, 23). He makes mention of this fact five times in this brief letter, but only three times in the much longer letter to the Colossians (Col. 4:3, 10, 18). Why does he do so? What interpersonal and pastoral leverage does this grant him?
- Note also his mention of his advanced age ("the aged," v. 9). Is Paul counting on personal sympathies to move Philemon's heart toward a particular response in the matters at hand?
- Note the way Paul builds accountability into this letter. Clearly Philemon is the primary recipient of the letter, but three times Paul turns to address the larger congregation which meets in Philemon's home (vv. 3, 22, 25). He speaks to Philemon, but he makes sure that he knows he is being spoken to in the context of congregational life. The choices to be made are his, but many are watching.
- Note the way Philemon (offended slave owner) and Onesimus (runaway, previously unbelieving slave) are made to stand on equal footing in their relationships to the Apostle Paul. They are both alike called "beloved brother" (vv. 1, 16). And this is not simply in relationship to Paul, but to one another (v. 16)!
- Note how Paul subtly builds an ethos of unity. In Colossians, which would have been delivered along with the letter to Philemon, Paul shows an affinity to words prefixed with σύν ("with"), using eight such words (cf. commentary on

Philem. 1). Then he does so again specifically here with regard to Philemon, designating him a "fellow worker" (συνεργῷ, v. 1).

- Paul begins with expressions of his gratitude for Philemon, noting the far-ranging reputation he enjoys as a servant of Christ and the personal benefit he has himself enjoyed by knowing this man (vv. 4-8). Will this reputation of grace hold true now, under these new circumstances with Onesimus?

- Paul specifically mentions how "the hearts of the saints have been refreshed" (v. 5) through Philemon. And now, using the same word, Paul asks him to do the same for him, through his response to Onesimus (v. 20).

- Knowing what weighs in the balance, the Apostle delicately emphasizes "love" as he writes. Elsewhere in his letters when the combination of "faith" and "love" are found, they are in just that order. But this time Paul reverses the order and places "love" before "faith" (v. 5). Was this intentional? Or was it simply the weight upon his heart pressing out the words as he prayerfully hoped toward a certain outcome in this dispute?

- Having noted Philemon's reputation as a servant of God (vv. 4-5), Paul reminds him that true Christian maturity and knowledge is realized in the context of our relationships (v. 6)—a gentle reminder that Philemon is not free to do as he pleases with Onesimus and still expect to go forward with Christ and His people.

- Paul's prayer in fact introduces many of the themes that will arise later in the body of the letter. This serves to lay a theological and psychological groundwork for the exhortations that follow. Onesimus would be the perfect test case to prove the reality of Philemon's faith.

- Note Paul's calculated use of the word σπλάγχνον (lit., "bowels," i.e., seat of the emotions). The word appears only eleven times in the NT, eight of which are by Paul. Of those eight usages by Paul, three are in this letter (vv. 7, 12, 20). Philemon has a long record of touching the "hearts" (v. 7) of the saints. Now he needs to know that Onesimus is "my very heart" (v. 12). So the Apostle pleads with Philemon: "refresh my heart" (v. 20)! This would happen precisely by the way he receives Onesimus!

- Note the juxtaposition of the dual roles Onesimus fulfills: Philemon's slave (v. 16) and Paul's child (v. 10).

- And note the gentle way Paul sets forward Onesimus's new standing as "my child" (v. 10a), even before making direct mention of his name (v. 10b). The artist's gentle brushwork provides hues and shades of finesse which communicate the intent of his heart.

- Paul carefully puts Philemon (offended slave owner) and Onesimus (offending, but newly converted, slave) on level ground by noting that apparently he was the human agent in the conversion of both (vv. 10, 19).

- There is also artful wordplay upon the name of Onesimus. His name means "useful" (v. 10). He has proven "useless" in the past, but now as a believing slave can prove "useful" in manifold ways, to both Philemon and Paul (v. 11). Additionally, note Philemon's role in letting Paul "benefit" (v. 20) from his response to Onesimus. Wright aptly says, "It is now Philemon's turn to be 'useful' to Paul."[988]

- Paul clearly wished for Onesimus to stay with him and to assist him in ministry (v. 13). Yet when noting the benefit Onesimus could be ("useful"), he was careful to put Philemon's claim before his own ("to you and to me," v. 11b). In this way the Apostle was careful not to assert his authority over Philemon, but respected the existing relationship between him and Onesimus.

- To forestall any anger in Philemon, Paul assured him that any delay in Onesimus's return was to be laid at the feet of the Apostle (v. 13).

---

[988] Wright, 189.

- Note the mention of how Onesimus was able to serve as a proxy for Philemon, providing the Apostle what he had been unable to provide personally (v. 13)!
- Paul wisely invites Philemon to enter into the same process of thoughtful choice that he himself had gone through (v. 14).
- Indeed, in the response Paul desired from Philemon, he was looking for more than raw obedience ("compulsion"), but for his glad and willing ("free will") choice (v. 14). This is a call for true "goodness," not mere moral compliance.
- Perhaps to overcome growing bitterness in Philemon, the Apostle hints that divine providence stood behind his "loss" (v. 15).
- Note again the psychological and spiritual pressure brought to bear upon Philemon when Paul designates Onesimus "a beloved brother" (v. 16). And note how he foists upon Philemon the logical implications of this transformation. Onesimus stands in this position "especially to me," says Paul. In this he uses elative language to spike the wondrous joy in his heart over this slave's conversion. But then he adds, "but how much more to you"! In this Paul has not only elevated Onesimus to a status equal to that of Philemon (as a "beloved brother," cf. v. 1), but he has elevated the newly converted slave to a status with Philemon that exceeds the one he enjoys with Paul himself.
- Paul is clear: Philemon is to receive Onesimus as if he were receiving the Apostle himself (ὡς ἐμέ, lit., "as me"; v. 17).
- Paul uses atonement language in calling upon Philemon to take any debt Onesimus owes him and "charge it to my account" (v. 18). In this way Paul subtly reminds Philemon that grace received must become grace extended.
- For all of his subtlety and finesse, "obedience" is the bottom line in all the Apostle has said (v. 21)! There is a way which Philemon is morally obligated to respond to Onesimus, a way that is "proper" (v. 8).

- Paul announces early that he has an "appeal" (vv. 9, 10) to make of Philemon. Yet he leaves the specifics of that appeal unstated as he pastorally and wisely builds the groundwork upon which that "appeal" needs to rest. Finally, he makes the specifics known in the form of three imperatives: "accept him as … me" (v. 17), "charge that to my account" (v. 18), and "refresh my heart" (v. 20).
- Indeed, in closing, the Apostle lays upon Philemon the possibility that he might actually do "even more" (v. 21) than Paul has asked!
- And in the end, Paul seals his letter by letting Philemon (and the church in Colossae) know that he will be coming to personally inspect how Onesimus has been received (v. 22).

Bibliography

See the bibliography in the introduction to Colossians as well as the annotated bibliography of commentaries in Appendix E.

PHILEMON

1 Paul, a prisoner of Christ Jesus, and Timothy our brother, To Philemon our beloved brother and fellow worker,

As in all thirteen of his NT epistles, "Paul" (Παῦλος) places his name at the lead of the opening sentence. He was born a Roman citizen (Acts 22:28). He had been given both a Roman ("Paul," Παῦλος) and a Hebrew name ("Saul," Σαῦλος). The latter predominates in the Bible's earlier references (e.g., Acts 7:58; 8:1, 3; 13:1, 2, 7, 9). This may be because he was at this time more commonly associated with the Jewish people. But when he was called and sent as a missionary to the Gentiles, his Roman name became the more common way for him to refer to himself.

Here Paul designates himself "a prisoner of Christ Jesus" (δέσμιος Χριστοῦ Ἰησοῦ). He uses precisely the same expression again in verse 9 (cf. the prepositional phrase in v. 23). But just what does Paul intend by this? How is the genitive (Χριστοῦ Ἰησοῦ, "of Christ Jesus") to be understood? If it is taken as a subjective genitive, it means "a prisoner for Jesus' sake." If it is taken as an objective genitive it means "one taken captive by Jesus Christ." The former was clearly true (Paul was in a literal, physical prison and

> **Ministry Maxim**
>
> Sometimes we make more progress by finding common ground than by pulling rank.

was there because of his faith in Christ Jesus), but the reference here could also be to the latter—in which case the latter is the ground of the former.

"Paul's heart had been taken captive by Christ the Lord, so much so that no matter what obedience brought his way—even imprisonment—he was first and foremost a captive of Christ" (cf. Eph. 3:1; 4:1; 2 Timothy 1:8; Philem. 9).[989] Moo says that this is "one of those hard-to-classify genitives that probably indicate a general relationship between 'prisoner' and 'Christ Jesus' that should not be confined to one particular nuance. Paul is in prison because he has been preaching Christ; he is in prison for the sake of Christ; he is a prisoner who belongs to Christ."[990]

It is remarkable that Paul makes no mention of his apostleship (the only others of his letters not to mention his apostleship in the salutation are Philippians and 1 and 2 Thessalonians) and thus add clout to his words. Rather he appeals to the recipients as fellow believers and on the ground of shared faith in Christ. Indeed, Harris writes: "This letter derives much of its potency from the fact that Paul appeals, directly or indirectly, (a) to his friendship with Philemon, rather than to his apostolic authority (vv. 7-9, 14, 17, 19, 20; but cf. v. 21); and (b) to his present circumstances as a prisoner (vv. 1, 9, 10, 13, 23)."[991]

Paul adds "and Timothy" (καὶ Τιμόθεος) as an evidence that he was not alone at the time of the epistle's writing. Timothy is also listed in the salutations of 2 Corinthians, Philippians, Colossians, and 1 and 2 Thessalonians. The Apostle first encountered Timothy and discovered him to be a disciple upon his return to Lystra (Acts 16:1-2). At the time of Paul's first visit to Lystra, he had been mistaken as a god by the populace after healing a lame man. But shortly after, the Jews stirred up the crowds and they stoned him nearly to death (Acts 14:8-20). Paul spent only a short time in Lystra before moving on. We have no explicit word of Timothy's conversion at that time. Had he been one toward the back of the crowd, listening intently as Paul preached? Is it possible that Timothy's heart was moved when he saw Paul's resolve in the face of death (2 Tim. 3:11) and that he subsequently put his faith in Christ? Whenever the precise time of his conversion and whatever the tipping point for his trust in Christ, he had gone public with his discipleship by the time of Paul's return. Paul found

---

[989] Kitchen, *The Pastoral Epistles for Pastors*, 316.
[990] Moo, 380.
[991] Harris, 244.

Timothy known in his hometown (the same locale where the citizenry had stoned Paul nearly to death!) and the surrounding region as an effective disciple of Christ (Acts 16:2). Paul wished for this effective young disciple to join him in the cause of the gospel, with hopes that he might further fashion him for ministry (Acts 16:3). Ten years may have passed between their initial meeting and the time of this epistle's writing. The two had lived, ministered, traveled, and shared much of life together by this time. Now, with Paul in a Roman prison, Timothy remains faithfully at his side. It does not appear that Timothy was also incarcerated. He was nevertheless present to attend to the needs of the Apostle and to do his bidding. Timothy had been present with Paul for at least some portion of his Ephesian ministry (Acts 19:22). It is likely that during this time Philemon met Paul and would likely therefore have come into acquaintance with Timothy as well.

As with the letter to the Colossians, we must ask: Does the expression ("and Timothy," καὶ Τιμόθεος) indicate that he had a hand in either the composition or recording of this letter? The expression could indicate that Timothy served as an amanuensis, recording the words as Paul dictated them. It is also possible that Paul may have provided the gist of his thoughts, leaving to Timothy the task of fleshing out a draft of the letter which the Apostle would later review and revise. Whatever the case, in the end, the Apostle laid claim to the letter and was responsible for its contents. Like Paul himself, Timothy appears not to have been known personally to the people of the church in Colossae, though surely they knew of him and his faithful ministry (perhaps even through Philemon). Though he deems it important to identify Timothy's presence with him (though others are present with Paul [cf. vv. 23-24] he makes mention only of Timothy in this salutation), the letter comes from Paul himself, for from verse 4 onward (other than verse 6), he uses the singular, and his name alone appears in verses 9 and 19.[992]

As he does in 2 Corinthians and Colossians, Paul designates Timothy "our brother" (ὁ ἀδελφός; more lit., "the brother"). This is the status Timothy holds toward Paul and the letter's recipients as they stand together in Christ. Elsewhere Paul, speaking of Timothy in relationship to himself personally, refers to him as "my true child in the faith" (1 Tim. 1:2), "my beloved son" (2 Tim. 1:2), and simply as "my son" (2 Tim. 2:1). One so

---

[992] Ibid.

well regarded by the Apostle would provide a good, objective witness to the ideas, claims, and statements made in this letter.

Paul dispatches the letter to four addressees, the first mentioned here and the others in verse 2. First he designates it "To Philemon" (Φιλήμονι), who seems clearly to be the focal point of the letter. Philemon was apparently a resident of the city of Colossae. He is called "our beloved brother and fellow worker" (τῷ ἀγαπητῷ καὶ συνεργῷ ἡμῶν). The two adjectives are used in a substantival way and are governed by a single definite article (τῷ).

When Paul calls Philemon "beloved" (τῷ ἀγαπητῷ), he uses an adjective employed often when speaking of fellow believers. Paul uses the adjective four times in Colossians, designating Epaphras as their "beloved fellow bond-servant" (1:7), Tychicus (4:7) and Onesimus (4:9) each as a "beloved brother," and Luke as "the beloved physician" (4:14). Thus we should understand Philemon as a disciple of Jesus Christ and, as such, one loved by Paul himself. Interestingly, Paul will shortly use the same word to describe the new status of Onesimus (v. 16), creating an interesting tension in the letter. The believing slave owner who, from an earthly perspective, has every right to punish his runaway slave is soon to be put on the same standing before Paul—and, implicitly, before God—as that now-believing slave.

Philemon is also designated a "fellow worker" (συνεργῷ). The noun is used by Paul twelve times in his letters (elsewhere only in 3 John 8). In Colossians the Apostle showed an affinity toward words beginning with σύν ("with"), such compounds appearing there twelve times. He has used eight different such compounds: "fellow bond-slave" (σύνδουλος, 1:7; 4:7), "understanding" (σύνεσις, 1:9; 2:2), "hold together" (συνίστημι, 1:17), "buried with" (συνθάπτω, 2:12), "raised up with" (συνεγείρω, 2:12; 3:1), "ligaments"/"bond of unity" (σύνδεσμος, 2:19; 3:14), "fellow prisoner" (συναιχμάλωτος, 4:10), and here, "fellow worker" (συνεργός). The word we encounter here is used also in Colossians 4:11 to refer to Aristarchus, Mark (v. 10), and "Jesus who is called Justus" (v. 11). He will use it again here in Philemon to describe Mark, Aristarchus, Demas and Luke (24). Thus we should also understand Philemon to have been an active servant in the church in Colossae.

2 and to Apphia our sister, and to Archippus our fellow soldier, and to the church in your house:

In addition (καὶ, "and") to Philemon (v. 2), Paul addressed the letter to two other individuals and one group. It is addressed also "to Apphia" ('Απφίᾳ). The consensus seems to be that Apphia was Philemon's wife.[993] Paul refers to her simply as "our sister" (τῇ ἀδελφῇ), indicating that she too had come to faith in Jesus. In this way he emphasizes Apphia's relationship to himself and other believers, not her marital status to Philemon. Most manuscripts have here τῇ ἀγαπητῇ ("beloved," cf. KJV) rather than τῇ ἀδελφῇ ("sister"). Perhaps this is because of the masculine form of the same adjective in verse 1. However, the earliest and strongest witnesses have τῇ ἀδελφῇ and thus it is attested as the correct reading.[994]

Then also the letter is addressed "to Archippus" ('Αρχίππῳ). Here the consensus seems to be that Archippus was the son of Philemon and Apphia.[995] What is explicit is that the Apostle dubs him "our fellow soldier" (τῷ συστρατιώτῃ ἡμῶν). Paul's only other use of this compound word is to describe Epaphroditus, who had come from the Philippian church to minister to his needs while in this imprisonment (Phil. 2:25). In the course of fulfilling this assignment Epaphroditus had fallen ill and nearly died (v. 27). If this is any indication, the designation "fellow solider" had a strong connotation of selflessness and sacrifice for the cause of Christ. It is clear that Paul considers him one of his trusted

Ministry Maxim
Sharing your home is a powerful way of sharing your faith.

ministry associates, enlisted in the same force, battling side-by-side with all true soldiers of the Lord (cf. 2 Tim. 2:3). It may be that Archippus was the leader of the church in Colossae. In this regard, consider our comments on Colossians 4:17. Given the way Paul singles him out in that passage and the way he is described here, it seems probable that his ministry had to do with a role of spiritual leadership in the church at Colossae. Epaphras had apparently founded the church in Colossae. He, however, is now with the

---

[993] E.g., BAGD, 103; Bruce, 206; Harris, 245; Lightfoot, 304, 306; Lohse, 190; Moo, 383; O'Brien, 273.
[994] NET Bible.
[995] E.g., Bruce, 206; Lightfoot, 306-307; Moo, 383; O'Brien, 273.

Apostle Paul (Col. 1:7; 4:2; Philem. 23). It seems reasonable then to conclude that Archippus had been given the charge of the congregation in this city.

Certainly the church (or one expression of it) met in the home of Philemon and Apphia, for the Apostle adds: "and to the church in your house" (καὶ τῇ κατ᾽ οἶκόν σου ἐκκλησίᾳ). As was the case in other localities, Christians usually met in the home of one of the believers. We have here a prepositional phrase (κατ᾽ οἶκόν σου, lit., "of your house") tucked between the noun and its definite article (τῇ ... ἐκκλησίᾳ, "the church"). Church buildings devoted to the worship and service of God and the gathering of His people were unknown at this early stage of the church's development. For this reason believers met together in the homes of those among them. Elsewhere the NT speaks of or alludes to house churches in the homes of Gaius (in Corinth, Rom. 16:3, 5), Aquila and Priscilla (in both Ephesus and Rome, 1 Cor. 16:19 and Rom. 16:3, 5 respectively), Lydia (in Philipi, Acts 16:15, 40), Nympha (in Laodicea, Col. 4:15), Mary (in Jerusalem, Acts 12:12), and Jason (in Thessalonica, Acts 17:5-6).[996]

In saying it was "your" (σου) house, the Apostle uses the singular form—thus referring to Philemon alone, not to what may have been his entire family. As would be expected in a patriarchal society, Philemon was seen as the head of the family and owner of the home. Philemon is clearly the primary recipient of this letter as the singular forms throughout the body of the letter attest; however, it appears Paul also wants the larger church listening in on this as well, for he uses the plural form of second-person personal pronoun in verses 3 ("grace to *you*"), 22 ("I hope that through your prayers I shall be given to *you*"), and 25 ("The grace of the Lord Jesus Christ be with *your* spirit").[997] This is a strong indication that Paul, while dealing personally with Philemon, wanted and utilized the accountability that the entire church body would bring to the matter.[998]

According to tradition Philemon, Apphia, Archippus and Onesimus were all martyred by stoning under the reign of Nero, though this has not been confirmed.

---

[996] Harris, 246.
[997] Emphases added; Moo, 383.
[998] Contra, Lightfoot, 279; O'Brien, 267-268.

3 Grace to you and peace from God our Father and the Lord Jesus Christ.

This precise sentence is used by the Apostle Paul to open eight of his thirteen epistles (Rom. 1:7; 1 Cor. 1:3; 2 Cor. 1:2; Gal. 1:3; Eph. 1:2; Phil. 1:2; 2 Thess. 1:2; Philem. 3). The combination of "grace" (χάρις) and "peace" (εἰρήνη) are found in the salutations of the remaining five (Col. 1:2; 1 Thess. 1:1; 1 Tim. 1:2; 2 Tim. 1:2; Titus 1:4). "Grace" (χάρις) may serve as a one-word summary of all Pauline theology. It both declares and reminds that all which comes to us from God in salvation is a free, unmerited gift. Paul uses it also to close this brief letter (v. 25), thus wrapping its contents in an inclusio of grace. The word "peace" (εἰρήνη) reverberates with echoes of the Hebrew *shalom*, the emphasis being not so much on an inward serenity of heart, but on the full-orbed wholeness of a life at rest with God. This the Apostle extends "to you" (ὑμῖν), using the plural form to address not only Philemon, but also Apphia and Archippus and perhaps the entire church that meets in his home (v. 2; cf. the plural pronouns in vv. 22 and 25).

> **Ministry Maxim**
>
> Ministering out of divine resources rather than our own is the first lesson of Christian service.

These are not graces that arise from within the Apostle himself or that can be drawn from some reserve of personal virtue. Rather they must come "from God our Father and the Lord Jesus Christ" (ἀπὸ θεοῦ πατρὸς ἡμῶν καὶ κυρίου Ἰησοῦ Χριστοῦ.). The single preposition (ἀπὸ) governs both "God our Father" and "the Lord Jesus Christ." Harris aptly observes that this "indicates not that God and Jesus are one and the same person (as though καὶ were epex[egetical]) but that they jointly form a single source of divine grace and peace. Of no mere human being could it be said that, together with God, he was the fount of spiritual blessing; the deity of Christ is thus implicitly affirmed."[999]

The first portion of this phrase (ἀπὸ θεοῦ πατρὸς ἡμῶν, "from God our Father") was used also in the salutation of Colossians (1:2), but there the customary "and the Lord Jesus Christ" (καὶ κυρίου Ἰησοῦ Χριστοῦ) is missing. In a letter so strongly Christological in focus, why would this be

---

[999] Harris, 246.

(see discussion on Col. 1:2)? A definitive answer eludes us, but we see here that Paul is not hesitant in sending the full and customary greeting to those within that same church. Paul grounds this grace and peace in the initiative of the Father and in the accomplishment of the Son. Nowhere in this letter does Paul make mention of the third member of the Trinity (cf. our comments on Col. 1:8).

Digging Deeper

1. Why do you think Paul did not mention his apostleship in the salutation to this letter?
2. What does Paul's twofold identification of Philemon in v. 1 tell us about the link between serving side-by-side and the growth of friendship?
3. What might the fact that the church met in Philemon's house tell us about his station in life and the state of his heart?
4. If Archippus was Philemon's son and if he was also the pastor of the church, how might that complicate things with regard to how Onesimus's return was handled within the church?

---

4 I thank my God always, making mention of you in my prayers,

As he does in so many of his letters (Rom. 1:8; 1 Cor. 1:4; Eph. 1:16; Phil. 1:3; Col. 1:3; 1 Thess. 1:2; 2 Thess. 1:3), Paul gives thanks for the recipient(s). This is the shortest such example in Paul's letters, partly because of the overall brief nature of the letter and partly because of its more personal nature.[1000] The sentence in Greek runs from verse 4 through verse 6. Verse 7 is not a part of the thanksgiving expression, but serves as an effective transition from the thanksgiving (vv. 4-6) to the main body of the letter.

The verb (Εὐχαριστῶ, "I thank") is in the present tense, pointing to the ongoing nature of the gratitude. The singular form reveals that, though he has included mention of Timothy in the salutation (v. 1), Paul speaks as the singular author of this letter. In this regard contrast the plural form used in Colossians 1:3 that may indicate that the thankfulness there expressed was

---

[1000] Moo, 384-385; O'Brien, 275.

shared in jointly by both Paul and Timothy (see discussion there). Here it is Paul who has the key relationship with Philemon, not Timothy, and is thus in a position to make the kinds of requests he will set forth later in the letter.

Thankfulness is a prominent theme throughout the letter to the Colossians (1:3, 12; 2:7; 3:15, 16, 17; 4:2). The Apostle's gratitude is directed to "my God" (τῷ θεῷ μου). The precise phrase is used also in Romans 1:8, 1 Corinthians 1:4, and Philippians 1:3. This is appropriate, for it is God who is the source and origin of that over which Paul delights. Rightly so, for God is the Giver of all good things (John 1:16; 1 Tim. 4:4; James 1:17) and all things are "from Him and through Him and to Him" (Rom. 11:36). For Paul, as he thinks of Philemon ("you" is singular in form), he is "always" (πάντοτε) expressing this thanksgiving. Technically the adverb could qualify the main verb "I thank" (thus the NASU's rendering), or it could be understood as qualifying the participle to follow (ποιούμενος, "making mention"; thus the NKJV: "making mention of you always"). Most English versions understand it as qualifying the main verb. Paul can speak both of always praying (Eph. 6:18; Col. 1:9; 1 Thess. 5:17; 2 Thess. 1:11) and of always giving thanks (Eph. 5:20; 1 Cor. 1:4; Eph. 5:20; 1 Thess. 1:2; Philem. 4). Paul is about to reveal that it is in prayer that his thanksgiving finds expression; therefore, there is little practical difference in saying "I thank my God always" (NASU) or I am "making mention of you always" (NKJV).

This gratitude, says Paul, finds expression by "making mention of you in my prayers" (μνείαν σου ποιούμενος ἐπὶ τῶν προσευχῶν μου). A woodenly literal rendering would yield: "remembrance of you making in the prayers of me." The noun μνείαν points to the mental act of consciously calling something to mind. It is used seven times in the NT, all by Paul. Six of those describe Paul's prayers, usually with regard to his expressions of thanksgiving (Rom. 1:9; Eph. 1:16; Phil. 1:3; 1 Thess. 1:2; 2 Tim. 1:3; Philem. 4). In four of those six, including this one, it appears in tandem with ποιέω ("making"). Here it is a present middle participle. The middle voice emphasizes that Paul acts upon himself, taking the initiative to offer these prayers. Once again, on this occasion the specific focal point of

> **Ministry Maxim**
>
> Grateful prayer is the first duty of Christian ministry.

his gratitude is Philemon (σου, "you" is singular). Among the several nouns used to describe prayer in the NT, this is a more general term, but it describes making a specific supplication.[1001] The sense may, then, be that whenever Paul is making supplication on Philemon's behalf, he always turns also to give thanks for him.

5 because I hear of your love and of the faith which you have toward the Lord Jesus and toward all the saints;

Paul's gratitude is "because" of something specific. There is, however, no corresponding conjunction in the original text. Rather we are met by a participle which is, by most English translations, interpreted as having a causal meaning. Alternatively the KJV and NKJV render it simply as "hearing" (ἀκούων). The present tense intends something like "because I *keep on* hearing" (contrast Col. 1:3-4 where it is aorist).[1002] Paul's information on Philemon is up to date. The source of that information may be Onesimus or perhaps Epaphras (Col. 1:7-8).[1003]

That of which Paul had been hearing and which formed the ground of his gratitude is twofold. First, it is "your love" (σου τὴν ἀγάπην). The personal pronoun (σου, "your") is singular, designating Philemon personally. It stands emphatically before the noun it

> **Ministry Maxim**
>
> The quality of one's human relationships testifies to the solidity of one's faith in Christ.

qualifies, adding extra punch to Paul's words.[1004] Note the presence of the definite article with the noun (τὴν ἀγάπην)—this is not just "love," but *the* "love" that distinctively arises from the life of one who has been made the object of divine love. Philemon's love, Paul will say in verse 7, had brought him "much joy and comfort," not because of its expressions to him personally, but because it had found concrete expression to other believers: "the hearts of the saints have been refreshed through you." It is precisely upon the basis of this love that the Apostle will make his appeal with regard to Onesimus (v. 9).

[1001] BAGD, 172.
[1002] Harris, 249.
[1003] Moo, 387.
[1004] Harris, 249.

Secondly (καὶ, "and") Paul is grateful for "the faith" (τὴν πίστιν). Note again the presence of the definite article with the noun. It is not just "faith" as a quality that Paul recognizes in Philemon, but "*the* faith." Yet, as the next verse will make clear, this is a *shared* faith—it is the faith once for all delivered to the saints, embraced in explicit, personal trust, and shared together by all such believers. Indeed, this is something "which you have" (ἣν ἔχεις). The present tense of the verb underscores the ongoing nature of Philemon's embrace of "the faith."

The relative pronoun (ἣν, "which") is singular in form, leading us to consider whether it refers to "the faith" alone or to both "the faith" and "love," each individually.[1005] The question is only compounded when we consider that they are said to be "toward the Lord Jesus" (πρὸς τὸν κύριον Ἰησοῦν) "and" (καὶ) yet also "toward all the saints" (εἰς πάντας τοὺς ἁγίους). One can easily see how both "faith" and "love" can be directed toward Christ, and one can see how love can be directed toward "the saints." But just what would Paul have in mind by saying that "faith" could be "toward all the saints"? Lightfoot suggests that Paul may have been employing a chiastic arrangement (cf. Gal. 4:4):

> A "your love"
> B "the faith"
> B "toward the Lord Jesus Christ"
> A "toward all the saints"[1006]

Whether by intentionally employing chiasm or not, it seems that Paul intends something like what he expresses to the whole of the Colossian church, but now with Philemon specifically in mind: "we heard of your faith in Christ Jesus and the love which you have for all the saints" (Col. 1:4; cf. Eph. 1:15). The NASU renders two different prepositions here as "toward" (first πρὸς and then εἰς). Nowhere in the NT do we find an example of Paul using πρὸς ("toward") with ἀγάπη ("love"). This, then, makes it unlikely that he does so here.[1007] Paul probably employed the two different prepositions (πρὸς with "the Lord Jesus" and εἰς with "all the

---

[1005] Moo, 387.
[1006] Lightfoot, 332-333; cf. Harris, 250; Lightfoot, 332-333; Lohse, 193; Moo, 388-389; O'Brien, 278-279; Robertson, *Word Pictures*, 4:465.
[1007] Harris, 250.

saints") not to differentiate specific shades of meaning, but to help signal the chiastic arrangement he intended. That which is at the core ("the faith which you have toward the Lord Jesus") gives rise to that which is on the periphery ("love ... toward all the saints"): "faith working through love" (Gal. 5:6).

It is worth noting that the order in which Paul makes mention of "love" and "faith" here are unusual—a reversal of his normal order when mentioning them (e.g., Col. 1:4; 1 Thess. 1:3; 2 Thess. 1:3; 2 Tim. 1:13). This is probably to be attributed to his intent in this letter to appeal to Philemon's "love" in his dealings with Onesimus (vv. 7, 9). Nowhere else in the letter does Paul make mention of or appeal to Philemon's "faith."[1008]

The name "Jesus" (Ἰησοῦς) appears six times in this brief letter (vv. 1, 3, 5, 9, 23, 25), while "Lord" (κύριος) appears five times (vv. 3, 5, 16, 20, 25). "Christ" (Χριστός) will be found eight times (vv. 1, 3, 6, 8, 9, 20, 23, 25). The plural form of the noun "the saints'" (τοὺς ἁγίους) is an oft-used expression, referring to believers in Jesus Christ generally. It refers to those declared righteous (justification) and being made holy (sanctification) by God.

6 and I pray that the fellowship of your faith may become effective through the knowledge of every good thing which is in you for Christ's sake.

The verse brings to closure the sentence begun in verse 4 and leads the way with the conjunction ὅπως. When used as a conjunction, it often identifies a purpose clause, but here it is used to designate the content of Paul's prayer (thus the words "and I pray" have been added by the translators to make clear the intent).[1009] It may be connected to "making mention of you" (μνείαν σου ποιούμενος) in verse 4 and thus introduce the substance of the intercession Paul speaks of there.[1010]

In understanding the Apostle's intent in this verse there are several questions to be settled. What does Paul mean by "the fellowship of your faith" (ἡ κοινωνία τῆς πίστεώς σου)? Does "may become effective" (ἐνεργὴς γένηται) mean "active" (NIV, NLT) or "effective" (ESV, KJV, NASU)?

[1008] Lohse, 193; Moo, 389; O'Brien, 278-279.
[1009] Harris, 250; Lohse, 193; O'Brien, 279.
[1010] BAGD, 577; Lightfoot, 333; O'Brien, 279; Robertson, *Word Pictures*, 4:465.

Does ἐν ἐπιγνώσει ("through the knowledge") refer to knowledge alone or also to experiencing what is known? What specifically does Paul have in mind when he speaks of "every good thing" (παντὸς ἀγαθοῦ)? Just how should εἰς Χριστόν ("for Christ's sake") be understood? Let's pursue an answer to each of these questions and thus build a composite understanding of the whole.

Right away we must deal with the question of just what is meant by "the fellowship of your faith" (ἡ κοινωνία τῆς πίστεώς σου). There really are two questions here. First, what does Paul intend by ἡ κοινωνία ("the fellowship")? Broadly speaking, the noun is used in three ways in the NT: *participation* (association by shared experience; 1 Cor. 10:16; Phil. 1:5; 2:1; 3:10), *fellowship* (association by shared life; 1 Cor. 1:9; 2 Cor. 6:14; 13:14 [13]; Gal. 2:9), and *giving* (association by shared goods, i.e., a gift/contribution; Rom. 15:26; 2 Cor. 8:14; 9:13), though the line of demarcation between the first two is not always easily drawn.[1011] While some think Paul has in mind Philemon's financial support of God's work, this seems to find little support in the remainder of the letter itself. Neither is there evidence for the notion of evangelism as hinted at by some translations (ESV, KJV, NKJV). Nor does he seem to be calling upon Philemon's connection through common experience. Rather, it seems more likely he has the broader and more active notion of the fellowship created among God's people by way of being joint sharers in the eternal life given by Jesus. This seems to best fit with Paul's use of a cognate of this word (κοινωνόν, "a partner") in verse 17.

The second question regards the expression "of your faith" (τῆς πίστεώς σου). It could be used objectively, referring to "the faith" (i.e., the Christian faith or the body of Christian truth).[1012] However, it is probably best understood as a subjective genitive, referring to the personal faith/trust Philemon has placed in Christ and by which he has been brought into fellowship with others of like faith.[1013] Thus the point of this opening clause would seem to be that Paul prays for Philemon's full participation in the shared life of Christ with all others of like faith.

[1011]   Little Kittel, 448.
[1012]   Lohse, 193; Rienecker, 659.
[1013]   Lenski, 957, Lightfoot, 333; Wallace, 116.

The Apostle prays that this fellowship by faith "may become effective" (ἐνεργὴς γένηται). The adjective can mean "effective," "active" or "powerful."[1014] It is used only two other times in the NT (1 Cor. 16:9; Heb. 4:12). Paul has just made the point that Philemon's faith is active (v. 5) and will do so again (v. 7).[1015] To pray that it would become so now would be odd. For this reason it seems best to understand the meaning "effective" here. The verb (γένηται, "may become") is an aorist subjunctive. The middle voice seems to call for the thing to "become effective" by itself or as a natural consequence of its use. The subjunctive mood describes that which is not necessarily yet reality, but which is potential and which Paul is anticipating through his intercession.[1016] Thus far the idea seems to be that Paul prays for Philemon's fellowship with God and man to grow ever more effectual.

Paul prays this will happen ἐν ἐπιγνώσει ("through knowledge"). The preposition (ἐν, "through") is understood by the translators of the NASU as describing the means by which Philemon's faith may become effectual. In contrast, the NIV takes it as expressing purpose ("so that you may have"). The former would intimate that our knowledge of every good thing in Christ leads to an effective fellowship (NASU, NLT, NRSV). The latter would suggest that it is effective fellowship with Christ and His people that leads to a growing knowledge of every good thing in Christ (ESV, NIV, RSV). Which is it?

Perhaps the preposition would be better understood as describing the sphere in which Philemon's active participation with other believers (brought about through his personal trust in Jesus) is to become effective.[1017] In this way the relationship between fellowship and knowledge could be understood as a *reciprocating* one—it is only as we begin to see every good thing that is ours in Christ that we are able to live in fellowship with one another, but on the other hand as we do indeed live effectively in fellowship with Christ and His people, we learn at ever deeper levels every good thing that is ours in Christ.

[1014] BAGD, 265.
[1015] O'Brien, 280.
[1016] Melick, 352.
[1017] Ibid.

The sphere in which Philemon's fellowship is to exist and grow is "the knowledge" (ἐπιγνώσει). The noun is used four times in Colossians (1:9, 10; 2:2; 3:10). The cognate verb is used in Colossians 1:6. It is a compound word (ἐπὶ, "upon" and γνῶσις, "knowledge"), the prefix of which intensifies the root and points to fullness, depth, and completeness of knowledge. The word is likely employed in Colossians in order to make a subtle point with regard to the false teacher's claim to secret knowledge available only to the initiated. Here the idea seems rather to be the increasing depth of experiential knowledge gained by the growing believer.

The verb is followed by a genitive, indicating the thing that is known (παντὸς ἀγαθοῦ, "of every good thing").[1018] Thus the subject of this knowledge is "of every good thing which is in you for Christ's sake" (παντὸς ἀγαθοῦ τοῦ ἐν ἡμῖν εἰς Χριστόν). The adjective πᾶς, when found with a singular, anarthrous noun, denotes "the individual members of the class denoted by the noun" and thus should be translated "every" or "each."[1019] These good things, according to the NASU, are found "in you." A question arises as to whether these are good things to be performed by Philemon[1020] or good things provided to him.[1021] While the noun (ἀγαθοῦ, "good thing") is often used to describe God's will for the believer (e.g., Rom. 15:2; Gal. 6:10; 1 Thess. 5:15) and might thus point to the former, the preposition (ἐν, "in") would seem to point to the latter.

> **Ministry Maxim**
>
> He who withdraws from God's people beggars himself.

There is a textual debate about whether the second-person singular pronoun (ὑμῖν, "you"; cf. NASU, NET, NKJV, KJV) or the first-person plural pronoun (ἡμῖν, "we" or "us"; cf. ESV, NIV, NLT) is the better reading. The evidence is fairly well divided between the two. In the end the meaning is not significantly changed, for what Paul may be suggesting Philemon has as a believer in Christ would be no different than what he would claim for himself and every other believer in Christ. If we choose the second-person singular form (ὑμῖν, "you"), Paul would be dialing in the focus upon Philemon in order to strengthen his case for him to act rightly in regards

---

[1018] BAGD, 291.
[1019] Ibid., 631.
[1020] Moo, 393.
[1021] Harris, 252; O'Brien, 280.

to Onesimus. If we choose the first-person plural form (ἡμῖν, "we"), Paul would simply be reminding Philemon that he is not asking of him anything more than he would ask of any other believer in Christ.

In this clause τοῦ "functions as a rel[ative] pron[oun] introducing a restrictive rel[ative] clause: 'that is in us,' 'that is ours' (RSV; sim. NAB), 'that we have' (sim. NIV)."[1022] These are provisions given to us "for Christ's sake" (εἰς Χριστόν). The phrase is used twelve times in the NT, ten of those by Paul. It might be woodenly rendered "unto Christ," but just what does the Apostle intend by this expression? Harris suggests five possible ways to understand the phrase.[1023] The NASU views it as expressing purpose: "for Christ's sake" (cf. ESV, NRSV).[1024] The NIV, NET, NLT, and RSV seem to view it as expressing location: "in Christ" (thus apparently as equivalent to ἐν Χριστῷ). Along this line, O'Brien suggests that the preposition may have been chosen simply as a style variation so as not to have three consecutive clauses beginning with ἐν.[1025] If this be the case, Paul would be stressing, as he so often does throughout his letters, that it is in relationship to Christ—being found, by God's grace, "in Christ"—that we have all these good things (cf. Eph. 1:3). This, of course, is true, but is it what Paul intended here? It seems the wiser course to take the wording as we have it without trying to read into the Apostle's motives for its use. Thus the preposition is probably best understood as expressing direction: "to," "toward," "for."[1026] The meaning would then be that all these good things that have been given to us in Christ and which are to be discovered and exercised in the context of Christian fellowship are ultimately given in order to point to Christ, or, as the NASU has said, they are give to us "for Christ's sake."

While these conclusions must of necessity be held with the humility that recognizes other possible answers for each question raised, it is our view that this makes the best sense of the Apostle's words. Here then is a paraphrase which seeks to gather up all these fragmentary conclusions and communicate the gist of Paul's thought: "I pray for you that your active participation in Christ's life among His people, which is yours through

---

[1022] Harris, 252.
[1023] Ibid., 252-253.
[1024] Lohse, 194-195.
[1025] O'Brien, 281; cf. Dunn, 320.
[1026] Moo, 394; cf. Lightfoot, 334.

faith, may prove productive as you dwell in a constantly growing knowledge and experience of every good thing which is in you for the glory of Christ."

Though we will only discover this later in the letter, the specific intent of this more general prayer has to do with Paul's call for Philemon to put his faith to work in receiving Onesimus in a forgiving spirit that will release him from punishment for his past sins. Paul's opening here lays the theological and psychological groundwork for the exhortation yet to come. Onesimus would prove the perfect test case for the reality of Philemon's profession of faith and participation in the shared life of Christ among His body.

Digging Deeper

1. How does the Apostle Paul's practice of prayer (v. 4) challenge yours?

2. If your close associates were to report about you to a far-distant and well-respected Christian leader, what tale would they likely tell (v. 5)?

3. In what ways does a growing knowledge of what is made ours in Christ help us live more effectively with one another?

4. In what ways does our shared life with one another help us grow in knowledge of what is ours in Christ?

---

7 For I have come to have much joy and comfort in your love, because the hearts of the saints have been refreshed through you, brother.

Paul elaborates on the reason (γὰρ, "For") for his thanksgiving with regard to Philemon (v. 4). In so doing he will transition effectively from his opening thanksgiving (vv. 4-6) to the main body of the letter (vv. 8-20). Paul says, "I have come to have much joy and comfort in your love" (χαρὰν ... πολλὴν ἔσχον καὶ παράκλησιν ἐπὶ τῇ ἀγάπῃ σου).

The verb (ἔσχον, "I have come to have") is in the aorist tense, understood here as an ingressive aorist[1027] stressing Paul's "entrance into a state" of being.[1028] This state into which Paul has come includes two things: "joy and

---

[1027] Robertson, *Word Pictures*, 4:465.
[1028] Wallace, 558-559.

comfort" (χαρὰν ... καὶ παράκλησιν). The first is coupled with the adjective "much" (πολλὴν). The adjective is used to mark the degree to which Paul experienced this joy.[1029] It could qualify both "joy" and "comfort,"[1030] or because of its position in the sentence it may qualify only "joy." Clearly, however, Paul also found "comfort" (παράκλησιν) in what he heard of Philemon. This noun is cognate to the more frequently used verb παρακαλέω (used in verse 9). It is a compound word meaning "to call" (καλέω) "alongside" (παρά). The noun has a range of meaning that spans from comfort (2 Cor. 1:3; Phil. 2:1) to admonition (Rom. 12:8; 1 Tim. 4:13). Paul clearly uses it here in the former sense.

> **Ministry Maxim**
>
> Praising past obedience and gazing down its continuing trajectory may be a powerful motivator.

The Apostle's "joy" and "comfort" find their impetus "in your love" (ἐπὶ τῇ ἀγάπῃ σου). The preposition (ἐπὶ, "in") is used here "of that upon which a state of being ... is based."[1031] The noun "love" (τῇ ἀγάπῃ) has just been used in verse 5 (to describe the basis of Paul's thanksgiving over Philemon) and will again in verse 9 (as the basis of Paul's appeal to Philemon regarding Onesimus). As it was in verse 5 and as it will be in verse 9, the noun is accompanied by the definite article. The use of "love" (τῇ ἀγάπῃ) signals another chiastic arrangement within the structure of Paul's composition:

> A Love (5)
> > B Faith (5)
> > B Faith (6)
> A Love (7)[1032]

This would seem to confirm that verse 7 should be read as a part of the thanksgiving section of the letter (vv. 4-7), rather than as a part of the opening of the body of the letter. Indeed, a number of the themes of the letter are presented here in capsule form (see the comments at the end of this verse). It is somewhat unusual for Paul to use the thanksgiving section of one of his letters to so thoroughly prepare the way for the body of

---

[1029] BAGD, 688.
[1030] Harris, 253.
[1031] BAGD, 287.
[1032] Dunn, 316; Moo, 385.

the letter.[1033] The Apostle is sincere in what he expresses by way of thanks-giving (vv. 4-7), but he will also employ that genuine gratitude as leverage in moving Philemon to a godly course of action.

Employing the conjunction ὅτι ("because"), the Apostle further elabo-rates upon just what he meant by "in your love" (ἐπὶ τῇ ἀγάπῃ σου), looking apparently to some specific instances of his "love ... toward all the saints" (v. 5).[1034] Through these acts "the hearts of the saints have been refreshed" (τὰ σπλάγχνα τῶν ἁγίων ἀναπέπαυται). The verb (ἀναπέπαυται, "have been refreshed") means to "cause to rest" or to "give (someone) rest, refresh, revive."[1035] This may have the intent of refreshing them or giving them rest with a view to renewing their labors.[1036] Paul will employ the same verb in verse 20 to ask Philemon to undertake this kind of ministry to the Apostle himself. The perfect tense here either looks to such acts of love that Philemon continues to undertake even as Paul writes or may refer to a standing state of effect brought about by past acts by Philemon.[1037] The passive voice sees Philemon acting upon the people of God.

The effect is found specifically upon "the hearts of the saints" (τὰ σπλάγχνα τῶν ἁγίων). The noun (τὰ σπλάγχνα, "the hearts") is used three times in this short letter (vv. 7, 12 and again with this same verb in v. 20). It refers more accurately to the "*bowels, intestines* (the heart, lungs, liver, etc.)."[1038] In the ancient world these were considered the seat of the emotions. For the Greek poets they were the center of "the more violent passions, such as anger and love, but by the Hebrews as the seat of the tenderer affections, especially kindness, benevolence, compassion."[1039]

Here it probably becomes "a very forceful term to signify an expression of the total personality at the deepest level."[1040] Paul will momentarily use the word to refer to Onesimus as "my very heart [σπλάγχνα]" (v. 12). In sending Onesimus back to Philemon, the Apostle was in essence sending his very self. It was to fellow members of the body of Christ (τῶν ἁγίων,

---

[1033] Moo, 385.
[1034] Harris, 253.
[1035] BAGD, 59.
[1036] Lightfoot, 334-335.
[1037] Harris, 254.
[1038] Thayer, 584.
[1039] Ibid.
[1040] Little Kittel, 1068.

"the saints") that Philemon had so ministered, and his acts of love had not gone without notice, their report reaching all the way to the Apostle himself (cf. v. 5).

And this, Paul can say to Philemon, has taken place "through you, brother" (διὰ σοῦ, ἀδελφέ). The conjunction (διὰ, "through") with the genitive (σοῦ, "you") points to agency.[1041] The vocative ἀδελφέ ("brother") is placed last in the sentence for emphasis.[1042] Paul was underscoring the intimacy and connectedness of their relationship. This was true, and it would become the basis from which he will next launch his efforts on behalf of Onesimus.

Verse 7, then, serves capably in the role of transition from Paul's opening salutation and thankful prayers (vv. 1-6) to his forceful exhortations in the body of the letter (vv. 8-22). Powerful currents that will run through the landscape of the letter find their head here: "love" (vv. 5, 7, 9); "hearts" (vv. 7, 12, 20); "refreshing" (vv. 7, 20); and "brother" (vv. 1, 7, 16, 20; verses 1 and 20 are the only time in Paul's writings that he uses the vocative singular of ἀδελφός[1043]).

8 Therefore, though I have enough confidence in Christ to order you to do what is proper,

The Apostle now uses an inferential conjunction (Διὸ, "Therefore") to make the move from his introductory expressions of gratitude and prayer (vv. 4-7) to the real reason for the letter (moving from gratitude for Philemon's love to Paul and the saints [v. 7] to the love he is to express toward Onesimus [v. 9]). The sentence structure is complicated and will run through verse 14. The main verb is "I ... appeal" (παρακαλῶ) in verse 9 (and it is repeated in v. 10 as Paul picks up his train of thought again after a brief parenthetical thought in v. 9b).

What we have here in verse 8 is a participial phrase which modifies that main verb. The present-tense participle (ἔχων, "though I have") is considered concessive by the translators of the NASU (*though* I have) and most other English translations (e.g., ESV, KJV, NKJV, NIV, NRSV, RSV).[1044]

[1041] Harris, 253; Lightfoot, 335; Moo, 396.

[1042] Rienecker, 659.

[1043] Dunn, 320; Moo, 396.

[1044] Lenski, 959; Rienecker, 659; Robertson, *Word Pictures*, 4:466.

That which Paul claims to have is "enough confidence in Christ" (πολλὴν ἐν Χριστῷ παρρησίαν). The noun is a compound made up of πᾶς ("all") and ῥῆσις ("speaking"). Woodenly rendered it might read, "to say it all." It thus describes "*outspokenness, frankness, plainness of speech, that conceals nothing and passes over nothing.*"[1045] Thus it is often rendered "boldness" or "confidence."[1046] But this developed into "*openness to the public, before whom speaking and actions take place,*" the sense it carries in Colossians 2:15.[1047]

By examining Paul's other uses of the noun, we discover that such confidence may be grounded in the hope of glory (2 Cor. 3:12), Christ's faithfulness (Eph. 3:12), the gospel itself (Eph. 6:19), the prayers of God's people (Eph. 6:19; Phil. 1:20), and faithful service to Christ (1 Tim. 3:13).

Here he grounds his confident boldness simply "in Christ" (ἐν Χριστῷ). Just what does Paul intend by this expression? Paul could easily have said something like "as an apostle of Christ," but instead he describes himself [and perhaps he hints at Philemon's standing as well] simply as one in union with Christ. The former would have been an authoritative command flowing down a hierarchical ladder. The latter served to underscore the rightness of the actions simply as things are "in Christ." Perhaps it carries the notion that, "As you and I, Philemon, stand together in Christ, you know that under His watchful gaze I could easily and rightly issue a command to you with regard to your reception of Onesimus." Such confidence is magnified even more for it is "great" (πολλὴν).

That which Paul could have confidently undertaken in Christ was "to order you to do what is proper" (ἐπιτάσσειν σοι τὸ ἀνῆκον). The present-tense infinitive (ἐπιτάσσειν, "to order") is a compound comprised of ἐπί ("upon") and τάσσω ("to assign/appoint"). The compound then means to order or command. Though the word is used ten times in the NT, surprisingly this is Paul's only usage. It is used of Jesus commanding the wind and waves (Luke 8:25), evil spirits (Mark 1:27; 9:25; Luke 4:36; 8:31), and crowds of

> **Ministry Maxim**
>
> What we *can* do is not always what we *should* do.

[1045] BAGD, 630.
[1046] Rienecker, 575.
[1047] BAGD, 630.

hungry people (Mark 6:39). It describes King Herod's orders to the executioner of John the Baptist (Mark 6:27), those of a master to a slave (Luke 14:22), and those of the High Priest, Ananias, to those who would strike Paul (Acts 23:2).

Clearly Paul felt, as an Apostle, he had the option of "laying down the law" to Philemon. The personal pronoun (σοι, "you") is singular, marking these words as individually addressed to Philemon. Only he, as Onesimus's master, could "do what is proper" (τὸ ἀνῆκον). The word is used impersonally in the NT and has the sense of that which is fitting or that which is one's duty.[1048] Such moral obligations extend to the arena of one's speech (Eph. 5:4) and one's relationships (Col. 3:18). Clearly Paul felt there was a course of action with regard to Onesimus to which Philemon as a follower of Christ was obligated. The world would likely have concluded, based on other allegiances, that an opposite course was required. Christ, however, turns the thinking of the world on its ear. The articular participle (τὸ ἀνῆκον, "what is proper") is used to express that which could be commanded.

Paul could easily have called out Philemon publicly, demanding what action he must take with regard to Onesimus, but, while assuring a certain course of action, it would not have yielded the lasting relationship that was even more desirable.

9 yet for love's sake I rather appeal to you — since I am such a person as Paul, the aged, and now also a prisoner of Christ Jesus —

Here then is the main verb of the sentence that began in verse 8 and extends through verse 14 (with colons at the end of verses 9 and 12): "I ... appeal" (παρακαλῶ). It is a compound word, coming from the verb καλέω ("to call") and the prepositional prefix παρά ("beside"). Woodenly rendered it might be translated "to call alongside." Paul uses it in every one of his letters except Galatians. Its range of meaning can swing from the softer sense of "comfort" to the sharper edge of "exhort." It is translated variously according to context by words such as "appeal" (Philem. 9, 10), "comfort" (2 Cor. 1:4, 6), "encourage" (1 Cor. 16:12), "exhort" (1 Cor. 1:10), "implore" (2 Cor. 12:8), and "urge" (Rom. 12:1). He has just used the cognate noun in verse 7 (παράκλησιν, "comfort"). The masculine singular

---

[1048]   Friberg, 55.

noun form became a title for the Holy Spirit (John 14:16, 26; 15:26; 16:7) and the Lord Jesus Christ (1 John 2:1).

Though Paul might have pulled rank on Philemon and ordered him to receive Onesimus (v. 8) his "appeal" is made "for love's sake" (διὰ τὴν ἀγάπην). The phrase might be more simply rendered "because [διὰ + the accusative] the love." Note the definite article with the noun—this is not just any love, but *the* "love" of all loves. This is the love which has been expressed to them by God in Christ and which now is to command their every thought, word, motive, and deed. This picks up on the use of the noun in verse 5 (Philemon's love toward all the saints) and verse 7

> **Ministry Maxim**
>
> Personal appeal may prove more powerful than authoritative command.

(Paul's own comfort in Philemon's love), hinting that Paul's carefully crafted introduction was intended to make way for the very appeal he introduces here. Paul says his "appeal" is "rather" (μᾶλλον) than the alternative of ordering Philemon with regard to Onesimus. The adverb modifies a verb which describes a course of action taken "instead" of an alternative course.[1049]

In what amounts to a parenthetical thought, the Apostle offers two appositional descriptions of himself (for other appositional descriptors in this letter see verses 10, 11, 12, 16, 19).[1050] They would seem to be offered to add weight to the appeal he is issuing. He says, "since I am such a person" (τοιοῦτος ὤν). The expression might simply be rendered "such a one being." It combines an adjective (τοιοῦτος, "such a person") and a present-tense participle (ὤν, "I am"). It could modify what has come before in verses 8 and 9a, in which case it would indicate Paul's decision to appeal to Philemon rather than command him. Yet it seems better to understand it as modifying Paul's description of himself which he is about to unfold.[1051] The participle itself may be either causal ("*since* I am," NASU) or concessive ("*although* I am").[1052]

He adds "as Paul the aged" (ὡς Παῦλος πρεσβύτης). Note the repeated use of the comparative particle ὡς ("as," cf. vv. 9, 14, 16, 17). It has here the idea of "in my character as."[1053] The noun translated "the aged" (πρεσβύτης)

[1049] BAGD, 489.
[1050] O'Brien, 289.
[1051] Harris, 259.
[1052] Ibid., O'Brien, 290; emphases added.
[1053] BAGD, 821.

refers to a man of some advanced age. Paul used the term elsewhere only in Titus 2:2 where it is a cognate of the term for "elders" (Titus 1:5), but does not designate an ecclesiastical office. It is also used to describe Zacharias when the angel appeared to him (Luke 1:18). Life in ancient times was divided into various stages of age, though there was not always agreement about when those stages began and ended. Philo used the word to speak of a man between 50 and 56 years of age.[1054] In Titus, Paul simply divided human age into two stages—"older" (2:2, 3) and "younger" (vv. 4, 6). The Apostle believed he was clearly a part of the older grouping. It has been estimated that Paul was about sixty years old at this time.[1055]

Paul has refused to call on his apostleship to back his directives with authority. Yet he appears to use this designation as a way of calling upon either Philemon's sympathies (don't withhold an old man's desire) or decency (respect your elders). Some prefer to render this as "ambassador," which would require either understanding πρεσβύτης as a alternate spelling of πρεσβευτής or taking this latter as the original reading with our current text understood as a corruption.[1056] Yet these seem to be unnecessary re-creations in an attempt to explain an otherwise nonexistent problem. It is argued further that if Paul wished to refer to himself as "the aged," he would have used definite articles both with his own name and the noun.[1057] Yet the anarthrous noun would seem only to underscore the qualitative nature of the reference (i.e., he does not use "the aged" as a title, but as a descriptor). Most English versions render it as a reference to the Apostle's age. The RSV rendered it "an ambassador," but the NRSV has "an old man" with a marginal note indicating that "an ambassador" is a possible rendering.

Added (δέ, "and") to Paul's advanced age is the fact that at present (νυνί, "now") he is "also a prisoner of Christ Jesus" (καὶ δέσμιος Χριστοῦ Ἰησοῦ). The expression "a prisoner of Christ Jesus" (δέσμιος Χριστοῦ Ἰησοῦ) is precisely the same as the one he used to open the letter (v. 1; cf. the prepositional phrase in v. 23). There are a variety of intricate possibilities with regard to how one might punctuate these lines. Harris offers a helpful

---

[1054] Ibid., 700.
[1055] Lenski, 961.
[1056] Harris, 259-260.
[1057] Ibid.

recap of those options.[1058] Paul mentions his status as "a prisoner" three times in this immediate context (vv. 9, 10, 13). Moo aptly observes that Paul "is doubly helpless: not only an old man, but an imprisoned old man."[1059]

10 I appeal to you for my child Onesimus, whom I have begotten in my imprisonment,

Having taken an aside via the long concession of verse 9b, Paul now returns to his main thought by repeating the main verb from verse 9a (παρακαλῶ, "I appeal"). The repetition serves not only to connect the line of thought to its original point, but also as a device to add emphasis to the Apostle's petition. What he left as simply understood in the previous verse, he now makes explicit—it is "to you" (σε, singular, i.e., Philemon) that his appeal is made.

Paul's appeal is "for my child" (περὶ τοῦ ἐμοῦ τέκνου). The preposition (περὶ, "for") normally would have the meaning "about" or "concerning," but here is more akin to ὑπέρ, meaning "on behalf of."[1060] The Apostle, of course, means to describe a deeply personal and spiritual bond between himself and Onesimus. The attributive position of the possessive adjective (ἐμοῦ, "my"), being tucked between the noun and its definite article, emphasizes the qualitative nature of the relationship. The possessive adjective makes more emphatic or powerful the sense of possession than would even the possessive pronoun.[1061]

Paul has proven he is not against such expressions of intimacy, having called Timothy "my true son in the faith" (1 Tim. 1:2, cf. v. 18), "my beloved son" (2 Tim. 1:2), "my son" (2:1), and "my beloved and faithful child in the Lord" (1 Cor. 4:17). He designated Titus "my true child in a common faith" (Titus 1:4). He called the Corinthian believers "my beloved children" (1 Cor. 4:14) and the Galatians "my children" (Gal. 4:19). He dealt with the Thessalonian believers as if they were his own children (1 Thess. 2:7, 11). Thus we can see that Onesimus had come under the tender care and influence of one who took seriously the bond formed by common faith and his responsibility in influencing those under his care. To Philemon Onesimus was a slave; to Paul he was "my child"!

[1058] Ibid., 260.
[1059] Moo, 406.
[1060] Harris, 261; Lohse, 199; Moo, 407; O'Brien, 290.
[1061] Harris, 261; Lenski, 962.

Despite the centrality of his place in the events that brought forth this letter, the name "Onesimus" (Ὀνήσιμον) occurs only here and in Colossians 4:9. There he is referred to as a "faithful and beloved brother, who is one of your number." His name is actually the last word of the verse, concerning which Harris says "in a delicate touch, Paul makes clear to Philemon the new status of Onesimus as a Christian before he mentions his name."[1062]

> **Ministry Maxim**
>
> Never let your physical circumstances dictate what you believe God can do.

While Paul could use the designation "my child" or "my son" somewhat freely, he refers uniquely here to Onesimus as one "whom I have begotten in my imprisonment" (ὃν ἐγέννησα ἐν τοῖς δεσμοῖς). The verb "I have begotten" (ἐγέννησα), when used literally, describes either a man becoming a father (Matt. 1:2) or a mother giving birth to a child (Luke 1:13). It enjoys a wide usage in metaphorical terms as well, as it does here. Paul uses the verb only seven times. He uses of it of literal, physical birth (Rom. 9:11; Gal. 4:23, 29). He also uses it to describe that which produces something else, whether it be an argument (2 Tim. 2:23) or a covenant (Gal. 4:24). But his usage here is more akin to how he employs it when he tells the Corinthian believers "in Christ Jesus I became your father through the gospel" (1 Cor. 4:15b).

Paul is indicating that he personally led Onesimus to faith in Christ. This would have put Onesimus and Philemon on common ground (cf. v. 19) as both being led to faith in Jesus Christ by the Apostle Paul—making brothers out of master and slave.[1063]

Though we could wish to know more detail concerning the conversion of Onesimus, all we are told is that this happened "in my imprisonment" (ἐν τοῖς δεσμοῖς). Did one of Paul's associates bump into Onesimus in the city of Rome and convince him to visit the Apostle in prison? Did Onesimus, so far now from home, seek out Paul on his own terms—perhaps out of loneliness, fear, or spiritual contrition? We do not know the circumstances of their meeting.

[1062] Harris, 261; cf. Lenski, 962; Lohse, 199; O'Brien, 290.
[1063] Lohse, 200; O'Brien, 291.

What is clear is that in a remarkable move of providence, God brought the two together in Rome, even in Paul's imprisonment, and used this to draw Onesimus to a saving relationship with God through Jesus Christ. The aorist tense of the verb used here points to that decisive moment of turning. The noun rendered "imprisonment" (δεσμοῖς) means simply "bond" or "fetter," but is often used, as it is here, as a metonymy for prison or imprisonment.[1064] The Apostle's words here prove what he would later write during his final imprisonment (and perhaps he thought of Onesimus even as he penned the words): "the word of God is not imprisoned" (2 Tim. 2:9). The messenger may be bound, "But God's word is not chained" (NIV).

The Apostle's words must have shaken Philemon. To Philemon, Onesimus was a thieving, runaway slave. To Paul, Onesimus was "my child" (and "my very heart," v. 12). Our labels for others are often misplaced, premature, or outdated. We must leave a place for grace to transform our conclusions about others.

11 who formerly was useless to you, but now is useful both to you and to me.

In a verbless clause which makes up this eleventh verse, the Apostle now speaks of the transformation of Onesimus by making wordplay on his name.

The name Onesimus means "useful" and was, for this reason, a common name among slaves of the first century.[1065] It may have been a burdensome name for Onesimus, for slaves from Phrygia (the region in which Colossae was located) notoriously carried a reputation of being lazy and worthless in productivity.[1066] In a play upon Onesimus's name (though using a different root word), Paul reminds Philemon that

> **Ministry Maxim**
>
> "Useful" is something we are made by grace, not something we are by nature.

his slave had once been "useless" (ἄχρηστον) to him. The adjective is used only here in the NT. It is formed by adding the α–privative to χράομαι ("to use").[1067] Paul does not explain in just what way Onesimus had once been "useless" to Philemon. He may have in mind the particular offense Onesimus

---

[1064] Friberg, 106.
[1065] BAGD, 570.
[1066] Lightfoot, 310.
[1067] Robertson, *Word Pictures*, 4:466-467.

committed in apparently stealing from Philemon and then running away, or he may have in mind a larger problem that existed prior to that event. Perhaps there had been strained relations between master and slave for some time— maybe over job performance. Any specificity remains a matter of speculation. What we do know is that "but now" (νυνὶ δὲ) a transformation has taken place within the runaway slave.

This transformation radically alters his relationship, says Paul, "both to you and to me" ([καὶ] σοὶ καὶ ἐμοὶ). The first instance of καὶ ("both") appears in a few manuscripts, but is missing in most. It could have been added later by copyists trying to conform it to νυνὶ δὲ καί ("but now also") in verse 9.[1068] If genuine it would underscore the double usefulness of Onesimus, "both" to Paul and to Philemon. Note the order in which Paul presents the advantage: "to you and to me" (σοὶ καὶ ἐμοὶ). In this way Paul may have aimed to underscore the priority of Philemon's relationship to Onesimus, even over his own, now dear, connection to the transformed slave.

To both parties Onesimus now had become "useful" (εὔχρηστον). The adjective is formed from the same root word (χράομαι, "to use") as the previous adjective, but has εὖ ("good") added as a prefix. The resulting adjective is used only three times in the NT, all by Paul. He uses it twice to speak of the characteristic of two individuals—Onesimus (here) and Mark (2 Tim. 4:11). Significantly, in both cases it described turnaround cases, in which individuals, for different reasons, once had been "useless," but had become "useful" in the end. The word points to that which is serviceable.[1069] Such a person has come to a position where he can be used to fulfill the purposes of God. Paul uses it also in 2 Timothy 2:21 to speak of the one who has fully dedicated himself to God and has thus become "useful to the Master" (εὔχρηστον τῷ δεσπότῃ). Clearly, none of us is naturally "useful" to God, but through the cleansing and sanctifying work of God we can be brought to that state by His grace. To be "useful" is the quest of every believer.

A second and far more subtle wordplay may be employed here as well. The root form of the two adjectives is χρηστός, which bears a striking resemblance to Χριστός ("Christ"). There is some evidence from other ancient usages to show that the two can be used in wordplay. Thus some commentators believe

---

[1068]   NET Bible.
[1069]   BAGD, 329.

that Paul is hinting at the fact that what made Onesimus's transformation from "useless" (ἄχρηστον) to "useful" (εὔχρηστον) was his conversion to faith in Christ (Χριστός).[1070] While surely this is Paul's point—as alluded to by the expression ποτέ ... νυνὶ δὲ ("formerly ... but now")—it is not clear that this was his intent by his use of these words in this particular context.[1071]

12 I have sent him back to you in person, that is, sending my very heart,

Though most English translations begin a new sentence here, the Greek text continues the sentence begun in verse 8 all the way through verse 14 (with colons at the ends of verses 9 and 12). The singular relative pronoun (ὄν) finds its antecedent in "Onesimus" in verse 10, with which it agrees in gender, case, and number. Onesimus, says Paul, "I have sent ... back" (ἀνέπεμψά). The verb is used only five times in the NT, the other four by Luke, three of those in the exchange between Pilate and Herod as they shuffled Jesus back and forth between them (Luke 23:7, 11, 15; Acts 25:21). It is a compound word comprised of ἀνά ("up/back/again") and πέμπω ("to send"). Some see here a technical meaning in which Paul is sending Onesimus back to Philemon (as to a higher authority) for him to render his verdict upon him and his actions. But it seems best to understand the verb in its simplest sense of "sent back." The aorist is epistolary, meaning that it might be translated as a present tense in English: "I am sending" (ESV, NIV, NKJV, NRSV, RSV).[1072] The direction of the sending is from Paul (spiritual father of Onesimus, Apostle, prisoner, old man) "to you" (σοι, Philemon—Onesimus's owner, master, and now fellow believer and spiritual brother).

> **Ministry Maxim**
>
> Risking my relationship with you for the sake of your relationship with another is proof of my love for you.

The NASU says that Paul sends Onesimus back "in person," which is a translation of the personal pronoun αὐτόν. Its appearance following the relative pronoun (ὄν) makes this an intensive use of this personal pronoun and thus the NASU's rendering is justified. Because it is difficult to bring

---

[1070] E.g., Dunn, 329; Lohse, 200; Wright, 182.
[1071] Lightfoot, 338; Moo, 409-410.
[1072] Rienecker, 660.

this emphasis over into English, most versions do not attempt to represent it in their translations.

Paul continues his thoughts regarding Onesimus, saying, "that is, ... my very heart" (τοῦτ' ἔστιν τὰ ἐμὰ σπλάγχνα). The NASU's "sending" is added by the translators in an attempt to make sense in English of a difficult Greek construction. A literal rendering might be "this one is the bowels of me." The demonstrative pronoun (τοῦτ', "that") is "used to call attention to a designated person or object, often with special emphasis."[1073] In this case, of course, it is Onesimus that it singles out. Its combination with the verb (ἔστιν, "is") becomes a standard way of saying "this/that is" in the NT.[1074]

Onesimus is "my very heart" (τὰ ἐμὰ σπλάγχνα), says the Apostle. Once again the possessive adjective is used (see verses 10 and 19) and it is emphatic here.[1075] Once again Paul uses the noun σπλάγχνον (lit., "bowels"; see verses 7 and 20). This is the only time in the NT that it is used in apposition to people.[1076] This probably led to a variety of textual variants using the verb προσλαβοῦ ("receive/accept") or the pronoun "you" (cf. KJV, NKJV). The difficult syntax of the verse may have motivated scribes to smooth the reading by the insertion of the verb, which is also found in verse 17.[1077]

By addressing the matter in the way he does here, the Apostle lays the burden of Philemon's response to Onesimus squarely upon his own relationship to Philemon, rather than resting its weight upon the relationship between Philemon and Onesimus.[1078] Köster says, "It is as if Paul, in the runaway slave, came to Philemon in person with his claim to experience love" (cf. "accept him as you would me," v. 17).[1079]

Though it seems tempting as a possibility, it appears unlikely that the regulations of the Mosaic Law had much bearing for the Apostle in the matter: "You shall not hand over to his master a slave who has escaped from his master to you. He shall live with you in your midst, in the place which

---

[1073] Friberg, 288.
[1074] BAGD, 223-224, 597.
[1075] Harris, 263.
[1076] NET Bible.
[1077] Ibid.
[1078] Moo, 411.
[1079] Quoted in O'Brien, 293.

he shall choose in one of your towns where it pleases him; you shall not mistreat him" (Deut. 23:15-16).[1080]

Digging Deeper:

1. Does Paul, by making mention of the authority he might have used, end up making use of it by mere suggestion (v. 8)?
2. What is love able to produce that authoritative command never can (v. 9)? Why is this so? How might this apply to your current ministry?
3. When is an appeal to one's negative circumstances ("the aged ... a prisoner," v. 9) a legitimate motivational device, and when does it become manipulative?
4. How does Onesimus exemplify that "useful" is something you *become by grace*, not *are by nature* (v. 11)? How might this perspective help you with some of the folks you shepherd right now? How might it help you view yourself?
5. To Philemon, Onesimus was a runaway slave and thief. To Paul he was "my child" (v. 10) and "my very heart" (v. 12). How might someone else label a person you have negative emotions toward right now? How does God label them?

---

13 whom I wished to keep with me, so that on your behalf he might minister to me in my imprisonment for the gospel;

The sentence in Greek has a colon at the end of verse 12, but the thought continues on here with a relative pronoun ("Ον, "whom") referring back to Onesimus ('Ονήσιμον, v. 10; as the same pronoun does at the beginning of v. 12), with whom it agrees in gender, case and number.

It was Onesimus, Paul says, "I wished to keep with me" (ἐγὼ ἐβουλόμην πρὸς ἐμαυτὸν κατέχειν). The "I" (ἐγὼ) is emphatic, perhaps stressing that it was Paul who is to blame for any delay in the return of Onesimus.[1081] The imperfect form of the verb (ἐβουλόμην, "I wish"), though understood by

---

[1080] Moo, 411; Wright, 182; though see Bruce, *Paul, Apostle of the Heart Set Free*, 399-400.
[1081] Dunn, 330.

387

some as epistolary[1082] (like the aorist tense verb of v. 12; i.e., written as if from the position of the arrival of the letter), is probably best understood as underscoring the ongoing nature of Paul's desire in the past, a desire subsequently set aside.[1083] This was no passing fancy, but an enduring desire on the part of the Apostle. The middle voice highlights the inward nature of Paul's struggle as he determined what he should do with Onesimus and the circumstances that circled around him.

The verb used here (βούλομαι, "I wished") is different from the one he will use in verse 14 (θέλω, "I did not *want*," emphasis added). As Thayer points out, the distinction between the two is that "the former seems to designate the will which follows deliberation, the latter the will which proceeds from inclination."[1084] That is to say βούλομαι expresses more strongly than θέλω the "deliberate exercise of the will."[1085] It describes "choice, purpose, or intention and desire or longing."[1086] Given that θέλω is used five times more frequently in the NT than βούλομαι, it would seem Paul had good reasons for using the verb he did in this case.[1087] Thus we may conclude that Paul is not describing here merely a "wish" he felt with regard to Onesimus, but a strong impulse for which he felt he could have marshaled firm foundations.[1088] The Apostle had carefully considered this possible course of action. That which Paul may have felt he had good reason to follow was "to keep" (κατέχειν) Onesimus. The present infinitive renders a word that is a compound: κατά ("down") and ἔχω ("to have/hold"). Here it has the notion of "hold back, hinder, prevent from going away."[1089] But it is not so much a withholding of Onesimus from Philemon that is pictured, but a keeping or holding of him "with me" (πρὸς ἐμαυτὸν).

That which stood behind Paul's inclination to keep Onesimus with him is now stated (ἵνα, "so that"): "on your behalf he might minister to me" (ὑπὲρ σοῦ μοι διακονῇ). The preposition ὑπὲρ ("on your behalf")

[1082]   Robertson, *Word Pictures*, 4:467.
[1083]   Harris, 263.
[1084]   Thayer, 286.
[1085]   Vine, 301, 1240-1241.
[1086]   Mounce, 773.
[1087]   Thayer, 286.
[1088]   Kitchen, *The Pastoral Epistles for Pastors*, 96-97.
[1089]   BAGD, 422.

underscores the notion of substitution.[1090] It means "in place of," "instead

of," "or "in the name of" another.[1091] If Philemon
(σοῦ, "your") had been present with Paul, he would
have surely ministered to his needs. Circumstances,
however, prevented that. But God in His providence
had put Onesimus there in Philemon's place. His
actions, had he been retained by the Apostle, would
have been done in Philemon's stead. At a time when
surely Philemon would have been bent on seeing
the vast differences between himself and Onesimus,
the Apostle was emphasizing their similarities—

Ministry Maxim
An ally may be found in the most unexpected of persons—don't judge too quickly the value of any person.

even to the point that Onesimus could fairly stand in Philemon's place.

The subjunctive mood of the verb (διακονῇ, "he might minister") is
used with the preposition (ἵνα) to form a purpose statement. The verb
itself is often translated generally with words like "serve" or "minister"
(e.g., Matt. 4:11; Luke 10:45). It was used originally to describe waiting
upon tables (e.g., Matt. 8:15; Luke 10:40; 12:37; John 12:2; Acts 6:2). It
is used also of the ministry of deacons (1 Tim. 3:10, 13), but is frequently
used more generally (e.g., 2 Tim. 1:18). Note that the two personal pronouns are juxtaposed one over against the other for emphasis (σοῦ μοι),
(lit., "of you to me").

Paul says Onesimus might have filled this role (in Philemon's stead) "in
my imprisonment for the gospel" (ἐν τοῖς δεσμοῖς τοῦ εὐαγγελίου). The
expression is more literally, "in the bonds/imprisonment of the gospel." The
noun (τοῖς δεσμοῖς, "imprisonment") was just used in verse 10 (see our
comments there).

The question becomes just how to understand the genitive (τοῦ
εὐαγγελίου, "of the gospel"). Moo is quick to point out that the genitive here
is difficult to classify.[1092] Should it be understood subjectively ("the imprisonment because of the gospel") or objectively ("the gospel's imprisonment")?
Clearly it cannot be the latter, for, as Paul said in his final letter (using this
very noun), "the word of God is not imprisoned" (2 Tim. 2:9). The genitive

---

[1090]   Wallace, 387.
[1091]   BAGD, 838.
[1092]   Moo, 415.

may be, then, understood as subjective: "indicating that his bonds arise from the gospel."[1093] It is possible that it could also be understood as a genitive of source,[1094] origin,[1095] reference/relation,[1096] or some combination of these. In comparing the subjective genitive and the genitive of origin, O'Brien says, "Probably both nuances are included and there is no need to choose between these alternatives."[1097]

14 but without your consent I did not want to do anything, so that your goodness would not be, in effect, by compulsion but of your own free will.

Paul had given thought to acting unilaterally and retaining Onesimus for his own personal benefit, maybe sending a letter of explanation to Philemon (v. 13). In contrast (δὲ, "but") to this contemplated course of action Paul says, "without your consent I did not want to do anything" (χωρὶς ... τῆς σῆς γνώμης οὐδὲν ἠθέλησα ποιῆσαι). The word translated "without" (χωρὶς) is an adverb used as an improper preposition and could mean either "apart fr[om] someone's activity or assistance" or "apart fr[om] the presence of someth[ing]."[1098] That without which Paul did not want to proceed was "your consent" (τῆς σῆς γνώμης). The noun has a broad usage, but here seems to describe "previous knowledge" or, as it is rendered here, "consent."[1099] Thus it indicates "not just agreement to a course of action, but agreement that arises from a considered opinion about the matter."[1100] The definite article (τῆς) and the possessive adjective (σῆς, "your") in the attributive position makes particular, specific, and emphatic that "consent" of which Paul is speaking.

Without this, says Paul, "I did not want to do anything" (οὐδὲν ἠθέλησα ποιῆσαι). In expressing his desire Paul uses a different verb here (ἠθέλησα, "I ... want") than he did in verse 13 (ἐβουλόμην, "I wished"). See our discussion there for the difference between the verbs. The tenses Paul chose in each case are significant. Whereas Paul chose an imperfect in

---

[1093] Moo, 415; Rienecker, 660.
[1094] Moo, 415.
[1095] Kent, 195; Lightfoot, 339.
[1096] Harris, 264; Lohse, 202.
[1097] O'Brien, 294.
[1098] BAGD, 890.
[1099] Ibid., 163.
[1100] Moo, 415.

verse 13 (describing his ongoing desire in the past), here he uses the aorist tense (which points to a specific decision). O'Brien says that the imperfect "describes a desire which Paul felt for a time while … [the] aorist, indicates his actual decision."[1101] Lightfoot adds, "The imperfect implies a tentative, inchoate process; while the aorist describes a definite and complete act."[1102] Paul had carefully considered his options; now he wanted Philemon to do the same before coming to a decision regarding Onesimus. The infinitive (ποιῆσαι, "to do") is also in the aorist tense, underscoring the emphasis of its main verb. The negation is categorical and absolute (οὐδὲν, "did not … anything").[1103]

Paul had apparently given significant thought to the possibility of retaining Onesimus at his side, a move that he may have been able to justify in his own mind. But he made a determination that he would not undertake such a course without first allowing Philemon the same process of thought and decision. Lightfoot says it so well: "The will stepped in and put an end to the inclinations of the mind."[1104]

This course was chosen to avoid a specific outcome (ἵνα μὴ, "so that … not"). The construction forms a negative purpose statement ("in order that … not," ESV). That which Paul wanted was that Philemon's "goodness would not be, in effect, by compulsion" (ὡς κατὰ ἀνάγκην τὸ ἀγαθόν σου ᾖ). The preposition (κατὰ, "by") describes "homogeneity" or conformity and can mean "*according to, in accordance with, in conformity with, corresponding to.*"[1105] But in this case that notion is combined with the idea of reason for an action, "so that *in accordance with* and *because of* are merged."[1106] The noun (ἀνάγκην) describes a "compulsion of any kind, outer or inner, brought about by the nature of things, a divine dispensation, some hoped-for advantage, custom, duty, etc."[1107] The entire phrase (ὡς κατὰ ἀνάγκην) could thus be rendered "as it were, by compulsion"[1108] or, as in the NASU, "in effect, by compulsion." The conjunction ὡς ("as"),

---

[1101] O'Brien, 293.
[1102] Lightfoot, 339.
[1103] Thayer, 408, 462.
[1104] Lightfoot, 339.
[1105] BAGD, 407.
[1106] Ibid.
[1107] Ibid., 52.
[1108] Ibid; NASB 1978.

placed as it is before κατὰ ἀνάγκην ("by compulsion"), "marks the *appearance* of necessity. Philemon's kindly reception of Onesimus must not even *seem* to be constrained."[1109]

That which is not to be coerced is "your goodness" (τὸ ἀγαθόν σου). The neuter definite article and adjective are used as a noun.[1110] The genitive

> **Ministry Maxim**
>
> Actions can be forced, but goodness can not.

pronoun (σου, "your") is rendered as possessive. This act of "goodness" has not yet been specified. Soon enough it will become clear that what Paul is calling for by way of "goodness" from Philemon is his glad and forgiving reception of Onesimus, indeed, a welcome that would be fitting for Paul himself (v. 17), perhaps even with the notion of Philemon then generously commissioning Onesimus to return to Paul's side as an aide to him in his ministry (vv. 13, 20-21).[1111]

Rather than coercion, Paul had another outcome in mind. By using the strong adversative (ἀλλὰ, "but"), Paul signals how powerful the set of his will had become in this matter. Instead of backing him into a corner, the Apostle tells Philemon that he wanted his actions to be "of your own free will" (κατὰ ἑκούσιον). Again he uses the preposition (κατὰ, "of") as he did in the previous clause. The adjective translated "free will" (ἑκούσιον) is used substantivally. It is found only here in the NT, but it appears in the LXX to describe a "freewill offering" (Num. 15:3; cf. the root adjective [ἑκών] in Rom. 8:20 and 1 Cor. 9:17). Paul wishes for willingness on Philemon's part, "as opposed to legal compulsion."[1112]

Forced goodness is not goodness at all, but mere moral conformity. Moral conformity may indeed be enforced, but moral goodness requires a change of heart. This is what the Apostle was seeking for Philemon. The slave's (Onesimus) heart had been transformed; now Paul was seeking a change in the heart of the master (Philemon).

[1109] Vincent, *Word Studies*, 3:521; cf. Lightfoot, 340; Lohse, 202; Moo, 416; O'Brien, 294.
[1110] Harris, 265.
[1111] Ibid.
[1112] BAGD, 243.

Digging Deeper:

1. What does Paul's processing of his desire (through thorough consideration) and his ultimate decision tell us about how to handle our own wishes and decisions in life and ministry?

2. How does Paul's method of gentle suggestion and personal respect illuminate the way for you in dealing with some difficult interpersonal circumstances right now?

3. How does the power of individual choice transform a person's actions? What does this suggest concerning your current challenges with others?

---

15 For perhaps he was for this reason separated from you for a while, that you would have him back forever,

Paul moves to explain further (γὰρ, "for") his reasoning for sending Onesimus back to Philemon. The first word in the sentence (Τάχα, "perhaps) is an adverb used in the NT only here and in Romans 5:7. It means perhaps, possibly, or probably.[1113] Paul employs it to offer gently a suggestion as to the possible purpose (διὰ τοῦτο, "for this reason"; pointing forward to the argument to be made in the second half of the verse[1114]) behind Onesimus' flight.

The verb (ἐχωρίσθη, "he was ... separated") in the active voice means divide or separate, but in the passive voice, as it is here, it means "*be taken away, take one's departure, go away.*"[1115] The aorist tense looks back to the event of separation. The passive voice pictures the subject (Onesimus) being acted upon. But this probably is not intended to say someone forcibly removed him from Philemon's home (i.e., stole him). More likely it pictures "the divine overruling and would be parallel to the 'divine pass[ive]' in Heb[rew] which was a mode of expression to denote the hidden action of God as an agent responsible for what is done."[1116]

[1113] Friberg, 375.
[1114] Wallace, 333.
[1115] BAGD, 890.
[1116] Rienecker, 660; cf. Harris, 265; Lightfoot, 335; Lohse, 202-203; Moo, 419; O'Brien, 295.

Commentators are quick to illustrate this verse by the example of Joseph, who was sold with evil intent by his brothers into slavery in Egypt.[1117] Yet in time Joseph came to see God's hand in all that transpired. "I am your brother Joseph, whom *you sold* into Egypt. Now do not be grieved or angry with yourselves, because *you sold me* here, for *God sent me* before you to preserve life .... *God sent me* before you to preserve for you a remnant in the earth, and to keep you alive by a great deliverance. Now, therefore, it *was not you who sent me* here, *but God*; and He has made me a father to Pharaoh and lord of all his household and ruler over all the land of Egypt" (Gen. 45:4b-5, 7-8, emphases added). Even further down the road Joseph would tell them, "As for you, *you meant evil* against me, but *God meant it for good* in order to bring about this present result, to preserve many people alive" (Gen. 50:20, emphases added).

It seems probable, then, that Onesimus himself initiated the separation (for what precise reason, we are not told), fleeing from the home of Philemon and in his flight finding his way to Rome and eventually, by some means we are unable to trace precisely, to the Apostle Paul. This separation, suggests Paul, was only "for a while" (πρὸς ὥραν) or, more literally, "for an hour." What Philemon (and perhaps Onesimus himself) thought was permanent, was, in the plan of God, only momentary. It ran with purpose in a direction none of them could have anticipated.

Now Paul is explicit as to the higher, divine purpose (ἵνα + subjunctive, "that") behind all these tumultuous events: "you would have him back forever" (αἰώνιον αὐτὸν ἀπέχῃς). The pronoun (αὐτὸν, "him") matches in case, gender, and number the one in verse 12 which in turn finds its antecedent in Onesimus ('Ονήσιμον, v. 10). The verb ("you would have .... back," ἀπέχῃς) is a compound word made up of "from" (ἀπό) and "to hold" (ἔχω). It was used as a technical term in commercial contexts to mean "*receive* a sum *in full* and give a receipt for it."[1118] Some interpret this as indication that Philemon will set Onesimus free; having received him back he can now free him forever. But

> **Ministry Maxim**
>
> Ultimate purposes are seldom easily identified nor found on the surface of things.

[1117] E.g., Moo, 419; O'Brien, 295; Wright, 185.
[1118] BAGD, 84-85.

it is not clear that Paul is using the term in its technical sense, for the construction of the sentence is unique, indicating that Paul may be using the verb in a more general sense.[1119]

O'Brien suggests that Paul may use the term simply because in the first century slaves were considered property.[1120] The notion here may be simply "to keep" or "to keep for one's self."[1121] The present tense probably points to continuous action. The verb is used by Paul only four other times (Phil. 4:18; 1 Thess. 4:3; 5:22; 1 Tim. 4:3).

Paul suggests that this humanly unforeseen, but divinely engineered, reunion may now last "forever" (αἰώνιον). In this context this may mean merely "for good" or "permanently,"[1122] but it is easy to see that Paul may have something even more enduring in mind (as the next verse will make clear). What had been a relationship limited to the temporal and commercial plane has in the grace of God become an eternal one as Onesimus and Philemon find themselves united as brothers in Christ, indwelt and bound together by the same eternal Spirit. Thus "forever" (αἰώνιον) stands in direct contrast to "for a while" (πρὸς ὥραν).

However much we might wish Paul to do so (to help clear the air on his views on slavery in general), he is not making a statement either about Philemon's obligation to free Onesimus or about the slave's obligation to remain permanently with his master. He is focusing on the transformation of a life and one of its relationships through the miracle of new birth in which both master and slave now share. The societal challenges and changes must arise from internal and spiritual transformation.

16 no longer as a slave, but more than a slave, a beloved brother, especially to me, but how much more to you, both in the flesh and in the Lord.

Paul continues the sentence, expanding upon just how Philemon would "have … back" (v. 15) Onesimus. The conjunction (ὡς, "as") sets up the comparison about to be made. The strength of this comparison is drawn out by the combination of the adverb οὐκέτι ("no longer") and the strong

---

[1119] Moo, 420.
[1120] O'Brien, 296.
[1121] Rienecker, 660.
[1122] Moule, 146.

adversative conjunction ἀλλ' ("but"). The adverb denies the matter simply and categorically.[1123] Lightfoot says, "The 'no more a slave' is an absolute fact, whether Philemon chooses to recognize it or not."[1124] When Onesimus fled the home of Philemon, he was simply "a slave" (δοῦλον)—a being without personal rights or the power of self-determination. But now, upon Onesimus's return, Philemon finds him "more than a slave" (ὑπὲρ δοῦλον). The preposition (ὑπὲρ, "more than") here has the sense of excelling or surpassing and might be translated "over and above, beyond, more than" a slave.[1125] This means that, as O'Brien says, "whether Onesimus remained a slave or not, he could no longer be regarded *as* a slave."[1126]

Something had happened to Onesimus in Rome which transformed him, and not only transformed him as an individual, but was so thoroughgoing that it must of necessity redefine the relationship between himself and his master. Indeed, through faith in Jesus Christ, Onesimus had become "a beloved brother" (ἀδελφὸν ἀγαπητόν). Paul has already used the same noun (ἀδελφὸν, "brother") to refer to his relationship with Philemon (v. 7) and will do so yet again (v. 20). So too he refers to Timothy (v. 1).

What a shock it must have been to Philemon—who no doubt had built up a case against Onesimus in his heart and mind during his absence—to hear the Apostle refer to him in this way! He was not merely "a brother," but "a *beloved* (ἀγαπητόν) brother." This is precisely how Paul addressed Philemon in the salutation to this letter (v. 1). With the simple sweep of his quill, the Apostle put both master and slave on the same relational ground before himself. This is both an act of great grace (to Onesimus) and a subtle rebuke (to Philemon).

This new standing of Onesimus as "a beloved brother," says Paul, is "especially to me" (μάλιστα ἐμοί). The adverb "especially" (μάλιστα) is a superlative of the adverb μάλα which means "very" or "very much."[1127] It is used here as an elative and points to "the highest point in the extent of something" and means something like "most of all," "especially," or "above all."[1128]

[1123] Thayer, 462.

[1124] Lightfoot, 341.

[1125] BAGD, 839.

[1126] O'Brien, 297.

[1127] BAGD, 488; Harris, 267.

[1128] Friberg, 252.

Because of the uniqueness of Onesimus's appearance in Paul's presence in his imprisonment in Rome and because of the clear hand of God upon his life and all the circumstances relating to his conversion (v. 10), the Apostle clearly feels a special and unique bond to this man. It may have been some source of pride or secondhand dignity to Philemon to have enjoyed a close relationship with the Apostle Paul (or at least to be receiving a personal letter from him, one read before the entire church!). But now his own slave—a runaway, problem slave—stands before him with written testimony of an intimacy of relationship with this very apostle which surpasses even something that he himself enjoyed with Paul.

The humbling effect upon Philemon must have been massive. But the superlative language used to describe Onesimus's relationship to Paul is now surpassed by the language used to describe his new relationship to Philemon himself: "but how much more to you" (πόσῳ δὲ μᾶλλον σοί). The combination of the interrogative adjective (πόσῳ, meaning something like "how great?") and the adverb (μᾶλλον) sends the comparison over the top. Lightfoot says, "Having first said 'most of all to me', he goes a step further, 'more than most of all to thee.'"[1129] Now, not only has Paul elevated Onesimus to a status parallel that of Philemon, but he has elevated the slave to a status

> **Ministry Maxim**
>
> The gospel resets all our relationships—so don't be surprised by the hard work it creates for you.

with Philemon that is greater even than that which he enjoys with Paul himself. This is grace—masterful, reconciling grace.

This new status functions in two realms—"both in the flesh and in the Lord" (καὶ ἐν σαρκὶ καὶ ἐν κυρίῳ). The double use of the conjunction (και ... καὶ, "both ... and") provides the framework of the comparison. The preposition (ἐν) may, in each instance, point to the sphere of the relationships—the sphere of the human, earthly relationships and the sphere of standing together before and in the presence of their common Lord. Thus by "in the flesh" (ἐν σαρκὶ) Paul seems to mean "as to earthly, human relationships—as slave to master," and by "in the Lord" (ἐν κυρίῳ) he seems to mean "as both standing before an infinitely greater Master."

[1129] Lightfoot, 341.

This emphasis serves as a reminder that no life—especially that of a Christ follower—is fully defined by their earthly, human relationships. It further reminds us that we do live in a double sphere—upon the earth in tangible realities and in the spiritual world in which Christ has rewritten the nature of our relationships. The spiritual rules the natural, but interestingly Paul does not draw out in detail just what this must mean for Philemon and Onesimus. Harris states it well: "Nowhere in the letter does Paul demand the release of Onesimus or even assume that Philemon will set him free. But although the apostle accepts slavery as a social condition and as a legal fact (he returns Onesimus to his rightful owner with a promissory note to cover any indebtedness), he indirectly undermines the institution of slavery by setting the master-slave relation on a new footing when he highlights Onesimus's true status as a dearly loved Christian brother."[1130]

The fact that Onesimus is now a believer in Christ does not change the fact that as he stands before Philemon at this moment, he remains his slave. But the fact that he is now a fellow believer with Philemon does transform the nature of the master-slave relationship—and, indeed, may move Philemon to release Onesimus from that relationship, though Paul does not overtly demand this. Rather than demanding that the new relationship to Christ—now shared by both master and slave—dissolve the already-standing human relationship, Paul indicates that it should transform it. God changes our relationships not primarily by subtraction (insisting that the slave's new relationship to Christ dissolves the master-slave relationship), but by addition (the newly shared spiritual relationship both have with Christ).

This is a reminder that we must first read the text of Scripture from the vantage point of its original author and readers, not from our own cultural context. Would Paul have spoken differently about slavery if he were writing the letter from nineteenth- or twentieth-century America? We do not know. Paul wasn't addressing the institution of slavery—even as it stood in the first century. He was addressing two particular lives—men he knew and both of whom he loved. He acted pastorally, not legislatively or as a social engineer. How he counseled them laid the foundation for a wider and much-needed social transformation.

[1130] Harris, 268.

We freight the Apostle's letter with baggage it was not designed to bear if we read it as a tract on different issues in different times. The desired transformation will be found at the *application* level (of the enduring and unchanging principles exhibited here while dealing with a unique, local, personal situation), not at the *interpretation* level (in an attempt to make Paul speak to circumstances which were not in his view at the time).

Digging Deeper:

1. What does Paul's tentativeness in drawing ultimate conclusions about the purpose of things (v. 15) suggest about our attempts to do so in our own lives or those of others?

2. How does Paul's contrast between the temporal/momentary ("for a while," v. 15a) and the lasting/eternal ("forever," v. 15b) guide us in dealing with galling circumstances in our own ministries?

3. Onesimus's transformation from a "slave" to "more than a slave, a beloved brother" demanded a difficult change in Philemon as well. Where does a change in another demand change in you or in the flock you lead? How and why is this change painful?

---

17 If then you regard me a partner, accept him as you would me.

Using the inferential conjunction (οὖν, "then"), Paul now draws a conclusion based upon the line of thought expressed above.[1131] Earlier the Apostle mentioned he had an "appeal" to make of Philemon (v. 10). He is finally about to spell it out. His conclusion is built upon a condition—one which he considered as already fulfilled: "If ... you regard me as a partner" (εἰ ... με ἔχεις κοινωνόν). The conditional conjunction (εἰ, "If") with the present indicative verb (ἔχεις, "you regard") forms a first-class condition, which is assumed to be true. The verb (ἔχεις, "regard") means simply, "have" or "hold." Perhaps the latter is the meaning here. Paul assumes, based on their relationship, that Onesimus considers Paul "a partner" (κοινωνόν). The term signifies "one who fellowships and shares something in common

---

[1131]   Moo, 425; contra, Harris, 271; Lohse, 203; O'Brien, 298.

with another."[1132] As Lightfoot says, it describes those "who have common interests, common feelings, common work."[1133] The kindred noun was used in verse 6 as Paul described his prayers for Philemon.

The protasis having been set forth, the Apostle now lays down the apodosis: "accept him as you would me" (προσλαβοῦ αὐτὸν ὡς ἐμέ.). Here we meet the first of three imperatives (vv. 17, 18, 20b) with which Paul draws the main body of the letter to a close.[1134] The aorist imperative demands action be taken immediately. The verb (προσλαβοῦ, "accept") is a compound made up of λαμβάνω ("to take/receive") and πρός ("to"). It can have a technical meaning of "receive or accept in one's society, in(to) one's home or circle of acquaintances."[1135] Paul uses it only four other times, either of God's reception of sinners (Rom. 14:3; 15:7b) or of Christians receiving one another (Rom. 14:1; 15:7a). The middle voice conveys the notion of "receive to yourself."[1136] The one to be thus accepted is Onesimus (αὐτὸν, "him"). The manner of the acceptance is "as ... me" (ὡς ἐμέ). The NASU translators add "you would" to smooth out the English rendering, but it is literally and simply "as me." It is not merely that Philemon should receive Onesimus in the same manner he would receive the Apostle Paul. It is that he should receive Onesimus as if he were Paul himself. It is as if Paul said, "Do not just treat him as you would me, but as if I myself had shown up at your door." Philemon was no longer to treat Onesimus as a mere slave, but as the Apostle of Christ with whom he shared all their relational history. After all, in sending Onesimus the Apostle says he is sending "my very heart" (v. 12).

> **Ministry Maxim**
>
> A good shepherd risks his own relationships to create Christ-honoring relationships between others.

Philemon was to Paul beloved (1), a fellow-worker (1), and brother (7). This should be the basis and starting point, then, for Philemon's new relationship to Onesimus.

Could the Apostle have found a more powerful way of making certain that Philemon did the right thing with regard to Onesimus, his past offenses,

---

[1132] Friberg, 233.
[1133] Lightfoot, 341.
[1134] Cf. also the optative of v. 20a, which clearly lays the Apostle's wish upon Philemon's will.
[1135] BAGD, 717.
[1136] Robertson, *Word Pictures*, 4:468.

his slavery, and his new standing as a brother in Christ? By this means Paul put Philemon's response purely upon spiritual, relational ground. Paul did not argue the abolition of slavery in theoretical terms; he did what he could on the personal level to eliminate its injustices by means of the gospel and its power to liberate both master and slave.

18 But if he has wronged you in any way or owes you anything, charge that to my account;

As in verse 17, the sentence begins with a conditional clause of the first class (εἰ, "if")—one which is assumed to be true. The postpositive conjunction (δέ) is normally either translated as it is here with an adversative ("But," NASU, NKJV) or is left untranslated (ESV, KJV, NIV, NLT, RSV, NRSV). That which Paul assumes to be the case is twofold.

First is the concern that "he has wronged you in any way" (τι ἠδίκησέν σε). The verb, when used intransitively, views the doing of wrong as a violation of a law, whether it is human or divine. Here, it probably has the sense of "injure."[1137] The aorist tense has in view the specific offense that Onesimus may have committed against Philemon (σε, "you"). Just what this may point to is uncertain, and Paul uses the indefinite pronoun (τι, "in any way") to generalize the reference and point to any and every wrong that could be imagined.

> **Ministry Maxim**
>
> A Christ follower, following his Master, willingly absorbs the debt of another in order to set them free.

Second (ἤ, "or") is the concern over whether Onesimus "owes you anything" (ὀφείλει). Paul has in mind any negative financial consequences for Philemon because of Onesimus's actions.[1138] The present tense of the verb pictures this as an outstanding, unresolved debt that has fallen to Philemon. Taken together, the two verbs may indicate that Onesimus had stolen from his master. Perhaps he did this as he fled the house, so as to have some means for his travels. Or maybe he fled because his theft had been discovered. This is the more traditional reconstruction of the events behind Onesimus's absence from Philemon and the cause of this letter. It is

---

[1137] BAGD, 17.
[1138] Ibid., 598.

possible, however, that Paul refers not to something stolen, but to the value of the labor lost while Onesimus was away.[1139]

Whatever the precise details may have been, Paul tells Philemon "charge that to my account" (τοῦτο ἐμοὶ ἐλλόγα). The verb is a commercial technical term.[1140] Its only other use in the NT is in Romans 5:13 where Paul declares "sin is not imputed [ἐλλογεῖται] when there is no law." The present-tense imperative calls for repeated or habitual action. The Apostle wanted the debt to fall to him (ἐμοὶ, "to me") now and forever.

Just how the Apostle would make good on the debt is purely a matter of speculation. Did Paul have a reserve of personal wealth? Did he have wealthy supporters upon whom he could call? Was he simply confident that Philemon would never require payment from him? We simply do not know. What is clear is the Apostle's willingness to assume responsibility for any debt the slave-and-now-brother Onesimus had outstanding with his master-brother Philemon.

19 I, Paul, am writing this with my own hand, I will repay it (not to mention to you that you owe to me even your own self as well).

Paul wants to make emphatic his offer and intent to pay for any financial hardship that Onesimus has caused Philemon (v. 18). To that end he first testifies to the genuineness of this letter: "I, Paul, am writing this with my own hand" (ἐγὼ Παῦλος ἔγραψα τῇ ἐμῇ χειρί). The emphatic personal pronoun (ἐγώ, "I") and his name (Παῦλος, "Paul") serve as a kind of authentication of his vow to repay any debt that Onesimus may have before Philemon (cf. 2 Cor. 10:1; Gal. 5:2; Eph. 3:1; Col. 1:23). The verb (ἔγραψα, "am writing") is an epistolary aorist—the author writing from the vantage point of the reader. The ink is applied to the parchment "with my own hand" (τῇ ἐμῇ χειρί). Paul's usual course of action may have been to have an amanuensis take down the letter at his dictation (e.g., Rom. 16:22; 1 Cor. 16:21; Col. 4:18; 2 Thess. 3:17). Some interpret this expression as a signal that Paul personally wrote the entire letter[1141] (perhaps because of the intensely personal nature of the correspondence and perhaps because of the

---

[1139] Lenski, 968-969; Lohse, 204; O'Brien, 299-300.
[1140] BAGD, 252.
[1141] Lightfoot, 342.

legality of including this very statement); others conclude that this signals only that he wrote this portion "with [his] own hand" (cf. Gal. 6:11).[1142] Still others say that this gives no clear signal either way.[1143]

That which draws forth this handwritten notice from the Apostle is his statement "I will repay it" (ἐγὼ ἀποτίσω). Again we meet the emphatic personal pronoun (ἐγώ, "I"). The verb (ἀποτίσω, "will repay") is used only here in the NT. It is a compound made up of ἀπό (here meaning "back" or perhaps "in full"[1144]) and τίνω ("pay"). It is a legal technical term referring to "damages to be paid off."[1145] Paul is underscoring the seriousness of his command in verse 18 ("charge that to my account") and offering proof of his intent to follow through. This letter, then, serves as Paul's promissory note[1146] or IOU.[1147] He does not intend the fulfillment of his promise to be indefinitely delayed, for Paul intends to come personally to Philemon upon his release from prison (v. 22).

Now Paul adds what the NASU regards as a parenthetical statement: "(not to mention to you that you owe to me even your own self as well)" (ἵνα μὴ λέγω σοι ὅτι καὶ σεαυτόν μοι προσοφείλεις). Some other translations mark it off as an ellipsis, using a dash to separate it from the main body of the sentence (ESV, NIV, NKJV, RSV). Still others set it apart with a colon (KJV) or as an independent sentence in English (NET, NLT, NRSV). Harris calls this as an example of paralipsis—a literary device where the writer feigns to pass over something that he then states plainly (cf. 2 Cor. 9:4).[1148]

Paul uses a negative purpose statement (ἵνα μὴ; cf. v. 14) to make his point. The verb is a compound form of the one just used in verse 18 (ὀφείλει, "owes"). It is made up of πρός ("to/toward/with") and ὀφείλω ("owe") and means "owe besides" or "owe in return."[1149] By saying "you owe to me even your own self," Paul doubtless refers to Philemon's very standing as a follower of Christ, with all its attendant hopes, graces, and benefits.

[1142] Dunn, 339-340.
[1143] Lohse, 204; O'Brien, 300.
[1144] Harris, 273.
[1145] Friberg, 72.
[1146] Robertson, *Word Pictures*, 4:468.
[1147] O'Brien, 300.
[1148] Harris, 274.
[1149] Friberg, 335.

Apparently the Apostle led Philemon to faith in Christ, probably during his extended ministry in Ephesus (Acts 19:10), which is the capital of the province of Asia Minor where Colossae is found. Details are not provided to us.

Ministry Maxim

All our demands for justice are to be measured against our own enjoyment of grace.

Paul, then, appears to be genuine in his willingness to personally take on any debt that Onesimus has before Philemon, but in his calculations he wants Philemon to take in the full sphere of all benefits gained and lost within the triangle of these relationships. Onesimus may owe Philemon something monetary, but Philemon owes Paul something money can never buy. In this regard it is instructive to read the parable of the unmerciful steward as background to the Apostle's words to Philemon (Matt. 18:21-35). Note especially Jesus' final words, after describing the torture the unmerciful steward eventually received: "This is how my heavenly Father will treat each of you unless you forgive your brother from your heart" (v. 35).

Digging Deeper:

1. In the context of your ministry, how might you risk one of your relationships in order to help another relationship be what it should?
2. When is that necessary? When is it unwise?
3. How are you being called upon to absorb the debt (and that not necessarily financial) of another for the glory of Christ?
4. Humanly speaking, to whom do you owe your relationship to Christ?
5. When was the last time you put your reputation on the line for someone else?

20 Yes, brother, let me benefit from you in the Lord; refresh my heart in Christ.

With these words, Paul puts a wrap on the main body of this letter.[1150] He signals that this is his intention by calling upon three words with which he opened the heart of the letter. One of those repetitions is his use of "brother" (ἀδελφέ, cf. v. 7) as a designation for Philemon. Along the way he has pulled the offending, but now converted, slave Onesimus into that circle of brotherhood as well (v. 16). Thus Paul's use of the word again here serves to remind Philemon of his standing alongside Onesimus as well as the obligations such grace brings.

In a set of relationships and circumstances in which it would have been easy for Philemon to stand over Onesimus and in which Paul could easily have stood above Philemon, Paul deliberately placed all three on equal footing "in the Lord" and "in Christ." Lightfoot aptly comments, "It is the entreaty of a brother to a brother on behalf of a brother."[1151] The particle ναὶ ("Yes") is used as an "emphatic repetition of one's own statement."[1152] This signals that Paul is not intending to say something new, but to reaffirm what it is he has already requested.

Paul says, "let me benefit from you" (ἐγώ σου ὀναίμην). The verb is in the aorist middle optative form (ὀναίμην, "let me benefit"). This is the only occurrence of the optative in the first-person in the NT (all others are in the third person).[1153] The optative mood expresses "an *obtainable wish* or a *prayer.*"[1154] Yet Paul clearly intends to lay this upon the will of Philemon. It might be, as Wallace says, a "*polite request* without necessarily a hint of doubting what the response will be."[1155] The aorist tense looks for a specific action that takes place at a definite point in time. Paul is seeking a particular action from Philemon. Though the verb is used only here in the NT, it is used regularly in the literature of the day as a formula meaning "*may I have joy* or *profit* or *benefit, may I enjoy.*"[1156]

[1150] Moo, 397-398; O'Brien, 301.
[1151] Lightfoot, 342.
[1152] BAGD, 533.
[1153] Dunn, 341; Harris, 275.
[1154] Wallace, 481-483.
[1155] Ibid., 481.
[1156] BAGD, 570.

The subject (σου, "you") and the object (ἐγώ, "me") are emphatically spelled out by use of the personal pronouns. In fact the genitive (σου, "you") is used in the formulaic statement to identify that which is to be the source of the joy.[1157] The question arises as to whether the verb chosen here is used as a pun upon Onesimus's name (i.e., ὀνίνημι = "benefit"; Ὀνήσιμος = "useful"; cf. v. 11). Some speak in the affirmative,[1158] others in the negative.[1159] Still others only concede that it is possible.[1160] Given the rarity of the word (only here in the NT) and of the form of the verb (the only first-person optative in the NT), it seems likely that Paul intended to make this turn of phrase and for Philemon to catch his drift. Wright aptly says, "It is now Philemon's turn to be 'useful' to Paul."[1161]

While Paul has expressed his wish and in the process ever so subtly laid the burden of its fulfillment at Philemon's feet, he knows that this benefit will be found and enjoyed only "in the Lord" (ἐν κυρίῳ). The preposition (ἐν, "in") describes the sphere in which this wish will be possible. Within that circle—no matter how uncomfortable and shocking this may be to Philemon—now clearly stand the Apostle, Philemon himself, and his slave-now-brother Onesimus. That circle, however, is not an artificial boundary created by the Apostle's words, but is the Lord Jesus Christ Himself into whom God has placed them all. It is in union with Christ that they are now bound together as brothers, and it is in union with Christ that they will find all that is necessary to live as such.

Moving from the subtlety of wish to the directness of command, Paul now issues the third of the three imperatives with which he draws the main body of this letter to a close (vv. 17, 18, 20): "refresh my heart" (ἀνάπαυσόν μου τὰ σπλάγχνα). With the use of the verb (ἀνάπαυσόν, "refresh"), Paul returns to another expression used in verse 7. As Philemon has refreshed the hearts of the saints of God (v. 7), so the Apostle wishes to be the object of Philemon's refreshing ministry. For more on the meaning of the verb, see our comments on verse 7. So too the object of this ministry is a repetition from verse 7: "my heart" (μου τὰ σπλάγχνα). Of the Apostle's eight

---

1157 Ibid.
1158 Bruce, 221; Dunn, 341; Moo, 432; Wright, 189.
1159 Lohse, 205; O'Brien, 302.
1160 Lightfoot, 343; Moule, 149.
1161 Wright, 189.

NT usages of the noun (σπλάγχνον), three of them appear in this brief letter. Again, turn to our comments on verse 7 for more on the meaning of this word.

The pronoun (μου, "my") is made emphatic by its placement in the sentence. Of note is the fact that Paul has called Onesimus "my very heart" (τὰ ἐμὰ σπλάγχνα, v. 17). So, in asking Philemon to "refresh my heart" (v. 20), is the Apostle asking Philemon to take action directly upon Onesimus and thus only indirectly upon the Apostle Paul? Or is he calling for something more directly aimed at Paul himself? The answer, of course, is found in understanding the nature of the body of Christ. By Philemon's grace and forgiveness extended to Onesimus (by receiving him as a brother and fulfilling the directives of this letter), Philemon will be refreshing the heart of the Apostle himself. This implies not only the closeness of the human relationship (between Paul and Onesimus), but the solidarity of the body of Christ itself.

> **Ministry Maxim**
>
> Only in a heart that has already been given away can one's personal refreshment be found in another's blessing.

What is done to a brother in Christ is, in a very real way, done to the whole of the body and to each member that makes it up. Indeed, this can only take place "in Christ" (ἐν Χριστῷ)—that is to say, in union with the living Christ. This parallels Paul's "in the Lord" (ἐν κυρίῳ) earlier in the sentence which was attached to the expression of his wish.

21 Having confidence in your obedience, I write to you, since I know that you will do even more than what I say.

The sentence that comprises verse 21 is made up of a main verb (ἔγραψά, "I write") and two participial clauses (Πεποιθὼς, "Having confidence"; εἰδὼς, "I know"), one of which precedes and the other of which follows the main verb in the order of the sentence. The main verb (ἔγραψά, "I write) is in the aorist tense. This again (as in v. 19 where he uses the same verb and tense) may be an occasion of the epistolary aorist, in which case Paul is viewing his writing from the vantage point of the reader who, as he reads it, will have a completed document in his hand (cf. also vv. 12, 19 for other examples of the epistolary aorist). The letter is again considered as being sent only to Philemon, evidenced by the singular personal pronoun (σοι, "to you").

The first participial clause precedes the main verb: "Having confidence in your obedience" (Πεποιθὼς τῇ ὑπακοῇ σου). The participle is perfect tense in form, though present tense in meaning.[1162] The word itself points toward trust, reliance, conviction, confidence, and assurance. It has the sense of "to convince someone to believe something and to act on the basis of what is recommended."[1163] With this assurance of Philemon's readiness to obey whatever directive the Lord may lay upon him, Paul could write this letter regarding Onesimus with confidence in his response. The participle seems to describe attendant circumstances—actions that take place alongside of or coterminous with those of the main verb.

That of which Paul was convinced as he wrote the letter was "your obedience" (τῇ ὑπακοῇ σου). Again the spotlight is squarely upon Philemon—for again the personal pronoun is singular in form (σου, "your"). The noun translated "obedience" (τῇ ὑπακοῇ) might sound out of place in a letter in which Paul has seemingly gone to great lengths *not* to make demands and in which he has stated his desire in the form of a wish (v. 20a). Indeed, Paul has appealed to Philemon (cf. v. 9), calling upon him to act on the basis of love (v. 9). Some, for these very reasons, insist on a milder side to the meaning of the word and opt for something like "compliance" in their translation.[1164] Yet what is a call for compliance, except for a gentle and yet insistent call for obedience? And why the presence of the definite article, if not to mark out the specificity of the response Paul says he is confident Philemon will make?

One might ask, then, "What precisely is it that Philemon is now expected to *obey*?" This serves to remind us that what the Apostle clearly holds forth as the appropriate and desired pathway with regard to Onesimus is ultimately more than a mere wish, though it has been expressed as such (see our comments on v. 20a).[1165] At least in this case, the Apostle's wish is God's command. Love requires Philemon to receive Onesimus as a brother.

[1162] BAGD, 639.

[1163] Louw and Nida, 33.301.

[1164] E.g., Robertson, *Word Pictures*, 4:469.

[1165] And the wish of v. 20a is packed among three imperatives (vv. 17, 18, 20b), though they are ultimately the fleshing out of Paul's "appeal" (vv. 9, 10).

Grace received demands that grace be extended. We ought to regard this then as another example of the Apostle's subtlety evident throughout the letter. He drops the "O"-word into the discussion as a gentle reminder to Philemon of the solid nature of the demand behind the velvety veil of gentleness. The word itself came from the verb ὑπακούω, which properly was used "of one who on a knock at the door comes to listen who it is."[1166] It came then, by popular usage, to describe one who hearkened to the voice of another, or, that is, listened to and obeyed what they were told.

The second participial phrase follows the main verb: "since I know that you will do even more than what I say" (εἰδὼς ὅτι καὶ ὑπὲρ ἃ λέγω ποιήσεις). Paul says, "I know" (εἰδὼς) something. It is a defective perfect which has a present-tense meaning. The participle appears to be causal; that is to say, it explains the ground of Paul's confidence ("since I know," NASU).[1167] Harris believes this participle qualifies the first participle ("Having confidence ... because I know ...") rather than the main verb, but the word order of the sentence would seem to work against such an understanding.[1168] It would seem rather to modify the main verb and have the sense of "I write [as I do] to you because I know that you will do even more than what I say." Paul often uses the combination of this verb and the conjunction ὅτι ("I know that") to introduce "a well-known fact that forms the basis ... of an exhortation or affirmation" (e.g., Rom. 5:3; 6:8-9; 2 Cor. 4:13-14; 5:6, 8).[1169]

In the expression καὶ ὑπὲρ ἃ λέγω ("even more than what I say"), καὶ ("even") qualifies and heightens ὑπὲρ ("more than"). As in verse 16, ὑπὲρ has the sense of excelling or surpassing and might be translated "over and above, beyond, more than."[1170] The relative pronoun ἃ ("what") assumes a missing demonstrative pronoun which would specify "these things" of which Paul is currently writing (λέγω, "I say").[1171] With all this intensifying and heightening of expectations, Paul finishes with "you will do" (ποιήσεις). The present tense pictures the simple, ongoing action of Philemon in regard to Onesimus. Only the embrace of divine grace produces an "even more

---

[1166] Thayer, 637-638.
[1167] Harris, 278.
[1168] Ibid.
[1169] Ibid., 185.
[1170] BAGD, 839.
[1171] Ibid. 469, 583; Harris, 278; Moo, 435.

than" ethic within the beloved. Such an orientation cannot be demanded, but only wooed. Jesus asked, " … what are you doing more than others?' (Matt. 5:47). He told a parable in which He concluded, "So you too, when you do all the things which are commanded you, say, 'We are unworthy slaves; we have done only that which we ought to have done'" (Luke 17:10).

The question, of course, is this: What is the "more than" Paul is so confident that Philemon will "do"? Several options present themselves. He may be confident that Philemon will receive Onesimus in an even more gracious manner than Paul has spoken of here.[1172] Or he may be confident that upon hearing the whole story, including the benefit Onesimus is to the Apostle, Philemon will return Onesimus to Paul for service to him in the ministry of the gospel.[1173] Or, thirdly, he may be confident that Philemon, in an act of brotherly, Christian love, will release Onesimus from his slavery and make him a freedman.[1174]

The first option seems agreeable enough, though it is not mutually exclusive from the others. As for the second, it would seem odd for the Apostle to imply his wish that Onesimus be allowed to return to him in Rome when in fact he expresses plans to visit Colossae upon his release in the next verse (v. 22).[1175] The same desire may be in mind, yet without the notion of a quick return trip by Onesimus to Rome. Perhaps upon the Apostle's visit to Colossae, Philemon would announce his willingness for Onesimus to travel with Paul in ministry.

> **Ministry Maxim**
>
> Ultimately this world is changed through individual choices made by free hearts bound by divine love, not by legalistic demands.

The third option, it seems to us, must be viewed as an ever-looming possibility, one which Paul does nothing to eradicate from the atmosphere of the letter. This, one would think, was Paul's ultimate hope. Yet we are probably correct to join those who conclude that, while the call upon Philemon is binding, with these words the Apostle leaves to Philemon the

---

[1172] Dunn, 345; Hendriksen, 224; Kent, 202; Lenski, 972.
[1173] O'Brien, 306.
[1174] Lightfoot, 343; Moo, 436; Wright, 189.
[1175] Kent, 201-202; Moo, 436.

specifics of what love requires.[1176] In this regard the words of Harris are particularly helpful:

> When Paul appeals to his position as Philemon's brother (vv. 7, 20) and spiritual father (v. 19), when he mentions Philemon's widely attested love (vv. 5, 7, 9) and his faith that prompts generosity (v. 6a), when he calls himself an imprisoned ambassador of Christ (vv. 1, 9, 10, 13), when he foregoes his apostolic right to give commands (vv. 8-9) and chooses to request Philemon's voluntary consent (v. 14), when he issues a promissory note to cover Onesimus's debts (vv. 18, 19a), when he expresses confidence in Philemon's compliance (v. 21) and intimates that he plans to visit Philemon after his anticipated release (and can thus personally reassure himself that Philemon has done his Christian duty, vv. 8, 22), then he is putting considerable psychological or spiritual pressure on Philemon to comply with his basic request (v. 17) and extend to Onesimus a ready welcome on his return to Colossae. Yet although he assumes Philemon's compliance with this basic request (v. 21), he leaves him free, beyond this, to follow the dictates of his Christian conscience in determining how his ἀγάπη (vv. 5, 7) should be expressed, and seriously entertains the possibility that Philemon might decide to retain the services of Onesimus as a slave permanently (vv. 15-16).[1177]

Digging Deeper:

1. What do Paul, Philemon, and Onesimus teach us about the ministry of mediation in fractured relationships?
2. When should we become involved in such a ministry? When should we not?
3. What risks do we run by becoming involved? What risks do we run by not becoming involved?
4. What new believer have you so invested yourself in that his being blessed by another refreshes your heart?
5. When was the last time you did even more than you were asked by someone? By God?

[1176] Harris, 278-279; Lohse, 206.
[1177] Harris, 278-279.

22 At the same time also prepare me a lodging, for I hope that through your prayers I will be given to you.

The Apostle Paul now asks that preparations be made for what he hoped was his release from prison and subsequent arrival in Colossae. This subtle and gentle move on Paul's part sends a signal to Philemon that he plans to gather firsthand evidence of his decisions and actions with regard to Onesimus.

The adverb ἅμα ("at the same time") denotes "the coincidence of two actions in time."[1178] While Philemon is busy welcoming Onesimus into his heart, his home and the fellowship of the church—doing "even more than what" Paul has said (v. 21)—he is "also" (καὶ) to make preparations (ἑτοίμαζέ μοι ξενίαν, "prepare me a lodging") for the presence of the great Apostle. The present-tense imperative demands that action be undertaken repeatedly, presumably until such preparations are in place (cf. "have a room ready," NEB).

The NASU leaves untranslated the postpositive conjunction δέ ("And" in NASB). The noun translated "a lodging" (ξενίαν) most often describes hospitality or the entertainment of a guest, but then at times comes to be used (as it is here) to describe the place the guest is given to occupy, "*the guest room.*"[1179] It is found in Acts 28:23 where it describes the quarters where Paul spent his house arrest in Rome and from which presumably he wrote this very letter.

One has to wonder what this word of Paul's visit did for the entire fellowship of believers in Colossae. To think that the great Apostle would now pay a visit to their inconspicuous town was probably thrilling. For Onesimus this was no doubt good news of a slightly different sort. And how precisely would this have struck Philemon himself?

Paul gives the ground beneath (γὰρ, "for") his request for hospitality, "I hope that through your prayers I will be given to you" (ἐλπίζω γὰρ ὅτι διὰ τῶν προσευχῶν ὑμῶν χαρισθήσομαι ὑμῖν). Paul says "I hope" (ἐλπίζω) something will transpire with regard to the future. The present tense underscores the abiding and ongoing nature of Paul's hope—a hope every prisoner no doubt entertains, but one made the more certain for the

---

[1178] BAGD, 42.
[1179] Ibid., 547.

Apostle because of the righteous nature of his cause and the prayers of God's people (cf. Col. 4:2-3). His hope is that "I will be given to you" (χαρισθήσομαι ὑμῖν). The verb has a broad range of meaning, but at root has the notion of giving freely or graciously. It can be used, as it is in Colossians 2:13 and 3:13, of forgiveness of sin by God (cf. Eph. 4:32), or of forgiveness extended by humans (Luke 7:42, 43; 2 Cor. 2:7, 10; 12:13). The former is always the fount and foundation of the latter (Eph. 4:32; Col. 3:13). But here it has its more generalized meaning of freely or graciously giving as a favor.[1180] In this case it is God (note the passive voice of the verb) who must graciously bestow the gift—a gift which is Paul himself!

> **Ministry Maxim**
>
> People do not what you expect, but what you inspect.

The personal pronouns have now become plural (ὑμῖν, "you"), something we have not seen since verse 3. Paul is not intending to visit just Philemon. It will be a visit with Philemon, his family, Onesimus, and the entire church that meets in his home. This will come about via the agency (διὰ, "through") of "your prayers" (τῶν προσευχῶν ὑμῶν). The pronoun is again plural, signaling that Paul is calling upon the entire church to pray for the release and supervisory visit from the Apostle. This subtle shift from the singular to the plural again (cf. comments on v. 2) places a gentle pressure upon Philemon to realize that, just as this letter was surely read before the entire church, so too its application would be under the scrutiny of the Apostle himself and of the whole of the church.

Such a visit to Colossae (and presumably the other churches of the Lycus Valley) represents a change in Paul's travel plans. In Romans 15:23-24 and 28 the Apostle makes clear that his plans, having finally visited Rome, were to continue on westward into lands that were as yet untouched by the gospel. But both here and in Philippians (1:25-26; 2:24), Paul signals a determination to return eastward toward some of the already-established churches. This may serve as a signal of the severity of the issues being faced in Colossae, not to mention other churches.

[1180] Ibid., 876.

23 Epaphras, my fellow prisoner in Christ Jesus, greets you,

The name "Epaphras" ('Επαφρᾶς) is an abbreviated form of the name Epaphroditus ('Επαφρόδιτος). By this time, however, it had become a recognizable name in its own right. The Epaphras we meet here is thus distinct from the Epaphroditus of Philippians 2:25 and 4:18. Epaphroditus is always associated with the Philippian church, while Epaphras is always connected to the Colossian church (Col. 1:7; 4:12). In his letter to the Colossians, the Apostle Paul calls Epaphras "one of your number" (Col. 4:12), and for this reason we are probably right in considering him a citizen of Colossae. Clearly, the heart of Epaphras was intertwined with the believers in Colossae, for Paul tells them that Epaphras was "always laboring earnestly for you in his prayers, that you may stand perfect and fully assured in all the will of God" (Col. 4:12).

It appears from the Apostle's words here (ὁ συναιχμάλωτός μου, "my fellow prisoner") that he had been imprisoned with the Apostle. Whether this implied the Apostle's present imprisonment (in Rome) or perhaps a past imprisonment, we cannot be certain, though the former seems more likely given that he sends his greetings to Philemon via the Apostle Paul at this time. This seems more probable also because clearly at this time Epaphras had been separated from his beloved Colossian believers and longed for their welfare and growth in grace.

> **Ministry Maxim**
>
> Greetings may help both connections within the body of Christ and obedience within individual hearts.

We are safe in surmising that Epaphras had proven a trustworthy fellow servant at Paul's side and had likely evangelized in and around Colossae during Paul's tenure of ministry in Ephesus. During that time we know that "all who lived in Asia heard the word of the Lord, both Jews and Greeks" (Acts 19:10). At that time Paul's adversary could testify, "not only in Ephesus, but in almost all of Asia, this Paul has persuaded and turned away a considerable number of people" (Acts 19:26). Much of that work was doubtless carried out by faithful colaborers like Epaphras who were trained and sent out by the Apostle. Epaphras may have been responsible for not only the founding of the Colossian church, but also for the churches in other cities of the Lycus valley, such as Laodicea and Hierapolis (Col. 4:13).

Epaphras's imprisonment, like that of the Apostle Paul (cf. v. 1), is "in Christ Jesus" (ἐν Χριστῷ Ἰησοῦ). In verses 1 and 9 Paul used the genitive and here he uses the prepositional phrase, but he seems to intend the same meaning by both forms. See our comments on verse 1. In this letter, as in most of his others, Paul is fond of using the preposition ἐν ("in") to describe the believer's union with the Lord (vv. 8, 16, 20 [2x], 23).

It is this Epaphras, says Paul, that now "greets you" (Ἀσπάζεταί σε). The pronoun is singular (σε, "you"), signifying that Philemon alone is in view here. Paul frequently uses the indicative form of the verb (as here) to convey his own personal greetings or those of others who are with him (e.g., Rom. 16:21-23; 1 Cor. 16:19-20; 2 Cor. 13:12; Phil. 4:21-22; Col. 4:10, 12, 14; Titus 3:15). He often employs the imperative form of the verb to command the recipients of his letters to thus "greet" others in the body of Christ (e.g., Rom. 16:3, 5-16; 1 Cor. 16:20; 2 Cor. 13:12; Phil. 4:21; Col. 4:15; 1 Thess. 5:26; Titus 3:15).

24 as do Mark, Aristarchus, Demas, Luke, my fellow workers.

Paul adds now to the "greetings" of Epaphras (v. 23) those of others apparently having contact with him at the time of his writing. Four are named specifically, and they are all designated by Paul as "my fellow workers" (οἱ συνεργοί μου). This is the same term used to describe Philemon himself in verse 1 (see our comments there).

The first individual is "Mark" (Μᾶρκος). In Paul's previous experience with Mark, the young man had proven unreliable. He had been selected to travel with Paul and Barnabas on their first missionary journey (Acts 13:5). It was not long, however, before he deserted Paul and Barnabas and returned to Jerusalem (13:13). As Paul and Barnabas were about to embark on their second missionary journey, Barnabas insisted that they bring Mark along again. Paul disagreed, and this led to a division between them (15:37-39). We do not know if Barnabas's insistence was an outgrowth of his heart as an encourager (4:36) or because Mark was his cousin (Col. 4:10). It is now over a decade later, and we are surprised to hear Paul speak again of Mark in positive terms. The Apostle's opinion of him has clearly changed (cf. also

Col. 4:10). Reconciliation has taken place, and Mark finds himself with Paul in the Apostle's first Roman imprisonment. At the end of his life, Paul commands Timothy, "Pick up Mark and bring him with you, for he is useful to me for service" (2 Tim. 4:11).

The next person to send greetings is "Aristarchus" ('Αρίσταρχος). He too is mentioned as sending greetings to the entire church in Colossians 4:10. Aristarchus hailed from Macedonia—Thessalonica, to be precise (Acts 20:4). He had been a member of the team accompanying Paul with the offering from Gentile believers back to Jerusalem. He had been present with the Apostle when the riot broke out in Ephesus. Indeed, he had been personally attacked in that encounter (Acts 19:29). He remained a part of the apostolic band, traveling with Paul when later a plot of the Jews was formed against him in Greece and evasive measures were necessary (Acts 20:4). He traveled with Paul on his voyage as a prisoner to Rome (Acts 27:2) and thus faced the fierce storm that nearly took all their lives. In connection with Colossians 4:10, Lightfoot conjectures that Aristarchus left the journey to Rome at Myra, but later rejoined Paul in Rome.[1181] Aristarchus was obviously a man who had faithfully stayed at the Apostle's side come what may. Indeed, in Colossians 4:10 Paul calls him, "my fellow prisoner" (ὁ συναιχμάλωτός μου), the same expression he uses of Epaphras in verse 23.

The third person to send greetings is "Demas" (Δημᾶς). He is mentioned in Colossians 4:14 and at the end of the Apostle Paul's life and ministry in 2 Timothy 4:10. Demas appears to have come to faith in Christ and grown in his faith to a place where the Apostle recognized in him gifts for ministry. He was selected to travel and serve alongside Paul on his missionary journeys. It is possible that Demas, like Aristarchus (Acts 20:4; 27:2), came from Thessalonica since they are mentioned side-by-side here. This could explain why, at the time of Paul's second Roman imprisonment and impending martyrdom, Demas departed and was said to have "gone to Thessalonica" (2 Tim. 4:10). Was he running for home? Paul had great affection for the church in Thessalonica (1 Thess. 2:7-8, 17-20; 3:9-10), and if Demas was chosen to represent them alongside the Apostle, it likely meant that he was

> **Ministry Maxim**
>
> Ministry as a team can be trying, but the rewards are terrific.

[1181] Lightfoot, 234.

himself a dear friend to the Apostle. The final, sad testimony of the Apostle with regard to Demas is that "having loved this present world, [he] has deserted me" (2 Tim. 4:10). But at the time of the composition of this letter, Demas appears to have been a faithful and appreciated coworker of Paul.

Finally, "Luke" (Λουκᾶς) is included in the greetings. He too, like Demas and Mark, is mentioned here and in Colossians (4:14) and 2 Timothy (4:11). The fellowship they shared had no doubt deepened through many shared experiences—both trials and triumphs. Luke, probably a Gentile, had likely also come to faith in Christ through the witness of the Apostle. He was frequently a companion of the Apostle Paul as he traveled the Mediterranean world in ministry for Christ (note the "we" sections of Acts; e.g., Acts 16:10ff.). As is clear here and in Colossians 4:14, Luke was with Paul in this his first Roman imprisonment. He was a physician, which was likely an aid to Paul, both personally and in ministry (Col. 4:14). He was an educated man, painstaking in his research and writing (Luke 1:1-4; Acts 1:1). Luke never makes mention of himself in either the Gospel of Luke or in Acts. He is the picture of the faithful, loyal friend and self-effacing coworker. At the close of his life, Paul can say that "Only Luke is with me" (2 Tim. 4:11). See our other comments on Colossians 4:14.

Think of this group of men attached to the Apostle Paul for purposes of the gospel's advance. We have one faithful gospel-soldier (Aristarchus); one previous defector, now restored (Mark); one soon-to-be defector (Demas); and another Gentile, medical doctor-author (Luke). Ministry as a team is never neat, easy, or painless—but the rewards paid out in fellowship and in increased productivity through the synergy of divine gifting are remarkable.

25 The grace of the Lord Jesus Christ be with your spirit.

The wording of this entire verse is identical to that of Philippians 4:23. The opening portion ('Η χάρις τοῦ κυρίου Ἰησοῦ Χριστοῦ, "The grace of our Lord Jesus Christ") is also identical to a portion of 2 Corinthians 13:13.

As Paul so often does in his letters, he opens and closes with "grace" (χάρις; cf. v. 3). The inclusio serves to wrap the entire letter with all its contents and challenges in "The grace of the Lord Jesus Christ." Some have suggested that the noun "Jesus" (Ἰησοῦ) should be separated out and understood as a fifth name (added to those from verse 24) referring to the man named "Jesus who is called Justus" (Col. 4:11) and thus bringing conformity between the two letters.[1182] But this conjecture appears fanciful and unnecessary.

The noun "spirit" (τοῦ πνεύματος) is singular while the pronoun (ὑμῶν, "your") is plural. The noun is to be understood as a distributive singular.[1183] The plural pronoun returns the attention to the wider audience of the opening of the letter, signaling that Paul sends his blessing to the wider circle he addressed in verses 1-3 and 22. The phrase "with your spirit" (μετὰ τοῦ πνεύματος ὑμῶν; cf. Gal. 6:18; Phil. 4:23; 2 Tim. 4:22) is probably not intended to have a more expansive meaning than the simpler "with you" (μεθ᾽ ὑμῶν; as in his other letters, e.g., Col. 4:18).[1184] Though many manuscripts conclude with "Amen" (ἀμήν; cf. KJV, NKJV), the best manuscripts omit it. Most manuscripts of NT letters contain such a tag to their conclusion, probably the addition of reverent scribes.

> **Ministry Maxim**
>
> Wrapped in grace, even the most difficult relationships can honor God.

It is easy to read such words with a casual flair—as if, because of Paul's common use of such language at the close of his letters, he really doesn't give them much thought or that he uses them as mere conventions. Yet Paul never in any of his writings makes light of "grace." It is absurd that he would do so here, in a letter where he has called upon Philemon to demonstrate grace in such a socially and personally difficult situation. No, all Paul's inward strength lies behind his pen as he sends this final grace-wish, for he knows that apart from it the reconciliation and welcome befitting Onesimus as a new believer in Christ will not be possible. But, with grace, nothing is beyond the reach of those who take up God's will.

[1182] Lohse, 207.
[1183] Harris, 281.
[1184] Moo, 442.

Digging Deeper:

1. In what way have the people you lead been falling short of your expectations? How can you add inspection to expectation without being overbearing or heavy-handed in your leadership?
2. Who has God given you to share side-by-side with in ministry? How have they been loyal and faithful co-laborers?
3. Who would identify you in that way?
4. In what way do those relationships require special grace from God?
5. In what way do those relationships bring special grace from God to you?

APPENDIX A

PREACHING AND
TEACHING COLOSSIANS

Preaching is one of the great privileges of a pastor. The NT has much to say about faithfully preaching God's Word (for starters see 2 Timothy 4:1-4). It is my conviction that expository preaching should be the regular practice of every local church pastor.[1185] Of course, even among those of similar conviction, there is not always consensus on just what constitutes expository preaching. Similarly, each pastor is comfortable preaching passages of different lengths and series of varying duration. Local circumstances also permit (or require) sermon series of differing lengths.

What follows are suggestive attempts at projecting both preaching series and their individual sermons. First, I offer an exegetical outline of Colossians. Then I offer three possibilities for preaching Colossians—a single message covering the entire book, a shorter series of messages, and a more extended series of messages. These may, of course, be expanded even further. In some cases you may divide the letter differently than I have suggested here. My hope is that these suggestions will provide fodder for your preaching of these portions of sacred Scripture. It is your duty as a servant of God to wrestle with the text of Scripture until God brings you forth with a message for His people which arises from His Word.

"I solemnly charge you in the presence of God and of Christ Jesus, who is to judge the living and the dead, and by His appearing and His kingdom: preach the word; be ready in season and out of season; reprove, rebuke, exhort, with great patience and instruction" (2 Tim. 4:1-2).

[1185]   See the author's *Revival in the Rubble* (chapter 9) for more on the primacy and practice of expository preaching.

Exegetical Outline: Colossians

I. **The Salutation (1:1-2)**
    A. The senders (1:1)
    B. The recipients (1:2a)
    C. The blessing (1:2b)

II. **Paul & Timothy's Prayer for the Colossian Believers (1:3-14)**
    A. Paul & Timothy's thanksgiving for the Colossian believers (1:3-8)
        1. The basis of their thanksgiving (1:3-4)
        2. The hope of their thanksgiving (1:5-8)
            a. Hope through the gospel (1:5)
            b. Hope throughout the world (1:6)
            c. Hope in Colossae (1:7-8)
    B. Paul & Timothy's intercession for the Colossian believers (1:9-14)
        1. The nature of prayer: "pray" and "ask" (1:9a)
        2. The content of prayer: "be filled with the knowledge of His will" (1:9b)
            a. The means of being filled: "in all spiritual wisdom and understanding" (1:9c)
            b. The goal of being filled: A walk that is worthy (1:10-14)
                i.   Bearing fruit (1:10a)
                ii. Growing (1:10b)
                iii. Being strengthened (1:11)
                iv. Giving thanks (1:12-14)
                     aa. Qualified for an inheritance in the light (1:12b)
                     bb. Rescued from the domain of darkness (1:13a)
                     cc. Transferred to a new kingdom (1:13b)

III. **The Preeminence of Christ (1:15-23)**
    A. Christ in relationship to God (1:15a)
        1. Christ is the image of the invisible God (1:15a)
    B. Christ in relationship to creation (1:15b-17)
        1. Christ is the firstborn over all creation (1:15b-16)
        2. Christ is the sustainer of all reality (1:17)
    C. Christ in relationship to the church (1:18-20)
        1. Christ is the head of the body (1:18a)
        2. Christ is the firstborn from the dead (1:18b)
        3. Christ is the fullness of God (1:19)
        4. Christ is the peacemaker (1:20)

D. Christ in relationship to the redeemed (1:21-23)
    1. Christ reconciled you through His death (21-22)
    2. Christ must remain the object of our faith (23)

IV. **The Principles of Paul's ministry (1:24-2:5)**
    A. Paul's ministry generally (1:24-29)
        1. Paul's joy in the midst of suffering (1:24)
        2. Paul's making known the mystery of Christ (1:25-28)
        3. Paul's struggle in all Christ's power (1:29)
    B. Paul's ministry to the Colossians (2:1-5)
        1. Paul's struggle for the Colossians and Laodiceans (2:1)
        2. Paul making known the mystery of Christ to them (2:2-3)
        3. Paul's joy over their growth in the face of challenges (2:4-5)

V. **The Practice of the Christian life (2:6-4:6)**
    A. The Christian life condensed (2:6-7)
        1. Walk in Christ (2:6b)
            a. As you have received Christ (2:6a)
            b. Having been firmly rooted in Christ (2:7a)
            c. Having been built up in Christ (2:7b)
            d. Now being established in your faith (2:7c)
            e. Continuously overflowing with gratitude (2:7d)
    B. The Christian life confused (2:8-23)
        1. A false reasoning (2:8-15)
            a. The false reasoning (2:8)
            b. The fullness of Christ (2:9-15)
                i. Christ in His fullness (2:9)
                ii. We in Christ's fullness (2:10-15)
                    aa. We are full in Christ who is head over all spirit beings (2:10)
                    bb. We are in union with Christ in His death (2:11)
                    cc. We are in union with Christ in His burial (2:12a)
                    dd. We are in union with Christ in His resurrection (2:12b-13a)
                        (i) In this union we are forgiven of sins and freed from demonic oppression (2:13b-15)
        2. A false legalism (2:16-17)
        3. A false spirituality (2:18-19)
        4. A false asceticism (2:20-23)

C. The Christian life clarified (3:1-4:6)
   1. In principle (3:1-17)
      a. Put your mind (3:1-4)
         i. Seeking the things above (3:1)
         ii. Setting your mind on things above (3:2)
         iii. Because you have died and your life is hidden with Christ in God (3:3)
         iv. When Christ is revealed, you will be revealed with Him in glory (3:4)
      b. Put off your old self (3:5-9)
         i. Think rightly about yourself and sin (3:5-7)
         ii. Throw off the acts of sin (3:8-9)
      c. Put on your new self (3:10-17)
         i. You have put on the new self (3:10-11)
         ii. So put on the life of the new self (3:12-14)
            aa. Let the peace of Christ rule over you (3:15)
            bb. Let the Word of Christ dwell in you (3:16)
            cc. Let the glory of Christ consume you (3:17)
   2. In relationships with believers (3:18-4:1)
      a. Wives and husbands (3:18-19)
         i. Wives (3:18)
         ii. Husbands (3:19)
      b. Children and fathers (3:20-21)
         i. Children (3:20)
         ii. Fathers (3:21)
      c. Slaves and masters (3:22-4:1)
         i. Slaves (3:22-25)
         ii. Masters (4:1)
   3. In relationships with nonbelievers (4:2-6)
      a. Prayer (4:2-4)
         i. Devotion to prayer (4:2)
         ii. Direction for prayer (4:3-4)
            aa. Prayer for opportunity to speak the gospel (4:3)
            bb. Prayer for clarity in speaking the gospel (4:4)
      b. Witness (4:5-6)
         i. The way we act toward unbelievers (5)
         ii. The way to speak to unbelievers (6)

VI. Paul's Greetings and Farewell (4:7-18)

    A.   Explanations and greetings (4:7-14)

        1.   Explanations (4:7-9)

            a.   Through Tychicus (4:7-8)

            b.   Through Onesimus (4:9)

        2.   Greetings (4:10-15)

            a.   Sent (4:10-14)

                i.   From Aristarchus (4:10a)

                ii.   From Mark (4:10b)

                iii.   From Jesus, called Justus (4:11)

                iv.   From Epaphras (4:12-13)

                v.   From Luke (4:14)

            b.   Commanded (4:15)

    B.   Instructions (4:16-17)

        1.   Share the letters (4:16)

        2.   Exhort Archippus (4:17)

    C.   Paul's farewell (4:18)

Preaching Colossians

Single Message

I. **We Must Pursue Right Ministry Paths (1:1-2:15)**
    A. The walk of a disciple (1:1-14)
    B. The exaltation of Christ (1:15-23)
    C. The maturity of God's people (1:24-2:5)
    D. The union of Christ and His people (2:6-15)

II. **We Must Avoid Wrong Ministry Paths (2:16-23)**
    A. Legalism (2:16-17)
    B. Spiritualism (2:18-19)
    C. Asceticism (2:20-23)

III. **We Must Pursue Right Maturity Paths (3:1-17)**
    A. Put your mind on truth (3:1-4)
    B. Put off your old self (3:5-11)
    C. Put on your new self (3:12-17)

IV. **We Must Pursue Right Ministry Relationships (3:18-4:18)**
    A. The relationship of husband and wife (3:18-19)
    B. The relationship of father and children (3:20-21)
    C. The relationship of employee and employer (3:22-4:1)
    D. The relationship of believer and unbeliever (4:2-6)
    E. The relationship of servant and fellow workers (4:7-18)

Shorter Series (9 Messages)

#1   1:1-14   The Gospel Makes All Things New
  I.   The Gospel Gives New Life (1-8)
         A. A new perspective to life (1-2)
             1. I live under divine authority (1a)
             2. I live within divine providence (1b)
             3. I live in spiritual relationships (1c-2a)
             4. I live by divine enablement (2b)
         B. A new process to life (3-6a)
             1. The gospel plants hope (5)
             2. Hope sprouts into faith (4b, 5)
             3. Faith blossoms as love (4c, 5)
             4. Love scents the air with the fragrance of
                 gratitude (3)
         C. A new pathway for life (6b-8)
             1. The gospel must be heard (6b)
             2. The gospel must be understood (6c)
             3. The gospel must be learned (7-8)
  II.   The Gospel Gives New Light (9-14)
         A. Light for knowing God's will (9-10a)
             1. Knowing God's will requires prayer (9a)
             2. Knowing God's will requires insight (10a)
             3. Knowing God's will requires obedience (10b)
         B. Light for doing God's will (10b-14)
             1. The goal of knowing God's will is bearing fruit
                 (10b)
             2. The goal of knowing God's will is knowing God
                 (10c)
             3. The goal of knowing God's will is steadfastness
                 (11)
             4. The goal of knowing God's will is giving thanks
                 (11b-14)

#2   1:15-23   Jesus 101
  I.   Jesus Is Supreme over This Creation (1:15-17)
         A. Jesus and God (15a)
         B. Jesus and Creation (15b-17)
             1. Christ is the King of creation (15b)
             2. Christ is the sphere of creation (16a)

        3.   Christ is the agent of creation (16b)
        4.   Christ is the goal of creation (16c)
        5.   Christ is the origin of creation (17a)
        6.   Christ is the sustainer of creation (17b)

II.   **Jesus Is Supreme over the New Creation (1:18-23)**
    A.   The Father's pleasure (18-20a)
        1.   Jesus is first over a new kind of life (18b)
        2.   Jesus is first over a new kind of people (18a)
        3.   Jesus is first over a new kind of creation (18c)
    B.   The Father's plan (20b-23)
        1.   The problem: rebellion (21)
        2.   The provision: peace with God (20b)
        3.   The path: reconciliation (22a)
        4.   The product: presentation before God (22b)
        5.   The prerequisite: remaining (23a)
        6.   The plan: planted in the gospel (23b)

#3   1:24-29   Working for Christ's Supremacy
  I.   Working for Christ's Supremacy Requires Suffering (24)
  II.   Working for Christ's Supremacy Requires Speaking (25-28)
    A.   We speak "the word of God" (25)
    B.   We speak "the mystery" of God (26-27)
    C.   We speak the Son of God (28)
  III.   Working for Christ's Supremacy Requires Striving (29)

#4   2:1-5   Wealth Worth Fighting For
  I.   A Wealth Worth Fighting for Is Found in ... (2-3)
    A.   *Fellowship*
    B.   *Committed* fellowship
    C.   *Loving,* committed fellowship
    D.   *Insightful,* loving, committed fellowship
    E.   *Christ-centered,* insightful, loving, committed fellowship
  II.   A Wealth Worth Fighting for Is Threatened by ... (4)
    A.   Popular deception
  III.   A Wealth Worth Fighting for Is Displayed in ... (5)
    A.   Orderly faith
    B.   Firm faith

#5   2:6-23   Gospel Thinking
    I.   Right Thinking (2:6-7)
    II.   Wrong Thinking (2:8-23)
        A. False thinking (2:8-15)
        B. False legalism (2:16-17)
        C. False spirituality (2:18-19)
        D. False asceticism (2:20-23)

#6   3:1-17   Living Rightly with Yourself
    I.   Thinking Rightly (3:1-4)
    II.   Walking Rightly (3:5-11)
    III. Relating Rightly (3:12-17)

#7   3:18-4:1   Living Rightly in Relationships
    I.   Transformed Marriages (3:18-19)
        A. Transformed wives (18)
        B. Transformed husbands (19)
    II.   Transformed Families (3:20-21)
        A. Transformed children (20)
        B. Transformed fathers (21)
    III. Transformed Workplaces (3:22-4:1)
        A. Transformed employees (3:22-25)
        B. Transformed employers (4:1)

#8   4:2-6   Living Rightly in the World
    I.   Getting Prayer Right (4:2-4)
        A. Devotion to prayer (2)
        B. Direction in prayer (3-4)
            1. Pray for opportunity to speak the gospel
            2. Pray for clarity in speaking the gospel
    II.   Getting Witness Right (4:5-6)
        A. The gospel changes the way we think (5)
            1. The gospel changes the way we think about others ("outsiders")
            2. The gospel changes the way we think about our interactions with others ("with wisdom")
            3. The gospel changes the way we think about the times in which we live ("the opportunity")

    B.   The gospel changes the way we act (5)
        1.   The gospel changes the movement of our lives ("walk")
        2.   The gospel changes the moments of our lives ("making the most of")
    C.   The gospel changes the way we speak (6)
        1.   The gospel changes the context and the content of our speaking ("your speech")
        2.   The gospel changes the flavor of our speaking ("always be with grace, as though seasoned with salt")
        3.   The gospel changes the effect of our speaking ("so that you will know how you should respond to each person")

#9   4:7-18   Living Rightly with Believers
    I.   The Principle of Involvement (7-8)
    II.   The Principle of Integration (9-10)
    III.   The Principle of Identity (11)
    IV.   The Principle of Intercession (12-13)
    V.   The Principle of Investment (14)
    VI.   The Principle of Interaction (15-16)
    VII. The Principle of Imperative (17)
    VIII. The Principle of Interruption (18)

Longer Series (21 Messages)

#1 1:1-8 **Gospel Newness**
I. The Gospel Imparts New Perspective (1-2)
   A. I live under divine authority (1a)
   B. I live within divine providence (1b)
   C. I live in spiritual relationships (1c-2a)
   D. I live by divine enablement (2b)
II. The Gospel Impels a New Process (3-6a)
   A. The gospel plants hope (5)
   B. Hope sprouts into faith (4b, 5)
   C. Faith blossoms as love (4c, 5)
   D. Love scents the air with the fragrance of gratitude (3)
III. The Gospel Illuminates a New Pathway (6b-8)
   A. The gospel must be heard (6b)
   B. The gospel must be understood (6c)
   C. The gospel must be learned (7-8)

#2 1:9-14 **Knowing and Doing the Will of God**
I. Knowing the Will of God (9-10a)
   A. Knowing God's will requires prayer (9a)
   B. Knowing God's will requires insight (10a)
   C. Knowing God's will requires obedience (10b)
II. Doing the Will of God (10b-14)
   A. The goal of knowing God's will is bearing fruit (10b)
   B. The goal of knowing God's will is knowing God (10c)
   C. The goal of knowing God's will is steadfastness (11)
   D. The goal of knowing God's will is giving thanks (11b-14)
      1. Thankful for a rich and undeserved inheritance (12)
      2. Thankful for a complete and total deliverance (13a)
      3. Thankful for a wonderful and glorious residence (13b-14)

#3   1:15-17   Christ's Supremacy over Creation
     I.   Christ and God (15a)
     II. Christ and Creation (15b-17)
          A. Christ is the King of creation (15b)
          B. Christ is the sphere of creation (16a)
          C. Christ is the agent of creation (16b)
          D. Christ is the goal of creation (16c)
          E. Christ is the origin of creation (17a)
          F. Christ is the sustainer of creation (17b)

#4   1:18-20   Christ's Supremacy over the New Creation
     I.   The Father's Pleasure (18-20a)
          A. To make Jesus first over a new life (18b)
          B. To make Jesus first over a new people (18a)
          C. To make Jesus first over a new creation (18c)
     II. The Father's Plan (19-20)
          A. Christ's Incarnation (19)
          B. Christ's Reconciliation (20)

#5   1:21-23   Christ's Supremacy over Me
     I.   The Problem: Rebellion (21)
          A. The provision: peace with God (20b)
     II. The Path: Reconciliation (22a)
          A. The product: presentation before God (22b)
     III. The Prerequisite: Remaining (23a)
          A. The plan: planted in the gospel (23b)

#6   1:24-29   Working for Christ's Supremacy
     I.   Working for Christ's Supremacy Requires Suffering (24)
     II. Working for Christ's Supremacy Requires Speaking (24-28)
          A. We speak "the word of God" (25)
          B. We speak "the mystery" of God (26-27)
          C. We speak the Son of God (28)
     III. Working for Christ's Supremacy Requires Striving (29)

#7 2:1-5 Wealth Worth Fighting For
I. A Wealth Worth Fighting for Is Found in ... (2-3)
   A. *Fellowship*
   B. *Committed* fellowship
   C. *Loving,* committed fellowship
   D. *Insightful,* loving, committed fellowship
   E. *Christ-centered,* insightful, loving, committed fellowship
II. A Wealth Worth Fighting for Is Threatened by ... (4)
   A. Popular deception
III. A Wealth Worth Fighting for Is Displayed in ... (5)
   A. Orderly faith
   B. Firm faith

#8 2:6-7 Walking the Walk
I. Walking the Walk Requires Beginning Correctly (6)
   A. Begin with the right focus ("Christ Jesus, the Lord")
   B. Begin with the right response ("you received")
II. Walking the Walk Requires Continuing Correctly (7)
   A. Metaphor #1
      1. Pathway: Rooted
      2. Metaphor: Horticultural
      3. Direction: Downward
      4. Destination: Stability
   B. Metaphor #2
      1. Pathway: Built up
      2. Metaphor: Architectural
      3. Direction: Upward
      4. Destination: Maturity
   C. Metaphor #3
      1. Pathway: Established
      2. Metaphor: Legal
      3. Direction: Inward and Outward
      4. Destination: Authenticity
   D. Metaphor #4
      1. Pathway: Abounding in Thanksgiving
      2. Metaphor: "Atmospheric"
      3. Direction: Upward
      4. Destination: Felicity

#9   2:8-10   Fuller Than Full
    I.   Christ Is Fuller than Full of Deity (9)
        A.   Christ was and is fully man
        B.   Christ was and is fully God
    II.   You Are Fuller Than Full in Christ (10)
    III. So Why Entertain Other Offers? (8)
        A.   Examine these other offers
            1.   They are not what they claim ("deceptive")
            2.   They cannot deliver what they promise ("hollow")
            3.   They produce the opposite of what they offer ("takes you captive")
        B.   Expose these other offers
            1.   They are human
            2.   They are spiritual

#10   2:11-15   A Victory Not of Our Making
    I.   You Are in Union with Christ (11-13a)
        A.   You have died with Christ (11)
        B.   You have been buried with Christ (12a)
        C.   You have been raised with Christ (12b-13a)
    II.   Therefore You Are Victorious with Christ (13b-15)
        A.   In Christ you are victorious over sin (13b-14)
            1.   In union with Christ your sin debt has been erased (14a)
            2.   In union with Christ your sin debt has been removed (14b)
            3.   In union with Christ your sin debt has been crucified (14c)
        B.   In Christ you are victorious over Satan (15)

#11   2:16-23   Failed Strategies for Spiritual Success
    I.   The Failed Strategy of Legalism (16-17)
        A.   Are you dwelling in the shadow?
        B.   Are you dwelling in the substance?
            1.   Legalism aims at victory through obeying
    II.   The Failed Strategy of Spiritualism (18-19)
        A.   Spiritualism promotes a false humility
        B.   Spiritualism promotes a false authority
        C.   Spiritualism promotes a false self-image

      D. Spiritualism promotes a false life

         1. Spiritualism aims at victory through substituting

   III. The Failed Strategy of Asceticism (20-23)

      A. Asceticism impels you to live a life to which you've already died (20a)

      B. Asceticism impels you to submit to an authority to which you've already died (20b)

      C. Asceticism impels you to dwell in an environment to which you've already died (20c)

      D. Asceticism impels you to come under a legal system to which you've already died (21)

         1. Asceticism aims at victory through denying

#12 3:1-4 Living Our New Life

   I. Realizing a New Life Involves the Search of Our Hearts (1)

   II. Realizing a New Life Involves the Set of Our Minds (2-3)

   III. Realizing a New Life Involves the Certainty of Our Hope (4)

#13 3:5-11 Real Change: From Root to Fruit

   I. Real Change Requires a Choice

      A. "Put to death" (5a)

      B. "Rid yourselves of" (8a)

   II. Real Change Requires a Foundation

      A. A New Identity: "you have taken off your old self ... and have put on the new self" (9b-10a)

      B. A New Possibility: "Christ is all" (11b)

   III. Real Change Requires a Target

      A. Sexual Idolatry (5) (See Appendix D)

      B. Social Destruction (8)

#14 3:12-14 Dress the Part!

   I. Gospel Grace – Foundation for God's Commands (12a)

      A. You are chosen

      B. You are holy

      C. You are loved

II. Gospel Demand – Fruit Arising from God's Foundation (12b)
   A. "Put on!"
III. Gospel Wardrobe – Attire (12c-14)
   A. Root – Inward (12c)
      1. Compassion
      2. Humility
      3. Patience
   B. Fruit – Outward (12c-13)
      1. Kindness
      2. Gentleness
      3. Forbearance and Forgiveness

#15 3:15-17 The Texture of Our Life Together
I. God's People Prize Three Treasures
   A. The peace of Christ (15)
   B. The word of Christ (16)
   C. The honor of Christ (17)
II. God's People Promise Three Things
   A. The peace of Christ will rule our interactions (15)
   B. The word of Christ will rule our attention (16)
   C. The honor of Christ will rule our actions (17)

#16 3:18-19 Transformed Marriages
I. Transformed Wives (18)
II. Transformed Husbands (19)

#17 3:20-21 Transformed Families
I. Transformed Children (20)
II. Transformed Fathers (21)

#18 3:22-4:1 Transformed Workplaces
I. Transformed Employees (3:22-25)
II. Transformed Employers (4:1)

#19 4:2-4 Devotion to Prayer
I. We must be devoted to prayer (2)
   A. We must be devoted to the discipline of prayer
   B. We must be devoted to a dependence upon prayer

II. We must have direction in prayer (3-4)
   A. We are to pray for opportunity to proclaim God's Word (3)
   B. We are to pray for clarity in proclaiming God's Word (4)

#20 4:5-6   Gospel Changes
   I. The Gospel Changes the Way We Think (5)
   A. The gospel changes the way we think about others ("outsiders")
   B. The gospel changes the way we think about our interactions with others ("with wisdom")
   C. The gospel changes the way we think about the times in which we live ("the opportunity")
   II. The Gospel Changes the Way We Act (5)
   A. The gospel changes the movement of our lives ("walk")
   B. The gospel changes the moments of our lives ("making the most of")
   III. The Gospel Changes the Way We Speak (6)
   A. The gospel changes the context and the content of our speaking ("your speech")
   B. The gospel changes the flavor of our speaking ("always be with grace, as though seasoned with salt")
   C. The gospel changes the effect of our speaking ("so that you will know how you should respond to each person")

#21 4:7-18   The Circle of Christian Relationships
   I. The Principle of Involvement (7-8)
   II. The Principle of Integration (9-10)
   III. The Principle of Identity (11)
   IV. The Principle of Intercession(12-13)
   V. The Principle of Investment (14)
   VI. The Principle of Interaction (15-16)
   VII. The Principle of Imperative (17)
   VIII. The Principle of Interruption (18)

APPENDIX B

PREACHING AND
TEACHING PHILEMON

Please see the beginning of Appendix A for my thoughts with regard to preaching generally.

When it comes to preaching the little letter to Philemon there are several legitimate approaches that can be taken. At first blush you may conclude that such a short letter is capable only of sustaining a single sermon or perhaps a brief series of sermons. I give you examples of both below. But I would challenge you to also consider the substantial things this letter has to say and the possibility of a longer series. I offer below fodder for your thought on this as well.

Exegetical Outline: Philemon

I.   **Paul's Salutation (1-3)**
    A.   The letter's author: Paul (1a)
    B.   The letter's recipients (1b-2)
        1.   Philemon (1b)
        2.   Apphia (2a)
        3.   Archippus (2b)
        4.   The church in their house (2c)
    C.   The author's blessing (3)

II. **Paul's Gratitude (4-7)**
    A.   The regularity of Paul's gratitude (4)
    B.   The reason for Paul's gratitude (5)
    C.   The result of Paul's gratitude (6)
    D.   The rationale of Paul's gratitude (7)

III. Paul's Appeal (8-20)
  A. Preparation for Paul's appeal (8-14)
    1. The foundation of Paul's appeal (8-9)
       a. Not based on authority (8)
       b. But based on love (9)
    2. The subject of Paul's appeal (10-11)
       a. Onesimus: Paul's child from prison (10)
       b. Onesimus: Useless turned useful (11)
    3. The explanation of Paul's actions (12-14)
       a. Sending Onesimus was painful for Paul (12-13)
       b. Sending Onesimus was deferring to Philemon (14)
  B. Perspective on Paul's appeal (15-16)
    1. Perhaps it happened that you might have him forever (15)
    2. Perhaps it happened that you might have him as a brother (16)
  C. Paul's actual appeal (17)
    1. Accept Onesimus as you would accept me
  D. Paul's promise (18-19)
    1. Paul's taking of Onesimus' debts (18)
    2. Paul's promises to repay Onesimus' debts (19)
  E. Paul's renewed appeal (20)
    1. Paul's appeal to benefit from Philemon (20a)
    2. Paul's appeal to be refreshed by Philemon (20b)

IV. Paul's Farewell (21-25)
  A. Paul's confidence in Philemon's obedience (21)
  B. Paul's plan to visit (22)
  C. Paul's associates' greetings (23-24)
    1. Epahras (23)
    2. Mark (24)
    3. Aristarchus (24)
    4. Demas (24)
    5. Luke (24)
  D. Paul's benediction (25)

Preaching Philemon

Single Message: *Graced and Gracing*

I. The Challenge of Grace
A. God's grace came to Paul
B. God's grace came to Philemon (through Paul's witness) (19)
C. God's grace came to Onesimus (through Paul's witness) (10)
D. Will God's grace come to Onesimus through Philemon? (17)

II. The Power of Grace
A. God's grace binds us (1a)
B. God's grace binds us together (1b-2)
C. God's grace binds us to gracing (3)

III. The Flow of Grace
A. Grace is inclusive (1, 7, 16, 20)
B. Grace is gentle (8-9)
C. Grace is empowering (11)
D. Grace is respectful (14)
E. Grace is insightful (15-16)
F. Grace is costly (17-19)
G. Grace is positive (20-21)
H. Grace is accountable (22-24)

Shorter Series (4 Messages)

#1   1-3   True Thinking
      I.   I live captive to Christ (1a)
      II.   I live in family (1b, 2a, c)
      III. I live at work (1c)
      IV. I live in combat (2b)
      V.   I live in dependence (3)

#2   4-7   True Gratitude
      I.   True gratitude grows when I think of you (4)
      II.   True gratitude grows when I hear about you (5)
      III. True gratitude grows when I pray for you (6)
      IV. True gratitude grows when I rejoice over you (7)

#3   8-20   **True Fellowship**
- I.   True fellowship has a pursuit (8-14)
  - A. A pursuit of love before authority (8-9)
  - B. A pursuit of the "useless" becoming "useful" (10-11)
  - C. A pursuit of my rights becoming your choice (12-14)
- II. True fellowship has a perspective (15-16)
  - A. An unexamined divine purpose (15)
  - B. An unexpected personal benefit (16)
- III. True fellowship has a price. (17-20)
  - A. The price of risking the relationship (17)
  - B. The price of taking the debt (18-19)
  - C. The price of making the request (20)

#4   21-25   **True Accountability**
- I.   True accountability explains expectations (21)
- II. True accountability explains inspection (22)
- III. True accountability exists in community (23-24)
- IV. True accountability extends resources (25)

Longer Series (6 Messages)

#1   1-3   **The Mind-set That Makes for Fellowship**
- I.   I live captive to Christ (1a)
- II. I live in family (1b, 2a, c)
- III. I live at work (1c)
- IV. I live in combat (2b)
- V. I live in dependence (3)

#2   4-7   **The Gratitude That Makes for Fellowship**
- I.   True gratitude grows when I think of you (4)
- II. True gratitude grows when I hear of you (5)
- III. True gratitude grows when I pray for you (6)
- IV. True gratitude grows when I rejoice over you (7)

#3   8-14   **The Intervention That Makes for Fellowship**
- I.   The intervention must use a new motive (8-9)
  - A. Eschew authority (8)
  - B. Embrace love (9)

II.   The intervention must offer new insight (10-11)
- A. Onesimus was useless (10)
- B. Onesimus is now useful (11)

III. The intervention must extend new respect (12-14)
- A. Embrace personal pain (12-13)
- B. Empower personal choice (14)

#4   15-16   **The Perspective That Makes for Fellowship**
- I.   I must look for a divine purpose (15)
- II. I must look for an unexpected benefit (16)

#5   17-20   **The Price That Makes for Fellowship**
- I.   The price tag of fellowship is risking the relationship (17)
- II. The price tag of fellowship is taking the debt (18-19)
- III. The price tag of fellowship is making the request (20)

#6   21-26   **The Accountability That Makes for Fellowship**
- I.   True accountability explains expectations (21)
- II. True accountability explains inspection (22)
- III. True accountability exists in community (23-24)
- IV. True accountability extends resources (25)

APPENDIX C

A TOPICAL INDEX
TO THE MINISTRY MAXIMS

What follows is a topical index of the Ministry Maxims found in each verse of the commentary. In many cases each verse could have multiple Ministry Maxims formulated for it, so this does not serve as a comprehensive index of all that Colossians and Philemon teach. Rather, this index serves as a quick guide to locating some of their teaching on various subjects, as capsulated in the Ministry Maxims. These topics may provide starting points in dealing with particular issues in your personal study or training church leaders.

Kingdom	Col. 1:13
Leadership	Philem. 7, 9, 13, 14, 17, 21, 22, 24
Legalism	Col. 2:16, 17; 3:5
Lordship	Col. 3:17, 22, 24; 4:1; Philem. 20
Love	Col. 1:4, 8; 3:14, 19; 4:7, 14; Philem. 5, 12
Maturity	Col. 1:7; 3:10; 4:12; Philem. 14, 20
Ministry	Col. 4:13, 14; Philem. 1, 3, 4, 11, 13, 14, 17, 18, 20, 21, 24
Missions	Col. 1:24, 28; 4:3, 6
Mystery	Col. 2:3, 9
Obedience	Col. 3:1, 5, 7, 8, 9, 18; 4:1, 5; Philem. 8
Opportunity	Col. 4:5
Pain	Col. 4:13, 14
Parenting	Col. 3:20, 21
Pastor	Col. 4:17; Philem. 1, 17, 24
Peace	Col. 2:14; 3:3, 15
Perspective	Col. 1:22; 3:2, 4, 5, 7, 8, 9, 10, 18; 4:1, 5, 9, 18; Philem. 13, 15
Philosophy	Col. 1:28
Pleasure	Col. 1:19
Power	Col. 1:11, 29; 3:7, 9; Philem. 3, 8, 11
Pragmatics	Col. 2:23; 3:5, 8, 18; Philem. 1
Prayer	Col. 1:3; 4:3, 12; Philem. 4
Preaching	Col. 1:5, 26; 2:4; 4:4, 16, 17

Reality	Col. 1:2, 5, 16, 17, 20, 22; 3:2, 5, 6, 18; 4:1
Redemption	Col. 1:14
Relationships	Col. 4:7, 8, 9, 10, 11, 13, 14, 15; Philem. 1, 5, 6, 8, 12, 13, 14, 16, 17, 18, 21, 23, 24, 25
Responsibility	Col. 2:1; 3:1, 6, 18; 4:1, 5, 8
Reward	Col. 3:25; Philem. 6, 24
Salvation	Col. 1:13, 21, 22; 2:6, 12, 14; 3:3
Sanctification	Col. 2:10, 11, 16, 17, 20, 23; 3:5, 6, 8, 9, 10, 18, 21
Scripture	Col. 2:3, 18; 3:1, 16; 4:16
Security	Col. 3:3, 20
Self-image	Col. 1:2, 21; 2:10, 11, 20; 3:4, 9, 10, 19; Philem. 11
Sin	Col. 1:21, 24; 2:13, 14, 20, 23; 3:5, 6, 7, 8, 9, 25
Speech	Col. 3:8
Submission	Col. 1:20; 2:20; Philem. 20
Suffering	Col. 1:24
Temptation	Col. 2:23; 3:5, 6, 8, 9, 18
Truth	Col. 2:4, 20, 21
Understanding	Col. 1:9; 3:4; Philem. 15
Union w/ Christ	Col. 1:27, 28; 3:9, 10
Walk	Col. 1:10; 2:8, 17
Wisdom	Col. 1:9; 2:3
Witness	Col. 1:6, 7, 23, 24, 28; 3:4, 11; 4:3, 6; Philem. 2, 5
Work	Col. 3:23, 24; 4:1
Wrath	Col. 3:6

APPENDIX D

ASSORTED CHARTS

The charts found here are referred to at several points in the commentary and are intended as educational and applicational aids.

The Hope of the Gospel

". . . to whom God willed to make known what is the riches of the glory of this mystery among the Gentiles, which is **Christ in you**, the hope of glory. We proclaim Him, admonishing every man and teaching every man with all wisdom, so that we may present **every man** complete **in Christ**."

(Colossians 1:27-28, emphasis added)

The Hope of the Gospel might be summarized this way:

You "in Christ"

Jesus lived to provide the righteousness you lack.
(Rom. 3:21-22; Phil. 3:9; 2 Cor. 5:21)

Jesus died to pay the penalty you incurred.
(Rom. 3:24-26; Gal. 3:13; 1 Pet. 2:24)

"Christ in you"

Jesus lives again to produce in and through you the life required of you. (Rom. 8:4, 10; Gal. 2:20; Eph. 3:17; Col. 1:27; 3:4)

"To be *in Christ*—that is redemption; but for Christ to be *in you*—that is sanctification! To be *in Christ*—that makes you fit for heaven; but for Christ to be *in you*—that makes you fit for earth! To be *in Christ*—that changes your destination; but for Christ to be *in you*—that changes your destiny! The one makes heaven your home—the other makes this world His workshop."
—Major W. Ian Thomas (*The Saving Life of Christ,* p.20)

Sexual Idolatry

"Therefore consider the members of your earthly body as dead to immorality, impurity, passion, evil desire, and greed, which amounts to idolatry."
—Colossians 3:5

Sexual idolatry moves from the general/inward ("greed") to the specific/outward (ultimately "immorality").
It moves along a line of:
Impulse → Desire → Lust → Obsessive Thoughts → Actions.

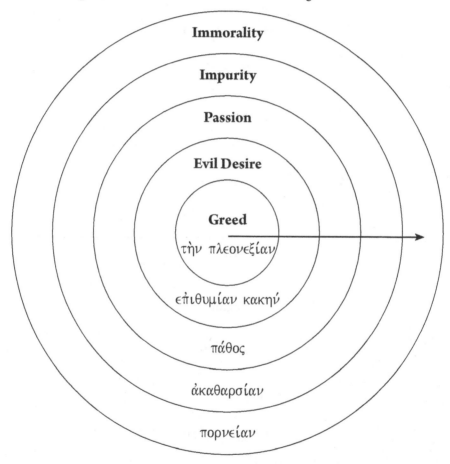

The most effective means to victory is to "put to death" the root motivation ("greed"). We must also "put to death" the more specific desires and actions that arise from it, but if we only go after the actions and do not take out the root motivation, we will be endlessly "pulling dandelion heads" and never truly finding victory.

Social Destruction

"But now you also, put them all aside: anger, wrath, malice, slander, and abusive speech from your mouth."
—Colossians 3:8

Social destruction moves from the general/inward ("anger") to the specific/outward (ultimately "abusive speech").
It moves along a line of:
Impulse → Desire → Lust → Obsessive Thoughts → Actions.

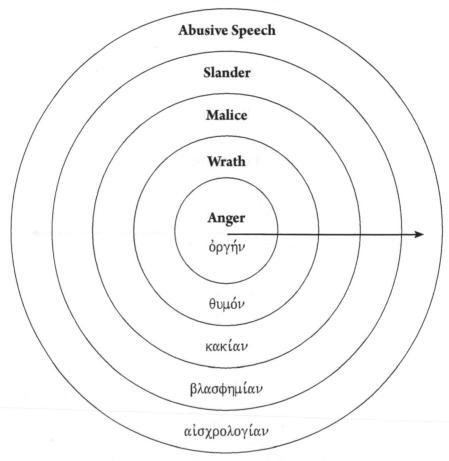

The most effective means to victory is to "put to death" the root motivation ("anger"). We must also "put to death" the more specific desires and actions that arise from it, but if we only go after the actions and do not take out the root motivation, we will be endlessly "pulling dandelion heads" and never truly finding victory.

Real Change: ROOT TO FRUIT

"Therefore consider the members of your earthly body as dead to immorality, impurity, passion, evil desire, and greed, which amounts to idolatry ... But now you also, put them all aside: anger, wrath, malice, slander, and abusive speech from your mouth."
(Colossians 3:5, 8)

Sexual idolatry moves from the general ("greed") to the specific (ultimately "immorality").
Social destruction moves from the general ("anger") to the specific (ultimately "abusive speech").
Our battle always moves along a line of:
Impulse → Desire → Lust → Obsessive Thoughts → Actions.

"But each one is tempted when he is carried away and enticed by his own lust. Then when lust has conceived, it gives birth to sin; and when sin is accomplished, it brings forth death." (James 1:14-15)

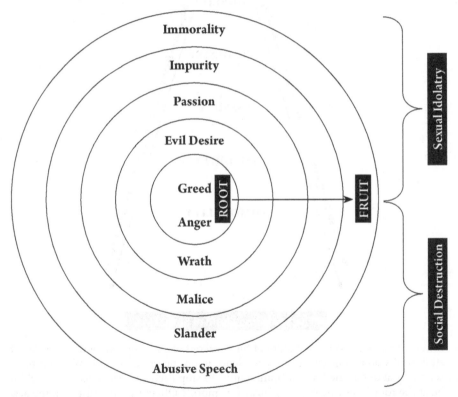

To move into true victory we must "put to death" these expressions of the flesh, beginning with the root impulses ("greed"/"anger"). Certainly we must also "put to death" the more specific desires and actions that arise from these roots, but if we only go after the actions and do not take out the root motivation, we will be endlessly "pulling dandelion heads" and never truly move into victory.

Breaking Free from Sexual Idolatry
Colossians 3:5

We find a hint of victorious strategy in the way Paul develops the list of vices here. He begins with the multiplicity of individual acts ("sexual immorality") and moves progressively toward the root motivation ("greed"). Viewing this in reverse order enables us to move from root to fruit and realize lasting change.

Picture this progression as a river at flood stage, breaking through the protective levies constructed to hold back its powerful waters.

River of impulses and desires

GREED

EVIL DESIRE

PASSION

IMPURITY

IMMORALITY

Impulse → Desire → Lust → Obsessive Thoughts → Actions

Impulse → Desire → Lust → Obsessive Thoughts → Actions

The Spreading Flood of Sexual Sin

If this provides an accurate picture of the breakout of sin, then where would we most strategically apply our efforts in dependence upon the grace of God? Would it be in scurrying about at the level of "immorality" to stop each and every act? Or would it be at the root level where "greed" lusts for "more"? Obviously we must stop the acts of sin. But our best hope of doing so is by nipping in the bud the impulses and desires from which the acts grow. We all have a river of base impulses and desires that still flows within us. Ultimately the most effective steps toward freedom from the tyranny of sexual idolatry are found in dealing with ("Put to death," NIV) the original impulse for "more" rather than in trying to just stop each individual act.

Leveraging A New Life
Colossians 3:1-14

Earthly Realities:
1. The world. (2:8, 20)
2. The flesh. (3:9)
3. The devil. (2:10, 15)
4. Sexual sins. (3:5)
5. Social sins. (3:8-9)

Heavenly Realities:
1. You have died with Christ. (3:3a)
2. You have risen with Christ. (3:1a)
3. You are seated with Christ. (3:1b)
4. You are hidden with Christ. (3:3b)
5. You will be revealed with Christ. (3:4)

Positively
Put On
(vv. 10, 12, 14)

Negatively
Put Off
(vv. 5, 8, 9)

"Set your hearts" & "Set your minds" (vv. 1, 2, NIV)

Heavenly
"the things above" (v2)
Realities

Earthly
Realities
"the things that are on earth" (v.2)

New Identity = you "in Christ" (1:2, 14, 28)
New Possibility = "Christ in you" (1:27)

APPENDIX E

ANNOTATED BIBLIOGRAPHY
OF COMMENTARIES

This annotated bibliography is provided to help pastors determine how to invest their money in commentaries before preaching either Colossians or Philemon. I believe a pastor should interact with the Greek text at the greatest depth his training and available tools afford him. My comments will come from this perspective.

As I prepare to preach a book of the NT, I seek several commentaries that work closely and carefully with the Greek text, engage in technical discussions, and provide in-depth insights into the original text. I then look for two or three commentaries that are more exegetical or theological in nature. Finally, I want one or two that are more expositional or homiletical in character. After my own exegetical work, I work through the commentaries in that order. Those in the first category help me with analysis (taking the pieces apart). Those in the second category assist in the transition from analysis to synthesis (putting the pieces back together). Those in the last category help me move from text to message. To that end, then, I would want to have (in addition to this current volume!):

> Technical Commentaries: O'Brien, Harris and Dunn
> Theological/Exegetical Commentaries: Moo and Bruce (NIC)
> Expositional Commentaries: Hughes and MacArthur

In the annotations that follow, my observations are personal reflections, and each reader may come to different conclusions about a given commentary.

Abbott, T. K. *The Epistles to the Ephesians and to the Colossians.* The
International Critical Commentary on the Holy Scriptures of
the Old and New Testaments. Edited by Samuel Rolles, Alfred
Plummer, and Charles Augustus Briggs. Edinburgh: T. & T. Clark,
n.d., last impression 1991.
Though an older work, it continues to provide helpful insight into
the Greek text. Given the price of its replacement volume in the
series (see below under Wilson), a used copy of this original work
will probably be more within the budget of the local church pastor.

Alford, Henry. *Alford's Greek Testament: An Exegetical and Critical
Commentary.* 5 vols. Grand Rapids, MI: Baker Book House, reprint
1980 from the 1871 version.
Based on the Greek text. Its age limits its usefulness, but there are
occasional gems to be found here.

Arnold, Clinton E. "Colossians." In *Zondervan Illustrated Bible Backgrounds
Commentary: Volume 3, Romans to Philemon.* Grand Rapids, MI:
Zondervan, 2002.
As one might suspect from the title, the commentary set offers
background information helpful in understanding the message
of each book of the NT. The commentary on Colossians is
valuable in this regard, with Arnold offering rich insights gathered
during his postdoctoral research. Arnold offers the insightful
recommendation that one particular false teacher (rather than a
multiplicity of teachers) may have been the problem in Colossae.
As it is part of a volume covering all of Paul's epistles, one would be
unlikely to purchase it just for its contribution on Colossians. Go
to a library, check out the entire set, and determine if it is valuable
enough to you to purchase the entire set. Better yet, return to the
library and use theirs as you do your preliminary, background work
in preparation for preaching.

Arnold, Clinton E. *The Colossian Syncretism*. Grand Rapids, MI: Baker
    Books, 1996.
    This is not a commentary *per se*, but rather a result of postdoctoral
    research into the particular nature of the false teaching in Colossae.
    Arnold suggests that the false teaching found its origin neither in
    Gnosticism nor mystical Judaism, but was a syncretistic blend of
    teaching from various backgrounds. He contends that "the worship
    of angels" (Col. 2:18) stems from a background in the local
    mystery religions in which angels were called upon for protection
    from other spirits. The work is probably more technical than the
    local pastor needs or is able to wade through in the course of his
    busy ministry. It is worth your time to breeze through the volume.
    Better yet, read Arnold's later contribution to the *Zondervan
    Illustrated Backgrounds Commentary* (see just above) which
    condenses his findings for the less scholastically inclined.

Barclay, William. *The Letters to the Philippians, Colossians, and Thessalonians*.
    The Daily Study Bible. Philadelphia: The Westminster Press, 1959.
    Barclay is not always where we would like him to be on some
    matters, but he occasionally provides excellent background
    material.

Barth, Markus and Helmut Blanke. *The Letter to Philemon*. Eerdmans
    Critical Commentary. Grand Rapids, MI: William B. Eerdmans,
    2000.
    A 560-page commentary on the little letter to Philemon!
    Obviously the authors leave no stone unturned as they exhaust the
    possibilities of the text. In their over 240 pages of introduction and
    background, they devote 100 pages to exploring and explaining the
    first-century world of slavery. There are approximately 250 pages
    devoted to actual commentary. Obviously the work is expansive,
    but the price of a new copy is probably more than the average
    pastor can spend as he prepares to preach a series out of this short
    letter.

Bruce, F. F. *The Epistles to the Colossians, to Philemon, and to the Ephesians.* The New International Commentary on the New Testament, F. F. Bruce, general editor. Grand Rapids, MI: William B. Eerdmans, 1984.

This renowned British NT scholar holds that "the Colossian heresy was basically Jewish," though not a Judaizing legalistic brand, but "a form of mysticism" (22). While he interacts with the Greek text (mostly in the footnotes), he offers a thoughtful theological commentary. He sees insufficient evidence to conclude that Onesimus was a runaway slave, thinking perhaps he had overstayed his limit while on an errand for his master (197). The commentary is valuable and worth having.

Carson, Herbert M. *The Epistles of Paul to the Colossians and Philemon: An Introduction and Commentary.* Tyndale New Testament Commentaries, R. V. G. Tasker, general editor. Grand Rapids, MI: William B. Eerdmans, 1960, reprint 1981.

The original contribution in this series. Carson's volume has been outdone by the newer volume by N. T. Wright (see below).

Davids, Peter H. "Colossians." In *Cornerstone Biblical Commentary – Volume 16: Ephesians-2 Thessalonians, Philemon.* Carol Stream, IL: Tyndale House, 2008. WORD*search* CROSS e-book.

These commentaries on Colossians and Philemon are part of one volume (covering six NT books) in a series eventually to cover the entire Bible. Davids believes Paul wrote these letters from an Ephesian imprisonment (234, 418). He suggests the issue in Colossae was Jewish in nature (238). The volume offers brief exegetical insights on each verse and then provides a more expansive section of commentary from a theological angle. Its greatest usefulness will likely come in bridging from your exegesis to your sermon-crafting and as you seek to identify appropriate application of the text to your contemporary audience.

Deibler, Edwin C. "Philemon." In *The Bible Knowledge Commentary: New Testament*. Edited by John F. Walvoord and Roy B. Zuck. Victor Books, 1983.
Solid, conservative, evangelical. Good as far as it goes, but too brief to be of substantive help to the serious expositor.

Demarest, Gary. *Colossians: The Mystery of Christ in Us*. Waco, TX: Word Books, 1979.
An expositional commentary on Colossians. Some helpful material as you think of moving from exegesis to sermon, though not an essential volume.

Deterding, Paul E. *Colossians*. Concordia Commentary: A Theological Exposition of Sacred Scripture. Saint Louis: Concordia, 2003.
A recent contribution from a Lutheran perspective. The author offers insight into the Greek text along with commentary, all in a way designed to make his insights accessible to a nonscholastic, ministry-based audience. Predictably the author argues for baptism replacing circumcision and for paedobaptism as the NT norm.

Dunn, James D. G. *The Epistles to the Colossians and to Philemon: A Commentary on the Greek Text*. Grand Rapids, MI: William B. Eerdmans, 1996.
Dunn believes the problem being confronted in Colossians was "a synagogue apologetic promoting itself as a credible philosophy more than capable of dealing with whatever heavenly powers might be thought to control human existence" (35). He believes the "most plausible solution is probably that the letter was ... composed by someone other than Paul" (38), though with his "explicit approval" (41). One finds here a careful and close unfolding of the Greek text. It can be quite helpful in wading through technical issues, Dunn's presuppositions notwithstanding.

Eadie, John. *A Commentary on the Greek Text of the Epistle of Paul to the Colossians*. Birmingham, AL: Solid Ground Christian Books, first published in 1885, new edition July 2005.

Though the volume is dated, one is regularly surprised by the help found in dealing with the Greek text. Though it is scholarly in tone, one appreciates the warmth of the insights and applications drawn. A valuable addition to the expositor's library.

Erdman, Charles R. *The Epistles of Paul to the Colossians and to Philemon: An Exposition*. Philadelphia: The Westminster Press, 1933.

This is a diminutive volume (141 pages) with some helpful insights from a beloved expositor. The author contends that the false teaching in Colossae was essentially Jewish in nature. Certainly not essential, but if you can find an inexpensive copy, you may find it worth your investment. Otherwise look elsewhere.

Felder, Cain Hope. "The Letter to Philemon." In *The New Interpreter's Bible*. Nashville, TN: Abingdon, 2000.

The comments come from a professor representing the United Methodist Church. Better help will be found elsewhere for the conservative expositor.

Garland, David E. *The NIV Application Commentary: Colossians and Philemon*. Grand Rapids, MI: Zondervan, 1998.

As with other volumes in the series, this commentator seeks to bridge from original meaning to contemporary significance. In this regard it may prove helpful for the preaching pastor as he moves from exegesis to exposition. The applications should be considered suggestive, rather than taking the place of your own prayerful, diligent work. The format of the series at times makes it difficult to locate comments on specific verses. Garland supports Pauline authorship of Colossians during his first Roman imprisonment. He believes the problem in Colossae was from rival Jews (28-32).

Geisler, Norman L. "Colossians." In *The Bible Knowledge Commentary: New Testament*. Edited by John F. Walvoord and Roy B. Zuck. Victor Books, 1983.
Conservative, evangelical, and reliable. Good as far as it goes, but too brief to be of great help to the serious expositor.

Gromacki, Robert G. *Stand Perfect in Wisdom: An Exposition of Colossians and Philemon*. The Woodlands, TX: Kress Biblical Resources, 2002.
A brief, but insightful collection of expositions. A good outline frames the comments. Best suited for adult Sunday School teachers and lay readers.

Guthrie, Donald. "Colossians." In *The New Bible Commentary: Revised*. Edited by Donald Guthrie and J. A. Motyer. Grand Rapids, MI: William B. Eerdmans, 1970.
Guthrie upholds Pauline authorship from a Roman imprisonment. He views the problem in Colossae as a syncretistic amalgam of pagan (pre-Gnostic) and Jewish ideas. As part of a one-volume commentary his comments are helpful, but are generally too brief to be of significant help to the serious expositor.

Guthrie, Donald. "Philemon." In *The New Bible Commentary: Revised*. Edited by Donald Guthrie and J. A. Motyer. Grand Rapids, MI: William B. Eerdmans, 1970.
See comments directly above.

Harris, Murray J. *Colossians and Philemon*. Exegetical Guide to the Greek New Testament. Edited by Murray J. Harris. Grand Rapids, MI: William B. Eerdmans, 1991.
Thankfully this work was reissued in a new edition by Broadman and Holman Publishers in 2010. While perhaps not exactly what some would classify as a commentary, it is one of a few indispensible tools for the careful study of these two Pauline letters. It is wonderfully helpful in dealing with the Greek text. It also provides an insightful, fresh paraphrase of the text to see how Harris's comments might find final expression. The suggestive preaching ideas are a benefit to the working pastor. Sell whatever you must, but find the money to get a copy of Harris's work.

Hendriksen, William. *Philippians, Colossians and Philemon.* New Testament
Commentary. Grand Rapids, MI: Baker Book House, 1962.
Trusted, evangelical, conversative. He upholds Pauline authorship
of both letters, coming from Paul's first Roman imprisonment. A
fine commentary filled with rich insights. Worth the investment.

Henry, Matthew. *Matthew Henry's Commentary on the Whole Bible:
Complete and Unabridged in One Volume.* Peabody, MA:
Hendrickson Publishers, 1991.
Dated, but devotionally warm and thus sometimes helpful in
homiletical development.

Hughes, R. Kent. *Colossians and Philemon: The Supremacy of Christ.*
Preaching the Word. Westchester, IL: Crossway Books, 1989.
A trusted expositor who is also the editor for the entire Preaching
the Word series. He offers excellent expositions of these two books
that will prove valuable as the pastor moves from his exegetical
work to the crafting of his sermon.

Ironside, H. A. *Lectures on the Epistles to the Colossians.* Neptune, NJ:
Loizeaux Brothers, 1981.
Classic but dated expositions.

Johnson, S. Lewis. A series of twelve expositions of Colossians in
Bibliotheca Sacra 118 (July, 1961) through 121 (October 1964).
(See the bibliography in the introduction to Colossians.)
While not a commentary in the usual sense of the word, Johnson's
insights are valuable and well worth the pastor's time to obtain. Ask
your friends or check a library to see if you can find the volumes.
Short of that, a one year's subscription to *Bibliotheca Sacra* will
grant you access not only to these excellent expositions, but to
every article ever published by the journal.

Kent, Homer A., Jr. *Treasures of Wisdom: Studies in Colossians and Philemon,*
    rev. ed.: Grand Rapids, MI: Baker Book House, 2006. First
    published 1978 by BMH Books, Winona Lake, IN.
    Kent affirms Pauline authorship of both letters, coming from his
    first Roman imprisonment. He sees the problem in Colossae as
    a combination of Jewish and other elements. Helpful exegetical
    outlines embedded in the text of the commentary. I consistently
    found valuable insights here.

King, Martha. *An Exegetical Summary of Colossians.* Dallas: Summer
    Institute of Linguistics, 1998.
    Not a commentary in the usual sense, this volume was prepared
    with Bible translators in mind. It gathers insights from twenty
    commentaries and reference works and presents the findings
    in a verse-by-verse format under two headings: "Lexicon" and
    "Question" (in which various answers to key questions related to
    the text are provided). This volume "makes available more sources
    of exegetical help than most translators have access to" (4). It can
    be helpful in concisely surveying the exegetical options on key
    questions concerning the text of Scripture.

Lenski, R. C. H. *The Interpretation of St. Paul's Epistles to the Colossians, to*
    the Thessalonians, to Timothy, to Titus and to Philemon. Minneapolis:
    Augsburg . Copyright 1937, Lutheran Book Concern; 1946, The
    Wartburg Press. Copyright assigned to Augsburg, 1961.
    The classic Lutheran commentator. Because of its age some
    newer developments are not touched upon, yet often helpful
    and intriguing on the Greek text. Helpful in giving a Lutheran
    perspective on the text. Often the source of a valuable nugget of
    insight.

Lightfoot, John B. *Saint Paul's Epistle to the Colossians and to Philemon.*
    London: MacMillian, 1892.
    Though an older volume, Lightfoot provides excellent help with
    the Greek text. Available at reasonable prices, this is a solid choice
    for the expositor, though you'll want to be sure to have one of the
    more recent technical commentaries as well.

Lincoln, Andrew T. "The Letter to the Colossians." In *The New Interpreter's Bible*. Nashville, TN: Abingdon, 2000.
The author believes the evidence goes against Pauline authorship. Conservative expositors will find a better return for their dollars elsewhere.

Lohse, Eduard. *Colossians and Philemon*. Hermeneia. Philadelphia: Fortress Press, 1971.
The introduction is surprisingly brief. He does not believe Paul wrote Colossians (167), though he does believe he penned Philemon from an Ephesian imprisonment (188). Lohse provides helpful background information gleaned from his extensive knowledge of scholarly articles related to Colossians. He is helpful in considering critical issues in difficult verses. You'll find him often cited by newer commentators. A new volume is expensive; but you should be able to find a used copy at a reasonable price. If so, you will likely find it a worthwhile investment.

Lucas, R. C. *Fullness & Freedom: The Message of Colossians and Philemon*. The Bible Speaks Today. Downers Grove, IL: IVP, 1980.
Helpful for thinking through the flow of thought in the two letters. A helpful resource as you do preliminary study and plan your preaching series.

MacArthur, John. *The MacArthur New Testament Commentary: Colossians and Philemon*. Chicago: Moody Press, 1995.
The introduction is characteristically brief, but as always MacArthur provides strong work in the text. As one would expect the volume is conservative and consistent. It is a valuable resource for the preaching pastor.

Martin, Ralph P. *Colossians and Philemon*. New Century Bible
  Commentary. Grand Rapids, MI: William B. Eerdmans, 1973.
  He upholds Pauline authorship from an Ephesian imprisonment
  for both letters (30, 147). He views the problem in Colossae as a
  syncretistic blend of "free thinking Judaism" and "the speculative
  ideas of Greek mystery-religion" (19). A good, solid, though
  somewhat brief commentary.

Melick, Richard R. *New American Commentary – Volume 32: Philippians,
  Colossians, Philemon*. Nashville, TN: Broadman Press, 1991.
  WORD*search* CROSS e-book.
  Melick assumes Pauline authorship of Colossians (165) from
  a Roman imprisonment (167) as he appears also to do with
  Philemon (335). This is a commentary likely to provide some good
  help to the pastor/expositor.

Moo, Douglas J. *The Letters to the Colossians and to Philemon*. The Pillar
  New Testament Commentary. Grand Rapids, MI: William B.
  Eerdmans, 2008.
  Moo believes Colossians is "an authentic letter of Paul" (40).
  He believes the false teachers were from within the Colossian
  community itself, "were bragging about their ability to find
  ultimate spiritual 'fulfillment' via their own program of visions and
  asceticism," and that there was a strong Jewish element in this (59).
  Moo is thorough, careful and insightful in dealing with the text
  of both Colossians and Philemon. He ably meets the goals of the
  Pillar commentary series in making the text of these letters clear
  and thus assisting serious pastors and teachers of the Scriptures
  to expound it to those under their charge. Do not preach or teach
  these letters without Moo's rich assistance.

Moule, C. F. D. *The Epistles to the Colossians and Philemon*. The Cambridge Greek Testament Commentary. Cambridge: Cambridge University Press, 1957.
>   This is a brief commentary working from the Greek text. He holds to Pauline authorship from a Roman imprisonment (13, 24). Moule provides some valuable insight for the pastor able to work from the original language.

Moule, Handley C. G. *Colossian and Philemon Studies*. London: Pickering and Inglis, Ltd, n.d.
>   An older work that has been surpassed by more recent commentators. One will occasionally find a newer commentary referencing Moule, and one can probably trust that they have gleaned most of the valuable contributions. If a friend offers you a copy or you find an inexpensive copy at a used book sale, grab it. Otherwise look for newer works.

Muller, Jac. J. *The Epistles of Paul to the Philippians and to Philemon*. New International Commentary. Grand Rapids, MI: Zondervan, 1955.
>   A careful study of Philemon that careful students of the Bible have appreciated. Muller's contribution on Philemon was later eclipsed by the work of F. F. Bruce in his New International Commentary volume on Colossians, Philemon, and Ephesians. You can find a used copy online for a very inexpensive price.

O'Brien, Peter T. *Colossians and Philemon*. Word Biblical Commentary, vol. 44. Nashville, TN: Nelson Reference & Electronic, 1982.
>   O'Brien supports Pauline authorship, probably from his first Roman imprisonment (liii). He sees the problem in Colossae not as "a clear-cut system with precise and definite points," but still something that is "basically Jewish" (xxxi, xxxii). This, however, does not rule out syncretism as a part of the falsehood (xxxiii). He is thorough, careful, and insightful in his work on the Greek text. Don't begin a preaching series in either book without this volume. This commentary is a must.

Parker, Joseph. *The Epistles to the Colossians and Thessalonians*. The
　　Devotional and Practical Commentary. Edited by W. Robertson
　　Nicoll. New York: A. C. Armstrong and Son, 1904.
　　An older contribution of expositions from a well-known preacher
　　of another era. The age and nature make it reasonable to pass on
　　this volume.

Peake, A. S., "The Epistle of Paul to the Colossians." In *Expositor's Greek
　　Testament*, vol. 3. 1903. 484-556.
　　The work is dated and Peake made disappointing concessions to
　　higher criticism and liberalism. Yet, if aware of these shortcomings,
　　one may still find some valuable insights into the Greek text. Given
　　that you can download it for free at Google Books it may be worth
　　your effort.

Rupprecht, Arthur A. "Philemon." In *The Expositor's Bible Commentary*, vol.
　　11. Grand Rapids, MI: Zondervan, 1978.
　　He supports Pauline authorship, possibly from an Ephesian
　　imprisonment. This is one contribution in a volume covering seven
　　NT books, but still Rupprecht's comments are exceedingly brief,
　　the actual commentary comprising a mere seven pages. Don't buy
　　the series for this one commentary, but if you have it in hand you
　　may find some help here.

Vaughan, Curtis. "Colossians." In *The Expositor's Bible Commentary*, vol. 11.
　　Grand Rapids, MI: Zondervan, 1978.
　　Supports Pauline authorship from his first Roman imprisonment.
　　He believes the problem confronting the Colossian believers was
　　a syncretistic blend of Jewish, pagan, and Christian ideas. Though
　　Vaughan's comments are necessarily brief as part of a multivolume
　　series, he consistently offers helpful insight that will prove valuable
　　to the preaching pastor.

Vincent, Marvin R. *A Critical and Exegetical Commentary on the Epistles to the Philippians and to Philemon.* The International Critical Commentary. Edinburgh: T. & T. Clark, 1897.
Vincent's contribution is dated, but still an outstanding help to the pastor as he wrestles with the Greek text. If you can find a used copy at a good price, it will be worth your investment.

Wall, Robert W. *Colossians and Philemon.* The IVP New Testament Commentary Series. Edited by Grant R. Osborne. Downers Grove, IL: InterVarsity Press, 1993.
The series intends to offer insightful, though brief, explanatory comments on the text and then move the reader toward application of the text to the life and ministry of believers in the church. To that end it can offer help to the expositor as he moves from exegesis to exposition. As outlined above, you'll want to gather one or two commentaries that aid in that transition, and this would be a valid choice in that regard.

Wiersbe, Warren W. "Colossians" and "Philemon." In *The Bible Exposition Commentary: New Testament,* vol. 2. Colorado Springs: Victor Books, 2001.
Wiersbe's reputation as an outstanding Bible teacher who faithfully opens the Scriptures for hungry hearts is well deserved. The size and nature of the volume necessitates that much technical material is left untouched, yet he seldom fails to provide some insightful and helpful homiletical tidbit.

Wilson, Robert McL. *Colossians and Philemon.* International Critical Commentary. London: T&T Clark International, 2005.
This is a substantive new work (512 pages) that replaces the early volume on Colossians by Abbott and the work on Philemon by Vincent. Wilson brings a lifetime of research into the issues related to Colossians to this long-anticipated commentary. Unfortunately it is priced well out of the budget of the average pastor, and it is too new for inexpensive used copies to be obtained.

Wright, N. T. *The Epistles of Paul to the Colossians and Philemon: An Introduction and Commentary.* Tyndale New Testament Commentaries, Leon Morris, general editor. Downers Grove, IL: IVP Academic, 1986.

Wright affirms Pauline authorship (34), probably from an Ephesian imprisonment (37). In Colossians, "Paul is warning the reader not to be taken in by the claims of Judaism" (24). Wright's comments are concise (as required by the series format), but thorough and worth the discerning pastor's time to investigate.